STANDARD OF LIVING

:: MARINA MOSKOWITZ ::

STANDARD OF LIVING

THE MEASURE OF
THE MIDDLE CLASS IN
MODERN AMERICA

The Johns Hopkins University Press

BALTIMORE AND LONDON

© 2004 The Johns Hopkins University Press
All rights reserved. Published 2004
Printed in the United States of America on acid-free paper
2 4 6 8 9 7 5 3 1

The Johns Hopkins University Press
2715 North Charles Street
Baltimore, Maryland 21218-4363
www.press.jhu.edu

Library of Congress Cataloging-in-Publication Data

Moskowitz, Marina, 1968–
Standard of living : the measure of the middle class in modern America /
Marina Moskowitz.
p. cm.
Includes bibliographical references and index.
ISBN 0-8018-7947-7 (alk. paper)
1. Middle class—United States—History. 2. Cost and standard of living—United
States—History. I. Title.
HT690.U6M67 2004
305.5′5′0973—dc22   2004000147

A catalog record for this book is available from the British Library.

Title page illustration: Detail from Good Housekeeping, 1910.
Library of Congress.

For my family,
"the primary social unit"

:: CONTENTS ::

Illustrations appear on pages 105–128

:: ACKNOWLEDGMENTS ::

This book has been a long time in the making! Throughout the process, I have amassed debts of gratitude that span ten years and two continents. The following words are a small start to thank the people who contributed in so many ways both to this project and to my own standard of living; I hope the book itself provides "the measure" of my appreciation.

This study of course began with research. While traipsing across the United States, I was assisted by a wonderful group of archivists and library staff. I would like to thank Brent Sverdloff, then at the Baker Library at Harvard Business School; Cheryl Prepster at the Kohler Company Archive; and Carole Prietto and David Straight at the Archives of Washington University in St. Louis. While I was in St. Louis, Susan Lammert was kind enough to introduce me to Eldridge Lovelace, whose insight into Harland Bartholomew's practice was illuminating. The team at the Clarke Historical Library at Central Michigan University—Frank Boles, Evelyn Leasher, and Deborah Minnis—were invaluable; Woodard Openo's cataloguing made my research possible and Susan Pyecroft checked details for me (on our shared favored topic of food). I would not have made my way to Mt. Pleasant in the first place without Robert Schweitzer's generous direction. At Yale, a very pleasant summer at the Beinecke Library was made all the more productive by Maureen Hehr, Bob Babcock, George Miles, and my old friend Ralph Franklin. I also want to thank the countless, and to me often nameless, staff members of the Sterling Memorial and Seeley Mudd Libraries at Yale, who make research in New Haven such a brilliant experience. While finishing this project, and in particular while gathering the images that illustrate this book, I was fortunate to have access to the Library of Congress and Smithsonian Institution Libraries, which provided all a scholar could ask for and more.

Research travel and writing time in the early phases of this project were supported by the McNeil Fund in American Material Culture, the John Enders Travel Grant, and the Beinecke Rare Book and Manuscript Library, all at Yale; the Harvard Business School; the American Historical Association; and the Newcomen Society. The manuscript was completed during a period of study leave from Glasgow University, during which I was a peripatetic scholar at the Warren Center at Harvard University, Dumbarton Oaks, and the Smithsonian. Finally, a generous publication grant from the Graham Foundation for Advanced Studies in the Fine Arts allowed me to obtain the illustrations that have inspired my research and will, I hope, convey to readers my enthusiasm for my subject. At the Johns Hopkins University Press, I thank Bob Brugger and his former assistant Melody Herr for their equal measures of enthusiasm and patience; JHUP's readers, most especially Daniel Horowitz, made this a more coherent and fluid book, as did Maria denBoer's careful copyediting. Susan Lantz has kept me calm and cheerful by being so herself throughout production; Louise OFarrell made this a beautiful book to look at.

I am grateful to audiences, both known and anonymous, who helped me sharpen my focus on everything from comparative studies of the middle class to the cultural meaning of net curtains. I encountered these helpful groups at the Yale Material Culture Study Group, Preservation Institute: Nantucket, Society for American City and Regional Planning History, Whitney Humanities Center, Organization of American Historians, the departments of History and Economic and Social History at the University of Glasgow, Cambridge American History Seminar, British Association for American Studies, and particularly the Business History Conference, whose institutional recognition (personified by Ken Lipartito, Pam Laird, Reggie Blaszczyk, and Chris McKenna) has been encouraging. While many commentators and participants have offered thought-provoking questions and comments, I want to single out Joseph Corn, who had a big impact on the final version of this project.

Another chance meeting, an airport coffee with Alison Isenberg on the way home from a conference, has resulted in a valued collegiality and friendship that I have relied on at pivotal moments in the creation of this book. Although Martha McNamara and I cannot even remember where we met, I feel a similar bond, fostered by egging each other on to finish our manuscripts. I'm not sure I've ever actually told Kevin Murphy how much I appreciate the ways in which our relationship seamlessly transcends the divide between work and play; this seems a good place to do so. Alison, Martha, and Kevin are all models to me of intellectual engagement and generosity. Other friends have charted this project from its inception; Mary Anne Caton, Patty Chang, Anna Graves, Eugene Hahm, Amy Hufnagel, Mary Lammert, Anne McBride, Victoria Sams, Gretchen Schmidt, Stephanie Schragger, and

Eric and Rita Henninger Steadman always seemed to know when to ask, and when not to ask, how this book was going.

This book is in many ways about the formation of communities, bound by everything from living in close proximity to reading the same books to sharing the same silverware pattern. I have been lucky to be situated in two incredible communities, of scholars and friends, during the time I have worked on this book. In New Haven, Yale's familiar parameters were entirely new and inspiring because they were shared with Catherine Allgor, Matthew Babcock, David Barquist, Elspeth Brown, Rob Campbell, Tripp Evans (whose amazing drawings grace this book!), Mike Haverland, Marni Kessler, Andrew Lewis, Ted Liazos, Steve Rice, Lori Rotskoff, Margaret Sabin, Beka Schreiber, and Jessica Smith. Tom Starr's vision as my personal designer is eclipsed only by his friendship over these years. To Jeff Hardwick and Cathy Gudis, simply, I could not have done this without you. I am at a bit of a loss for words as to how to express to Jean-Christophe Agnew what an important influence he has been, and continues to be, as a thinker, teacher, and friend; I can only hope that the 100,000 or so contained between the covers of this book exhibit how much he is a mentor. But the wonderful thing about Yale is the depth of its resources, including personal ones: Ned Cooke, Johnny Faragher, Dolores Hayden, Bryan Wolf, and especially Matt Jacobson were, each in their own way, a great help.

I moved home base across the Atlantic in 1999 and my colleagues and friends at the University of Glasgow have made that transition easier than I imagined possible. I landed in the History Department, which, under the guidance of David Bates and Thomas Munck, has been a remarkably congenial home. Lynn Abrams, Simon Ball, Evan Mawdsley, Alan Smith, and most especially Phil O'Brien have made it a pleasure to come to the office, but also provided creative reasons for leaving it; my students will not realize when little bits of this book work their way into lectures and seminars, but their engagement at those moments encourages me. Marguerite Dupree (another chance meeting that in retrospect seems like fate), Mike French, David Hopkin, and Duncan Ross have helped close the gap between the various houses on University Gardens. Margo Hunter and Alison Peden manage to make everything I do at work that much easier and therefore that much more enjoyable. Susan Castillo literally took me in upon my arrival, and she, Andrew Hook, Alice Jenkins, Helen Marlborough, Kristen Whissel, and the Selby family have shown what a good thing interdisciplinary socializing can be. Simon Newman has made Glasgow home, in so many ways.

As much as I have written about communities, I have also written about the importance of the family. Mine has grown over the course of writing this book, to encompass new members in Philadelphia, London, and the Trimleys. I thank everyone on this transatlantic axis for eagerly anticipating this book along with me (even if the little ones "read" only the pictures). At the heart of this ever-widening circle are Dan, Else, and Luise Moskowitz, who have made my standard of living so high, and to whom this book is dedicated.

STANDARD OF LIVING

THE STANDARD OF LIVING

Definitions, or Lack Thereof

The room displayed a modest and pleasant color-scheme, after one of the best standard designs of the decorator who "did the interiors" for most of the speculative-builders' houses in Zenith. The walls were gray, the wood-work white, the rug a serene blue; and very much like mahogany was the furniture . . . the plain twin beds, between them a small table holding a standard electric bedside lamp, a glass for water, and a standard bedside book. . . . It was a master-piece among bedrooms, right out of Cheerful Modern Houses for Medium Incomes . . . It had the air of being a very good room in a very good hotel . . .

Every second home in Floral Heights had a bedroom precisely like this.

—Sinclair Lewis, *Babbitt*, 1922

In his novel *Babbitt,* Sinclair Lewis explored the character of a midwestern real estate salesman living in a rapidly growing American city in the early twentieth century. As important as George F. Babbitt's interactions with family members, business acquaintances, and those he considers to be the bohemian element of his hometown are in defining his identity, they are matched in significance by his physical environment, the settings for those interactions. Lewis shares with the reader the standards by which Babbitt evaluates the objects within his and his acquaintances' homes, offices, and clubs, as well as those structures themselves, and the larger environs of the neighborhoods, city, and region in which they are located. Although Lewis's

1

writing can be taken as a parody, for that parody to be effective, the main character, a quintessential member of the American middle class, and his identifying environs needed to be familiar to readers. In presenting this portrait, Lewis revealed the concept of the standard of living, the yardstick by which middle-class Americans measured their material well-being.

The standard of living was one expression of the increasingly shared national culture that stemmed from the proliferation of both material culture and middle-class communities at the turn of the twentieth century. A quality of life to which many Americans aspired, the standard of living was dynamic and difficult to define or quantify, but it was materialized in the settings of everyday life. Material culture, defined broadly to encompass things or spaces made or manipulated by humans, was freighted with a broad array of cultural associations and meanings. While material culture certainly did not create the middle class, it did identify the growing group, both to themselves and to others, on a national scale. This study considers the processes by which certain objects, structures, and landscapes became "standard" possessions of and settings for Americans by the 1920s. The epigraph above raises the central questions surrounding the construction of these standards: Who chose the "best standard designs"? How did people find out about "cheerful modern houses"? What else did people with a "medium income" share? Were "very good hotels" and other public spaces important means of spreading design ideals? If "every second home in Floral Heights" had a bedroom just like the one described, did every second American city have a subdivision just like Floral Heights?

The standardization of everyday environments can be considered the nationalization of material culture—the simple fact that people in Massachusetts, Illinois, and California could all own the same furnishings, live in houses of the same plan, and work and play in towns that were ordered remarkably alike. This geographic sense of standardization was a by-product of new, large-scale distribution systems. The marketing and physical distribution of goods and design services mediated the relationship between middle-class communities and their material culture. In this marketing process, sales pitches both reinforced and were reinforced by the teachings of cultural educators. Manufacturers and wholesalers worked, whether consciously or unwittingly, in collaboration with other individuals or groups to promote the values and morals associated with certain products or services. These collaborators—advocates of middle-class values such as etiquette, public health and hygiene, good business sense, domestic and civic order, and a focus on the family—were themselves potential consumers.[1] Thus, the commercial process of distribution paralleled the cultural process of establishing a standard of living. Neither producers nor consumers alone could create the standard of living; it was a by-product of the marketplace itself. From this nexus of exchange, and the cultural ideals and marketing practices that informed it, the standard of living arose.

As people across the country had access to the same goods, placed them in similar spaces, and arranged those spaces into similar communities, they shared more than taste or design sense; rather, they shared a way of organizing life. Taken together, the elements of the material environment, along with the values that those elements symbolized, made up a quality of life increasingly referred to as the standard of living. The term that supplies the title for this book is, admittedly, a slippery one. The standard of living is a measure, but a qualitative rather than quantitative one. It is at once personal, applied to an individual or household, and collective, shared by groupings as large as a class or a nation. It is felt or perceived more accurately than it can be enumerated or articulated. It changes over time, and sometimes from place to place. Yet, despite being such a vague entity, the standard of living retains a powerful hold on the culture and economy of the United States— most Americans would know it when they see it. Economist Edward Devine wrote of the standard of living in 1924, "Elusive and kaleidoscopic though it may be, nevertheless the conception represented by this phrase is a definite and powerful reality."[2] In this study, I show that while a contemporary standard of living cannot be expressed as a complete list or "bundle of goods," it can be, and frequently is, represented by material culture. As a cultural ideal driving both production and consumption, the standard of living played a similar role at the turn of the century to the one that the American Dream assumed during the Great Depression and afterward.

Although the term *standard of living* gained both popular and social scientific usage at the turn of the century, its definition was open to debate.[3] As late as 1934, Carl Brinkman wrote in the *Encyclopaedia of the Social Sciences:*

The concept of the standard of living has yet to be worked into definitive form. It was used by the classical economists largely in discussion of the cost of labor as one of the factors of production; the Austrian school gave formal expression to the importance of the standard of living for a theory of consumption; but it was not until the influence of historical and anthropological studies that led economists to adopt a broader approach that there occurred any real analysis of the concept itself.[4]

The standard of living was a product of this gray area between production and consumption. Thus, the term was tied to the distribution that took place between these two phases of the market. A standard could be shared only when goods and design ideals could be both physically transported and culturally valued across the country. At the same time, the standard inspired a level of productivity that made consumption possible. As Brinkman noted, the standards of living "derive their greatest economic and social significance . . . from the ways in which these conditions are reacted upon and developed, so that they result in cultural instead of natural minima."[5] These cultural minima were a form of marketing not for specific products, brands, or designs, but for the concept of consumption.

Though the term *standard of living* was sometimes used to describe a level of wages thought appropriate for American workers, the term was frequently associated with the middle class and their material culture. Rather than a level of earnings, the standard of living increasingly became defined through consumer goods and the spaces established and maintained to contain these goods.[6] The distribution of standardized products did not cause this shift, but did make it possible, as elements of life aside from money could be equated across the country. The new standard dictated the ways in which money was usually or normally spent. Purchasing power, not income, became the measure by which Americans evaluated their status. Divorcing the notion of what one might buy from the notion of what one earned showed an important distinction in the domestic economy at the turn of the century as opposed to earlier decades: the widespread acceptance of credit. As economist Ira S. Wile explained to a national conference on home economics in 1913, "the installment business has made possible the acquisition of well-furnished homes that would otherwise be impossible."[7] While there had long been networks of credit, in local contexts, these systems were gradually removed from daily, face-to-face negotiations between buyers and sellers. Particularly in the arena of homeownership, debt was accepted as a necessary measure to purchase a family home. If debt was wisely concentrated in a long-term investment such as private real estate, it became as important and valuable as a base of savings might be.[8]

Thus, the standard of living was separate from the concept of the cost of living or, another common phrase of the early twentieth century, planes of living. Many contemporary social scientists sought to sort out the different planes on which Americans lived; although different theorists used slightly different terminology, a common scheme included four planes: subsistence, convenience, comfort, and luxury. As essayist F. Spencer Baldwin defined these terms in 1899, "a necessary is something indispensable to physical health; a convenience is something that relieves from slight pain or annoyance . . . ; a comfort . . . is a common and inexpensive means of enjoyment; a luxury . . . is an unusual and expensive means of enjoyment." The standard of living was usually defined both by social scientists and in the public imagination to encompass the first three of these levels, leaving luxury for those who could not only meet but also surpass the standard.[9]

The standard of living was not a measure of how people lived, according to what they could afford—it was a measure of how people wanted to live, according to shared cultural minima. These wants outpaced their attainment, creating an ever-shifting bar against which Americans evaluated their material well-being. As economist Frank Streightoff wrote, "there is an 'ideal' standard of living which is always in advance of achieved satisfaction."[10] Certainly the cultural sense of how Americans "should" live was rising. While the standard of living was understood to be dynamic, and tied to the conditions of history, prior to the Depression of the 1930s, its trend was assumed to be ever-upward. Ira Wile explained simply, "Standards level upwards. The luxuries of yesterday are the necessities of today . . . There is no absolute standard of living save as an ideal; and when the highest standards of today are realized, they will fall short of the standards that will then be used."[11] Thus, the standard of living was a mark of a particular era.

If the character of George F. Babbitt approached middle age with the novel's publication in 1922, he would have been born around 1880. The years of his maturation corresponded to an expanding national culture; the development of the character's standard of living was, of course, set in a larger national context. A nexus of technological, economic, and cultural factors, which correlate with the historical designations of the Gilded Age and the Progressive Era, helps explain how and why the concept of the standard of living developed in the decades between the 1870s and the 1920s. The completion of the transcontinental railroad in 1869, physically linking the country from coast to coast, and the brief recovery from the Panic of 1873 contributed to the moment when a conscious image of national culture, and the means to express and distribute it in the form of material culture, took hold.

By the end of the 1920s, competing forms of national communications media, such as radio and film, had grown in importance, while the precipitous drop in the economy after 1929 made this competition all the more acute.

Babbitt's youth would have been lived in what Mark Twain and Charles Dudley Warner presciently labeled the "Gilded Age" in 1873, the years of the late nineteenth century in which the effects of American industrialization became entrenched.[12] The era announced itself in part at the Centennial Exposition, a display of not only postbellum national unity, but also the country's industrial breadth and strength. While the great Corliss Engine stood as a reminder of the technological power driving production, surely as overwhelming to many visitors was the sheer abundance of finished consumer goods, displayed according to materials and modes of manufacture as they had been at industrial exhibitions common to the second half of the nineteenth century. While perhaps only the wealthiest industrialists could afford the glittering goods and palaces that lent the era its name, their companies mass-produced more affordable versions of goods and their riches underwrote the large institutions in which a broader public might mix. These goods and spaces, both necessities and luxuries, were accessible to a growing middle class, who for their part increasingly took what had been considered the latter and recast it as the former.[13] In fact, the country was not always prosperous in this generation; in both the early 1870s and the early 1890s, widespread financial distress settled on the nation. But even then, those who were able masked those financial conditions with the abundant production, and consumption, of material culture. By the turn of the century, the novelty of standardized mass-production methods was already wearing off, but the proliferation and availability of goods and services were not yet taken for granted.

Industrialization brought changes not only to the material environment but to the social and demographic landscape as well. Large-scale employment, or the promise of it, attracted thousands of new residents, particularly to expanding cities. Farmers struggling with the changing economy, African Americans beginning a migration northward at the end of Reconstruction, and European immigrants facing political and economic upheaval in their homelands all sought to establish new life patterns. At the same time, some who had long lived in urban areas transformed the traditional "walking city" into a landscape linked by transit routes, at the terminal points of which they formed new suburban housing developments. These shifting social and political boundaries, and the inevitable tensions that arose from them, may have been most keenly experienced in metropolitan areas, but were certainly perceived across the country. Many Americans were deeply ambivalent about the course of industrialization, appreciating the security it brought the national economy and material well-being, but also striving to contain its physical presence and social influence.

The increasing disparity between the power—political, economic, and consumer—of the richest and poorest strata of the country, as expressed in their material environments, became a cause for concern as the nineteenth century gave way to the twentieth and the Gilded Age ceded to what is now known as the Progressive Era. Characterized broadly as an "age of reform" or "search for order" by historians, the first generation of the twentieth century saw a rise in the civic concern of the managerial classes.[14] They sought not a passive existence between the wealthy industrialists and the poor who labored for them, but an active mediation between the groups in everyday life, as they did in the industrial settings they managed. Centered primarily on urban concerns, progressives adopted a wide variety of tools to try to effect change, ranging from settlement houses to the playground movement to changes in municipal government structure. While their do-gooder instinct ran strong, embodied in such noted persons as Jane Addams and Jacob Riis, the progressives often stood to gain in economic and political terms from their efforts. They could be as patronizing in domestic matters as they accused the captains of industry of being in the workplace; in fact, they relied on these captains for philanthropic funding of their causes. Rather than eradicating stratification, then, reformers sought to improve all tiers and encourage upward mobility, while largely maintaining the status quo in terms of the organization of industrial life. The push for betterment and progress did not stay the tide of material goods and the creation of new environments, but rather encouraged it, as long as production and distribution of goods were well managed and regulated. While the progressives might have questioned the gilded luxuries of the previous generation's elite, they also sought to raise the quality of life for many Americans, including their material circumstances.

The scrutiny of society common to the Progressive Era was supported by the work of social scientists, presented in both academic and popular venues. Studies of the standard of living proliferated at the turn of the century, as the burgeoning social sciences applied survey and observation techniques to groups within the United States. Early studies, such as Helen

Campbell's *Prisoners of Poverty* (1887), Walter Wyckoff's *The Workers* (1897), and Robert Chapin's *The Standard of Living of Workingmen's Families in New York* (1909), concentrated on the working class, but by the 1910s and 1920s, studies of middle-class living standards and household budgets were common in sources ranging from Robert and Helen Merrell Lynd's classic text, *Middletown,* to women's magazines.[15] The standard of living emerged at a point when new disciplines promoted a self-conscious study of daily life.

While an exhaustive study of the many different strands of American society, politics, and culture at the turn of the twentieth century would be necessary to explain *why* the standard of living emerged when it did, this study of the expanding commercial and cultural exchange of the period attempts to explain *how* it emerged on a national scale. If standards of living were historically situated, they were no longer geographically situated within the boundaries of the United States: consumer goods and the mechanisms to buy them were distributed across the country. In particular, the distinction between urban and rural markets was eroding. As the consumption theorist Christine Frederick wrote in 1924, "Time was when well-to-do farmers' sons spent a lot of money on fancy watches, guns, clothes; but it is automobiles today . . . The farm woman once wore little else but gingham and black alpaca. She buys copies of Fifth Avenue models today, and her daughter, whose face was innocent of aught but freckles, now possesses the standard female laboratory of toilet articles."[16] Frederick's examples were seconded in a variety of media. American author Edna Ferber chronicled this broadening of the middle-class market in her novels depicting American commercial life. In *Fanny Herself,* the story of a woman working in a large mail-order firm, Ferber described a typical destination for the firm's goods:

> Winnebago was one of those wealthy little Mid-Western towns whose people appreciate the best and set out to acquire it for themselves. The Winnebagoans seem to know what is being served and worn, from salad to veilings, surprisingly soon after New York has informed itself of those subjects. The 7:52 Northwestern morning train out of Winnebago was always pretty comfortably crowded with shoppers who were taking a five-hour run down to Chicago to get a hat and see the new musical show at the Illinois.[17]

The seamlessness between urban, small town, and rural communities made for a larger, more unified market not only for goods, but also for marketing services themselves. In the mid-1920s, the *Des Moines Register* started a campaign geared at potential advertisers, letting them know that the newspaper's circulation figures included numerous out-of-town readers. This audience nevertheless shopped in Des Moines or by catalogue, and was worth courting. In a series of full-page ads with titles such as "The Fable of the Cigar Store Indian that Moved to the Happy Hunting Ground" and "The Fable of the State Fair Excursion," the *Register* combated the idea that rural and small town dwellers lived in an isolated past. Rather, due to the car, Rural Free Delivery, and the daily newspaper, among other influences, these communities were markets that were guided by a national standard of living.[18]

Commerce was a key mechanism through which the standard of living was defined, disseminated, and perceived. The exchange at the heart of the commercial enterprise was defined through marketing. While modern business usage refers to a coordinated campaign of promotion, usually from a purveyor to a purchaser, earlier meanings of the word invoke the consumer's act of buying. Still, in establishing the standard of living, actual consumption was less important than a general awareness of the market. Potential consumers who strove for goods and services were as important as those who purchased them. The distribution phase linking production and consumption reveals the varied influences within the marketplace. As much as firms may influence consumption patterns through their marketing efforts, they are also directed by those patterns when planning production and sales efforts. The cyclical communications between producers and consumers—the collaboration between commercial and cultural interests—constitute distribution.[19]

Distribution can be considered in two distinct but interrelated ways. First, I consider the actual distribution mechanisms of goods and services. Changes in transportation technology, most notably the completion of the transcontinental rail line in 1869, greatly enhanced the ability of producers to distribute their goods to a broader geographic base of consumers. Transportation, of course, not only shipped goods, but also moved people in new commercial roles such as salespeople and wholesalers.[20] The increased reliability of mail service, particularly after the establishment of Rural Free Delivery in 1896, was another mechanical factor in the spread of goods.[21] These growing distribution patterns contributed to the standardized settings for middle-class life.[22]

Second, and of equal importance, I examine the distribution of not only designed products, but also the ideas about those designs. Producers created those ideas or images through advertising, catalogues, and other marketing tools. In addition, wholesalers and retailers contributed to advertising campaigns and issued catalogues, such as the Sears, Roebuck and Montgomery Ward "wish books." In cities and towns across the country, stores, particularly department stores, also created images of ideal design through window displays and showrooms.[23] In the competition for consumer dollars, firms vied with not only other manufacturers or service providers in their own field, but also with any other firm trying to gain a place in the domestic or institutional budget. Through their advertising, many businesses promoted not only their own specific type or brand of whatever product they sold, but also that product in general. As economist Newel Comish wrote in 1923, "Measured in dollars and cents, advertising is the most important form of education in the United States"; he went on to say that $1 billion was spent annually on American advertising, considerably more than the total spent for all other forms of education, taking into account public and private institutions from grade school through universities.[24] Many aimed to make their goods or services essential, or highly prized comforts, and not optional luxuries. While luxury was still of course a virtue for high-end firms targeting a wealthier but significantly smaller market, many manufacturers sought to make their products necessary, if not through actual function then through the values or morals these products represented. Thus, to be classed as "necessary," a product may not have been a physical necessity for survival, but a perceived necessity for the survival of middle-class culture.

Still, this process of marketing was larger than the direct communication from sellers to buyers. Other cultural productions also contributed to the ideas about consumer goods, buildings, and urban design that Americans held at the turn of the century. New magazines, appealing primarily to women and promoting ideals of domestic design, proliferated in the late nineteenth century. New printing technologies allowed magazine editors, as well as mail-order catalogue purveyors, to picture the objects and plans they were discussing. For example, the monthly feature of architectural plans in Edward Bok's *Ladies' Home Journal* may have lent familiarity and even legitimacy to the growing house-plan and kit-house companies. Popular literature was another venue that depicted the possessions and environments of middle-class characters. *Babbitt,* and Sinclair Lewis's other masterwork, *Main Street,* were immensely popular in their day and popular fiction in general flourished in the period.[25] I draw on such source material, not as empirical evidence of ownership of certain goods, but to show that certain goods were broadly recognized and discussed. All of these genres distributed ideas about consumer goods to potential buyers across the country, and in doing so, helped Americans formulate their sense of the standard of living.

The changes to which these authors pointed did not mean that all Americans achieved a higher, more comfortable way of life, but that there was a broader agreement about how they hoped to live. Social conflicts in the Gilded Age and Progressive Era, often emerging along the fault lines of class, ethnicity, race, and gender, centered on issues of access to and achievement of a shared quality of life. Whoever the players in such disputes, whether large-scale labor uprisings or conflicts over Jim Crow laws, the opposing sides had in common a core belief that an American standard of living did exist. This belief, I argue, would not have been so widely shared prior to the 1870s, when the commercial, technological, and cultural mechanisms that linked citizens across the country began to emerge.

The standard of living was not a measure of achievement, but a measure of aspiration. Just as a standard weight or measure is the example against which all others are evaluated, so too is the standard of living an ideal rather than real measure.[26] Americans might live on a variety of planes of living, but they could aspire to a national standard. This aspiration was not the pinnacle of material life—Americans still shied away from the luxurious ways of living believed to abound in European capitals—but a high degree of comfort that became associated with the American middle class. While obviously a small percentage of the population lived above this standard and was not engaged by it, and another larger percentage lived so far below it that they might not have sensed its existence, this notion of aspiration made middle-class ideals available to many. As Wile stated, "It is but natural that aspiration, imitation, and emulation should serve as incentives to raise the lower standards to the higher levels."[27] That the standard of living was often considered to be set, and most often met, by the middle class was in fact also why it was considered representative of the nation.

Writing in the *American Magazine*, essayist Joseph Jacobs imagined the middle American, a typical citizen of the United States who was characterized as the median of every measurable quality, ranging from height and weight, to location in the country, to income. Jacobs explained the reason for such an exercise: "The value of such a figure, if we could obtain it, is great, especially for comparative purposes . . . To compare the bulk of one nation with another, our only method seems to be to compare the Middle Man of each nation with that of the other." Thus, though the standard of living was said to transcend regional differences in economy and culture within the United States, its limits were set at the country's boundaries; a standard of living was seen as a national measure, at once uniting the country's material culture and providing a comparison to other nations.[28]

If Jacobs used the median to create his typical citizen, an alternative vision of the mode arose, at least in the eyes of citizens themselves. In recent generations, as many as 90 percent of all Americans identified themselves as members of the middle class.[29] Recent cultural history and theory have recast the categories of race and gender as social and cultural constructs, regardless of the biological or physiognomic traits that originally defined them.[30] Similarly, the category of class needs to be augmented beyond its tie to measurable economic and social conditions. While perhaps technically true, that there are those whose income and assets are worth both more and less than this "middle" 90 percent, and whose economic and social status either determines or is determined by this group, this self-definition is all but worthless. The gradations of financial stability, purchasing power, and earnings among this massive group are too large for a single categorization to be meaningful in solely economic terms.

However, when one considers factors such as aspirations, organization of life, and sense of commonalty to others, the category does becomes more meaningful; though these factors are impossible to quantify, or perhaps *because* they are impossible to quantify, they are nonetheless important. The physical environment—how it is organized, used, and represented—becomes a means of gauging the less tangible shared attributes of a community that calls itself the middle class.[31] The shared material markers of the standard of living were particularly important in providing a sense of middle-class identity in places such as Edna Ferber's Winnebago, in which there were less obvious gradations of economic status. In many of the towns and small cities that the majority of Americans populated throughout the period of this study, the extremes of wealth and poverty that provided economic benchmarks against which the middle class measured itself were absent. Self-identification as "middle Americans" came through comparison and association on a national level.

If the middle class can be conceived as a national community with a shared standard of living, it is also made up of countless smaller communities. The varying scales and distribution methods of material culture enable community formation on a variety of scales as well. While a small object may impinge upon only its owner and perhaps his or her family or close associates, the development of a municipality requires negotiation on a much larger scale. These negotiations were situated not only in growing metropolitan districts but also in communities like the fictional Zenith— small cities and towns in every region of the country. While much of the scholarly conversation about middle-class consolidation has been set in a metropolitan context, I expand that view to include small cities and even rural towns, and argue that in these communities in particular, access to material goods was a route to inclusion in a national middle class.

While size and space connote one type of community, this type is ultimately determined by geographic proximity; a nuclear family, a suburban housing subdivision, or an entire municipality may seem to be radically different communities in their organization and purpose, but these units are all in some sense local. I am interested here in the roles of both these local communities and the national ones, based on common affinities and modes of life, and the interplay between local and national affiliations, in the establishment of the standard of living. In their landmark social survey, *Middletown*, Robert and Helen Merrell Lynd wrote:

> Small worlds of all sorts are forever forming, shifting, and dissolving . . . Some of these groupings are temporary—a table at bridge, a grand jury, a dinner committee; others are permanent—the white race, the Presbyterian Church, relatives of John Murray. Some are local—depositors in the Merchants' Bank, the Bide-a-Wee Club, friends of Ed Jones, residents of the South Side; others are as wide as the country, the state, the nation, or the world.[32]

Material culture goes far in defining and reflecting these different types of communities.

At the turn of the twentieth century, many material goods and the structures that housed them were manufactured—even improvements to cities had to be carried out by large-scale labor—and their manufacturing process was often a selling point. The concept of standardization has been studied extensively in the context of nineteenth-century industrialization, relating in particular to technological advancements, management and organization of the work process, and the experience of workers. In these studies, standardization has been looked at as a means of rationalization of the industrial process.[33] The proliferation of standardized goods was not the cause of a heightened awareness of the standard of living, but it was a necessary precondition. The production of standardized goods encouraged a discipline, structure, and organization in industrial settings that became models for other facets of daily life. Also, only standardized goods could be produced in large enough quantities for their distribution to contribute to the increasingly similar settings that Americans created for their everyday activities.

In order to explore the dynamic relationship between the distribution of standardized goods and design services and the standard of living, I have selected four case studies. They span the scales of material culture from small objects and fixtures to architecture and urban planning; my focus on them ranges chronologically from the 1870s through the 1920s. I examine silverplate flatware, bathroom fixtures, mass-produced foursquare dwellings, and early zoning plans. Each chapter traces the ways in which marketing and sales efforts within the trade were interwoven with the promotion of a variety of middle-class values and organizing principles by an array of cultural arbiters, including magazine editors, public health officials, popular authors, financial and legal advisers, social scientists, and writers of prescriptive literature. The products examined here were tied in the public imagination to specific values or modes of behavior, such as codes of etiquette, cleanliness and proper hygiene, wise investment, and a focus on the family. The chapters begin with discussions of the larger cultural contexts in which manufacturers and marketers made decisions about the production and sale of their goods and designs. While the products themselves contributed to the material expression of the standard of living, these ways of and reasons for using them contributed to the less tangible quality of daily life.

Each chapter then moves to the production and sales processes in each trade, concentrating on a specific firm. Depending on the type of goods being created or services being offered, producers used a variety of approaches to reach the swelling middle-class market. For some items, such as silverplate flatware, designers created a plethora of styles and patterns, trying to appeal to as many potential consumers as possible. In other areas, such as comprehensive city planning, consultants for the most part tried to streamline their ideas into one or a few basic versions that might appeal broadly to their potential clientele. This latter approach became more common as the early twentieth century wore on, particularly after World War I, which brought an increased acceptance of standardization in a variety of realms.[34] The chapters also chart four different approaches to the distribution of designed goods and design services, ranging from direct sales from the manufacturer by mail to a drawn-out chain of sales through several intermediary steps of wholesalers and retailers. Salespeople and cultural educators learned themes and methods from one another and together promoted a newly codified standard of living. Thus, for each case study, I explore, in turn, the cultural and commercial perspectives on the product, and then the collaborative moment in which these two perspectives meet in the marketplace.

While businesses offered their goods and services to American consumers, they also offered themselves as cultural models. If the organization of industry created the managerial and professional positions that supported a middle-class economy, then the establishment of similar modes of organization in other spheres, from specialized tools for dining to the separation of the functions within a zoned city, defined a middle-class culture and community. In this study, I examine how four scales of material culture contribute to the creation of four types of settings for everyday life, ranging from the intimacy of the dining table to the relative anonymity of a municipality. Each of these settings is described by its constituent material elements and by the behavior that becomes commonly accepted in those settings. The specific objects or spaces and their cultural associations reinforced one another and were encompassed by the standard of living at the turn of the twentieth century.[35]

In Chapter 1, "The Standard of Good Conduct," I examine silverplate flatware and its distribution to and use by middle-class families and institutions. Flatware defines a small community, a group of people who dine together using matching implements to signify their bonds, whether based in family, business, or other associations. Advertising for flatware often stressed its role as a family heirloom and encouraged its status as a popular gift for weddings, which established new lines of kinship. However, flatware also represented the larger social circles in which families found themselves, governed by codes of social conduct and etiquette. The very process of eating with flatware, and the social settings in which such eating would occur, whether at a family table or the public venue of a restaurant or hotel, was highly prescribed by these codes. In fact, for some, usage of these goods was learned in public settings and then incorporated into domestic use. Using these goods, then, implied knowledge of the codes and membership in the groups governed by them. While the experience of social communities might have been primarily on a local scale, the etiquette books and advice columns of magazines that promoted good conduct had an increasingly national readership. The arbiters of good manners wrote largely for a middle-class audience, adopting codes that had perhaps earlier been shared by an elite, and likely metropolitan, social group, but were now adapted to

a broader swath of the country. Similarly, the challenge for those selling silverplate flatware was to recast it from its status as a luxury item to a purchase that fit within the middle-class standard of living.

While dining in public contexts was increasingly accepted at the turn of
the century, other personal activities, particularly those connected to bodily hygiene, were withdrawn from public view. Chapter 2, "The Standard of
Health and Decency," focuses on bathroom fixtures and the designation of
a room to house them, whether in domestic or public settings. The turn of
the century witnessed the proliferation of bathrooms, which were notewor-
thy for both their concentration on the single function of hygiene and their
new place *within* buildings. These qualities lent importance to the activities
carried on within bathrooms, while simultaneously hiding them from view.
Manufacturers of enameled cast-iron and sanitary pottery fixtures sold not
only their products but also the idea of cleanliness. In an era with such a
strong focus on sanitation, hygiene, and health, bathing was to become a
regular activity on par with any other that occurred within the home. A
variety of educators, from public health officials to magazine editors, promoted the importance of bathing; its status as a personal activity, worthy of
privacy, was not a luxury, but at the core of a healthy lifestyle. The creation
of spotless interior settings for the display of sanitary wares was a concern
among parties who sold the goods. Within the fixture industry, the concentration on interior spaces applied not only to the final consumer but also to
the variety of showrooms and display areas in which the goods were sold.

The ability to create distinct domestic interiors in one's home was greatly
aided if one, in fact, owned the home and thus controlled its interior spaces
and decor. If the standard of living was applied in the household, then owning a house was a crucial element of that standard. Chapter 3, "The Standard
of Investment," charts the attempt to democratize homeownership as envisioned by the mail-order architecture trade in the first quarter of the twentieth century. Working with economies of scale to mass-produce the parts
that could then be joined to build a fairly wide variety of houses, these kit-
house firms sold the very idea of homeownership along with their houses.
While some of the mail-order market would not have been able to buy a
home any other way, others could have access to bigger or more elaborate
houses than they might have otherwise. Foursquare dwellings, rising two
stories from a square (or almost square) footprint to a hipped roof, were
particularly popular, easily adapted to a variety of sizes and, thus, price
ranges. "Affording" to buy a house, however, meant not just the availability

of a fixed amount of money, but also an inclination to spend that money in a particular way, and often, a willingness to incur debt through a mortgage. The mail-order architecture firms encouraged their prospective buyers to consider their family unit as a business and conduct that business in a way that made the most long-term financial sense. At the same time, these companies presented themselves as businesses with all the moral and compassionate qualities of a family, and as channels through which a sense of community could be fostered among homeowners across the country. Homeownership was advocated on a variety of fronts, ranging from shelter magazines to the U.S. Department of Commerce, all suggesting that this local investment would result in larger civic investment and even national patriotism.

If families were encouraged to consider themselves as businesses, so too were entire cities and towns. Business leaders and municipal government officials persuaded one another to manage the cities in which they lived just as they would a business, envisioning cities on industrial models. Chapter 4, "The Standard of Management," examines the rapid spread of the planning principle of zoning, usually designed by a consulting urban planner. Zoning placed the use of even private property under the long-term guidance of a municipal ordinance, which regulated the height, area, and, most notably, use of structures on any given lot. Cities and towns were divided into districts for industrial, commercial, and residential uses, with corresponding building sizes and heights in each area. Zoning served as a spatial equivalent to the tenets of scientific management, as popularized by Frederick Winslow Taylor. The end result of zoning was not only the plan itself, with recommendations centering on a map of districts, but an image of the municipality as a progressive, financially successful place, which could be marketed by town leaders and chambers of commerce to attract additional industry, commerce, and residents. Urban planners presented their work as necessary oversight of the growth of American cities, rather than superfluous schemes for beautification and ornamentation. Ironically, while industry provided an economic base for the prevalent standard of living, its physical presence was seen as a challenge, or even a threat, to middle-class culture. With its emphasis on the single-family home as the pinnacle of land use, zoning would foster and protect the standard of living.

The family home, however, was not the haven from the world of commerce that planning advocates painted it. If the standard of living was measured in the home, it was learned and developed in the public spheres of social institutions and the marketplace. These case studies all bridge the dichotomy between Victorian domesticity and Gilded Age business culture, often posed by historians as rivals for the attention of the American family, by showing the ways in which the home and public institutions in fact echoed one another in organization and decor. The middle-class home and the spectacle of the department store, hotel, or railroad car reflected one another in their furnishings, as described in the similarity of Babbitt's bedroom to "a very good room in a very good hotel," while larger ideas about order and planning were exchanged between the domestic and civic realms. Still, although goods and design services were marketed to a variety of institutional customers, including corporations, hotels, schools, and whole municipalities, at the core of the market for many products and services was the domestic consumer. The family stood simultaneously as the basic unit of middle-class communities and the basic unit of the consumer market, around whom in fact the world of commerce revolved. As such, the family was also usually the basic unit for any study or measure of the standard of living.[36]

At the heart of the organization of middle-class spaces, whether domestic or public, was a belief in environmental determinism, that the material world not only reflected the status of those who lived in it, but could in fact help shape that status. Aspirations for material goods and physical environments would result in behavior and shared values appropriate to middle-class life, according to much of the public sentiment of the day. Material possessions and the organization of the physical environment were a means to express an increasingly shared national experience, and also to introduce the tenets of that experience to those not yet sharing it. Objects and spaces were freighted with, and thus carried, significant values of middle-class life, such as the importance of etiquette and social codes, privacy and interiority, investment, and careful management. That some of these values were borrowed from business parlance is not accidental. The growth of the middle class, in both quantitative and geographical terms, with its ranks of clerks, managers, merchants, and professionals, was tied to the rise of American business and industry at the turn of the twentieth century. It is important to remember that there were not clear divisions between those who marketed specific products and services; those who depicted them for prescriptive, artistic, and academic purposes; and those who consumed them. Individuals might play different roles in the market at different times and for varying reasons. The standard of living grew out of these negotiations in the marketplace.

CHAPTER ONE

THE STANDARD OF ETIQUETTE

Silverplate Flatware

The November 1891 issue of *Ladies' Home Journal* shared with its readers "How Delmonico Sets a Table." While few, if any, of these readers would have eaten at New York City's renowned Delmonico's restaurant, one of the oldest in the country, many would have heard of it. Asking "How many persons know how to give a dinner, set a table properly, and serve food and wines as they should be served, in an orderly, appetizing way?," author Foster Coates shared the proprietor's suggestions for doing so, using the public space of the restaurant as a model for domestic space. Coates admitted that "all people cannot have rare foods, served on gold or silver plates, and not all of us possess handsomely decorated dining-rooms, and for the lack of these we must make up in less expensive ways. And one of the most important is a well set and attractive board, snowy napery, polished glass and china, and brightly burnished silverware, if you possess it."[1] The article not only explained the "correct" manner for table service, but also lent exposure and popularity to the New York restaurateur Delmonico as an arbiter of taste for these settings.

In addition to teaching "how to set the table," Delmonico and fellow restaurant proprietors also taught, by example, with what. Manufacturers of interior furnishings and fittings competed with one another for the prize commissions from public institutions—those places well-enough known that their use of a particular company's goods could be influential. Indeed, in some instances companies went so far as to take a loss on sales to their institutional customers, recognizing that there were added benefits. For ex-

ample, as early as 1877, an executive at the Reed & Barton Company, manufacturers of silverplate goods, directed the company's New York branch manager to make a very low bid for some pieces needed by Delmonico's: "There
would be no money in them at this price but we would like to have them in
Delmonico's as an advertisement."[2] When the *Ladies' Home Journal* recommended the use of "brightly burnished" tableware, they would have referred
to either Britannia ware or, more likely, silverplate. Silverplate flatware was
presented as one way of creating a well-appointed setting in "less expensive
ways," a middle-class alternative to the "gold and silver" of the wealthy.

In contemporary Western society, most people use some sort of flatware
to consume at least some of their food. While this basic means of elementary technology is shared widely, there is a plethora of distinctions within
that broad category of flatware. What is it made of? How is it made? What
does it look like? Do different pieces share elements of design or material
that suggest visual unity? Does one person's flatware resemble another's?
And perhaps most important, why and how are the answers to these questions so varied? On the one hand, flatware seems to be a personal object.
Forks, spoons, and knives of all sizes and shapes are used as extensions of
the human body to convey food from whatever vessel in which it is stored,
cooked, or served to the mouth. They are used to protect the body from extreme heat or cold, to give form to liquids, to break apart solids—in a general sense to aid the process of eating. And yet eating is often not a solitary
activity. Flatware is often produced in sets of matching items, visually suggesting that it also has some collective or social aspect.[3]

While knives were the earliest tools of the three basic forms, the spoon
was the first implement designed for eating; knives were later modified for
domestic use. Forks were introduced in Western culture first for serving,
between 700 and 1000, and later adapted for eating, between 1300 and 1500.
While the implements could be cast or forged by local metalsmiths, some
concentrations of producers did arise in what had formerly been specifically
centers for cutlery, such as Solingen, Germany, and Sheffield, England. Until
the end of the seventeenth century, these personal tools were often owned
and used by the same person or by people in close contact with one another.
They were carried in small cases, and taken out for meals both at and away
from home.

Over time, however, flatware became associated not so much with person as with place, not so much with the user but with the server or host.
Louis XIV is credited with commissioning the first complete set of flat-

ware—matching utensils made of gold with the royal insignia on them. All forms for all users shared aesthetic elements and could be recognized as a unit.[4] An obvious display of wealth and hospitality, this set of flatware also provided a way to define a group of people. With this innovation a group of people could not only eat meals together, sharing food, but also share the physical markers of a meal. As food service styles changed from communal serving dishes to individual plates, the need to identify one's access to food through personal flatware faded, while the importance of a "place setting" arose. Those using the matched sets of flatware were those invited to a meal, presumably of a shared social rank, brought into a grouping of some sort, often also symbolized by places around a table. Everyone dining together could now "have a place" at the table. Any sense of possession was of space, even if only temporarily, and no longer needed to be marked by specific utensils; rather, the utensils could provide the sense of the larger community within which that "place" was taken.

Of course, not everyone dined in the manner of the king of France and his court. For the majority of Westerners, particularly those not traveling from meal to meal, flatware might be shared in families or other small communities, made of easily accessible materials, and not used ceremonially, but rather for the utmost necessity. Still, a standard for aspiration had been established, and over the next two centuries, this collective manner of flatware use became increasingly common. Across the European Continent, through Britain, and across the Atlantic Ocean to the American colonies, and later, the United States, flatware became associated more with a home, a family, or a public institution where dining occurred than with an individual. An initial aspiration was for a few "good pieces"—for example, a spoon made of coin silver used by the most honored family member or guest for a special meal. In time, a matching set of flatware with a broad variety of forms and serving pieces emerged as an ideal possession for the home.[5]

In the American colonies, flatware was often made locally of forged iron for knife blades, spoon bowls, and, increasingly, fork tines, and wood for handles. At the upper echelons of merchant society, flatware was custom-made on commission from silversmiths, both locally and abroad. Pewter was another durable option for flatware. Experimentation with metals led to the development of Britannia ware; while pewter is composed of 80 percent tin and 20 percent lead or copper, Britannia is 91 percent tin, 7 percent antimony, and 2 percent copper.[6] Britannia ware was more durable and able to be polished more highly for a shinier finish; though not silver, it lent an

element of luxury to its surroundings and the meals eaten in them. Following experimentation in England, particularly Sheffield, American producers
began to test different ways of coating a base of Britannia ware or other metal
with silver. The earliest methods of plating, known for its center of development, Sheffield, had fused together sheets of metals, usually some white
metal sandwiched between thin veneers of silver, and then formed pieces
from these sandwiched sheets. Successful processes for electroplating were
developed in the 1840s by a variety of manufacturers, and the silverware
industry blossomed. Electroplating involved taking pieces already formed
of white metal and placing them in a silver bath where an electrical charge
would deposit silver on the piece no matter how intricate its detailing. The
base pieces for early electroplating were often made of Britannia ware, and
then later of nickel silver, also called German silver, an alloy made of copper,
zinc, and nickel. Electroplating was ultimately a much more durable method
of silverplating; the silver might wear off with heavy use, but the metals
could not come apart, because they had been fused by a chemical rather
than a mechanical process. By the 1860s, as much as 90 percent of silverware
produced in Britain and the United States was estimated to be silverplate.
American innovations in the industrial process for making bases and plating them led to a decrease in prices from British plate that in turn made
wares more accessible to both first-time buyers and those seeking to replace
old goods with new styles.[7]

A source within the American tableware industry wrote in the 1880s,
"Articles of table service especially are made in exquisite patterns, while recent improvements in the plating processes render them lasting and almost
indestructible. The plated ware made to-day by manufacturers of established reputations will last a lifetime without betraying the fact that the
silver surface has a foundation of white metal."[8] The very idea of coating a
white metal with a thin veneer of silver suggests the value placed on the aesthetics of the object. While durability, comfort, and the ability to perform
the basic function of dining (was the spoon bowl deep enough? the fork
tines close enough together?) were criteria of evaluation, some interest in
how the piece looked is evidenced in this composite material.

One of the early American silverplate manufacturers was the Reed & Barton Company, situated in Taunton, Massachusetts. The south shore of Massachusetts and the region around Providence, Rhode Island, grew into a
fancy goods center, housing both the Reed & Barton and Gorham silver
companies, as well as a number of smaller jewelry manufacturers.[9] Reed &

Barton, after going through various partnerships, was one of the pioneers in silverplating. The company grew rapidly in the 1870s and 1880s, with the number of employees doubling to about 800 at the end of the 1880s and the wares produced and sold increasing. The company also enjoyed financial stability in these years.[10] Reed & Barton was an innovator not only technically but also in terms of its business practices and, through these burgeoning marketing techniques, appealed to a variety of customers. Reed & Barton, and other silverware manufacturers, envisioned a broad domestic market made up of families who would eat together with matching flatware.

At the same time, these companies recognized that as the nineteenth century gave way to the twentieth, American lives were increasingly lived in public. The growing split between work and leisure time during the industrial era contributed to a proliferation of public spaces such as clubs and restaurants. The rise of the railroad, particularly after the completion of the first transcontinental line in 1869, meant the possible transport of both goods and people. Traveling salesmen established routes across the country for the distribution of goods, and a slowly burgeoning tourist trade emerged.[11] Temporary lodgings for these travelers provided a new market for the producers of furnishings, as did, of course, the dining cars of the railroads. All of these developments provided new settings in which daily life, including eating, occurred; railroad cars, hotels, restaurants, clubs, apartment buildings, college dining halls, and other spaces provided institutional buyers for table wares.[12] Known collectively as "the hotel trade," this sector of the market had a significant influence on the structure of the silverplate industry in the 1870s.

The domestic and public markets for silverplate flatware were in fact intertwined, in both the companies' production and marketing systems and consumers' everyday experiences. Not only the choice in furnishings for dining spaces, but also the behavior expected within them, circulated between the home and the public institution. The broad distribution of silverplate flatware, starting as early as the 1870s, predated the common use of the term *standard of living*. Yet the distribution process serves as a precedent for the negotiations between manufacturers, marketers, cultural educators, and consumers that resulted in the widespread use of these objects. The task for all of these groups at the end of the nineteenth century was to transform silverplate flatware from a luxury good into one that had a place in everyday life. By the first decades of the twentieth century, Americans had succeeded in this task.

THE RULES FOR DINING

Silverplate flatware might indicate dining rather than just eating, even for a seemingly simple meal. The rise of silverplate flatware echoed that of separate spaces designated for dining; the pieces were among the important furnishings for these new spaces, whether domestic dining rooms or larger banquet areas of clubs, hotels, and restaurants.[13] Though still an extension of the human body, flatware also symbolized the space in which dining took place. Special patterns created for specific public spaces or monogrammed pieces designating a family home were a means of unifying the experience of those dining in a specific place, marked by their eating with matching utensils. In the domestic context, this creation of a small community could foster either symbols of the primacy of the family unit, or could be a testament to the hospitality of the owner or household head as host of a larger circle. The use of such specially designated spaces also indicated a place within the broader middle-class community. The popular American novelist Robert Herrick explained the significance of such a space in his description of a family mealtime in *The Real World* (1901): "Their father and Jack wished to eat in the kitchen, as the most labor-saving method, but Mary, who was nearly fifteen, was loyal to the prejudices of both sides of the family, and insisted upon setting the table in the dining room." As the novel continues, the boy Jack leaves home and eventually falls in love with the daughter of a silverplate manufacturer, who inspires him in his quest to join the "great middle class."[14]

Along with the distribution of silverplate and the increasing use of a distinct dining room, the acceptance and availability of certain kinds of food was shared broadly across the country. New trends in both the structure and content of a meal were reflected in the overwhelming specificity of flatware forms. For example, the introduction of salad, particularly as a special course, led to the lettuce fork. The incredible popularity of oysters in the United States in the late nineteenth century called for the delicate but sharp oyster fork.[15] Much of the specialized silverware produced in the late Victorian era appeared to presume usage at formal dinner parties, which were in fact themselves a newly popular form of entertaining. And yet, the most basic forms of silverplate flatware were used on a daily basis in homes across the country. Wherever it took place, dining was a ritual, in specialized places with specialized tools.

Of course, participating in these rituals meant not only having a place at the table, but knowing the codes that governed the event—etiquette. Dining was bound into a set of rules, not the least of which was what piece of flatware to use for what course or food item, and the correct way to hold it. The tools for eating could express rules of social conduct, and knowing those rules was one way in which a community could recognize itself; etiquette went beyond just knowing the proper uses of flatware to a way of arranging middle-class life.[16] The table itself represented the orderliness of an ideal life in the industrial era; Robert De Valcourt wrote in an 1865 etiquette manual, "The table should be set straight and orderly. A table set askew is provoking to all people of regular habits."[17] The matched set of flatware might be a way of defining a circle—whether a family, a group of close friends, or a professional sector eating together at a club or restaurant. It would also indicate the refining element of etiquette, the rules and regulations to which that circle tacitly agreed to adhere.[18] De Valcourt explained the importance of these codes in language that applied equally well to the flatware that symbolized the rules of etiquette: "Our whole life and society needs re-forming . . . refining, and polishing, to bring out its highest use and beauty."[19] Social standards were played out with standardized goods.

Etiquette was a form of mediation between private and public life. As middle-class Americans increasingly shared a public stage, they needed a common denominator for their behavior on it. Some admitted that it was hard to say exactly how these codes had evolved. Writing in *Harper's Bazar* in 1900, Anna Wentworth Sears admitted, "I believe many of us wonder, too, in thinking over the problem of what and who set the standard for table etiquette. The forms often seem arbitrary"; nonetheless, these codes were social standards.[20] On the one hand, the home was seen as the practice ground for learning the rules of etiquette that would inevitably be evaluated in public. As one *Ladies' Home Journal* columnist wrote of table etiquette specifically, "It is at the home . . . that reform should begin. Rehearsal behind the scenes is necessary to appear well before the footlights."[21] On the other hand, despite these expectations of performance, the best way to act in public was, according to similar guidance, to project the ease of behavior associated with the home.

The standard for public behavior was set at the private dinner party, which required both hosts and guests to recognize social customs. A host (or, more likely, hostess) needed to know how to set the table while guests needed to know how to use the tools laid out before them.[22] Convention implied that the invitation would be reciprocated at some future point, thus ensuring that all parties knew all sets of rules. While the dinner party was said to have "a stately character possessed by no other social function," it was also seen to benefit the family.[23] Writing in the *Ladies' Home Journal,* Mrs. Burton Kingsland explained, "Entertaining visitors unifies a family, all being pledged to the same end—the gratification of the guest."[24] Families were instructed to use the company standard on a daily basis, so that it would in fact become everyday behavior. In language that belied the industrial era in which these etiquette standards were disseminated, Christine Terhune Herrick, who wrote frequently about table manners in *Harper's Bazar,* said, "Again let me emphasize the importance of everything being managed with the same precision when the family is alone as when guests are expected."[25]

The private dinner was the bar not only for family dinners but for public ones as well. For example, De Valcourt explained the tricky status of the hotel: "A public hotel is your house for the time being; but your own room is the only place where you can feel at entire liberty . . . It is a common visiting place, where to a certain degree you are on visiting etiquette. So the table d'hote has many of the elements of a private dinner party, and at some of our hotels is quite as ceremonious."[26] Writers of etiquette manuals in the last quarter of the nineteenth century recognized that the frequency with which Americans encountered one another in public required knowledge of all social codes, including those associated with the dining table. One 1874 guide to manners addressed readers by stating, "you may not go into what is technically called 'society' at all, and yet you are liable, at a hotel, on board a steamer, on some extraordinary occasion, to be placed in a position to which ignorance of dinner etiquette will be very mortifying."[27] Because, in the words of another tutor in 1895, "in these days few, if any, are wholly outside the world of social usage and convention," etiquette books addressed a broad audience.[28]

While etiquette manuals advocated that the perfect setting for learning these codes was in the home, many Americans' experience did not live up to this ideal, leaving them uneasy in public places. As De Valcourt admitted in his text, "one of the most trying things to a novice in society is to dine in elegant company."[29] In his 1911 work *Jennie Gerhardt,* novelist Theodore Dreiser depicted this trying experience, showing the title character's lack of familiarity with these codes, even while she was aware of their existence. Describing Jennie's dinner in a hotel restaurant with Lester Kane, the son of a wealthy industrialist, Dreiser wrote, "Another time in the Southern hotel in St. Louis he watched her pretending a loss of appetite because she thought her lack of table manners was being observed by nearby diners. She could not always be sure of the right forks and knives, and the strange-looking dishes bothered her; how did one eat asparagus and artichokes?" When Lester assures her that her "table manners are all right," Jennie admits to feeling "a little nervous at times." Still, in Dreiser's depiction, through these occasions, "Jennie grew into an understanding of the usages and customs of comfortable existence."[30] If Dreiser's scene showed the subtlety with which anxiety over social status could manifest itself, contemporary author Eleanor Abbott clearly stated the link between class and forms of eating in her 1913 novel *The White Linen Nurse*. The title character, Rae, is surprised by a marriage proposal from a man she believes to be her social superior, and looks for ways to convince him that the match would not be suitable:

> "Why, I'm not in your world, sir! Why, I'm not in your class! Why—my folks aren't like your folks! Oh, we're just as good as you—of course—but we aren't as nice! Oh, we're not nice at all! Really and truly we're not!" Desperately through her mind she rummaged up and down for some one conclusive fact that would close this torturing argument for all time. "Why—my father— eats with his knife," she asserted triumphantly.[31]

Such authors as Dreiser and Abbot not only reflected the standards of the middle-class communities of which they wrote, but also reinforced those standards.

While manuals and periodicals such as *Ladies' Home Journal* advised owners of flatware sets, and popular novels reflected the social circumstances in which they were used, the companies that produced them were also helping consumers to create a place for a set of flatware in their lives. In these ways, the manufacturers and arbiters of public taste reinforced one another. Etiquette manuals, dining guides, cookbooks, and columns on all these topics in popular periodicals suggested to readers that sets of flatware were a required purchase to establish a new household or refine an older one.[32] Similarly, silverware manufacturers joined the public education campaigns of late Victorian life, issuing pamphlets or including in their advertising much of the same information on "how to set the table." The fancy goods industry as a whole entered the public realm in the 1880s by offering a column from the trade journal, *Jewelers' Circular and Horological Review*, to the press at large. The journal encouraged jewelers to request advance copies of the "Fashions in Jewelry" column, authored by "Elsie Bee," and get them placed in local newspapers, stimulating interest in new forms and styles, which would then presumably be in demand from that jeweler. As one testimonial letter attested, "I have sold a number of bills of quite respectable amounts that I know were the direct result of reprinting some of 'Elsie Bee's' paragraphs in our home paper." Elsie Bee frequently discussed silverware in her columns, as well as jewelry, and focused on issues of design and novelty, discussed in a pragmatic tone. As one column touted, "All the better class of silver plate ware reproduces the leading styles made in sterling silver, and thus affords to a large class of people, at comparatively small cost, the benefits of beautiful as well as enduring goods. Silver plate, as it is made nowadays by our best manufacturers, will last indefinitely with ordinary care."[33]

The "large class of people" who, according to Elsie Bee, had access to silverplate flatware also had access to the quality of life that was believed to go along with such a purchase. A circle of diners represented the larger sector of the population who arranged their mealtimes, and their daily lives, in similar ways.[34] As industrial and professional occupations split work and leisure time from one another, mealtimes had to be coded one or the other. The emphasis on aesthetic qualities, in both its material and its design, made silverplate carry a hallmark of luxury without the price, and also indicated that its use was for leisure time. A Meriden Britannia Company promotional graphic showed a woman cooking with a spoon, with the warning: "CAUTION: This is not the way to use Plated Spoons and Forks."[35] Silverplate was not for the production of food, but rather for a leisurely manner of consumption. Eating with luxury goods—or luxury versions of necessary goods—was a way to insert a leisure break into a workday, in places distinguished from work settings. The concept of luxury was itself often defined or explained in the era in terms of dining, the act in which economic consumption of accoutrements and bodily consumption of food are combined into one. One role of silverware manufacturers, aided by arbiters of etiquette and deportment, was to redefine these acts from scenes of luxury into everyday occurrences, experienced broadly across the country.

DESIGN AND DISPLAY

To the extent that silverware connoted luxury, the association was defended on educational grounds. Certainly beautiful household furnishings would encourage an appreciation for high aesthetic standards, or so argued those in the trade, whose interest necessitated such a position. The *Jewelers' Cir-*

cular breathlessly described the public auction of the household of Mrs. Mary J. Morgan in 1886: "There were gathered at this display examples of pretty much everything that a person of the most extravagant taste could think of to place upon a dinner table, either for practical service or mere ornamentation; and there was a great profusion of every thing, fanciful knives and forks in numerous patterns and in quantities; spoons by the score; fish knives in elaborate designs and rich in ornamentation." While some might consider this "profusion" an example of excess, the author explained the benefits of the sale: "It is unfortunate that it [the collection] is scattered, but the specimens will probably do more separately to stimulate appreciation of art than they would in a single collection." The interest in the sale showed that this appreciation "is not confined to any particular section nor exclusively to persons of great wealth; but on the contrary, that it pervades the entire community, and is extending rapidly." Auctions such as Morgan's, and the press coverage of them, were in fact one way in which members of the middle class might come in contact with the splendor of the silver manufacturers' wares; they were a context in which the private domestic realm became public.[36] Such public settings showcased the extent to which the trade focused on design, as well as functional use, of its wares.

The electroplating industry captured the imagination of the popular press, perhaps because of the seeming disjunction between industrial methods and the beautiful, delicate, and decorative objects those processes produced. While a design phase and some handcraft finishing of products were common in late nineteenth-century manufacturing, the silverplate trade stressed these qualities. Articles about the trade touted both the industrial process that enabled the comparatively low cost of the wares and the imagination and handwork that went into design and finishing. One author wrote, "The American manufacturers have introduced methods of simplifying and expediting work by use of machinery, employing handwork for all the processes of finishing. They draw the best workmen from Europe, by paying the highest wages, and they also, in the large establishments, educate young Americans to a wonderful degree of skill in special branches of designing and the production of mechanical effects."[37] At the Sydney International Exposition of 1879, Reed & Barton, and several of the other well-known firms, won awards in both the art department and the manufactures department, Reed & Barton taking first-place awards in the appropriate subsets of each classification.[38] The company used this dual approach in its promotions, combining enthusiasm for both mechanization and design. A

Christmas brochure circulated from the New York office in 1881 stated, "Employing only artists of established talent in the department of design, the most skilled workmen and the most improved machinery in the manufacture, and with unsurpassed facilities, we are enabled with our long experience to produce ware unrivaled in design, unequaled in workmanship and durability."[39] The adaptation of handcraft and industrial methods to one another allowed silverplate wares to reach a broader audience.

Flatware, like so many items, began to be produced in large quantities by industrial methods in the early nineteenth century. The innovation of Britannia metal contributed to this development, as it was durable enough to be stamped more effectively than pewter, a softer alloy. Spoons and forks were stamped out of metal sheets rather than spun on forms as hollowware was. Machines cut the sheets of metal into strips with the approximate proportions of the pieces to be made. Presses formed these blanks into the rough shapes of spoons and forks and then steel dies created the final shapes and stamped patterns into the handles. Steel knife blades were machine hammered and inserted into handles. William Gale's invention of a roller die—rollers with patterns sunk into them that could be forcefully stamped onto the blanks—increased production potential as early as the 1820s; when the patent for the roller die expired twenty years later, this technology was adopted by many firms. In the 1850s, John Gorham, head of the American firm that bore his family name, traveled to England to purchase a steam-powered drop press for making flatware, signaling increased mechanization in the silverware industry.

The dies that created forms and patterns, whether placed on a roller or a steam press, were of critical importance to the production process. The workers who engraved the dies were both highly skilled and highly paid, and the dies themselves were estimated at high values in company inventories. Though handwork was still done, particularly with the finishing processes of polishing and burnishing, spoons and forks were the subsets of silverware most easily adapted to industrial processes. Sets of matching pieces, perhaps the greatest challenge to a hand craftsman, were more easily achieved by mechanized means.[40] Because the numbers of goods of any one form or pattern were relatively small, silverware manufacturers used what has been termed "batch" or "flexible" production, with groupings of skilled workers running adaptable machinery. Nonetheless, of the different sectors of the silver industry, flatware production most closely approached what might be considered at least bulk if not mass production, in that the process was a relatively linear one and dies were made specifically for each form and pattern.[41]

In its first decades, the silverplate industry exhibited some specialization in goods between its makers. While manufacturers could plate wares relatively easily, the actual production of white metal bases was an expensive process, and few companies could afford to create dies and other machines for a wide range of objects. Smaller firms tended to concentrate their production on the stamping processes that produced flatware, while larger firms made more hollowware and presentation pieces. Firms bought base wares from one another, and plated and stamped them with their own marks, in order to have broader lines to distribute. Over time, this system began to show its flaws. Companies had little quality control over goods issued under their own name, and were encountering their own goods in competition with other firms' stamps on them. At the same time, the burgeoning hotel trade made large quantities of relatively spare goods a lucrative prospect. For trade with larger institutions than an individual family, it was to a manufacturer's advantage to supply a complete line; rather than going to one manufacturer for flatware and another for hollowware, those placing large orders were more likely to want a complete service ranging from flatware to tea and coffee sets to serving dishes. Particularly in the flatware trade, these institutional commissions were significant sales, leading companies to consider how best to supply them; at Reed & Barton, flatware sales escalated over the course of the 1860s to over $100,000.[42]

The 1870s brought an overwhelming proliferation of silverplate flatware: numerous permutations of new patterns for handles and new forms for both eating and serving, all available in a range of grades of plating. Two major factors in this proliferation were the availability of silver and the ability to transport it. In the 1870s, the mining of the Comstock Lode of silver ore in Nevada, first discovered in 1859, made the United States a major silver producer. The ability to transport silver east for production and back across the country for consumption in all forms of flatware and hollowware was eased by the newly completed transcontinental railroad.[43] Flatware in particular could be packed efficiently, transported by train, and distributed by salesmen, jewelers, and other stores, even by mail order, bringing small luxuries into homes and public settings across the country.

Though originally focusing its own production on hollowware while buying up flatware from smaller houses such as the Hartford Manufacturing

Company or Rogers & Brothers, Reed & Barton invested in creating production space and mechanisms for flatware. In 1880–81, a new spoon mill was
constructed, leading the credit ratings firm of R. G. Dun and Company to
record "Keep building additions to [their] premises & [business] demands
it."[44] In its 1885 catalogue, the company announced this new plant: "By recent
addition of a new Factory built expressly for and devoted entirely to this
[flatware] branch, fitted up with the most expensive and latest improved
machinery, our facilities have been increased till now they are unsurpassed."[45]
With a large investment in the new "spoon room," the company sought to
capitalize on its economies of scale and ensure the broadest possible market
for its flatware. Having expanded its production capabilities to meet the
hotel market, the company, and its competitors, sought to then expand distribution to individual or family purchasers.[46] At about the same time, the
company started issuing new flatware designs exclusive to Reed & Barton,
as it expanded from the few flatware patterns that had long been shared by
electroplate producers; these standard patterns, such as Plain, Tipped, Oval,
Fiddle, French, and Olive, were originally designed for coin silver pieces.
Henry Reed designed the earliest of his company's original patterns, Roman
Medallion, in 1868. Roman Medallion was followed quickly by the Reed &
Barton exclusive patterns of Gem, Pearl, Unique, Orient, and Brilliant.[47]

Even before this plant was completed, Reed & Barton began phasing out
the practice of selling goods that the company had not manufactured. Because of the wide variety of forms customers sought, the company sometimes came up short. For example, in 1878, the salesman Wheeler ordered a
dozen each of mustard spoons and salt spoons in the Fiddle pattern, items
that the company did not produce. M. T. Rogers, in handling the order at
the home office, sent out the dozen salt spoons made by another company
that he "happened to have . . . on hand," but would not go so far as to buy
the dozen mustard spoons from another company to then resell.[48] The new
regime also meant not supplying other companies with its goods, as indicated in the following correspondence from a manager named Fiske to
Calvin Harris in New York: "We are in receipt of the enclosed letter from
Messrs. Rogers & Bros. but as you can see they do not state whether the
goods are wanted plated or in metal. I am instructed to request you to see
them & quote them such prices as will be high enough so they will not want
them as we dont [sic] like to sell them on account of always meeting the
goods in competition afterward & to R&B's disadvantage in price."[49] On
another occasion Rogers wrote to Harris in the New York office that in

putting together a big order, he substituted the Gem pattern for the Olive pattern, because otherwise he would have had to buy Olive pieces from Rogers & Smith Company.[50] Reed & Barton agents tried to direct their flatware sales into patterns like Gem and Pearl, which were the company's own designs, rather than the older shared patterns. However, even in arranging orders of their own patterns, Rogers and Harris sometimes had to make adjustments to reflect the particular forms available in certain patterns. Arranging an assortment of knives to add to a case being shipped, Rogers explained that the bulk of the order had to be filled with the Gem pattern, as opposed to the Pearl pattern, because hollow handle knives were not available in Pearl.[51] These substitutions show the firm's emphasis on goods of its own production (even at times as a higher priority than the original desires of its wholesale clients) but also of goods that were designed more recently and distinctively than the earlier patterns.

Thus, design also became a business principle; when producing goods exclusive to the company, the issue of meeting its own standard designs in trade did not arise. This shift in business practice coincided with the introduction of brand names in mass-produced goods. As one Reed & Barton catalogue explained, "It is a well established fact that in the manufacture of Silver and Gold Plate the integrity of the manufacturer is the only sure guarantee of quality." Markings on and advertisements for silverplated ware were an intersection between the long-held tradition of stamping metalwork with maker's marks and the newfound practice of selling corporate identification with goods through brand names.[52]

Design was a cumulative process, with various stages of input and literal trips back to the drawing board. Consultation with sales staff appears to have been standard practice for the silver designers. Correspondence between the manager Fiske in Taunton and Calvin Harris in New York exemplify these negotiations:

- We are duly in receipt of your letter in regard to the sketch of 2160 reduced size & note your suggestions.
  Mr. Beattie [the chief designer] has made another embodying as near as possible your ideas which will we trust be satisfactory.
- I send you tonight the drawing of the small size 3160 . . . changed according to your suggestion & return the other to show the points of difference.[53]

Though their work was not autonomous, designers held a high status within the industry.

Designers could be considered both the first and last steps of the production cycle, creating goods but also being asked to adjust them to popular taste.[54] In the early 1870s, Henry Reed and William Parkin, a die sinker by training, designed for the company. In 1874, W. C. Beattie was hired from England as the company's first full-time designer; he served as head designer until 1889, when Austin F. Jackson, also from England, replaced him. The design department at Reed & Barton grew quickly in the 1870s and 1880s, at the end of which there were twenty-four designers and modelers on staff. The same years witnessed the establishment and growth of American art schools, such as the Cooper Union (founded 1857) and Rhode Island School of Design (1877), training potential employees. By the 1880s, the industry would tout its own hiring of native design talent: "A prominent characteristic of American goods is their originality. Our workmen are no longer dependent upon the older countries for their designs any more than they are for the mechanical skill that gives them shape and form." Designers were well-known figures in the industry; they were well-paid and occasionally lured from one company to another.[55] Their workspaces, though so different from the manufacturing floors that made up most of a plant, were considered by many to be the heart of the factory. The Reed & Barton design room was described in *Appleton's Journal* as a "quiet sanctum" for those who originally conceived of the wares. The author continued: "It was difficult to draw the artist away from the congenial atmosphere of the room. The soft light streaming in from the half-curtained windows on casts and photographs, pencil-drawings and *bric-a-brac,* while on a side table a copy of the ART JOURNAL lay open for ready reference, had almost too great an attraction for him to be readily overcome."[56]

The designers created the rapid and at times overwhelming proliferation of flatware patterns that went hand in hand with the development of silverplating. Industrial production made the aesthetic aspect of the pieces accessible to a broader sector of the population, the new middle-class market. While there had always been some slight variations in shapes of the "functional" parts of flatware, handles (and sometimes the backs of spoon and fork bases) were usually the place for some aesthetic expression; this expression could be inherent in the material, such as pearl-handled knives, or in the care taken with the form and ornamentation of the handle. With these enhancements, functional objects could lend the quality of luxury to an otherwise modest setting or event. Though flatware was usually marketed, and considered by consumers, as a once in a lifetime purchase, the relatively low cost of silverplate allowed some purchasers to replace their goods with an eye to style. As one author in the popular press wrote, "The cheapness of the American makes enabled the buyers to get new styles as soon as the articles began to wear out, and thus a taste for novelty in designs was stimulated."[57] In the 1870s the development of decorative handle designs, created specifically for certain companies and protected by patent, grew and continued at a rapid pace into the twentieth century.

Despite these protections and exclusivity, manufacturers managed to create surprisingly similar designs. The standard patterns of the 1860s continued to be made, shared by the companies, or with variations so slight that the average buyer would have a hard time distinguishing between them. Some stylistic traits can be attributed to specific designers, but there appears to have been interchange between the different companies. For example, within a few years of one another around 1900, several companies introduced new designs featuring clusters of grapes. Another design tactic was to combine relatively similar elements of shape or ornamentation in different ways—almost an industrial approach to design in which "parts" or specific design elements were interchangeable.[58] As one article from *Jewelers' Circular* applauded, "The fact that American silversmiths have dared to go out of the old beaten track after original ideas, have dared select the best from all time-honored methods and adopt them, one, two, three or more differing styles in one article if need be, accounts for the wonderful progress made in American silverware, and the honor with which the country's art work is everywhere received."[59] Ironically, despite the incredible variety of patented designs, these shared design elements, and similar basic proportions for each form, resulted in a similar visual effect. A lengthy series of articles in *Jewelers' Circular* in 1895 detailed the spoon patterns of American silver producers; the author stated from the start of the series that although he would describe hundreds of patterns, the vast majority of them shared their basic outlines with one of the three traditional patterns, Oval Thread, Fiddle Thread, or Kings.[60] Distinctiveness in design does not seem to have been as important to the manufacturers as trying to appeal to the largest possible share of the market. Design was a selling point for the silver industry, as the numerous references to World's Fair and other competition prizes attest, but distinctive design was apparently not a necessity.

Companies tried to learn about each other's newest lines; salesmen on the road and in the jewelry stores were given the task of trying to ferret out what designs other companies had in production. The branch offices, in addition to acting as sales centers, also served as information-gathering points for Reed & Barton. Geographically remote from much of their competition, Reed & Barton managers were kept informed by their agents in trade centers such as New York and Philadelphia. For example, wanting to keep abreast of flatware patterns of their competitors (without seeming too eager to do so), managers sent out local agents to find new patterns in stores. In 1902, George Howard in Philadelphia was asked to investigate a new Gorham pattern; he replied that it was not yet available at either Bailey, Banks, and Biddle or Caldwells (the two major Philadelphia retailers in the jewelry trade) but that he would keep looking until he could secure a sample. He was successful, however, at finding the new Cat Tail pattern made by the William B. Durgin Company of New Hampshire. He sent impressions of the "fancy" pieces, including serving pieces and any form other than the standard place setting, in which Cat Tail was being produced, and predicted that it would soon be made in all fancy pieces; in Philadelphia, it was being handled at the time only by Bailey, Banks, and Biddle. Howard also learned the following design and pricing news:

> In re of Gorham's new pattern will say that I have talked with one of Bailey's salesmen who has seen it and from his description it is very much like their old "Meadow" design, it is designed to take the place of the Buttercup pattern that they brought out some time past, Bailey have adopted the new pattern and it will be on sale the latter part of the month, from what I could learn the price is to be about the same as the "Buttercup."[61]

Howard's description shows the practice of making small changes in existing designs, trying to strike a balance between old favorites and the desire to promote something new.

In addition to the variety of designs, there was also a proliferation of different forms in which those designs might be produced. Increasingly, specialized wares included not just a fork and spoon, but many sizes of forks and spoons, based on a presumption of different courses of food. One could buy not just any fork but a dessert fork, not just a dessert fork but a berry fork. One Reed & Barton listing from the 1870s included salt spoons, mustard spoons, teaspoons, desk spoons, tablespoons, bar spoons, coffee spoons, berry spoons, preserve spoons, rice spoons, mustache spoons, sherbet spoons, child's spoons, egg spoons, table forks, medium forks, dessert forks, child's forks, fish forks, lined fish forks, oyster forks, pickle forks, long pickle spears, short pickle spears, twisted pickle spears, oyster spears, butter knives, cake knives, cake servers, cheese knives, child's knives, crumb knives, fish knives, fruit knives, pie knives, desk knives, bon bon tongs, sugar tongs, sugar shells, sugar shovels, medium ladles, oyster ladles, soup ladles, gravy ladles, cream ladles, nut picks, julep strainer, and cheese scoops.[62] That the extreme specification of the wares could lead to increased sales was apparent to those both inside and outside the trade. The multiauthored novel *The Whole Family,* featuring a central character who owned a silverplate firm, provides a popular perspective; a friend of the silverplate manufacturer inquires after the state of trade: "'And the factory?' I asked. 'How does the business of metallic humbug thrive?'" The entrepreneur responds, "All right . . . There's a little slackening in chafing-dishes just now, but ice-cream knives are going off like hot cakes. The factory is on a solid basis; hard times won't hurt us."[63] Innovation in forms was a way to attract attention to a particular line of wares, even in times of economic downturn. The 1880s and 1890s brought still more pieces into production. The industrial notion of separation of functions, with specialized tools to perform each task, appears to have been applied to flatware.[64] While in some instances, manufacturers may have introduced new forms to the public, they may also have been responding to consumer demand; as the *Jewelers' Circular* explained in 1885, "The demand for . . . novelties in household decoration apparently does not abate, and there is such a pressure for novelties that designers in all parts of the world, from Boston to Yokohama, are kept busy pushing their inventiveness to the last degree to turn out new combinations. Every manufacturer who caters to this taste in any way keeps a designer, whose ears are burdened with the demand for something new."[65]

With this increasing specialization, Reed & Barton sought to make pieces best-adapted to the task at hand, while still retaining an emphasis on design. In 1869, the company patented its "improved cutting fork" with thicker and slightly rounded outside tines, providing a firmer edge for cutting food, but also adding a heightened symmetry to the design of the fork. The company touted the benefits of the fork, stating in a catalogue:

> The peculiar and well-proportioned shape of the tines, besides adding to the beauty of the fork by giving it a graceful outline, also makes it better adapted to meet all the requirements of a table fork than any other now in use . . . Great firmness and durability, besides symmetry and adaptation to practical use, are secured by the distinctive form of the outer tines. These tines it is impossible to bend in the process of cutting, thereby bringing the ends together and destroying all grace of outline, as so often happens with the ordinary fork.[66]

Thus, even the form itself, apart from the design of the handle, could contribute to the overall aesthetic effect.

Silverplate flatware was also produced in different grades, corresponding to the amount of silver deposited on the piece or the duration of the electrical charge that deposited the silver on the piece. Reed & Barton used four grades, the highest of which was referred to as "hotel grade," of particularly heavy plating to stand up to frequent use. In the 1870s, manufacturers developed modes of plating that added extra deposits of silver to areas of heavy ware. Meriden Britannia developed a method called "sectional" or XII plating, which placed extra deposits of silver on the backs of spoons, fork tines, and ends of handles. In 1878, Reed & Barton started searching for information about the patent for this process, and when it would expire, to see when it could adopt it.[67] The large firms such as Reed & Barton produced goods of relatively high grade; even their lowest grade was a high-quality product. Even on their lower-end products, Reed & Barton maintained a relatively high level of plating quality, sheltering its reputation. M. T. Rogers wrote to Calvin Harris at the New York office in 1878, "We received a line from JDB Paine 14 Pine St NY a few days ago calling for tea spoon at $1.25 per doz we have written him that we did not make that class of goods & did not know who did. Please drop him a line informing him who does as we advised him you would confer with him."[68] Rogers expressed the differentiation among producers of flatware, in this instance focusing on the grade of silver plating. He was insulated in Taunton from the numerous producers in New York, particularly firms specializing in flatware, who did serve the market that the wholesaler Paine was looking to supply.

Pieces were generally sold in dozens or half dozens until the 1920s, when sets of eight were popularized, in part by International Silver Company's "Pieces of Eight" promotions.[69] A "set" could mean anything from six matching coffee spoons to an elaborate velvet-lined case furnished with a dozen place settings each consisting of numerous pieces, as well as serving pieces. The production of cases to hold certain permutations of goods was another way in which the silverware industry belied its industrial base; the notion that each piece should have a particular housing and that the set should fit together into a cohesive whole bridged aesthetic and pragmatic concerns. As one article in *Jewelers' Circular* noted:

> Silver wedding presents in cases have had a great run, for the cases, being designed with reference to the special character of the contents, greatly en-

hance the appearance of the articles, however elegant these may be in themselves. There are great chests of solid mahogany, olive and other polished
woods, lined with satin or plush, and containing in sundry drawers and trays
an entire collection of table silver, beginning with tea spoons and running
through a diversified catalogue.[70]

Cases were another source of income for the companies, and helped identify a group of silverplate as a set. One Gorham Company advertisement
from 1885 introduced its new pattern, Nuremberg, stating that the case was
"an actually indispensable feature of the set."[71] Though for the most part silverplate flatware was a one-time purchase, sets could always be added to,
with serving pieces, additional place settings, or specialized novelty pieces.[72]

In the years following the discovery of the Comstock Lode, prices eventually fell low enough that sterling silver wares were actually in price competition with silverplate wares. Silverplate producers began to enter the sterling market. With an industrial system already established, it was easier for
the silverplate manufacturers to adapt their processes to the new material,
or the exclusive use of the material already in service, than it was for silversmiths who had worked exclusively in sterling but on a smaller scale, to
adapt to a larger market.[73] While even industrially produced silver retained
a considerable amount of handwork, flatware was the most easily mechanized of the pieces made. As *The Independent* explained near the end of the
century, "The low price of silver bullion gives nearly everyone an opportunity to buy silverware at a very great reduction from former prices, and it
has also stirred up manufacturers to increase the number of articles manufactured by them and in a wider variety of designs."[74]

The structure of the silverware industry, producing a broad range of
designs, forms, and grades, lent itself to a broad marketing. A set of flatware
was a durable good, likely to be bought once in a lifetime, if at all. In the estimation of the *Jewelers' Circular,* in 1885, "The number of persons who can
afford the luxuries of life and to indulge their refined tastes is constantly
increasing as the country grows older and adds to its wealth."[75] The challenge was to convince this growing market to buy these durable goods without considering them an "indulgence." Trying to pinpoint whom might be
persuaded to buy, when in their life they would do so, and whether such a
purchase might be for their own family or for a gift were the major questions of burgeoning marketing departments.

Competition between companies for sales was waged in the arenas of price, design, and reputation. In order to build that reputation, however, companies engaged in other forms of competition, for example, at industrial exhibitions or World's Fairs.[76] At these exhibitions, companies used not just their wares but also the displays as examples of their design skills.[77] Reed & Barton's leaders were firm believers in marketing methods, and displaying in public venues such as World's Fairs was one form of these practices. In the fall of 1875, Reed & Barton began negotiating with Henry Pettit, chief of the Bureau of Administration for the Centennial Exposition, for exhibit space at the Philadelphia World's Fair of 1876. Though asked to exhibit with other Massachusetts manufacturers by the Massachusetts Board of Managers for the fair, Reed & Barton, along with other silverware manufacturers, went directly to Pettit with its request for a large space allocation. Reed & Barton proposed the installation of a "Rosewood & French Plate Glass Case & Base" measuring 27×8 feet, and 10 feet high. The company requested that "the case should be placed where there is good light and should have a wide passage completely round it," obviously intending to design the space so that it could be viewed from all sides. Pettit wrote back, saying, "Make your exhibit as handsome as possible—we will give you as good a location as we can."

The company proposed to include over a thousand objects, valued at $24,500, and estimated spending an additional $15,250 on exhibit expenses. Clearly, the company's $39,750 investment in the Centennial Exposition was expected to bring it some gain.[78] The centerpiece of the exhibit was the Progress Vase, a 3×4 feet silverwork depicting scenes from the fifteenth and nineteenth centuries, drawing attention to the display. But it was the smaller objects, particularly flatware and sets of hollowware, that might have been within financial reach of the visitors to the exposition. Reed & Barton exhibited numerous examples of its Gem, Florence, French, and Roman Medallion flatware patterns, as well as the new patterns introduced around that time, Unique and Brilliant. In addition to the forks, knives, and spoons in various sizes, the patterns were displayed in "fancy pieces" ranging from gravy ladles to sugar shells to carving knives to pickle spears, and including their new patented cutting forks, with wider outer tines.[79] The jewelry and silversmithing trade for years to come would look back to the example of Philadelphia as the greatest exposition of national design.

Smaller fairs were useful for introducing goods to specific regions, as the publicity surrounding an 1885 exposition in New Orleans shows. The *Jewelers' Circular and Horological Review,* one of the major trade periodicals for the silverware trade, explained that while not as convenient as Philadelphia, there were merits to the site:

> the location is the great distributing center of an extensive section of the country, that is far behind the north and west in industrial and commercial development, and that offers a rich field for cultivation by the enterprising business men of the other sections. The south has had a hard struggle since the war . . . [but] twenty years have done much to improve it, and the times and the people seem ripe for a greater prosperity than they have ever known . . . visitors, many of them strangers to such exhibitions, will have an opportunity of seeing what progress has been made in this country in the . . . silversmiths' art.

Meriden Britannia exhibited extensively in New Orleans, using display cases from the centennial, but including such educational exhibits as one that showed the different states in the manufacture of a fork. Still, most of the other manufacturers waited for larger, better-attended opportunities for display.[80]

The *Jewelers' Circular* concluded, "From the Philadelphia Exposition dates what may be termed a 'boom' in art matters in this country, which has been worth millions of dollars to our artists and manufacturers."[81] In order to maintain this boom as long as possible, images of the Centennial Exposition were circulated. By the end of 1876, Reed & Barton was advertising its success at the Centennial in journals such as *Harper's Weekly*. Its advertisements included excerpts from the comments of the judges who granted three awards to the company:

> An Extensive Display of Silver-Plated Goods, including all varieties of household table ware.
> Their hollow ware, plated upon white metal, is of high excellence, with designs of good taste and quality, and finish of superior character.
> Their many patterns of knives, forks, and spoons are of great excellence.
> Their historical vase, PROGRESS, illustrating phases of the 15th and 19th centuries, an original and elaborate composition of striking character and praiseworthy excellence both in design and execution.[82]

While obvious competition at the fair may have been centered on the Progress Vase and Tiffany and Gorham's masterworks, the first excerpts in the advertisement were in fact about "household" use. Reed & Barton, at least for the consideration of *Harper's Weekly* readers, was a company that made silverplate goods that could be incorporated into the settings of daily life. The Centennial was clearly a site to spread the word about the company's wares, not only among those viewing the extensive display in Philadelphia, but those reading about it and those being reminded of what occurred there, regardless of whether they attended. In 1877, Reed & Barton sent the wholesalers Arkell & Tufts stereo views of its installation at Philadelphia along with information and photographs about goods from the fair lot that were still available for purchase. The stereo views were also distributed to Reed & Barton's salesmen to take with them on the road.[83] As the first hints of organizing the Columbian Exposition arose, the trade periodicals looked back fondly to Philadelphia, a time when workers from the various manufacturers were brought to Philadelphia at the expense of the companies to be inspired by the beautiful displays of work.

Along with other medals from fairs and expositions, the Centennial medals became a standard feature of Reed & Barton's promotional materials in the years following the fair. An 1880 flatware catalogue announced:

> We present you herewith our New Illustrated Spoon and Fork Price List, embracing all the latest patterns to date and respectfully solicit your patronage. The superiority of our goods which have been before the public for so many years is fully confirmed by the recent award of the MEDAL OF PROGRESS, the HIGHEST AWARD EVER GRANTED FOR SILVER PLATED WARE, and the still more recent testimony from the SYDNEY INTERNATIONAL EXHIBITION, where a SPECIAL AWARD has just been received in addition to the FIRST PREMIUM in competition with goods from all countries.[84]

In order to put together its trade catalogues, the firm rounded up images of the medals, and had new prints made so they would be on hand in the future. For example, the firm contacted the newspaper *El Espejo* for an image of a medal won at a Chilean fair. It was particularly important to company partner George Brabrook that the medals be displayed actual-size, no smaller or bigger, and that they be consistent in their representation, whether they were line drawings or shaded; even the image of the company's design awards was to be carefully designed.[85]

The process of advertising unique success was paralleled by an evolution in responsibility for sales; as silverplate companies moved away from using wholesalers toward having their own sales staff, goods became more easily identified with their original manufacturer. The companies sought to introduce to a broad public both their own name and design quality and the idea of a matching set of silverplate flatware to consumers who might not otherwise have considered such an investment. They brought their wares before the public eye in a variety of ways, particularly designed to stress the aesthetic element of their product. The trade journal *Jewelers' Circular* called for manufacturers to produce their own catalogue, rather than relying on jobbers to do so, just one of the ways in which company identification could be made.[86] The silverware firms needed to produce not only flatware, but also images of it, to be distributed across the country.

IMPRINTS OF SILVER

The distribution of these images was just one of the ways in which the work of designers and salesmen came together in the variety of promotional materials that displayed representations of Reed & Barton silverware. The company issued numerous trade cards, placards for jewelry stores, small pamphlets of seasonal poetry, and other ephemera, containing either images of specific wares or scenes evocative of leisure time, even if not specifically related to dining.[87] The artists responsible for creating these images worked at the intersection of design and marketing. For illustrations of specific wares, artists completed wood engravings of objects, which were then reproduced by means of electrotypography, an innovation of the 1850s. Producers of these engravings were different from the original designers, and usually had long-term relationships with the companies who used their services. These artists were responsible for the huge catalogues of electrotypes produced in the 1870s and 1880s; in addition to depicting wares, these books were valued for their own artistry and were a testament to the companies' overall attention to art and design. This means of illustration helped expand the potential audience for the company's wares in subsequent years; representations of goods were, of course, more easily circulated than the wares themselves and could have a broader distribution. As one Reed & Barton salesman wrote to the home office, of his jewelry store clients, "These people *all* ask for *books* . . . They need a book to which a ready reference can be had to anything you make."[88]

In 1877, bowing to its competitors, Reed & Barton issued its first large-scale catalogue showing a complete line of wares. The Meriden Britannia Company had started the trend toward large catalogues of wood engravings as early as 1855; with engravers on staff, Meriden was continually improving its production of images, as well as its products.[89] For Reed & Barton, securing the images for the 1877 catalogue took considerable coordination. Reed & Barton escalated its preexisting relationship with Oscar W. Maddaus, a New York engraver, to provide woodcuts for the 1877 catalogue. Photographs of goods were taken in Taunton and forwarded to New York to have engravings made, though frequently, actual wares were provided as well to ensure a more accurate representation. Engravings from Maddaus went through Harris in the New York office to Fiske in Taunton, where page layouts were decided upon and gathered into forms and then passed on to Appleton's printers in Springfield, Massachusetts.[90] The process of laying out the catalogue was similar to designing exhibits at World's Fairs or other exhibitions; each piece had to be shown to its best advantage, while also creating an aesthetically pleasing whole.

As Fiske and Brabrook determined the layout and order of the eight-page forms, they often realized they needed images cut in different ways, and went back to Maddaus for new electros. Or they might want certain features stressed in the drawing, as when they wrote, "you can tell Maddaus that we have not crossed them out on account of their being plain, small, or easy to cut but on [account] of the position for they now face the wrong way. The Sp[oons] & Forks that were crossed out are the extra heavy & we wanted them all together so as to have them cut with special reference to making them show the thickness of the metal particularly." On another occasion, Brabrook sent word to display images of the Tipped and Fiddle teaspoons with the words "New Dies" under them.[91] This direction shows that even in the production of traditional patterns, the firm stressed that the goods were up-to-date and well-made. It was a way to compete with other companies that were also manufacturing the standard patterns; Reed & Barton could make them more crisply and cleanly in its new dies. "New Dies" suggested that Reed & Barton was making these patterns itself, signaling an end to the practice of buying blanks from other firms and plating and stamping them.

While a steady stream of designs was sent to Maddaus for engraving over the course of the year, at times the management was unhappy with his work and threatened to take the potentially large commission elsewhere. For example, for cuts for the Pearl flatware pattern, Fiske asked Harris to include a full-size photo, the spoon itself, and find "the very best person you know of . . . some party who is used to cutting human figures & can do it well for Maddaus doesn't seem to excel in this." A second engraver apparently proved satisfactory to the company's management, and Fiske told Harris to con-

tinue to use him for all electros to be used in "the book"—the 1877 catalogue—but that if they requested copies of electros to be given away for
advertising or sales purposes, they could be of a cheaper grade. As the process
of putting together the catalogue reached a fever pitch, Fiske requested suggestions from Maddaus for someone in the Taunton area who could do wood
engravings of fine quality, because Reed & Barton might consider hiring an
engraver on a full-time basis.[92] Over time, Reed & Barton's plant in Taunton
included not just the whole industrial process but also design and ultimately
the means of advertising their wares through representations of them. An
1885 article in *The Evangelist* stated, "Everything is done by them at their
works; their photographic gallery, bureau of engravings, designing rooms,
and all the manual skill and machinery used in the production of goods; and
they make their own goods and roll their metals."[93] This author promoted
not just Reed & Barton's production of wares, but also its production of
images.

Regardless of who did the engravings, whether commissioned or on Reed
& Barton's staff, those persons still had to negotiate the representations with
Reed & Barton's chief designer Beattie. In a typical exchange, Fiske wrote
from Taunton, "The *drawing* of the Pearl Fork was very well liked & if it is
finished up to look as well I think it will be quite satisfactory. You had better have it done & send a proof. Mr. Beattie thinks there is a *little* too much
light on the knee of the figure." Though Maddaus's and the other engravers'
work was the backbone of the catalogue, it was meant to be "transparent"—
it was not their art, but the art of the wares themselves, the art of the designers, that was on display. Fiske wrote to Harris, "Mr. Brabrook says you can
let Appleton [the printer] cut out Maddaus' name whenever he can as we
have no particular desire to advertise for him."[94] The only "advertisement"
was to be for the company.

The catalogue was obviously supposed to compete with existing examples of the arts of the book; Fiske wrote that the type chosen will look good
"when printed as well as in *Picturesque Europe*," an expensive parlor book
of the day. Within this elaborate context, the sections of the catalogue devoted to flatware were designed in a more spartan manner. Apparently the
spoon and fork listings were seen as the humbler parts of the catalogue, or
perhaps the complexity of listing all patterns, forms, and grades demanded
a different approach than the rest of the catalogue. Fiske wrote, "Mr.
B[rabrook] says the Spoon & Fork Price List in the new book should be
printed in very *plain* figures and the other type should be so as to be easily

read. In other respects it should correspond with the general style of the book."[95]

The 1877 publication was only a trial run for Reed & Barton's grand catalogue of 1885. The introduction to the latter catalogue explained the importance of the circulation of images: "To meet the constantly increasing inquiry for Illustrations of the Latest Designs in Silver and Gold Plate, and to give a somewhat adequate idea of the Complete and Extensive Line of our Productions answering to the present advanced artistic standard, adapted to the requirements of the General Public, we offer this Catalogue."[96] The 1885 catalogue served as the basis of a public relations campaign perhaps even more than it could function as an actual sales tool. It is hard to imagine the 16 pound, 11×14 inch, 372-page volume getting daily use among the company's salesmen and distributors. The number of engravings, close to 4,000, seems almost too many for a salesman to use conveniently when looking for an example of a specific ware to show a customer. However, the volume became not just an object but an event. The company sent out leaflets to announce the catalogue to its most favored clientele:

> We are just receiving from the publishers finished copies of our new Illustrated Catalogue and take great pleasure in advising you that we have forwarded a copy to your address by express.
>
> We take this opportunity to extend our thanks for your many past favors, and ask your acceptance of this New Catalogue, containing illustrations of all our latest productions, embracing a line sufficiently comprehensive to meet every requirement of your trade.
>
> With the firmly established reputation of our goods for superior quality, we feel confident it will be to your interest, before placing your orders for the season, to await the possession of this catalogue, replete with all the latest novelties.[97]

Touted as the most expensive book published in the United States to date (besting even the 1882 art book *Picturesque America*), with estimates ranging from $30,000 to $70,000, the 1885 catalogue was treated as news, not only in trade circles but in local newspapers, the popular press, and perhaps even popular literature. In *The Whole Family*, the character of a printer pines over a commission for a catalogue from the silverplate manufacturer who lives next door; though written a generation after the height of the silver industry's competition in printed matter, the example clearly still rang true to readers. In describing the son of the family firm, the printer says, "Talbert's son is in the business with him, and will probably succeed him in it . . . he still does some sketching outside, and putters over the aesthetic details in the business, the new designs for plated ware, and the illustrated catalogues which the house publishes every year; I am in hopes that we shall get the printing, after we have got the facilities."[98] The real commission to which the fictional printer aspired was certainly a grand one.

Part of the story was told in the statistics about the book: its size, the weight and cost of the paper and ink, the use of color and gilding, and labor involved, with more than twenty engravers working two to three years (accounts varied) on the engravings. But the breathless prose also sought words to describe the artistic nature of both the wares and the representations of them. One local newspaper wrote, "Some of the designs are printed in colors and gilded giving them a rich appearance. No gift book ever printed equals it in magnificence," while another periodical stated, "this catalogue stands without rival as an art publication and as an example of American bookmaking." A third acknowledged the book's origins as a business tool: "The 'art of advertising' is a well-worn phrase, but it is peculiarly applicable to the handsome illustrated catalogue published by Messrs. Reed and Barton . . . To convey any adequate impression of the many beautiful objects so exquisitely represented in this volume would take a volume of itself."[99] In fact, Reed & Barton was describing its own work in these ways, offering as a press release several descriptions of its catalogue under the heading, "To The Editor: If any one of the following articles would be an acceptable contribution, and of sufficient interest to the general reader to warrant an insertion, please give it space."[100] The obvious implication of its efforts was that if such a high level of design skill was put into the catalogue, certainly equal if not superior effort would be put into the silverwares themselves.

The press referred to not only the design of Reed & Barton's magnum opus, but also the company's abilities to distribute that design: "Distributed, as it will be, all over this country, and in all the principal cities of the world, it is destined to exert a wide-spread influence, and reflects the highest credit on Messrs. Reed & Barton." Again, the catalogue served as a stand-in for the goods; if it could be distributed widely, so could Reed & Barton's wares.[101] The 1885 catalogue was also a testament to the company's financial security; if Reed & Barton was willing to spend this much money on a promotional effort, surely it would not skimp at any point in the manufacture of silverplate. In fact, R. G. Dun and Company wrote in its credit rating for the year that even with the catalogue expenditures the company was in fine shape, though it may not have made any profits that year:

> Last year they went to [considerable] expense in the way of advertising. They issued a large & handsome volume containing cuts of their wares which they distributed throughout the country. They had about 7000 struck off & it is reported that they cost $10.00 per vol. this item taken with dull times makes it altogether probable that they made no money on last year's [business] . . . Are still [considered] strong & [good] enough & their paper passes readily with the banks here.[102]

The 1885 catalogue was the culmination of the engraved trade catalogue for Reed & Barton, after which it adopted photographic images. The Gorham Company had been an innovator in the use of photography, introducing the process into the factory as early as the 1850s and maintaining a photographic department by the 1860s. Though Reed & Barton had used photographs in-house or as the basis for the engraved plates, the company began using photographic images even in its presentations to the public. Looseleaf books of photographs could be sent back to the factory and updated by inserting new images of wares into the ring or tie bindings.[103]

The books were prized as important information, especially if they contained prices; keeping track of them was a form of corporate security. While the circulation of images was necessary to trade, that circulation also needed to be managed. When Charles Flood left Reed & Barton's Philadelphia office, his replacement, George Howard, sent him repeated letters with increasing urgency to get the photo books back from him, wanting to avoid their unauthorized circulation.[104] Photograph books and catalogues were guarded carefully and sent only to members of the trade deemed worthy by Reed & Barton, whether in terms of their good credit or their reputation for high-quality goods. A typical letter from the home office in Taunton to the New York store, where such information was more readily obtainable, read, "Who did you get this card from? What do you know of the parties? If you find them worthy of a book please advise us & we will send it." The books were fastidiously accounted for and apparently local firms were charged for at least the shipping of such volumes.[105] Drawings and photographs were also sent out individually, for a variety of purposes. In addition to offering designs for local stores for review and possible orders, drawings and photographs were also used to attract high-end customers. For potentially large orders or commissions, salesmen might send images to prospective clients for their review, eliminating the middleman.[106] A stock of images was needed on hand to supply these potential buyers, as well as for advertisements.

Advertising in popular periodicals was contested within the industry; not surprisingly, trade periodicals advocated using their pages as the best space for manufacturers' advertisements, upholding a system in which manufacturers dealt with jobbers and retailers and maintaining that those groups should be responsible for the final communication to customers.[107] However, this system of advertising was increasingly unrealistic, as manufacturers looked to create not just their own wares but also an audience for them.

Reed & Barton's first print advertisement was in a local business directory in the 1860s, but its first national campaign was in 1868, in *Harper's Weekly*.[108] The company experimented in its early advertising practices, reaching different types of markets through different types of periodicals. For example, in 1878 and 1879, Reed & Barton advertised extensively in religious periodicals. Print advertising peaked after the Philadelphia Centennial, dropped off again in the late 1880s and early 1890s, in accord with the national economy, and then rose again at the end of the century. In addition to introducing the Reed & Barton name, many of the company's advertisements highlighted the concept of owning a set of flatware.[109]

In a domestic context, as silverware symbolized the family circle, it was also a family purchase, and might be a family gift, particularly for a newly married couple. In one explanation of the new process of making hollow handle knives, the company described the pieces by stating, "They are of the heaviest grade of Plate, are light, strong and durable, and are without exception the best adapted for family use of any Knife in the market."[110] Repeatedly, Reed & Barton reminded readers of high-end periodicals that providing silver was the duty of close relatives of the bride and groom, and should be seen as an investment in creating a family heirloom. The advertising copy read, "It is the one essential gift, the foundation of the 'family silver'—the heirloom of the future."[111]

In presenting its goods as the means to begin a family tradition, Reed & Barton also helped specify the broad market that it wished to cultivate. Prospective purchasers were likely to be those just attaining a new social status demarcated by such luxury goods; these buyers wished to pass on that status to subsequent generations in material form. For those who might already own heirloom silver, Reed & Barton proposed a second set of flatware. For example, Reed & Barton addressed those who already owned sterling, or were at least considering either option, with text exclaiming: "SILVER-PLATED WARES: For every day home use, where sterling silver is not desired, there is no ware as satisfactory or serviceable as the Reed & Barton silver plate."[112]

For companies producing both silverplate and sterling, there was a surprisingly slow move to distinguish the possible audiences for these pieces. Though advertising in the first years of the twentieth century in high-end periodicals such as *Vogue, Cosmopolitan,* and *Rider and Driver,* Reed & Barton still offered both sterling silver and silverplated sets in the same advertisements, selling the concept of a complete matching set of flatware, regardless of the price level. The company needed to show that on the one hand silverplate was a worthwhile investment as an alternative to unplated Britannia ware and on the other hand silverplate was an acceptable and lasting alternative to sterling silver.[113] As Elsie Bee remarked in support of this intricate balancing act, "The reasonable prices at which the best plated ware is now put on the market brings it within the reach of the popular trade, while the artistic forms and attractive finish with which it is presented, appeals to many who can afford the luxury of sterling silver. Indeed, in many cases, the solid silver service is in some safe deposit down-town while the family are dining up-town off plated ware."[114] Finally, accent pieces like sets of coffee spoons were also heavily marketed, whether for those not able to buy a larger set of flatware or those looking to extend their silver services.

Manufacturers and local retailers, though each responsible for placing their own advertising, did work in conjunction with one another. The home office in Taunton coordinated the effort to place not just Reed & Barton products into jewelers' stores, but also images of their products into jewelers' advertisements. Fiske wrote to Harris in New York in 1878: "Please send me some copies of R&B's *Ads*—that have been inserted within a year as we have none here. I want one now for a single column if possible."[115] In this way, the advertisements taken out in New York papers, for Reed & Barton's own retail store, appear to have served as models for jewelry stores in other areas. Reed & Barton also distributed electrotypes to jewelers to use in advertising in local newspapers. One of the trade magazines for the silverware industry, *Jewelers' Circular and Horological Review,* advised in an article in 1885, "Illustrations of specialties convey a better idea of style and construction than any long-winded description; accompanied by a few words of necessary explanation, they constitute the most attractive advertisement."[116] As early as the 1870s, the company sent these images, primarily of its new flat-ware patterns, to a remarkably broad network of jewelers, stretching to cities and towns of all sizes from the East Coast all the way to Honolulu. In light of this broad reach, the company used these images to retain some control over the advertising practices of the local jewelers. In 1877, trying to push the Pearl flatware pattern, Fiske asked Harris to send the largest electrotype of a Pearl pattern fork possible, saying he had already changed the copy for the ad to discuss the Pearl piece. Fiske was worried that if the electrotype were not received in time, the local firm would go ahead and use an old electrotype it had of a Gem piece.[117] Reed & Barton even made up advertisements with examples of flatware patterns, medals won at exhibitions, and quotations from the judges' comments from these events, with a space at the bottom of the ad for the local jeweler to insert its store name after the words "Sold By."[118] Reed & Barton managed the display of its wares and images of them in a variety of locations, which reached varied sectors of the public.

Toward the end of the nineteenth century, the major silverplate manu-facturers took different approaches toward defining their markets. The Gorham Company and Tiffany Company sought to appeal primarily to a high-end market. In contrast, to attract a broader-based market, Meriden Britannia and sixteen other producers combined into the International Sil-ver Company in 1898, with different divisions targeting different types of sales; the manufacturing group used an array of retailers, including the mail-order house, Sears, Roebuck.[119] Reed & Barton took a middle approach, try-ing to foster sales to a wider segment of the market than Gorham, but not merging with other companies or growing as large as International.[120] One tool that Reed & Barton used to distinguish its market broadly was to sell through jewelers.

As late as the 1900s, Reed & Barton still insisted on selling only through jewelers, and even more so, the jewelers insisted on it as well. Part of the effort of maintaining good relations with the local jewelry stores meant not engaging in trade with their burgeoning competitors, department stores. The issue of dealing with department stores came up again and again in the trade papers, with most concerns coming down against them, at least in the jewelry trade.[121] These middlemen seemed to exert a fair amount of power over the sales process, as evidenced in Philadelphia in 1902. The experience of Reed & Barton's agent, George Howard, was instructive for the company. Howard had been in his post only a couple of months when, in his perusal of a morning newspaper, he ran across an advertisement placed by Strawbridge and Clothier, a major Philadelphia department store, featuring Reed & Barton wares, at a substantial discount from the regular retail prices. Shocked, knowing that he had not supplied the goods himself, and trying to find out who had, he was soon faced with angry jewelers, who followed those ads equally closely, threatening to close their accounts. Howard seems to have smoothed the ruffled feathers of the local retailers by assuring them that selling to department stores "is *not our intention* and that it is our *wish* and our *intention* to support the *legitimate Jewelry trade.*" He even considered buying up the goods at Strawbridge's, if only as a good faith gesture to the local trade, but he could not ensure that the scenario would not happen again. Howard recognized that if a wholesaler went on to sell to a department store behind the Reed & Barton's agent back, he could not necessarily stop that practice. When he did learn of the middleman in the Strawbridge deal, Howard stopped trading with him. And he rejected outright the Strawbridge buyer's offer to sell directly to him.[122] Nonetheless, other silverware manufacturers were selling through other retail outlets; throughout the last quarter of the nineteenth century, the trade debated the issue in its trade journals, recognizing the potential for more sales beyond the jewelry store, and also advocating more advertising at the level of the retailer, in order to keep exclusive hold on the trade.[123]

The influence of the major retailers on the company could be large, as their buyers were seen as a window onto consumers' choices. Thus, agents might confer with buyers at the big retailers for their opinions on prospective merchandise. George Howard related to the home office the information that Bailey, Banks, and Biddle was planning to discontinue six patterns, and would therefore be in the market for new ones. Howard offered a new design for a flatware pattern to the store's buyer, Mr. Jaquete, who was apparently not impressed with it. The matter was to be put off for the visit of Henry Reed, still a primary designer at the firm, as well as one of its partners.[124] Buyers might give suggestions for pieces in the making. Howard wrote the home office in Taunton with a small order of La Parisienne flatware for Caldwell & Co., stating that if it sold well, the firm would order more. But he also added that the buyer, a Mr. Thomas, "suggests that you will 'dry buff' the backs of the handles and on the front, particularly the space for the engraving, this will relieve the work somewhat and take away what he terms the dead appearance of the present finish."[125] In the estimation of such buyers, the design of the pieces, their aesthetic value as opposed to their utility, was their primary selling point.

While earlier in the nineteenth century the company had relied primarily on wholesalers to sell its goods, when dealing with middlemen, the silverware companies had to offer lower prices, so that the middle agent could still make a profit. The incident with Strawbridge's confirmed that the company was better off dealing directly with the retail trade using its own sales staff. As early as the 1870s and 1880s, the responsibility of selling was brought into the company.[126] Salesmen were the front line of the marketing effort, seeing what bought and sold and reporting back to headquarters about the popularity of various lines. They might also negotiate with jewelers about local advertising, and even make some decisions, while on the road, of when and where to go and attempt sales. Many of the salesmen worked their way up through the company, ensuring their familiarity with the products to be sold. Salesmen were the highest-paid group of employees at Reed & Barton, and the expense of their salaries and extensive travel was seen as a necessary part of marketing expenditures.

THE SALESMEN'S REACH

In February 1875, Reed & Barton sales agent Joseph H. Rines established himself at the Grand Hotel in San Francisco with an important mission. Rines was determined to win the prize commission of silverware for William Ralston and Warren Leland's new Palace Hotel. Ralston was president of the Bank of California and one of San Francisco's biggest boosters; he wanted the city to host one of the world's grandest hotels and set out to build the 755-room hotel on an entire city block. Leland was one of the five brothers who were rapidly making names for themselves in the American hotel business.[127] The salesman Rines seemed to realize that this commission symbolized a major new market for his company, and that with clients as well known as Ralston and Leland, the hotel trade, and perhaps more individual purchasers, would come to trust Reed & Barton's wares.

Though Rines originally expected to be able to offer a bid for the contract in February, his visit stretched out longer. Construction on the Palace went more slowly than had been anticipated, and silverware appeared to be far from Leland's first priority among all the decisions he had to make about his new hotel. Unfortunately, Rines's trip was not otherwise useful to Reed & Barton, as a drop in mining stocks had depressed the retail trade in San Francisco at the same time. As Leland stalled, more silverware manufacturers learned of the opportunity and gravitated toward San Francisco. In a letter to the home office on 17 February, Rines mentioned that both the Tiffany Company and "an english house" had arrived to furnish samples for Leland, as he had earlier been asked to do; later he mentioned both the Gorham Company and Meriden Britannia as main competitors.

Leland further frustrated Rines by not stating explicitly what he was looking for in the way of furnishings for the hotel. In the meantime, Rines made it his business to examine Leland's choices in other appointments for the hotel. Rines predicted that a variety of patterns would be acceptable, as long as they "seem best and prettiest." It was not until over a month later, on 22 March, that Rines first had the opportunity to show Leland the Reed & Barton samples. Rines believed that his company's wares fared well in Leland's estimation, but still without a list of goods needed, he had a hard time gauging the proprietor's interest. This meeting was also his first opportunity to see what his competitors were offering for the Palace. On the grounds of design, Rines dismissed the competition: "After seeing the samples of all parties I think you have a fair chance with the rest. Tiffany has no show at all and the Meriden offer nothing stylish unless they are keeping back other patterns." But he also realized that the commission would be won largely on price, and began to strategize about the bid he would soon have to submit. Rines expressed doubts about Leland's business practice, saying, "They have acted about ordering other goods in a manner that I don't call 'square' so that if they like your samples and others will promise to furnish them for less than you offer you will lose the order."

Rines was an excellent sales agent. As he looked to earn this commission, he took a broad view of what it could mean for the company. The mounting anxiety that was expressed in his letters to sales manager George Brabrook at the home office in Taunton, Massachusetts, stemmed from his belief that this one commission could, if won, substantially further the company's business. In Rines's estimation, the financial cost of placing a low bid would pay off in the end; he wrote, "They say today that they expect to give the entire order to *one* party. I would rather lose a trifle now than not get it and if they divide it up there will be no honor about taking it nor will the advertisement be of any account." Thus, Rines was already viewing his potential sale as fodder for more, perhaps both within the hotel trade and without. He wrote later that same day, with the order numbers in hand, "Adding both lots together for Dining Room and private rooms and it makes quite a large order. Gorham is very anxious to get it. The dealers here all enquire every day if it is decided yet and I would prefer you should not lose the order as your sales would probably be affected by it." In flatware alone, the order would include 1,800 medium forks, 2,000 teaspoons, 1,800 tablespoons, and 150 butter knives, among a host of other wares. It was presumed by the agents that Leland would invest in nickel silver bases for the silverplate, the highest grade possible.

On the day before bids were due, Rines was trying to pursue every possible scenario for the commission. He figured his bid, including an additional discount if Leland would guarantee the whole order to Reed & Barton, all the while agonizing that Gorham, "anxious" for the commission, would bid low and have wonderful wares. At the same time, he began to wonder about taking only part of the order, just to make sure to get something; Rines asked Brabrook, "Do you think it any advantage for me to offer to take any part of the order I can get so that any one can come in at the last moment and take just enough to say they helped furnish it or that they really furnished it since your strongest competitions will not yield till he knows they can not get it?" Again, Rines was driven by the knowledge that the commission would provide advertising material for whatever company secured it. The next day, Rines wrote out his estimate, gave it to Leland, and sent it to the home office, asking Brabrook to look it over and telegraph him at once if possible to lower it still farther. He predicted a speedy decision, because in fact all the sample wares were being held "in one suite of rooms where Mr. Ralston and Mr. Leland sleep so I think they will wish to have it out of their way soon as possible." Again applying his knowledge of Leland's other purchases, Rines thought the competition might yet be decided on the basis of the goods themselves, but that the winning company would be forced to match the lowest bid offered by competitors; for example, Leland "may offer it to Gorham at the Meriden's prices." Rines also explained possible factors not relating to the wares at all: "There is strong intimation here that H. Wilcox [head of Meriden Britannia] was smart enough to buy up some months ago the influence of parties who have something to do with the selection."

Rines recognized Leland as a difficult customer, predicting that he would want to keep samples of all goods ordered, and might require changes on the design to other objects; he wrote at one point during his trial in San Francisco, "they want to see every piece they buy and are not willing to rely a farthings worth on the word or honor of any one or any company." But he still believed the commission worth the effort. He stated outright, "They will give you lots of fuss yet about odd pieces still it would help you sell lots of goods I think in years to come if you can secure it. It is known everywhere

that the competition is between the best houses of the country." Furnishing
the Palace Hotel was a competition between the leading silverplate manufacturers, and if won, the publicity surrounding Leland and the Palace could
translate into publicity for Reed & Barton. Rines's hard work indeed paid off
for Reed & Barton, who won the commission.[128]

Joseph Rines's experience in San Francisco in 1875 reveals many of the
issues involved in the manufacturing, selling, and purchasing of silverplated
wares, and durable goods in general, in the last quarter of the nineteenth
century. While the forms of flatware were functional, used in the daily experience of eating, silverplate versions were suitable for the finest hotel. In evaluating these objects that had both functional and decorative components,
potential purchasers of silverplate flatware weighed pragmatic concerns of
cost and durability with aesthetic judgment of the pieces' design. While a
low bid was an important element in the "competition," with Leland's ability to manipulate prices, the aesthetic qualities—what was deemed "best and
prettiest"—emerged as the actual grounds for the decision. In special instances such as this one, customers might even influence the design of goods
and would certainly determine quantities produced. Rines's lengthy stay in
San Francisco demonstrates the importance of the hotel trade, a new sector
of public spaces, to manufacturers of furnishings that might at first be considered "domestic goods." Not only the Palace Hotel, but also the Grand
Hotel where Rines stayed, were evidence of increasing access to travel, of
both people and goods. Mechanisms of transportation and communication,
from the train on which Rines brought samples to California to the telegraph
he used when information from the home office was critical, made a national
distribution network possible. The rising importance of early forms of publicity, marketing, and company identity also figured in this story. While
Leland would not trust "the honor of . . . any company," Rines presumed
that other potential purchasers might trust Leland's judgment of the wares,
and perhaps by extension, Reed & Barton.

Placing its wares in public settings was one way for Reed & Barton to help
educate the public about the possible settings and uses of its products.
While the design exhibitions of industrial fairs and World's Fairs were one
type of setting, another important category were public spaces where the
goods were actually in use. Railroads, hotels, clubs, restaurants, hospitals,
and schools all had the need for large quantities of silverware for their particular community of clients. Institutional commissions were an important
part of a business's sales, and not only in monetary terms. They served man-

ufacturers on three levels. At the most general, potential purchasers might become accustomed to the ideal of a matching set of flatware defining the community that dines together. But they also might learn to trust a particular company's wares if used by a large institution, or they might even grow fond of a particular flatware pattern and seek it out for their own home or other setting.[129]

The hotel trade might also be a testing ground for new forms. A series of letters to the *Jewelers' Circular* in 1885 explained developments in steel knife blades set into decorative silverplate handles, as a corrective to earlier complaints that when knife blades were dulled, customers attributed their difficulty cutting to the quality of the food rather than the furnishings.[130] Reed & Barton introduced its patent cutting-fork to the hotel trade before it was included in their general merchandise catalogues; it appeared in an 1882 catalogue with the explanation, "In our line of Flat Ware especially adapted for Hotels, Steamboats, etc.,etc., we have introduced the Improved Forks, and their superior strength and durability have already been fully tested, with perfect satisfaction in all cases."[131] Customers with commercial interests were a good test because they had more at stake in providing high-quality furnishings.

Having started in the hotel trade early on, Reed & Barton maintained its interest in this sector of the market, furnishing not only hotels, but all kinds of public spaces, including railroad dining cars, clubs, schools, steamships, and the new apartment houses being built across the country. It was not until 1883 that Reed & Barton actually began producing the hotel line in a separate division of the company, with separate inventorying and accounting.[132] Even when the production of the hotel and domestic wares were divided, however, their marketing was still unified. Until the first decade of the twentieth century, sales agents appear to have incorporated the hotel trade into their regional routes, rather than divide lines of wares between them.[133] Jewelers might act as middlemen for these large orders, just as they did with individual purchasers. For example, Reed & Barton's southern agent H. W. Graves worked with a local jeweler to win the commission for the Piney Woods Hotel. Still, the home office in Taunton certainly helped manage the process, keeping track of hotels furnished and new hotels under construction.[134]

Since there were concentrations of these public venues in metropolitan areas, the Reed & Barton branch offices also coordinated this marketing effort. George M. Howard, running a branch office for Reed & Barton in

Philadelphia in the opening years of the twentieth century, made it his business to keep abreast of construction of new public spaces and solicit commissions for silverware. He explained to prospective clients that "we firmly believe that our goods will give the greatest satisfaction, and will outwear any others on the market that may be offered you, this belief is based on the fact of our securing more hotel orders than any of our competitors." Particularly for flatware, the commissions were large; for example, a bid put together for William H. Woodward of the Hamilton Court Apartment House in Philadelphia in 1902, included such large quantities of flatware as 50 dozen teaspoons, 12 dozen tablespoons, 20 dozen dessert spoons, 16 2/3 dozen soup spoons, 10 dozen bouillon spoons, 16 2/3 dozen butter spreads, 25 dozen dessert forks, 25 dozen medium forks, 25 dozen medium knives, 25 dozen dessert knives, 16 2/3 dozen Tiger coffee spoons, 16 2/3 dozen oyster forks, 10 dozen orange spoons, 4 dozen sugar tongs, 5 dozen salt spoons, 5 dozen gravy ladles, 3 dozen sauce ladles, and 4 dozen punch ladles. Howard went on to describe to Woodward the sectional plating used for commercial wares: "These goods to be made of the very highest grade of Nickel Silver with the extreme of heavy Silver Plating . . . , the Flatware to have extra Silver applied to the most exposed part of the principal pieces, such as the tips of the handles and the backs of the bowls and tines." Howard sought new hotel commissions at the growing resort town of Atlantic City, visiting hotels under construction, hoping to place new bids, as well as hotels the company had furnished in the past, for reorders.[135]

Howard's solicitation letters were tailored to give examples of Reed & Barton's work in that particular line of public space; for example, a letter to Col. W. G. Price, developer of a new apartment house in Pittsburgh, Pennsylvania, listed these details: "Among some of the Hotels and Apartment Houses we have supplied we may mention The Plaza, Manhattan, The Ansonia, Majestic and various others in New York, The Rittenhouse, Gladstone, Colonnade, Bartram and Greens in Philadelphia, The Raleigh, New Willards, and The Dewey of Washington, and several others through out the country." Beyond this commercial trade, Howard also handled accounts with the Pennsylvania Hospital and local schools. He solicited accounts, writing, for example, to the president of Bryn Mawr College, "We desire to call your attention to the fact that we are now represented in Philadelphia with a full line of samples of goods suitable for the table service of Schools and colleges." Similar letters went to the presidents of the State Normal School in East Stroudsburg and Dickinson College in Carlisle.[136]

Whether or not the institutions were specifically schools, they were often nonetheless sites of education in middle-class ways of life. The actual settings of the businessman's hotel, Masonic lodge, or department store tearoom of small cities were one level of influence, while written accounts of the grander spaces of large cities provided another level. Even when people might not actually go to well-known restaurants or hotels, such as Delmonico's or the Palace Hotel, popular periodicals' coverage of them as significant public places could still plant ideas in the minds of the public far away.

Geographically, the reach of companies like Reed & Barton was remarkably broad. As the 1885 catalogue announced, "In compiling this volume our aim has been to make it sufficiently comprehensive to meet the demands of all sections of this, as well as of foreign countries."[137] Even though Reed & Barton was not selling through mail-order channels as Meriden Britannia did, a fleet of salesmen dispersed across the country serving even the smallest towns in all regions. The New York office, which had been established in 1867, served as a headquarters for the salesmen on the road; order books and other supplies were gathered there.[138] Also requested from the New York office were maps—what better symbol of the company's distribution system? Fiske wrote to the office, "Please send me 12 Maps of the *United States* with all the places on them—loose so I can trace out each travelers route on one. It takes several states for each so we will have to have the whole U.S. Get those mounted on cloth if you can," and added, "Rand & MacNally have them on cloth." Fiske later asked what some of the population designations on the maps meant, clearly searching out more towns with potential markets.[139] Over time, additional regional offices were established, for example, in Philadelphia in 1891 and Chicago in 1892. Just as the *Jewelers' Circular* predicted, as the country grew, so too would the need for regional trade centers beyond the East Coast. Branch offices were particularly important in the flatware trade; companies might not send out a complete line of samples of hollowware, for financial and storage reasons, but would certainly have representative flatware pieces on hand.[140]

As their manager kept track of them on Rand MacNally maps, Reed & Barton salesmen reported back to the home office through letters and telegrams. The salesmen traveled with "books" of images, first electrotypes and later photographs, as well as cases of actual samples. It appears that Reed & Barton manufactured goods on the basis of advance sales, or at least that these orders could outpace production. Correspondence from M. T. Rogers to the salesman Wheeler in 1878 informed him that the goods he had ordered were not yet made but would be produced in about a month. Obviously Wheeler was traveling with images or samples made up without a full run to back them up.[141] Salesmen's orders had to include not just what wares were needed, but the finish of these wares, whether they were to be engraved, what arrangements for shipping had been made, and other details. The company relied on a variety of communications and transportation mechanisms, but, in the 1870s, much of this ordering was still done by mail. After consultation with the local post master and the superintendent of the New England Mail Service, Fiske advised Harris that he had to mail his letters at the main post office in New York to ensure they reached Taunton the next morning.[142] The trade catalogues introduced a telegraph code, assigning each piece of silverware a short word to be used in orders. And in 1879, the company installed its first telephones into the factory at Taunton.[143]

Planning an efficient travel route was part of the task of the sales staff. The salesmen were indebted to rail connections and other transport modes for trade, but were also at their mercy. The silverware and jewelry trade kept close watch on the expansion of rail lines, believing that railroad tracks opened the landscape to "civilization and cultivation," two musts for the luxury goods trade.[144] In addition to accessibility, travelers had to keep abreast of the specific conditions of their sales region, ranging from the local economy to climate. For example, southern salesman H. W. Graves wrote from Columbus, Georgia, to the home office in the spring of 1881:

> Collections through the section south are very slow on [account] of the wet season, roads are only getting passable. Steam Boats have brought very little cotton & only the last trips have had paying freights—Capt Cameron has *laid up* the See until fall trade, all business men are complaining—The Corn & cotton crops so far are looking remarkably well and every one is looking forward to large crops—[Merchants] have been buying but little, running off their stock as low as possible for fall purchase & will be north early.[145]

Salesmen in industrial areas encountered other issues. In the summer of 1902, George Howard explained the rationale behind his fall selling trips in Pennsylvania, "in regard to the places in the eastern part of the Penna. will say that they are nearly all situated in the 'Strike' region and it will not be advisable to visit them until after same is settled."[146] Salesmen sent word of their upcoming visit to jewelers, sending, for example, decorative postcards advising "I shall visit you soon with an unusually large line of new and elegant designs. I think you would do well to examine my samples before placing your orders for holiday goods."[147] Routes were established, but then were often modified if requests from a particular area came in. For example, upon receiving a letter of interest from a jeweler at Antioch, Virginia, Fiske wrote his regional agent Oxton to see how close to the town he went, and if he could possibly go, as it "seems a pity if this party is good for anything not to get this order."[148]

Reed & Barton's sales force tried to gauge the regional popularity of different wares, and send them out for review accordingly. Manager M. T. Rogers, writing to Calvin Harris of the New York office in 1878, told him of a request for a "sample roll" of flatware placed by Arkell, Tufts, and Company, wholesalers. He asked Harris, "will you please go in and see them and find out the patterns which would be most likely to sell in the section of the country they intend the goods for." Rogers went on to ask Harris if they want the "sample put up on chamois skin and generally arranged like our sample rolls," an indication of the extent to which Reed & Barton maintained control over display of its goods, even when sending them to far-flung distributors.[149]

Though sales were certainly higher in metropolitan districts, significant enough sales were accrued in small towns to keep salesmen going there. For example, Graves's trip south took him to the towns of Enfalla, Americus, and Macon, Georgia; Milledgeville and Chester, South Carolina; Wilmington and Greensboro, North Carolina; and Danville and Petersburg, Virginia, in addition to larger markets such as Charleston, South Carolina, and Richmond, Virginia.[150] Though the small towns certainly were approached as significant sales sites, salesmen made distinctions between different markets. Howard wrote the home office in late summer of 1902, suggesting a travel schedule that would bring him back to Philadelphia when the urban buyers would place their orders, and requesting samples for both trades. Howard wrote, "I would suggest putting a line of the 'Regular' goods on which I can sell at net prices . . . I should also like to have a line of samples for the Philadelphia trade, this of the new goods you are bringing out this Fall."[151] Thus, while developing both urban and small town markets, Reed & Barton offered the wares on different time schedules.[152]

In recognizing the broadening market for their wares in communities of various sizes arrayed across the country, the Reed & Barton sales team was in accord with the teachings of American etiquette and advice manuals. An author of one such guide justified its usefulness by writing, "politeness and urbanity are no longer confined to the walled cities, where they originated, but flourish even more luxuriantly in the rural districts."[153] At the same time, the salesmen's own experiences exemplified one extreme of the extent to which daily life was lived in public. These two trajectories, of increasingly uniform and increasingly public modes of life, resulted in a growing market for certain consumer goods, including silverplate flatware. From its origins in the luxury of court behavior, these tablewares became a symbol of a comfortable, but not excessive, way of living.

Owning a matching set of silverplate flatware did become a recognized standard of home furnishing for the middle class. In the first decade of the twentieth century, Robert Chapin, who would become one of the most recognized names in studies of the standard of living, wrote:

> One of the evidences of a general rise of real wages in the nineteenth century is the increase in the number and kind of good things that are within reach of the ordinary man, and actually in his possession. We know, that is, that the rise of the standard of living so as to include trolley-rides and daily newspapers and silver-plated ware must be the result of a general increase in family income.[154]

The widespread distribution of silverplate flatware that began in the 1870s grew into, by the 1920s, an assumption of everyday use of the objects by the broadest swath of Americans possible. In the early 1920s, the Bureau of Labor Statistics enumerated "necessary household equipment" for a household of five. A set of silverware for six, with the specification "quadruple plated," was part of this equipment.[155] The workings of both salesmen and arbiters of American manners transformed silverplate flatware from "hotel grade" goods into "necessary equipment" for the national standard of living.

Over the course of the late nineteenth century, a variety of voices, ranging from manufacturers to restaurateurs, convinced Americans that silverplate flatware was not a luxury good. It was a possession appropriate to everyday life in the United States. The extreme specificity of the tools for dining was a reflection of the industrial era, and was echoed in a plethora of other manufactured goods and designed spaces. The situation of flatware in both private, or domestic, and public, or institutional, spaces showed its significance in defining both a familial unit and larger social groupings. The potential influence of public spaces in guiding domestic design was not unique to tableware, of course; even prosaic items such as washbasins might be adopted in the home after experience in public spaces. The objects were on the scale of the person; a matched set thus emphasized relationships between people and encouraged common ways of using them, guided by standards of etiquette.

As the goods were used in a variety of settings, proper etiquette was expected in a variety of settings, both private and public. Prescriptive literature remarked that it was in fact the increase in public interaction that made shared codes of behavior so important. Promoters of etiquette argued that rather than being exclusive, having a common denominator of social behavior actually enabled the cohesion of larger groupings. Flatware created boundaries—at the level of an individual's place at the table or in echoing the boundary of a table—while unifying those sitting at the table. The flatware did not of course cause these social groupings, but rather reflected them, and perhaps made them more apparent. Whether people owned the hallmarks of these social codes or not, they could still share the codes. But in the eyes of manufacturers, people who knew these codes might be looking to express that knowledge in material ways. Thus cultural arbiters and manufacturers reinforced one another's messages, while also consolidating a middle-class community.

The market for flatware was certainly hierarchical, but also broadening, which encouraged companies to experiment with different types of sales outlets. Reed & Barton's choice of salesman to jeweler was simply one option. Other companies worked with even more elaborate steps between company and final consumer, while some eliminated middlemen entirely. The amazing reach of the Reed & Barton salesmen serves as just one example of the larger trend of nurturing national markets. The expanding national infrastructure, particularly of railroad lines and telegraph wires, enlarged this expansion in the potential consumer base in geographic terms. A cultural infrastructure, rooted in improvements in print technology and manifest in magazines, popular fiction, and a wealth of visual ephemera, also contributed to increased awareness of new consumer goods. These same tools of distribution were put to use by manufacturers of bathroom fixtures, similarly striving to associate their goods with behavioral norms, in their case, the ideals of cleanliness and good hygiene.

THE STANDARD OF HEALTH AND DECENCY

Bathroom Fixtures

In his 1874 etiquette manual, F. Oswald guided readers to one distinction between work environments and social spaces: "Soiled hands and even a begrimed face are badges of honor in the field, the workshop, or the kitchen, but there is no excuse for carrying them into the parlor or the dining-room."[1] In order to move from one setting to another, therefore, it was necessary to pass through a mediating space in which one could remove the soil and grime of work, and present one's neatest and cleanest self to family, friends, or the public. This intermediate space might range from an elaborate dressing room to an outdoor water pump, depending on where one fell on the socioeconomic ladder, but over the last quarter of the nineteenth century and first quarter of the twentieth, Americans had increasing access to a designated, interior space for bathing. Bathing, however, went beyond aesthetics or social graces, and into the realm of hygiene and health. By the 1920s, economist Newel Comish could write, in a statement echoed by numerous others, "It is felt that a housing standard which is to provide health and decency must include a complete bathroom"—a bathtub, sink, toilet, and perhaps shower.[2]

Although a bathroom incorporated into the home was an ideal, a public institution or workplace might also provide access to a space for bathing. Oswald's few words cover a variety of work situations: agrarian, artisanal, and industrial; within the home or in a separate location; and tasks of both sexes. When work occurred outside the home, it was said to be in the interest of the employer to make a space for bathing available for workers. If cleanliness ensured good health, good health might ensure efficient workers. As the hygiene expert Seneca Egbert wrote, "Health means ability to work and to earn good wages; and a healthy community means more business, more money, and more comforts."[3] The employer might accrue public relations benefits as well. If the firm was in a field related to hygiene or sanitation, these benefits were all the more important. The Kohler Company, a producer of enamel cast-iron bathroom fixtures, was one such firm that made every effort to promote its wares, both within and outside of the company.[4] In the first years of making enamelware in the 1880s, the Kohler, Hayssen & Stehn Company installed "shower baths" in the factory where workmen could bathe at the end of the workday. A local newspaper, the *Sheboygan Times,* took up the company's cause, rhapsodizing of the improvement: "'Cleanliness is next to godliness' and if working men in all of the big establishments have a chance to get these baths, the *Times* predicts that it will be the means of saving doctor bills and making better men. For who has not felt that exhilarating feeling of contentment and good will toward all mankind after a bath."

A few years later, John Michael Kohler tried to use bathtubs as a form of recompense, although it is unlikely he achieved "good will" with his plan. With the economic downturn of the 1890s, and the fact that his burgeoning lines of bathtubs were not yet considered essential goods, Kohler needed to either cut wages or close the factory for a period of time. He offered this no-win alternative to his workers who produced bathtubs. The *Sheboygan Herald* explained, "It is understood however, that Mr. Kohler, head of the firm, graciously donated one of the tubs in question to each of those employed in the manufacturing of same as a recompense for the cut to be made."[5] Thus, while needing to cut production on a line that had not yet proven itself financially, he also took the opportunity to imply the importance of that very object. In later years, after the establishment of the company town, Kohler Village, workers were encouraged to invest in homes, all of which were built with Kohler fixtures installed from the start, even at a time when many homes of similar size across the country did not yet have indoor plumbing. In line with the example of Henry Ford, the Kohlers tried to transform their producers into their consumers. Finally, in the 1920s, Walter Kohler would enthusiastically support the Better Homes in America movement, which promoted homeownership and modern domestic conditions.[6] Thus, part of the company's promotional effort was to bolster the ideals that would make their products appear to be necessities for everyday life.

No matter what promotions Kohler or its major competitors such as Standard Sanitary Manufacturing Company and Wolff Corporation conceived of, they alone could not create the booming market for bathroom fixtures of either enamel cast iron or vitreous china. The manufacturers were in many ways beholden to the broader cultural movements toward improved cleanliness and hygiene as the cornerstone to improved public health. The spokespeople for this movement, including social reformers, doctors, and civic officials, became indirect promoters for the products that contributed to the cleanliness campaign. For example, in 1903, John Jegi wrote in a text on physiology and hygiene, "The one important condition of public health is cleanliness. Health demands not only clean air, clean, pure water, clean wholesome, unadulterated foods, but, in addition to these, clean streets and alleys, clean public buildings and parks, clean private residences and yards, and cleanliness of person and clothing."[7] Those who studied and advocated principles of hygiene frequently drew this connection between personal habits and public welfare. Egbert offered definitions for the key terms:

> Hygiene may be defined as the art and science that considers the preservation, promotion, and improvement of health and the prevention of disease ... Sanitation or Sanitary Science is usually taken to be concerned with matters pertaining to the general public health, while Personal or Domestic Hygiene is more closely related to the affairs of the individual or the household.[8]

Lessons about cleanliness were directed at all socioeconomic groups, but high standards of cleanliness were often seen as a marker of middle-class values, and were aggressively introduced as aspirations for the working classes, particularly through the social reform programs of the Progressive Era. As tied to the public good, personal cleanliness was a responsibility to the larger community. One hygiene manual explained this larger service: "individuals owe a duty to themselves, their families and the public, in the matter of personal hygiene, and of so conducting or regulating their habits of life as to promote a normal and healthy existence."[9] Educators not surprisingly put stock in their own teachings as most important in improving domestic hygiene. This education, though, was put in social rather than scientific terms; in rather condescending language, hygiene expert Frederick Smith wrote in 1908, "The masses of people must, therefore, have a better knowledge, not necessarily of disease and bacteriology, which they do not understand, but of the practical advantages of health, cleanliness and favorable environment, which they can comprehend, and to which they can attach a social and commercial value."[10]

While bathing could be achieved anywhere with a basin of water, having a designated space within the house for the purpose of washing oneself lent an importance to the act that it might not otherwise have and allowed for a greater degree of privacy for actions increasingly construed as personal. Social worker Florence Nesbitt wrote of the importance of privacy, even within the family context:

> There should be toilet facilities in good condition with a door which can be locked, for the use of the family alone; running water in at least one room in the house besides the toilet. A bathroom is highly desirable and should be included wherever possible. It may be considered essential in families where there are a number of older children in rooms which would not otherwise permit the necessary privacy for bathing.[11]

At the same time, as it became more common to hook bathing vessels to pipes of running water, these vessels needed to be fixed in a specific place. Whether interior plumbing was linked to municipal water and sewage systems or private wells and septic tanks, the receptacles for water—bathtubs, toilets, sinks—were, of necessity, fixed in place. The convenience of running water and the rising standards of privacy together contributed to the acceptance of the bathroom as a necessary use of interior space, worthy of specialized furnishings. The fixtures at the core of that space were an aspiration associated with middle-class life.[12]

The items available for a bathroom expanded quickly in the 1890s to include not only a bathtub, a lavatory, and a water closet, but also a sitz bath, a foot bath, a separate low receptor for a shower, and, slightly later, various accessories such as towel racks, cup holders, and lighting fixtures. Similar to the proliferation of flatware forms, these different vessels for different types of bathing suggested a carryover of the ideas of specificity of function from the industrial workplace. They also contributed to the most sanitary of bathing experiences, and were in their own way "efficient" ways of bathing. Like the flatware standard place setting, however, a standard bathroom of a reasonably coordinated bathtub, lavatory, and toilet eventually emerged.

In addition to proliferating forms, proliferating styles also arose. The different manufacturers usually named their bathtubs, lavatories, and other forms of bathing devices, to distinguish designs from one another. While in some ways reminiscent of the naming of flatware patterns, the names for fixtures were even less obviously related to the objects, as the latter did not have representational motifs or stylistic associations. As with the flatware patterns, names needed to be unique to one company to avoid consumer confusion. In one instance, in the preparation for Kohler's 1914 catalogue, one of the company heads discovered that Standard Sanitary Manufacturing Company had just published a catalogue using a name for a bathtub, "Walton," that Kohler was planning to use. The company had time before the printing of its own catalogue to change the product name to "Cardinal."[13]

If the purpose of a bathroom was to provide space for the transformation to cleanliness, the space itself had to be impeccably clean. Because salesmen could not carry with them the fixtures that furnished these rooms, they established spaces in which to store, display, and sell them—showrooms, branch offices, even warehouses. These sales spaces had to exemplify the cleanliness that provided both the impetus for and the end result of the purchase. Each phase of the industry from manufacturing through marketing had to uphold the message of the importance of personal hygiene. Both manufacturers and educators recognized that they were inculcating new standards in both cleanliness and the means to achieve it. The consumption theorist Simon Patten acknowledged that expectations rose over time: "Many today living in the modern two-story house with its porch and sanitary plumbing, enamel bath tub, running hot and cold water, and steam heat, are enjoying luxuries denied to kings in the Middle Ages."[14] Most authors promoting these developments, however, took the "sanitary plumbing" and "enamel tub" out of the realm of luxuries and placed them in the standard of living. In an article in the *American Journal of Sociology*, William Allen described the access to a personal space for bathing as the pinnacle of both "Sanitation and Social Progress." As Allen wrote to sum up his argument, "sanitary conditions offer a criterion of the standard of life." This contemporary phase he called "democratic sanitation."[15]

SELLING ENAMEL

In the collaboration between bathroom manufacturers and public health and hygiene advocates, the players had one important advantage—the material of the fixtures was a sanitary product because of its hard, slick, nonporous surface. Martha Cutler explained to readers of *Harper's Bazar* in 1907 what they should look for in hygienic and affordable fixtures:

> For our tubs and wash-basins we must have a material which is non-absorbent, one which makes cracks and joints unnecessary, and which looks clean and may be easily kept clean. The ideal material answering these requirements is solid white porcelain, since we do not aspire to the hollowed out blocks of marble of princes and millionaires. Even the solid porcelain tubs are very expensive, however, and sometimes too heavy for a floor not prepared especially for them. A material . . . answering the requirements as well as the solid porcelain, is that known as porcelain-enamelled ware. This is a peculiar combination of porcelain enamel and prepared iron, which is warranted not to crack or discolor. The basins and tubs all come in one solid piece without joints, and there are innumerable graceful designs.[16]

As much as it produced an ideal material for sanitary ware, enameling was a sensitive process, and it proved difficult to achieve consistent appearance and quality. As the Kohler Company explained it, "Enameling the surface of an iron or steel vessel signifies that it is coated with a porcelain-like finish, which is a composition of chemicals and minerals melted together by a secret process, applied to metal and then fused in by a heat of about 1200 degrees temperature. The finish is hard, smooth and glossy, and having united with the metal it is almost impossible to break or chip it off."[17]

The vague language of this "definition" exhibits the extent to which enameling was a trade secret; new formulas for enameling powder and new methods for applying it were constantly being tested to improve the product, particularly in comparison with other firms. In an industry in which there was often familiarity in visible design features, the secret of any company's enamel formula was its one claim to something no one else could have. The specific formula of enameling powder and the evenness of its application determined the quality of the wares. The virtues of enameled cast iron were simple but important ones, as explained by Kohler: "Vessels coated in this manner are easy to keep clean (while plain iron ones are not) and they will not rust or corrode."[18] Though enamelware could be prone to chips and crazing when not well-made, high-quality products were durable for the long haul.

As far as the Kohler Company is concerned, bathroom fixtures had a humble beginning. On a late nineteenth-century advertising broadside, the

Kohler, Hayssen & Stehn Company featured, amid other agricultural implements, "Cast Iron Enameled Water Troughs and Hog Scalders." A note at the
bottom of the illustration read, "When furnished with Legs can be used as
a bathing tub."[19] Originating as a maker of agricultural implements, the
company branched in two directions: decorative ironwork, such as ceme-
tery gates, and enameled ironwork, in the form of kitchen pots and pans,
cuspidors, and tubs, reservoirs, and sinks. It was the second of these processes that proved the company's true calling. Kohler, Hayssen & Stehn began
producing "hollowware and enameled goods," as it termed the latter experiment, in 1883 and one year later, the product line accounted for approximately 40 percent of its sales. While sales of agricultural implements and
general foundry work held steady in the 1880s, the hollowware and enameled goods line expanded quickly, bringing in over $50,000 in 1887, or over
70 percent of the company's total sales. Having an already-established market of rural dwellers whom the company had served with large-scale farm
equipment, the transition to smaller-scale equipment and goods for the
home was apparently a successful one.[20]

Though originally the majority of Kohler's enamelware were kitchen
implements, the material's durability may have encouraged the company to
begin shifting its focus to larger-scale fixtures, a marriage of the enameling
process and the company's earlier reliance on large castings for agricultural
settings. Prevention of rust and corrosion meant enamelware was well-
adapted to goods that held water for long periods of time. And increased
attention to cleanliness and hygiene brought demand for fixed spaces and
vessels designated for personal hygiene in both domestic and public buildings. The appeal of a bathtub originally intended to be a hog scalder was
limited. These qualities of enamelware all lent themselves to a concentration
on bathroom and kitchen fixtures, if possible, linked to water pipes and
sewer systems. The glossy finish of enamel, especially in pure white, connoted not only hygiene but also well-designed domestic goods, like the
porcelain with which it was associated.

By the mid-1890s, Kohler had phased out its production of hollowware
for kitchen use and focused its enamel work on large-scale receptacles for
water; at the end of the decade, plumbing ware accounted for around 90
percent of the company's total sales. The company's growth in the first
decade of the twentieth century was staggering, with total sales jumping to
almost $500,000 in 1905. By the 1910s, Kohler had concentrated its entire
product line on all manner of bathing tubs and showers, along with toilets,

lavatories (the industry name for bathroom sinks), kitchen sinks, laundry tubs, and drinking fountains, and was making the transition from a regional to a national market. Kohler's shift in production and consequent growth paralleled the growth of the enamelware and plumbing equipment industries in general.[21]

The earliest Kohler tubs and sinks did not have attachments for running water. The hog scalder and its immediate successors, between the mid-1880s and 1890s, were simply durable receptacles into which water that had been heated elsewhere could be poured, and then later bailed out. A low-level crude drain, essentially a faucet placed on the outside of the tub, was later incorporated, but water still needed to be collected and removed. During the 1890s, however, manufacturers increasingly assumed that their products would be fixed in an interior space, in either a domestic or public setting, and attached to some sort of permanent piping system; fixtures were designed accordingly. The shift from isolated pieces to fixed parts of a system of plumbing was encapsulated by the Kohler Company's own descriptions of its trade. In the mid-1890s, the company began using a billhead with an image of an ornate bathtub captioned by the words "Bath Tubs & Sinks A Specialty." By its 1902 catalogue, however, J. M. Kohler Sons referred to its products as "Plumbers' Enameled Ware," implying that the fixtures were designed to receive from and drain to fixed sets of pipes, and stated that it had been making these goods for "about ten years."[22]

In the 1900s and 1910s, the Kohler Company produced dozens of styles for bathtubs and lavatories, and many of these styles came in multiple sizes. Because of the relatively high level of skilled handwork that went into making the cast-iron fixtures, and particularly the enameling process, the company worked with batch production. Still claiming economies of scale as a method of keeping costs low, relatively small numbers of a multitude of pieces could be produced by this system, pooling the cost of materials and labor, even if not using an "assembly line" per se.[23] Pieces could be finished with enamel all over, or only on the inside, producing a variety of grades similar to the grades of silverplate. Different types of fittings could be paired with different fixtures as well. One element of the pieces was not variable: the color. Until the mid-1920s, Kohler, and most of the other companies, produced wares in white only.[24] In fact, competition between companies arose over the issue of who could create the whitest enameling powder.

If the processes of enameling were trade secrets, the basic products that were coated with enamel were obviously not, and the companies sought protection in the competition with one another. They obtained patents not only for actual improvements to the functioning of the wares but also for shape and form, much as silverware companies did for their flatware patterns. Though patent infringement was a problem within the industry, the big companies kept careful watch over their own designs, and were most concerned about encroachment from the other major firms. When it came to lesser competitors, Walter Kohler exhibited more of an amused detachment than a desire for compensation. On a trip to California in 1914, Kohler visited the factories of the Pacific Porcelain Ware Company and Pacific Sanitary Manufacturing Company, where he met with the general manager, Mr. Euphrat. He wrote of Euphrat, "He was very frank in stating that we made the best enamel ware in the country, and that they were trying to imitate it as closely as possible. In making up new fixtures they did not bother about creating new designs, or new patterns, but faithfully copied ours." Kohler noted that the enamelware branch replicated Kohler's Universal tub, several lavatories, and even a sink outlet that had been patented by the company. He continued, "In fact, in looking around their warehouse, it showed that they told the truth when they stated that they were copying our designs literally, and they have undoubtedly taken our castings and finished them in the patterns . . . they are following us in everything."[25] Larger companies, such as Kohler and Standard Sanitary, avoided this practice of identical design by producing large and varied lines of wares, in an attempt to appeal to the largest possible sector of the market. The fixture manufacturers' design practices display the tension between achieving distinctive design and trying to appeal to the same markets as one's competitors.[26]

Despite being an apparently weak protection from duplications by other companies, patents were still a selling point as proof of the company's originality. An early advertisement for Kohler, Hayssen & Stehn lavatories referred to both a design patent and a regular one in the very name of the piece: "Superior Porcelain Enameled Iron One Piece Lavatory Patented Slab, Bowl and Back in One Piece with Patent Overflow."[27] Even applying for a patent suggested confidence in the unique qualities of one's own products. In one instance, the Kohler executives debated whether to add the words "Patent Applied For" to certain pages of a new product catalogue, no doubt in part to impress customers while also dissuading competing companies from adopting a new design as their own. In the case of the Universal tub, "Mr. Caldwell [the company's lawyer] said that he did not believe we had anything here that was patentable outside of perhaps a design and he would not advise our applying for a design patent. However, he stated that he thought it might be worth our while to apply for a patent and print on all our literature 'patent applied for' and get what advantage there might be in that."[28] Thus, the patenting process could be as important to the marketing end of the firm as it was to the design and production divisions.

The Kohler Company emphasized three main qualities of its goods, which in fact were interrelated. As one early advertisement claimed, one of its fixtures was the "handsomest, most durable and sanitary Lavatory ever placed on the market."[29] Around the turn of the century, many of the fixture companies' claims to both design and sanitation stemmed from the development of one-piece lavatories and bathtubs. Until that time "built-in" bathtubs were cast in two pieces, the interior tub and a separate apron, which were pieced together by plumbers at the time of installation; not only were the fixtures placed into the wall space, but they were also fitted together. While these pieces were functional, over time cracks could develop along the seams; the seams also created angular edges that made the piece harder to keep clean. If cast all in one piece, the fixtures could be more curvilinear than if they needed to be fit together. For example, a sink bowl set into a slab that acted as a countertop would have to have a seam that no amount of sanding could make into the smoothly curved surface of a one-piece lavatory. The same held true for bathtubs set into aprons as opposed to cast as one piece. While this casting might make a more attractive line possible, it also diminished the chances of cracks that would prove hard to keep clean. As these fixtures contributed to personal hygiene, it followed, of course, that maintaining their cleanliness was of great importance.

Kohler introduced the Universal (1908) and the Viceroy (1914) bathtubs as lines that could be adapted to fit into a variety of wall configurations, even though they were built in. While each of these configurations was depicted separately to illustrate the many possible settings for the piece, they were all united, by both their design elements and their name, as a common family of fixtures. Thus the name could begin to be promoted, and recognized, as a secondary brand name, particularly with the start of a major advertising campaign in 1915, which focused attention on the Viceroy tub.

Even when promoting specific lines, the name *Kohler* was still the company trademark, printed faintly in blue on the white enamel at the end of bathtubs or side of sinks. Only high-quality goods were marked and guaranteed; others were sold as seconds. Walter Kohler felt strongly about producing only one line of goods, while some companies sold goods with either five-year or two-year guarantees. And eventually, Kohler led the industry by not selling seconds or unguaranteed goods, realizing that these wares might hurt the company name in the long run, even if in the short run they might add to a yearly sales total. Just as Reed & Barton had learned that it was not worth risking the company's name on a lower-end market, so too did the Kohlers consolidate their production and marketing on a single high-quality product.[30]

While Kohler products also had a paper label and the company name cast in raised letters on the bottom of fixtures, it was the name embedded in the enamel that was invested with the most meaning, much like the maker's mark on flatware. As the company explained to dealers, "This trade-mark is permanently incorporated in the enamel. It will last as long as the fixture lasts—a lifetime." The national advertising campaign started by the company in the 1910s featured this trademark by reproducing it the same size it appeared on fixtures and then using arrows to point out where it would appear on the actual fixtures, as depicted in the ads. The company sold its products at least in part on the perfection of its enamel, which in turn provided the durability and sanitary quality of the fixtures; embedding the company name in it made the enamel itself speak for the product. One of the company's other prominent slogans was, in fact, "It's In the Kohler Enamel," with the word *it* representing everything from the whiteness and durability of the ware to the claimed superiority over other brands. As the company explained to dealers, the trademark "is inconspicuous and will in no sense detract from the beauty of the fixture. At the same time, it will serve as a guarantee that the purchaser gets what he pays for, and it is also an evidence of our faith in the superiority of our product." The trademark symbolized "Pure White Enamel. Hygienic, artistic design. One-Piece construction. Highest quality. Fair dealing with the trade and with the public. Lasting satisfaction to the purchaser."[31] Thus the wares themselves served as their own assurance to prospective buyers.

MOVING IRON

If enamel lent itself to a broad cultural distribution through its association with hygiene, the iron bases of bathroom fixtures created a challenge of physical distribution. With its start as a purveyor of agricultural implements, Kohler retained an original market base that was predominantly rural and for the most part local. In the early years of the company, John Michael

Kohler traveled around with a cart of smaller wares and sold directly to farmers, though the firm also sold to dealers who might have carried their goods to a wider radius. Even when buying larger rakes and plows, most customers were close enough to visit the firm in Sheboygan. The company's later concentration on large fixtures necessitated a different system of distribution, simply due to the size and weight of the objects being sold; fixtures also demanded skilled workers, or at least some knowledge of plumbing, to install them. And their durability encouraged the company to seek a wider distribution network, since repeat sales could be expected only decades apart, if at all.

Traveling salesmen could not carry around samples of bathtubs, but in a field where the scientific vagaries of the enameling process led to huge distinctions in the quality of wares, illustrated catalogues were only an entrée into the market. Rather than rely on a fleet of salaried salesmen, companies sold fixtures through wholesalers, or jobbers, who could visit either the factory in Sheboygan or one of the regional branch offices that the company established as early as the 1890s. In areas where they did not have branches, the fixture companies also contracted with manufacturer's representatives, who would then sell to jobbers. At the end of the nineteenth century, Kohler, Hayssen & Stehn advertised in the *Plumbers' Trade Journal,* listing branch offices in New York, Chicago, and Toronto, and a manufacturer's representative in San Francisco.[32] A few years later, the company had shifted to using representatives, still concentrated in the trade centers of New York, Chicago, and San Francisco.[33] The wholesalers in turn sold to plumbers, builders, or architects, who fitted them into buildings for the eventual consumer.

The company management explained to its workers and potential consumers, "It is the policy of our company to confine the sale of our ware to jobbers of plumbing supplies or wholesale houses, who handle plumbing ware, pipe . . . and all other accessories, and, in turn, sell them to the retail dealer or plumber."[34] These "straight lines of Manufacturer to Wholesaler to Retailer to Consumer," as described by one Kohler representative, was the American norm of distribution for such fixtures, with the manufacturer's representative serving as an added initial step in the process and plumbers and architects often acting as the "retailer."[35] For this chain of sales to function properly, each member of it could buy from and sell to only the next in line on the chain. This chain was even presented to the popular imagination, for example, in the tale "Inside the House that Jack Built," which ran in *Country Life* magazine in 1913. Commenting on the sales process but also the importance of each step to eventual sales, the author, architect George Leland Hunter, depicted a conversation as two men share with their wives their experience outfitting a new bathroom for one of their homes:

> "Jack and I really had a very interesting afternoon when we started out to study up on the bathroom equipment," said Tom. "The salesman was especially well informed."
>
> "I shouldn't call him a salesman," said Jack. "He wouldn't sell us anything, but referred us to our plumbers."
>
> "Nevertheless, we afterward bought just about what he recommended."[36]

Hunter's story of home decorating taught readers of *Country Life* what to expect when remodeling their own homes, and where to go for advice.

The companies relied heavily on their representatives to manage the display of wares and to negotiate prices and discounts with jobbers. The representatives also served the same role as traveling salesmen in ferreting out the new wares and lines of competing companies, gathering information from the buyers with whom they traded. For Kohler, the "one to beat" was the Standard Sanitary Manufacturing Company and it asked representatives such as C. W. Armes in San Francisco to find out what he could about a new sink that Standard had devised in 1909. Armes wrote to the company headquarters of the sink's new features and which were patented, and how the product compared to Kohler's, including drawings of the whole fixture and its special features. Still, the company wanted to keep a rein on the activities of these representatives. In one instance, Armes learned of an additional discount that another company, believed to be Standard Sanitary, was extending to local buyers, and offered a similar cut on Kohler ware. Walter Kohler had authorized such a discount only if the competitor was Standard, and on only two railroad cars' worth of goods. When Armes made the sale for three cars and later admitted that the competitor may have been another company, Kohler rebuked him sharply for "exceeding his authority."[37]

Recognizing the prominent position these individuals held, Kohler phased out using manufacturers' representatives on commission and looked instead for employees to work on salary. As Walter Kohler wrote to a prospective sales agent, "We cannot consider the sale of our goods . . . on a commission basis, as we are gradually getting away from that method of marketing our product."[38] The company also experimented with incorporating separate companies to handle sales of Kohler wares in certain regions, with the local company president serving the role of a branch manager, but the plan was short-lived; the first attempt, the Kohler-Smith Company in Chicago, with distribution rights and responsibilities for the state of Illinois, existed only between 1903 and 1905. In the long run, it would be hard for Kohler to oversee the affairs of all these regional companies; the company preferred to have its sales staff in its own employ.[39] Although salaried positions may not have offered the same incentives as commission posts, the company clearly wanted to foster new types of relations with loyal employees, who would not divide their time among a variety of lines of products.

Kohler increasingly handled business through company-managed branches, located in regional distribution centers. Walter Kohler wrote of the Chicago office in relation to the Chicago-based wholesaler the firm had been relying on: "The fixed charges of the office will, including Mr. [Murphy's] salary, be a trifle more on the year than we paid [Murphy-Dugger-Clark Company, Kohler's previous representative in Chicago] but I feel that we will get better results."[40] While the company attributed the need for these branch offices to the "growth of our business and the development of our trade throughout the country," it is also likely that at least some of these offices, particularly on the two coasts, were in fact placed to foster business, rather than serve an already thriving trade.[41] In 1908, the company offered William H. Barth a position as a branch manager in New York City, hoping to drum up sales on the East Coast, a region with poor Kohler representation in comparison with some of the other leading companies.[42]

By the mid-1910s, Kohler had established fourteen branch offices across the country and one in London, and also had one remaining manufacturer's representative in Salt Lake City. These locations, including Boston, New York, Philadelphia, Pittsburgh, Atlanta, Detroit, Indianapolis, Chicago, St. Louis, St. Paul, Houston, Seattle, San Francisco, and Los Angeles, served as regional distribution centers for smaller towns and surrounding rural areas. With branch managers focusing exclusively on the company's wares, they could also approach a broader range of geographic locales. Within a regional radius, these branch managers might act as salesmen. For example, though hired to direct the New York office, Barth wrote enthusiastically of his knowledge of the entire mid-Atlantic corridor:

> I am very well acquainted with the Jobbers in the East having lived in New York City where I was raised the greater part of my life & have every reason to believe that I could renew the pleasant relations that formerly existed there am also fairly well acquainted in Albany Troy Utica Syracuse Rochester Buffalo

Bridgeport New Haven Hartford Providence Springfield Boston Wooster Philadelphia Battavia & Washington & have traveled through parts of Virginia & have every reason to believe that I could make a good success in that territory.[43]

Thus, the Kohler Company established itself across the country in terms of both the breadth of its geographic reach and the variety of communities it served.

As the company administration told its workers, "As a result of this method of distribution and our sales work, KOHLER WARE can be seen on display in all parts of the country. Go into any city and you will be able to see a KOHLER bath tub, lavatory or sink. Window displays and cards advertising our products are evident in even some of the smallest towns and villages."[44] While bathroom fixtures might appear to "trickle down" from urban to rural areas, Kohler appears to have started its trade with the rural market and moved to the urban one. As it became more common for bathroom fixtures to be fixed in place and tied to pipes, they relied more heavily on the infrastructure of water and sewer lines available in urban areas. Nonetheless, interior piping could also be fitted to septic tanks built for the use of a particular property where municipal lines might not reach, and thus Kohler addressed these areas as well.[45]

The local branches also served as regional showrooms, and, not surprisingly, the New York office emerged as one of the most important to the company. Walter Kohler seems to have learned quickly what made for appropriate displays and display space. Corresponding with Barth about the location of the store in the Bryant Park Arcade Building, Kohler explained that in front of one of the possible locations, the sidewalk narrowed, "which influences traffic toward curb and hurts value [of the] show window," and to try to obtain a street frontage on the wider sidewalk.[46] Once an appropriate site had been secured, Barth's challenge was to arrange pristine samples in an attractive display, made up primarily of the company's high-end goods. He was reminded by Kohler, "You are a long ways from the home office and we are paying a heavy rental for the New York store, largely for show room purposes, and we want you to make at all times such suggestions as you think will improve the show and be for the good of our business."[47] Similarly, the company took care in the siting of its Chicago branch; having hired his former wholesaler Murphy to be the branch manager, Kohler set out looking for appropriate space. In December 1907, Kohler wrote back to the headquarters that he had "finally decided on a good sized room, about 450 sq ft on the 5th floor of the 1st Natl. Bank Bldg. The rent is 90.00 a month, which seems pretty high, but the extra cost is warranted I think, and we will certainly have a representative location."[48] In the task of trying to convince purchasers to invest in new interior spaces within their homes, the interior space of the showroom could serve as an important model.

While the branch offices acted as salesrooms, the company also established auxiliary warehouses in Boston, New York, and San Francisco, from which products could be shipped to the surrounding regions, reducing the all-important freight costs. Geographic location made a particular difference in the business of selling fixtures, objects large and heavy enough that transportation costs made up a significant part of each step in the chain of sales. When Walter Kohler sought for ways to gain a foothold in the West Coast market, he looked for specific locations to which shipping charges might beat out those that Standard Sanitary, the regional leader, could offer. Writing from Spokane, Washington, in 1911, Kohler explained that he thought the company might be able to get a contract with a local wholesaler, Hughes and Co., because freight rates were cheaper to Spokane from Sheboygan than from Pittsburgh, the home of Standard Sanitary. He instructed his executives to investigate other ways of potentially beating Standard's freight charges; for example, knowing that Standard shipped to the Pacific Northwest by a combination of lake and train routes, he wondered whether an all-rail route on one of the transcontinental lines might work out to be a cheaper alternative. At issue was not only the transport of goods from Sheboygan but the transit of people to it. In order to get wholesalers interested in its products in the first place, Kohler needed to attract them to see its wares. Walter Kohler felt at a geographic disadvantage in this respect; he wrote, "jobbers from all over the country passing through Chicago or Pittsburgh will, because it is convenient, visit Wolff or Standard, while it requires a day to come to Sheboygan so they pass it up."[49]

Walter Kohler carefully weighed keeping the company's holdings together in Riverside (later to be called Kohler) on the outskirts of Sheboygan. Seemingly happy with his ability to oversee the production side of the company, he did realize that for the sake of broader distribution, branch plants might mean better access to coastal markets. In 1911, he toured an enameling plant in Elizabeth, New Jersey, owned by the Colwell Lead Company. In a memo to his associates, Kohler wrote, "There was nothing new or novel to me about the entire plant, and its only value for consideration by Western manufacturers is that it is located in the East, and its purchase might give the new owner an outlet for the product and an established market through the Colwell Lead Co's four jobbing houses in New York City, which handle approximately $400,000 worth of enameled ware during the year."[50] Nonetheless, for a firm that relied on skilled labor and careful inspection systems, the detriment of splitting the production base outweighed the benefits of easier distribution. Concentrated production also allowed the company to claim that "the Kohler factory is the largest in the world devoted exclusively to the production of enameled plumbing ware," as it did in promotional materials for jobbers in the 1910s.[51]

Good relations in the trade depended on the chain of sales from manufacturer to wholesaler to plumber or contractor to customer being kept intact. In areas where the company did not have representatives or branch offices, the company executives dealt directly with wholesalers, and negotiated an arrangement not only for price but also for dealing with competition. Both parties tried to balance the advantages of exclusive contracts with the need for flexibility in times of economic instability. While the manufacturer wanted wholesalers to carry only its goods and no goods of its competitors, the wholesalers wanted an exclusive contract for a manufacturer's goods in a certain region. While it may have seemed an even trade, adjustments were often necessary; for example, if a manufacturer did not make a certain type of ware that a competing firm did, and could not quickly put it into production, it might concede purchase of that one item to the wholesaler. For manufacturers, exclusive contracts were considered in relation to sales conditions in the wholesaler's district. Walter Kohler wrote to Hughes & Company of Spokane, Washington:

> While it has not been our policy to grant exclusive accounts for the sale of our product, we have considered carefully the question, particularly as it relates to Spokane, and have decided to offer you the following proposition—On condition that you give us 90% of your business on enameled ware in baths, lavatories, sinks, etc., we will give you the exclusive sale of our product in the city of Spokane, and give you, at all times, our best prices and attention. You have considerable experience with our goods and will admit that they are equal to any on the market.[52]

In other locales, particularly bigger cities, Kohler voted against an exclusive contract, believing that one wholesaler could not provide the volume of sales the company set as its goal. Looking in particular to expand its West

Coast market, the company reconsidered an exclusive contract it had had with the Morris Stulsaft Company in San Francisco, believing that "in this city it is not desirable, unless it should be our own show, as we are not getting anywhere near the amount of business we could get."[53] The arrangements between manufacturer and wholesaler varied from location to location and from firm to firm.

Beyond the contracts that regulated their business dealings, manufacturers sought additional influence over jobbers, particularly in the actual sites of their trade. Exclusive contracts were particularly important in trade with large jobbers who operated their own showrooms, places where the identification of certain jobbers with certain manufacturers could be fostered. For example, the company offered jobbing houses large prints of its factory to adorn their walls, showing them to be a Kohler representative.[54] On the West Coast, Kohler worked hard to achieve a foothold where the Standard Sanitary Manufacturing Company dominated the market, and treasured jobbers such as Boynton's in Los Angeles, who featured the Kohler line prominently. Walter Kohler described the Boynton facility to his executives: "They have a pretty good show room, and with the exception of a few pieces show only Kohler enamel ware, in addition to which they feature Trenton Pottery Co's goods [made of vitreous china, and thus, not a direct competitor]. Their show room organization is friendly and loyal to us, as they have had much less trouble with our ware than with Standard's."[55] As long as the Boynton showroom served, in effect, as a Kohler showroom, such evaluations would be crucial to continued trade between the two firms.

Because the wholesalers were such an important part of the chain of sales, with their facilities, organization, and sales staff often acting as Kohler's front line, the company tried to keep careful watch over these businesses. Company executives were particularly concerned with the appearance of the wholesalers' premises, seeking the association of cleanliness throughout the sales chain. In 1914, Walter Kohler took an extended trip to the West Coast, meeting with and inspecting the facilities of many of the company's distributors. Finding it was a "general condition among the plumbing supply jobbers" that their places of business were "not kept in a very tidy manner," he was particularly pleased to visit a firm like Boynton's or the Western National Supply Company in San Diego, California. The latter company, he wrote in his evaluation for the home office, was "one of the exceptional in their warehousing facilities, and in the method, order and cleanliness which prevailed throughout their institution. They have a splendid building and keep all of the ware in exceptionally clean shape."[56] The lines of influence worked both ways, however. To maintain their "loyalty," Kohler also needed to offer the jobbers what they wanted to sell, particularly in terms of creating complete lines of coordinating goods and having as many types of wares as its competitors produced. Though bathroom fixtures were not designed in matching sets, as flatware was, consumers certainly looked for groupings of products that would harmonize with one another. Boynton requested that Kohler consider making a sitz bath "where the fixtures come through the rim to conform to rim fixture baths" and a foot bath "which should be made on legs and base for the same reason," products already produced by Standard Sanitary.[57]

Other enamelware manufacturers were not the only competitors for a share of the bathroom fixture industry; producers of vitreous china, or sanitary pottery, as it came to be called in the trade, were also important players. On the advice of a West Coast jobber, Walter Kohler suggested some changes to roll rim lavatories, in order to keep up with the selling features of counterparts made of vitreous china. He suggested that flattening out the rim would not only create a more functional surface but would also "make a better looking fixture," as he had noted on vitreous china lavatories.[58] As early as the 1910s, Walter Kohler considered adding a vitreous china plant to the company's holdings. Upon touring the facilities of the Pacific Porcelain Ware Company, he wrote to the home office, "It is very interesting to go through this plant, as it illustrated that a comparatively small investment is necessary. Experience, however, is a very important factor, but the labor in the manufacturing end is no doubt available. It is a kindred line to the enamel ware, and the other two leading manufacturers, viz. Wolff and Standard, have found it desirable to have a plant."[59] It was not until the 1920s, however, that Kohler decided to go through with the expansion to include a vitreous china line, first buying a factory in the established pottery manufacturing center of Trenton, New Jersey, and later transferring production to the town of Kohler. Until this development, the company focused on ways to draw attention, of both the trade and public, to its tradition of enamel cast-iron fixtures.

COURTING THE SALESMEN

Throughout the first quarter of the twentieth century, Kohler maintained a centralized production base and decentralized distribution system. While

competing companies were opening regional manufacturing centers, the
Kohler Company expanded its plant in Wisconsin, and instead opened
branch sales offices. Decentralized sales offices provided for concentrated
shipping points, lowering overall freight charges, and allowed for more oversight of jobbers and local plumbers and architects. Around the same time
that the company began opening more branch offices, Walter Kohler also
reorganized the company to give equal weight to the Sales Department,
along with Production and Accounting, in part anticipating the new tasks
of coordinating the branch offices and expecting a higher volume of sales.
Under the new structure, begun in 1911, the Sales Department was responsible for all phases of distribution from initial advertising to handling customers' orders to shipping. The Order Division handled "quotation, grant-
ing of credit, placing of product orders with factory, registry of orders,
acknowledgment of orders, adjustment of orders, notification of shipments,
routing of shipments, invoicing, collections, purchasing of jobbing goods
and office supplies, traffic matters, all correspondence relating to above, correspondence with branch offices." The Advertising Division would oversee
"making of catalog copy, making of copy for advertisements, photographing of fixtures, all correspondence relating to advertising, engravings cuts
and printing work, distribution of catalogs and all other advertising matter"; here Kohler was no doubt looking ahead to production of more elaborate catalogues.[60]

Walter Kohler believed that a new catalogue would be particularly important for the design-minded audience of architects and builders who,
along with plumbers, acted as the de facto salesmen for the company. With
the company reorganization, Kohler started planning a catalogue that would
be a "large book, similar in size to Standards—Crane—Mott & Wolff for use
of jobber & master plumber." Starting in 1912, the company began photographing and engraving wares to be included. Early on it decided to work
with a Chicago printer, Rogers & Company, and met with them to find
"someone that has had practical experience in compiling catalogs and knows
the photographing, engraving and printing game pretty well." This person
would handle the details of assembling the catalogue, and work with Rogers,
while engravings could be handled by a local Sheboygan firm. Rogers &
Company in fact "lent" one of its own staff members, to work temporarily
on the Kohler payroll until the completion of the project. The printers
sold themselves as the premier firm of the West. Though Standard Sanitary
Manufacturing Company had suggested that their next catalogue might be

granted to Rogers, the printers assured the Kohler staff that if they received the Kohler contract they would turn down the Standard one as a matter of course, only working on catalogues for one firm in any particular line of manufacture. The company poured money into the production of what would become the 1914 catalogue; Walter Kohler wrote to Clark, "The new catalog . . . will prove of inestimable benefit in soliciting business from the architects. They do not care to bother with small books and leaflets and our new book will be one of the handsomest catalogs ever made for any one in the plumbing business, and there is nothing that can anywhere approach it outside of the Standard catalog."

The company's executives believed that one could in fact judge a book, and the products it represented, by its cover, and invested money in a decorative design for the cover. While Walter Kohler was away on a business trip to the West Coast in the early part of 1914, company secretary Oscar Kroos handled the matter of keeping the printer on schedule. Kroos wrote to Kohler:

> Under separate cover we are mailing you a velox print showing design of the cover as Rogers now have it worked out. They spent between 2 and 3 weeks in getting up the design, which is emblematic of water or sanitation, representing 2 dolphins and a sea wave in the center.
>
> There is no question but what it adds to the attractiveness of the cover and unless you advise us to the contrary by wire we will go ahead and have them put it on.[61]

The competition for the "handsomest" catalogue, even of prosaic goods, suggests a concern for the decor of their setting; if the bathroom fixtures could be made to look good in print, they could be made to look good in one's home as well.

The one change the company requested in the cover design was to remove the year, 1914, and instead print "Catalog K," suggested by Chicago branch manager Murphy. Walter Kohler approved of the "handsome" design, and also agreed with Murphy's recommendations, recognizing that bathroom fixtures were a long-term purchase in classic, timeless designs. He responded to Kroos, "Showing the year 1914 conspicuously is much like the automobile idea of an annual new production, and it is possible that the ultimate consumer seeing this catalogue after 1914 might get the idea that he is getting out of date designs."[62] The company needed to balance a timelessness inherent to the long-term purchase that ultimate consumers were making with a sense of modernity and innovation; of the catalogue, Kohler wrote, "Without it, they [the trade] will think us behind the times."[63] Thus, Kohler looked to a variety of audiences with its catalogue: the building and plumbing trades that were essential to its business, and also the ultimate consumer.

The first few pages of the catalogue depicted modern bathrooms with a wide range of appointments, shown in photographs of actual rooms. In contrast, these pages also had line drawings of various scenes of bathing, washing, drinking, and other activities that suggested a need for running water. The drawings were paired so that the images on facing pages loosely corresponded to one another, but suggested different eras in the settings and implements for bathing. The eras were not necessarily fixed in histori-cal time, but clearly showed "before" and "after" stages of a certain develop-ment: the incorporation of interior plumbing into modern bathrooms. On one page a group of boys is shown bathing in a pond, splashing riotously. On the facing page, two small children are shown in a bathroom: a boy sits in a bathtub while a girl combs her hair at a mirror above a sink—both are smiling somewhat mischievously. While both sets of children are bathing, and both sets seem to be enjoying themselves, in the second image the actions are more contained, quite literally, by the room itself and the fur-nishings or fixtures in it. Although the first image has no negative connota-tions, the second implies a consistency in the experience of bathing indoors, unaffected by climate or time of day. An interior bathroom encourages, or even rewards, the enjoyment of bathing.

Not only has this activity moved indoors but it has moved to its own space, a distinction made clear on another set of pages. On one page a woman bathes a small boy in a wooden tub. The drawing suggests a hearth in the background and a wooden chair sits to the side. The simple style of the chair and the woman's dress, along with the reliance on the hearth, sug-gest an earlier era, or at least a locale without modern amenities. The facing page shows a woman bathing a small boy in a modern built-in bathtub in a tiled room; the woman is dressed in a maid's uniform. While the first scene shows the positive associations of hearth and home, the second shows con-venience; there is no need for a hearth to warm the water before pouring it into the wooden tub, because running water is readily available at any temperature. The room is designed to accept splashes without a problem. Again, neither site is criticized; the act of bathing is depicted in charming fashion in both drawings, but in the second, it is shown to warrant its own space. The uniformed figure of the maid suggests a higher socioeconomic status of the family whose bathing facilities are shown, and links that status to a separate bathroom with modern fixtures.[64] Taken together, the range of bathing experiences in these drawings visually complemented countless hygiene manuals and articles in popular periodicals, which outlined different types of bathing for different effects. Educators of personal hygiene explained the different types of baths—requiring equipment ranging from a pitcher of water to a steam tank—but their advice usually assumed access to the standard suite of a bathtub, toilet, and sink.[65] The images showed that Robert De Valcourt's prediction of generations earlier had come true: "the time is not far distant, when no dwelling, or hotel, will be considered complete, which does not afford to every inmate facilities for daily ablutions."[66]

The drawings in the 1914 catalogue enforced a three-part message that supported any potential purchase of bathroom fixtures. First, the vessels for bathing were worthy of protection indoors. Second, they should have their own designated space within a building. Third, and most important, cleanliness and personal hygiene justified a major expenditure for home, office, or other public space in the form of large-scale bathroom fixtures. Fixtures, as their name implied, were to be permanent interior furnishings, and would set the tone for the room that housed them. American novelist Booth Tarkington humorously captured this shift toward indoor plumbing in his 1918 book, *The Magnificent Ambersons*: "during the seventies there developed an appreciation of the necessity for a bathroom. Therefore the architects placed bathrooms in the new houses, and the older houses tore out a cupboard or two, set up a boiler beside the kitchen stove, and sought a new godliness, each with its own bathroom. The great American plumber joke, that many-branched evergreen, was planted at that time."[67] The architects and plumbers to whom Tarkington refers were indeed partners to the fixture companies in presenting the ideal bathroom.

The company debated how to handle the distribution of catalogues, believing that a personal visit to architects or plumbers might contribute to the positive association the catalogue was meant to produce. The catalogues were often still distributed through the wholesalers to the architects, much as the wares were. In response to requests from wholesalers, the company looked into printing the names of jobbing houses, or architects and builders, on the catalogue in gold, in the first instance to give the wholesaler a stake in the transactions and in the second instance to personalize the "gift" from the company. In any case, these specialized copies would add to the decorative effect of the catalogue and show the individual attention that the company could foster. But in the 1910s, along with the rise of branch offices and direct consumer advertising, the company began to send its own branch managers out to hand-deliver the catalogues, especially to architects. Walter Kohler explained to the executives:

> In San Francisco Mr. Finch prefers to distribute the catalogs to the architects in person, which I think is a very good plan. It is possible that he may be able to do this also at Los Angeles, and to some of the important architects in the other towns. With the advent of this catalog it will undoubtedly be necessary for us to pay more attention to the architects than we have in the past, and we may need additional representation at the other branch house to attend to that end of the business. The same plan of having a personal representative deliver these catalogs to the big architects will be profitable at all of the branches.

On the other hand, Kohler was happy to have wholesalers distribute the catalogue to plumbers, and believed wholesalers would be pleased with this arrangement as well.[68] Because the plumbers were essentially the intermediate purchasers of goods, they would be more concerned with the actual logistics of sales that the wholesalers could provide. Architects might specify Kohler wares in the designs that would be passed on to contractors, but would not be involved with the actual passage of the fixtures through the chain of sales. Thus the approach to catalogue distribution mirrored the distribution of the actual wares.

In addition to production expenses, the 1914 catalogue generated large distribution costs; there were 25,000 copies, each weighing six pounds. Batches were shipped with the company's product in railroad cars to jobbers or branch offices to distribute in their area. Rail transport held the cost of distribution at $3,000 to $3,500.[69] Despite the considerable expense of producing and distributing the 1914 catalogue, the company received positive reinforcement for carrying out the project; as a member of another Sheboygan manufacturing firm wrote upon seeing the prospectus for the catalogue, "I can not help but believe that your catalog will have a selling help which will at least pay for a good portion of the cost. The effect of an issue of this kind, I believe, will remain in the minds of the buyers long after you have charged off a high cost for the work and forgotten about it."[70] The 1914 catalogue was just one step in a larger marketing effort the Kohler Company undertook in the 1910s.

The initial appeal that manufacturers and wholesalers had to make was to architects and plumbers, and through them to the ultimate consumers. As early as the 1880s, plumbers wielded their power over manufacturers when the National Association of Master Plumbers threatened to boycott any manufacturer who sold to plumbers who were not members of the association. In the 1890s, the Central Supply Association, a coalition of midwestern manufacturers and jobbers formed in part to combat this threat, agreed to provide any licensed plumber with goods, regardless of association membership status. In essence, the manufacturers did not want to be placed in the middle of a battle between factions of plumbers; still, they recognized the importance of the trade to their sales.[71] Reminiscent of the Philadelphia jewelers' reaction to finding Reed & Barton goods at Strawbridge's, some plumbers apparently believed that Kohler was selling directly to consumers, or allowing their jobbers to do so. Company secretary Oscar Kroos was dispatched to a plumbing association convention in 1912 to assuage these fears and foster good will toward the Kohler name. First, he explained that the jobber in question had actually bought very little from the company of late, so if he were selling directly to consumers it was either another firm's goods or Kohler goods he had bought from some other wholesaler. In either case, it was not Kohler's lack of oversight that had caused this potentially disloyal situation. Kroos wrote of a conversation with Frank Patterson, a member of the national executive committee and president of the Illinois Association of Plumbers, saying, "I explained to him our attitude toward the plumber, saying that we had no desire to willfully antagonize him, as we realized that he is the natural distributor for our goods. He was very much pleased to learn our position." Allowing company goods to be sold directly to the consumer was, in Kroos's words, "putting the ware practically in competition with Sears, Roebuck, and other mail order houses," a state of affairs that clearly carried negative connotations for the plumbers.[72]

The appeals to plumbers' associations continued over time, with branch managers taking responsibility for representing the company. When the thirty-sixth Annual Convention of the National Association of Master Plumbers met in St. Louis in June 1918, Stephen Gilmore, the local branch manager, coordinated a display of Kohler products. Gilmore sought to familiarize the "natural distributors" with the company's newest lines, particularly the Viceroy bathtub, of which three different versions were shown with different configurations of fittings and wall placements. The company also passed out souvenirs of small enameled tags with the Kohler trademark on it. The convention display booth was decorated with red, white, and blue bunting, representing Kohler's part in the war effort, and large framed photographs of sites in Kohler Village, such as newly built workers' homes, which were all outfitted with Kohler products. This part of the display was intended to inspire confidence in the company's workings, as well as its products, and assure prospective dealers that the company's own workers were counted among its consumers.[73]

Architects were another audience for Kohler's promotional push. As early as 1907, the company considered hiring a representative in the Chicago branch office to deal primarily with soliciting interest, if not direct business, from architects. W. B. Clark explained:

> Architects look for quality, style, workmanship and finish and we understand they specify and insist on a certain Ware regardless of the price involved, provided of course that price is not out of the question. Oftentimes they have a certain amount in the Estimates for Baths and Lavatories which allows them to go *above* the competitive line and into something of a higher grade. If we can get the Architects to visit us, we feel sure our fine Catalogue, nice Office and beautiful Samples will interest them.[74]

While Clark believed that architects were the key to the high-quality market, approaching these designers also involved practical considerations. If architects specified Kohler wares in floor plans, with the appropriate roughing-in measurements, it was likely that developers and builders would use these products, rather than finding products of other companies to fit the specifications. On a trip to the West Coast, Kohler found that architects more commonly specified Standard Sanitary wares, encouraging wholesalers to carry their goods.[75] One change Kohler could make was to standardize its roughing-in measurements, among its own lines, and also to accord more generally with the size and shape of Standard Sanitary wares. As Walter Kohler wrote emphatically to the company headquarters, "*Must be standard* on *all* staples if we want to do business on [west] coast . . . *Complaint* is general on that feature and it has affected our lavatory business in this section."[76] In order to get the wholesalers' business, the Kohler Company had to make its products as convenient for architects and plumbers as possible. In the eyes of Kohler executives, architects would be the link to consumers in the high-end residential sector, building new homes with modern plumbing, while plumbers would be more likely to retro-fit older housing stock or make decisions for builder-designed houses.

The architect was also an important entree into the nonresidential market. Public buildings required large numbers of fixtures and served as sites of exposure for these large-scale goods. Just as with flatware, sales to hotels, schools, hospitals, and other institutions were not only good money for Kohler but good advertising as well. The emphasis on reaching architects directly resulted in commissions for public buildings that might inspire confidence in other purchasers. This exposure, however, also meant that the quality of the wares in these locations had to be as close to flawless as possible (a task difficult to achieve in the enamel industry). On a western trip, Walter Kohler stopped at the well-known Brown Palace Hotel in Denver, and saw a chip in one of the lavatories in the barber shop; he suggested a small change in the design of the pedestal to make it less likely that such flaws would happen again.[77] In its catalogue and advertising images, particularly for lavatories, Kohler displayed banks of the fixtures, to show how they would look in a public setting. The sinks could be arrayed in one long row against a wall, or in pairs set back to back toward the center of a room. One unit, named "Tonsor" for its projected use in barber shops, was made with a "Combination Basin and Shampoo Fixture with China Handles, Rubber Hose and Sprinkler"; another had two sink bowls back to back on the same slab, all designed for use in public spaces.[78]

By the time the company started publishing the in-house newsletter *Kohler of Kohler News* in 1916, it could run a monthly column devoted to these commissions in public "buildings that are modern in every respect." The different types of buildings that housed Kohler fixtures highlighted a range of consumer concerns, from aesthetic design to low maintenance to sanitary quality. The company particularly highlighted its commissions for apartment buildings and hotels, but also included such varied building types as a monastery, a golf club, and a Masonic temple, as well as hospitals, a comment on Kohler's hygienic standards. The features noted the number of Kohler fixtures in each building, and any special attributes of either the building or the wares that made them well suited to one another, usually focusing on modernity and cleanliness. For example, in describing renovations to the Windsor Hotel in Jacksonville, Florida, an article stated, "As the dominant idea in remodeling was to introduce modern conveniences and unusual features, 51 'Viceroy' baths were added to the hotel's bathroom equipment." The company could tout these commissions all over the country, and clearly made a point of exhibiting the geographic breadth of its distribution network, reaching from Anchorage, Alaska, to New York City. Trying to reach the broadest possible market, particularly in regions where other companies had an advantage, these public buildings were good publicity for the company, which exclaimed with a new slogan, "soon we will be able to say 'KOHLER WARE is Everywhere'—in every part of the land where the highest quality of plumbing ware is demanded."[79]

Kohler courted the developers for these public spaces by displaying its wares at appropriate sites and conventions, much as it did with architects and plumbers. For example, in December 1918, the Kohler Company exhibited at the Hotel Men's Exposition at Madison Square Garden in New York City. Coordinated by Kohler's New York branch manager W. H. Barth, the exhibit addressed the "thousands of hotel men from all over the world who are progressive and eager to become acquainted with the best facilities and appliances for the convenience of their patrons." The company recognized, as did these visitors, that "good plumbing fixtures represent an increasingly important part of a modern hotel equipment." For this display, rather than trying to fit a range of the company's goods into a small space, Barth constructed a model bathroom, as it might appear in a hotel, with all built-in fixtures and additional amenities such as a medicine cabinet and towel rack. The inclusion of the Viceroy bathtub model was a reminder of the style being adopted in hotels across the country, most notably in the vast Commodore and Pennsylvania hotels, which, because newly opened and no doubt toured by many of the exposition visitors, also served as Kohler displays.[80] American novelist Sinclair Lewis commented on this new form of tourism and its benefits to manufacturers in *Babbitt* (1922). On his way to Maine from his hometown in the mid-sized, midwestern city of Zenith, the title character of George F. Babbitt makes a stop in New York. Lewis explains his primary destination: "They had four hours in New York between trains. The one thing Babbitt wished to see was the Pennsylvania Hotel, which had been built since his last visit. He stared up at it, muttering, 'Twenty-two hundred rooms and twenty-two hundred baths! That's got everything in the world beat.'"[81] Thus, not only might they feature a particular brand of product, but hotels introduced guests to the very idea of having a private bathroom. The company featured its large hotel commissions in advertising run in the architectural and other trade journals, using that forum to build confidence with the professionals who might promote its products. Hotels and other public spaces were also advertisements in and of themselves, but with placement determined by architects.

Although the consumer of bathroom fixtures for domestic or work spaces did not buy directly from the manufacturer, there was no question that the firm was ultimately responsible for the products. On a trip to the West Coast in 1914, Walter Kohler wrote to the home office underscoring this fact; he advised, "Be very careful in finishing up high grade ware, as the inspection is quite keen. I saw . . . a Wilmore, delivered to a very beautiful home, which showed a series of grinding marks on the inside of the tub, and was consequently rejected by the house owner."[82] The person "who is building or remodeling and wishes to install plumbing fixtures" was the final customer in the eyes of the company, and all sales efforts aimed at middlemen were an attempt to reach this ultimate consumer. As much as plumbers or architects might recommend certain lines of goods, consumers were also "educated" by advertising or by visiting local showrooms where "people intending to install such goods make a selection . . . and then place their order with the plumber."[83]

Kohler looked for other means to get its products before the public eye. While in California in 1914, Walter Kohler toured the site of the Panama Pacific Exhibition in San Francisco, considering whether Kohler should exhibit there. He believed that a display there could be of "considerable value" to the company, and noted that Standard Sanitary had not yet expressed an interest in display space, making Kohler's exposure there all the more worthwhile. In any case, he planned that Kohler fixtures would furnish the Wisconsin State Building.[84] In addition to this type of company-sponsored exhibit, Kohler benefited from the more local displays of its wholesalers. Plumbing supply companies might exhibit at state or county fairs, and feature a particular manufacturer's wares, as when Buschman and Sons of Indianapolis displayed a variety of Kohler bathtubs and lavatories at the Indiana State Fair in 1916.[85] Thus, the manufacturer worked with its distributors to increase familiarity with its products at all levels of distribution. The traditional form of inspiring name recognition, though, was print advertising.

SELLING BATHROOMS

While the chain of *sales* was inviolable, the chain of *selling* was not. With Standard Sanitary Manufacturing Company so often setting the pace for the industry, Kohler was always looking to learn whatever it could from the larger company. One important lesson was direct advertising to the consumer, even though the company did not sell directly to the consumer. As Walter Kohler wrote in assessing the West Coast market, "While we will get some business out of Los Angeles it is questionable how much . . . because of the extraordinary strength of the Standard, due to its advertising. Most of the jobbers find that it is easier to sell Standard goods because it has been so advertised."[86] Of course, the importance of national advertising and brand-name recognition had been learned from very different trades than ones that produced large fixtures. Companies such as Standard Sanitary and Kohler had to adapt the marketing strategies and goals used by manufacturers of small, consumable goods in order to make them reasonable for large durable items. While consumers might be tempted to try a new soap or canned soup, and might be convinced to repeat their purchases frequently, the purchase of bathroom fixtures for their home was a major investment (no matter how competitively priced they were) that would likely occur only once or twice in a lifetime.[87]

Although advertising for consumables might translate more directly into sales, the product would then be judged on its own merits. Advertising for durables had to be geared toward a much longer-range result; because the purchase was largely irreversible, advertising had to instill confidence. One Kohler marketer wrote:

> The value of good will, created by advertising, may be reflected in the ability to get better prices or to sell the finer and more expensive fixtures, to insure the future volume of business, and prepare for times when there is less activity in the line than now, to get the interest and co-operation of dealers and the pride of our own organization, and to advertise the Kohler name in such a way as to make it of value no matter what products it may be identified with.[88]

Creating brand-name recognition would enable consumers to request the Kohler name of their plumber, builder, or architect, who in turn would request that name from wholesalers. At Kohler, advertising expenditures increased from year to year during the first part of the twentieth century, reaching a peak of $75,000 budgeted in 1916 for print advertisements in popular and trade magazines and other promotional materials.[89]

Kohler started a full-fledged national advertising campaign in the 1910s, for the most part centered around the Viceroy bathtub. The campaign was run, in slightly different forms, in six national mass-circulation magazines, two architectural journals, and five journals in the building and plumbing trades. Together these journals were said to have a combined circulation of over four million readers, with approximately two million of this total coming from the *Saturday Evening Post. Collier's Weekly, Leslie's Weekly, Literary Digest, Good Housekeeping,* and *House Beautiful* rounded out the popular magazines, while the design and building trades were approached through *American Architect, Architectural Record, Domestic Engineering, Plumbers' Trade Journal, American Carpenter and Builder, Building Age,* and *Metal Worker.* Kohler focused on this rather small group of periodicals, but invested in continuous advertising, placing ads at the very least every other month, but usually in each issue for the year. An advertising manager explained the approach at the end of this first large-scale campaign:

> Where good will and prestige are the objects aimed at, continuity has a very great value. In fact, the good will created by a series of advertisements becomes practically an investment requiring continuity for its protection. If the series is broken off for a few months, much of what was gained is probably lost again because the public forgets. There are many instances of products that were universally known a few years ago but which the average person today never thinks of.[90]

The aim for continuity meant not necessarily the same exact advertisement in every issue of a magazine, but rather varied ads featuring similar, recognizable themes and prominent placement and repetition of the company name.

While the campaign featured the benefits of Kohler products, the advertisements also promoted the idea of the bathroom as an important domestic interior that no middle-class family should be without. Popular magazines reinforced this message in their editorial as well as advertising pages, presenting the bathroom as a domestic space worthy of attention in home decorating. For example, *House and Garden* presented a photo essay of "The Well-Equipped Bath," with images of every possible furnishing, ranging from the major fixtures to embroidered towels to a hamper to hand-painted bottles for toiletries such as boric acid, mouth wash, and almond cream. The words *attractive* and *decorative* appeared frequently in the descriptions of these wares, along with *sanitary* and *convenient.* This combination showed that the bathroom was not only a space for important hygienic functions, but was, like the rest of the house, a place to display good taste and aesthetic sensibilities.[91] A story in *Country Life* centered on the process of creating the aesthetically pleasing and convenient bathroom. The protagonist's closest friend pronounces the space "the most convenient and useful bathroom I ever saw," but in doing so, notes not the major fixtures of the room but "the variety of towel racks and sponge holders and soap holders and mirrored medicine cabinets."[92] Recognizing that these types of wares completed the image of the bathroom as an important interior space, Kohler began selling some of these lesser fittings, such as soap dishes, towel rods, and glass shelving, which lent the utilitarian space an aesthetic quality. In this way, the company sold not only fixtures, but also complete bathrooms.[93]

An article in *The Delineator* in 1913 explained the increasing attention to the accoutrements of the interior, addressing the owner of an older house: "When you built your house, the bathroom wasn't considered a place for decoration; it was such a luxury in itself that you didn't consider its esthetic side. Now when you go into a new house, you envy its mistress her shining white bathroom more than anything."[94] Martha Cutler explained that in bathrooms, beauty and utility were one, writing in *Harper's Bazar*: "Shining cleanliness is in itself beautiful, but when we add to that the attraction of white porcelain and tiles, white woodwork, polished nickel-plated fixtures, and the dainty light colors of walls and furnishings in general which the sanitary laws encourage for the sake of cleanliness, we need not fear that we must sacrifice beauty to utility and hygiene in this case at least."[95]

This desire for a modern bathroom was inculcated not only through these shelter and women's magazines, but also more subtly in contemporary popular fiction. For example, in his 1923 novel *Bread*, author Charles Norris tackled issues of adequate income and living standards, at one point given material form in a bathroom. One of the main characters aspires to an elegant bathroom:

> the bathroom floor was solid marquetry of small octagonal tiles embedded in cement, and glossy tiling rose glistened with shining nickel and flawless porcelain; the bathtub was sumptuous and had a shower arrangement with a rubber sheeting on rings to envelop the bather. Martin had grinned when his eye took in these details. He swore in his enthusiasm: by god, he certainly would enjoy a bathroom like that; it certainly would be great.[96]

It was this enviable bathroom that Kohler presented as a goal in its advertising.

Almost all of the print advertisements in the Kohler campaign featured children bathing, most often a small boy with a mischievous grin and water streaming out of his hair. This depiction of children promoted the family context in which the purchase was to be considered; as one ad featuring a small boy and girl stated, "The beauty of Kohler bathtubs, lavatories and other enameled plumbing ware makes a wonderful appeal to every family."[97] Even when not stated explicitly, guiding the next generation into habits of good hygiene and cleanliness was implicit in the entire campaign. As the company itself explicated one advertisement, featuring two small boys peering into a bathtub, "The playful 'youngsters' shown in the illustration make a special appeal to parents. The text of the advertisement, bringing out the high quality of Kohler Enamel, the hygienic designs, and the other distinctive features of Kohler fixtures, will not fail to influence the reader—especially since his sympathy has already been awakened by the picture."[98] This appeal to parents raised the issue of teaching children the importance of cleanliness and hygiene. Numerous manuals were written specifically for children, bolstering the message of these advertisements.[99]

The company always featured a bathtub and lavatory, and stressed the act of bathing. While of course Kohler and the other companies sold toilets, and only with them could a "complete bath" be achieved, they were not pictured in the 1915 campaign. The rooms were sketched in half or three-quarter view excluding the toilet, which might call to mind indelicate activities. Instead, everyone could rally around an image of small children bathing, and sales of baths and sinks would no doubt imply the appointment of an entire suite of furnishings and accessories. While the campaign stressed the special qualities of the Viceroy tub, the scenes depicted displayed an entire room setting, encouraging consumers to purchase a whole "set" of fixtures.

The emphasis on children in advertising not only conjured up the notion of family and appeal to the "parent" in a potential purchaser, but also was an appropriate view of a person in a bathroom. While a rare advertisement or catalogue sketch might depict a woman at her toilette, only a cute child, totally desexualized, would suffice to actually show a person in a bathtub at the turn of the century. Only children were exempt from the requirement of privacy that bathing increasingly demanded in the middle-class lifestyle. Readers of magazines could pose as "parents" to the children depicted, but could only be voyeurs of any other persons shown.

Because they could be depicted in little or no clothing, and with no other identifying personal accessories, children also allowed for a broader range of socioeconomic associations than adult models. Instead, the company defined its market through the depictions of interior appointments and the frames through which these rooms were presented. For example, in one advertisement, the central image of a small boy in a Viceroy bathtub was seen in a fuzzy-edged bubble, representing the imaginations of a man and a woman. The man was apparently an architect, pointing with one hand to the plans for a bathroom and with the other to the Kohler tub. The female client looked at the architect but was clearly envisioning her small child in the new bathroom. The text addressed the client, saying, "Your architect knows—let him specify KOHLER enameled Plumbing Ware for your bathroom," establishing both the authority of the architect and the client's right to the best possible products. Stating that the Viceroy was "just what you . . . want for your home," the copy highlighted the appearance, the hygienic qualities, the easy maintenance, and the low cost. The tub would "add materially to the attractiveness of your home," also presumably adding materially to the value of the home. This advertisement addressed a clientele well enough off to hire an architect for new home designs or renovations, but still clearly concerned with good value.[100]

Another of the ads also featured a man and a woman, but this time apparently a husband and wife—together they are considering a book entitled *Kohler of Kohler,* while between them float the words, "These Are The Bath Room Fixtures We Want." The ad offered to send the same book to readers, suggesting that "if you are building a house or an apartment or remodeling your home, write us at once for a free copy of our new book." This advertisement might have been targeted to those using the services of builders and contractors, rather than architects—a market distinction that encompassed not only financial status, but also differences in community type and available services.

The title of the consumer promotional book depicted, *Kohler of Kohler,* was significant. The company promoted its association with the town in which the wares were made, presented as a progressive, cohesive community; the very fact that those who resided there had voted to name the town for the company showed the good spirit emanating from the workplace. One advertisement explained, "When you buy a piece of Kohler enameled plumbing ware, you secure the product of an enthusiastic, efficient organization imbued with high ideals."[101] The design sense of the burgeoning garden city of Kohler Village was also linked to the products made there. Many of the ads stated that at Kohler, the process of enameling had been made a "finer art." At the same time that the artistic quality of the manufacturing process was touted, the company also claimed its large-scale factory, and resulting scale of production, as a means of keeping costs down. While addressing homeowners, the advertisement did allow for a broad range of possible settings for Kohler products; again featuring the Viceroy, the copy read, "This attractive bath has been adopted for many of the finest hotels and apartments, as well as for thousands of homes ranging from cosy bungalows to elaborate mansions."[102] This one sentence revealed the breadth of Kohler's market base.

While several of the advertisements showed children alone, two also portrayed an adult female figure. In one case a woman, presumably the child's mother, stands at the edge of the tub dousing her small son with a sprayer attachment. In another, the woman is a maid, dressed in a traditional, white-aproned uniform; she enters the bathroom to find two children apparently playing hide and seek in and around the bathtub. While this advertisement might have been addressing an upper bracket that still employed domestic help, in other ways, it invoked stylistic tradition in the home—this ad featured a Collonna ball-and-claw foot tub and small wall-mounted lavatory set in a room with woodwork and a transom above the door, suggestive of Victorian interior furnishings. While claiming that every "Kohler plumbing fixture is an expression of Twentieth Century ideas in construction and enameling," this ad did not make any claims for modern design; Kohler ware would fit just as easily into a remodeled nineteenth-century home as a new house that championed modernity. In contrast, another advertisement, featuring the slogan "Build your home around your bathroom," depicted a grand house in the prairie style (seemingly fronted by a large pond with lily pads), while the copy read "A beautiful bathroom containing modern hygienic plumbing fixtures adds to the value and attractiveness of any house or apartment, whether it is large or small, elaborate or inexpensive." The drawing of the house was almost identical to an illustration of a Frank Lloyd Wright design that had appeared in *The Delineator* a few years earlier. Thus, while appealing to different economic brackets, the campaign also had to appeal to differing personal taste.[103]

Many of the advertisements for the building and plumbing trade journals incorporated small-scale versions of those run in the national magazines, essentially selling to jobbers not only Kohler's products but the fact that these products came with already built-in brand-name recognition that could add clout to the local dealer. The company needed to promote itself at each step of the sales chain in order to achieve the highest possible sales.

In doing so, however, it also had to coordinate these promotions. Walter Kohler wrote to the home office about suggestions made by a wholesaler in Los Angeles, who reminded him to be sure to inform jobbers in advance of consumer advertising, so that they would be prepared to answer questions about the advertised goods. In response to such suggestions, the company began a campaign for jobbers that went along with its consumer advertising campaign, explained in a large-format booklet entitled *Kohler Sales Helps.* The basic advertising campaign of the 1910s, focusing on the Viceroy bathtub, "is so developed that any Kohler jobber or plumber can localize the advertising and get its full benefit." Because their own business was so closely intertwined with those of the jobbing and plumbing trades, the company stated the aim of the new campaign: "We are ready to do everything possible which will be of assistance in building up the business of the jobber and plumber and establishing it permanently upon a sound basis. To this end we cordially invite the co-operation of everyone who is interested in the trade." The company's goal was thorough coordination of all its promotional materials, whether they originated from the company, wholesalers, or plumbers, in order to "impart influences which will tend to stabilize trade conditions." To achieve this coordination, the company prepared a variety of promotional materials that could incorporate the name of the local dealer and be displayed in local contexts. Advertising was in itself seen as a mark of quality: that a company would spend money on national advertising campaigns and make large claims for its wares in print was significant. As Kohler explained its layered advertising campaign, "Let the property owners and prospective builders in your community know that you sell the best Enameled Plumbing Ware made—the kind that is advertised."[104]

The most typical of these "sales helps" were electrotypes for local newspaper advertising that would echo, in word and image, the advertisements being placed in the national magazines by the parent company. While the national ads might be in full color, the local ads would reproduce the same picture in a black-and-white line drawing. A more innovative idea was to distribute lantern slides that could be shown in between motion picture screenings; Kohler offered to add the name of the local dealer at the bottom of the slides. These images would remind moviegoers of magazine ads they might have seen, but attach a local context, perhaps providing more of a spur to investigate the product depicted. The company provided mailing pieces in standard envelope sizes, as well as electrotypes of Kohler fixtures or advertising images to be incorporated into local dealers' letterhead or billheads.

Large display cards were available for store windows, sales offices, or street-car advertising. The company's attention to show windows, evident when looking for branch office space, was renewed in this campaign; in addition to these cards, the company created a large-format folding panel display for store windows. As Kohler described it:

> This is the most beautiful window display that has ever been produced for the purpose of attracting attention to Enameled Plumbing Ware.
>
> In addition to the excellence of the general design, the combination of a large number of colors will make the display a feature that cannot fail to cause favorable comment.
>
> No one will be likely to pass a window in which this card is exhibited, without stopping to admire it and the fixtures it advertises.
>
> This Window Display will pull people into every establishment in which it is shown.[105]

All of these pieces were furnished by Kohler free of charge in exchange for the local jobber's or plumber's willingness to advertise for the company.

Sharing the emphasis on advertising with the local dealers was also a way to be able to better track the impact of their promotions. National advertising was certainly a boost to the company in brand-name recognition and specification, and the association of the product with quality in design and durability. But it was difficult to ascribe actual sales to these efforts. While the company could keep track of consumer responses to national advertising—for example, how many readers, upon seeing the image of the husband and wife looking over their *Kohler of Kohler* book, sent in for one of their own—these numbers were almost negligible in light of the overall circulation of the images. For the first nine months of the national advertising campaign in 1915 and 1916, the company received responses from a total of 775 readers of *Saturday Evening Post, Collier's Weekly, Leslie's Weekly,* and *Literary Digest,* to which magazines it ascribed a combined circulation of 3,565,000 (though of course some of this circulation would overlap) and to which it was paying combined advertising rates of over $45,000. While these statistics might seem discouraging, the company did not really hold the expectation of direct communication with the ultimate consumer. There would not even be an easy way to follow up on whether those 775 inquiries resulted in sales, because the sales would occur at the level of the dealer. Thus, echoing the national advertising in local dealers' ads whose effectiveness could more easily be linked to actual sales figures was one way, however imprecise, of gauging the overall effectiveness of the national campaign. As one advertising executive wrote at the close of the 1910s, "The principal purpose of our advertising has not been so much to make immediate sales as to build up good will and prestige. Doubtless, it would be at times very desirable to have our advertising clinch sales quickly . . . It probably never can be true because our distance from the consumer would make it too difficult and costly to clinch matters and we, accordingly, must build up a name that will assist somebody else in making sales for us."[106] The integrated advertising campaign and the *Kohler Sales Helps* offered just such assistance.

The "good will and prestige" accrued through advertising were ascribed to the company not only through its products and business dealings, but in its civic spirit as well. World War I offered the company the opportunity to promote its part in the war effort as well as the importance of sanitary plumbing as a necessary part of the American home. Kohler sold large quantities of its wares to companies building emergency war housing for increased ranks of workers and thus linked its name to the drive for "efficient" settings for production. As the company wrote in its newsletter, "The great demands upon labor for efficient work in winning the war have led to the construction, under government auspices, of large numbers of houses for workingmen. It is realized that a man cannot produce the most and the best unless he lives in a condition of comfort, decency, and health. And among the requirements for getting good living conditions, sanitary plumbing has, of course, an important place." Along with the inspirational words to the company employees about the value of their work, the *Kohler of Kohler News* ran a photograph of a construction site for employee housing for the American Brake Shoe and Foundry Company of Erie, Pennsylvania, reprinted from *Domestic Engineering*. The foreground of the photo showed dozens of newly unpacked bathtubs arranged in flanks on end, waiting to be installed, contributing not only to the effort of the Great War, but also to the fight for improved sanitation. Kohler thus associated its products with a standard of living that the nation should aspire to, one of "comfort, decency and health."[107]

Kohler was supported in these claims by members of the home economics and public health movements, who looked to evaluate the material means that might ensure the "health, longevity, industrial ability, comfort and welfare of human beings." These words, in the opinion of John R. Commons, a professor of political economy at the University of Wisconsin, represented the "units of output" to be measured in relation to the "units of cost" com-

prised of "food, shelter, clothing, occupation, education," when trying to
evaluate the workings of the home along standardized lines, just as engineers
might evaluate the workings of a factory. In an address to the American
Home Economics Association in 1910, Commons created a 100-point scale
for grading dwelling houses, with points allotted to various necessary qualities and attributes. A quarter of these points could be earned in the category of "House Appurtenances," which included a private bath, a private
water closet, the condition of these fixtures and their piping, accessibility of
running water, and the quality of that water for both drinking and bathing.[108]

In the early 1920s, the Kohler Company would make the association
between its products and the standard of living even more explicit, using the
phrase in its advertising. A 1922 advertisement depicted a bathroom with a
built-in Viceroy tub, a wall-mounted lavatory, and low tank toilet, headed
by the phrase "The Index to Your Standards of Living." This headline, an
obvious reference to contemporary attempts to enumerate a standard of living for American families, took the "bundle of goods" that normally comprised the index and reduced it to one item—the household bathroom,
described in the copy as the "one room in every home which is the key to
the real standards of living of that household." In contrast to the early
national advertisements of the mid-1910s, this one featured an image of the
room itself, with no people in it. The message here was not about introducing good habits of hygiene to one's family; the message here was that the
objects themselves, when placed in a proper setting, brought a certain status to the family that owned them.

The advertisement used three main appeals in its sales pitch: aesthetic,
pragmatic, and psychological or competitive. In the first case, Kohler ware
was described as "attractive," as "beautiful," and as "glistening, snow-white"
fixtures. As the "one room" that represented a family's standard of living, the
bathroom should be as well and thoughtfully decorated as the rest of the
household, and Kohler's complete and coordinated line of products could
help achieve this end. The second level of the advertisement addressed economic concerns. The company explained that the high Kohler quality was
attainable at a "surprisingly low cost"; because of its durability, the long-
term investment value of Kohler Ware was sound. The advertisement coun-
seled readers to either contact a "Kohler plumber" for "useful information"
or write the company directly for an "interesting, free booklet" with "many
valuable ideas."

But perhaps the most compelling address was the more personal one, appealing to readers' instincts to provide their family with the highest-quality goods possible, especially in comparison with high-class hotels and other people's homes, mentioned twice within the ad copy. At one point, the comparative desire to "keep up with the Joneses" was addressed directly: "You know Kohler Ware is used in the world's finest hotels and in countless thousands of homes and apartments. You, too, can enjoy their beauty." This last appeal was to the readers' pride, as stated explicitly within the advertisement: "The furnishings in the rest of your home reflect, from necessity, the limitations of your income. But whether this one room in question reflects your sense of refinement, your ideals of hygiene and sanitation, is a matter, not of money, but of pride." For such a purchase to transcend the realm of money, it had to be classed as a necessity, as a standard possession.

Though the aim of the advertisement was clear, the audience was actually somewhat imprecise. On the one hand, Kohler tried to appeal to those "of the most modest purse" but on the other hand, the issue was "replacing your old plumbing fixtures," not incorporating them anew. And further, the ad addressed those who "have admired [Kohler goods] in hotels of the first class." Those of truly modest purses would not have had the experiences described, including having any permanent plumbing fixtures, but through the ad copy, could aspire to them. With its picture of the "index to your standards of living" Kohler assumed that the "standard" was a common aspiration and promoted its products as the necessary first step toward achieving that goal. Because of the connection to a family's "health and decency," implied by the rhetoric of hygiene in the home, such a purchase could be justified as a necessity rather than a luxury. As "the index" to a family's standard of living, Kohler implied that this one purchase could establish a family's place within the middle class that shared that standard.[109]

Bathroom fixtures, particularly if plumbed into place, implied a certain organization of space in which hygienic processes were separated from other daily activities; this separation gave the act of bathing privacy and value in a way it had not had earlier. At the upper echelons of the market, the act of bathing could even be separated into constituent parts of the body with a bathtub, footbath, sitz bath, and shower. These ideas of separation of functions, even in the most routine of activities, were shared broadly in the industrial era. As with silverplate flatware, public settings—hotels, clubs, restaurants, offices—as sites of both work and leisure could also be sites of exposure to the design of bathroom fixtures and their use for individuals.

The infrastructure for distribution was even more important in the fixture industry than it had been with flatware. The weight and size of the objects magnified the logistical details and financial investment to move them from place to place. To spread these costs out and move goods to where they were needed, fixture companies developed chains of selling that moved from company to wholesaler to plumber to consumer. These different agents in the selling process also shared responsibility for publicizing their shared product.

Advertisements stressed that bathroom fixtures were a family decision; the bathroom would be not just a site for bathing but also a classroom for teaching hygiene, particularly to children. Although the act of bathing was personal, it had larger merits in the eyes of hygiene experts and public health officials. Cleanliness contributed to personal health, collective cleanliness to public health. As manufacturers looked to expand their market, they promoted the same ideals as the proponents of good hygiene. The very material with which the fixtures were coated emphasized their function. The enamel was impervious to embedded dirt or germs; it was a perfectly smooth and thus easy-to-clean surface. At the same time, fixed receptacles and plumbed water made bathing more convenient and symbolized its value. This collaboration between manufacturers and promoters of good health is encapsulated in Kohler's "Index" advertisement.

The modern bathroom was only one facet of an efficient and up-to-date household. The Kohler Company's provision of fixtures in employee housing in the company town was a form of promotion for not only their own wares but also modern housing in general. Walter Kohler was a supporter of initiatives such as the Better Homes in America program, which coordinated a variety of governmental, commercial, and social messages into a unified campaign for homeownership. Housing manufacturers would answer this call with innovations in standardized homes.

The family circle. *Good Housekeeping,* 1910. Library of Congress.

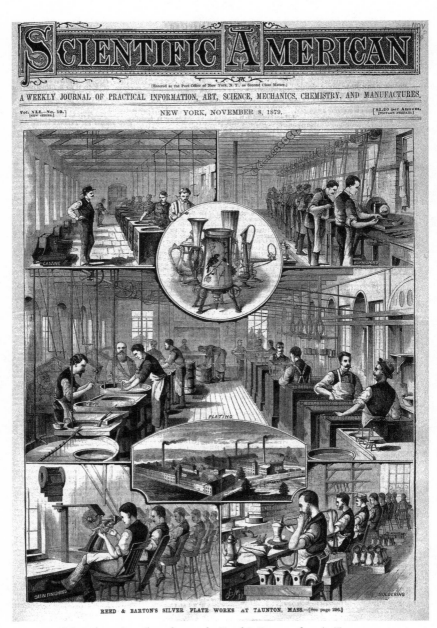

Manufacturing silverplate at the Reed & Barton plant in Taunton, Massachusetts. *Scientific American,* 1879. National Museum of American History, Smithsonian Institution.

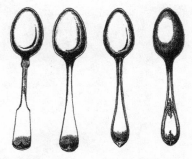

Early silverplate spoon patterns, 1860s–1870s.
Original drawing by R. Tripp Evans.

Spoon patterns designed for Reed & Barton, 1870s–1880s.
Original drawing by R. Tripp Evans.

Setting the table. *Good Housekeeping,* 1910. Library of Congress.

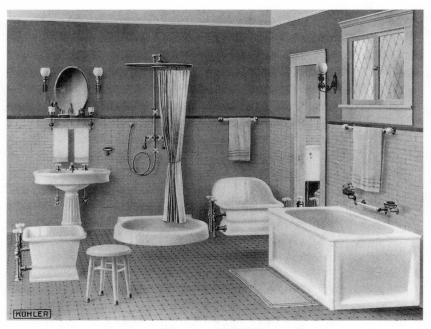

The complete bathroom, as depicted in a 1914 Kohler Company catalogue.
Kohler Company Archives.

The evolution of
bathtubs, 1880s–1900s.
Kohler Company
Archives.

Bathing children with and without fixed plumbing. Catalogue illustrations, 1914. Kohler Company Archives.

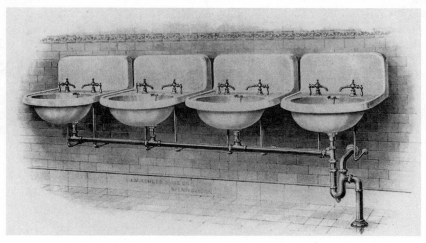

Plumbing for public institutions, 1904. Kohler Company Archives.

Advice from an architect. Advertisement from 1915.
Kohler Company Archives.

The varied venues of advertising for the plumbing trade. Cover of
Kohler Sales Helps, 1915. Kohler Company Archives.

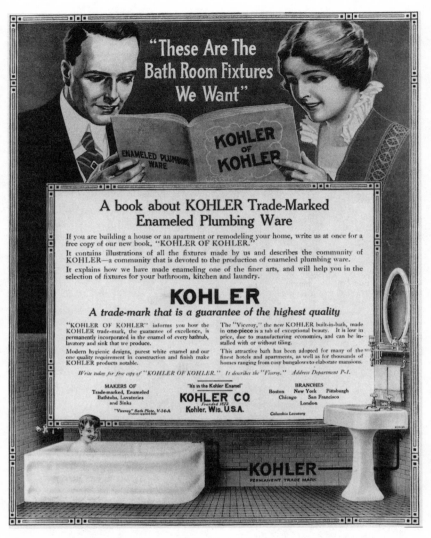

The dream of parents everywhere. Advertisement from 1915.
Kohler Company Archives.

On facing page: The symbiotic relationship of magazines and advertisers. The Kohler Company featured the modern architecture of Frank Lloyd Wright in a 1915 advertisement; a similar view was included in *The Delineator* of 1913. Kohler Company Archives and National Museum of American History, Smithsonian Institution.

Build your home around your bathroom

The bathroom should receive careful consideration when the plans for your home are being made.

A beautiful bathroom containing modern hygienic plumbing fixtures adds to the value and attractiveness of any house or apartment, whether it is large or small, elaborate or inexpensive.

KOHLER
Trade-Marked Enameled Plumbing Ware is an expression of 20th century ideas

One-piece construction and enamel of purest white give distinction to KOHLER products, which are *always* of the highest quality.

The trade-mark, permanent in the enamel of every KOHLER bathtub, lavatory and sink, is our guarantee of excellence, and your safe guide in the selection of plumbing ware. Be sure to look for it.

The "Viceroy," our latest built-in bath, has won exceptional popularity.

It is made in **one-piece**; can be installed without tiling; is low in price, due to manufacturing economies.

This beautiful bath has been installed in thousands of homes, ranging from cozy bungalows to the most elaborate apartments.

If you are building or remodeling, write for our free book, "KOHLER of KOHLER." It tells you how we have made enameling one of the finer arts. Address Dept. S-3.

MAKERS OF
Trade-marked, Enameled
Bathtubs, Lavatories
and Sinks

"It's in the Kohler Enamel"
KOHLER CO.
Founded 1873
Kohler. Wis. U.S.A.

BRANCHES
Boston — St. Paul
Pittsburgh — St. Louis
San Francisco — Seattle
Philadelphia — New York
Detroit — Chicago
Atlanta — London

Belmore Lavatory, Plate K-18-EA

KOHLER

"Viceroy" Bath Plate K-18-A
(Patent Applied For)

Advertisement from *Saturday Evening Post*, 1922. Library of Congress.

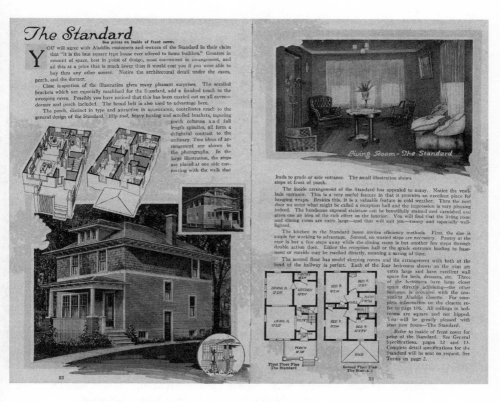

The "standard" American home, 1919. Aladdin Company Archive, Clarke Historical Library, Central Michigan University.

A vision of home, from the house organ of the Aladdin Company, 1915. Aladdin
Company Archive, Clarke Historical Library, Central Michigan University.

Direct from the Producer

An appeal to the rural market, from the house organ of the Aladdin Company, 1913. Aladdin Company Archive, Clarke Historical Library, Central Michigan University.

Anti-Landlord Issue

The anti-rent campaign, personified, 1920. Aladdin Company Archive, Clarke Historical Library, Central Michigan University.

Small Town Preferred

One sector of the market in new houses, 1920. Aladdin Company Archive, Clarke Historical Library, Central Michigan University.

The Herford

$836.00

Price, $880.00
Cash discount, 5%
Net price, $836.00

First Floor Plan
The Herford

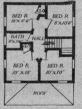

Second Floor Plan
The Herford

THE Herford is an achievement in building a two-story, four-bedroom house at a price less than nine hundred dollars, yet the convenience and attractive appearance of this design is not impaired in the least. A large living room across the entire front, large square dining room and kitchen make an exceptionally convenient and roomy first floor plan. The second floor has four bedrooms and bath, with clothes closets. The large porch across the front and the grade cellar entrance, are features of this design seldom found in a house at this price. Handsome front door with three-quarter length glass and wide window front the house. You couldn't possibly better the design and arrangement of the Herford, try as you might and it would be utterly impossible to find better lumber than is furnished, for it doesn't grow in any forest.

The carefully built semi-open stairway with circle first step, newel post and beautifully grained Fir lumber add a pleasing tone to the interior woodwork. All woodwork is very carefully sanded and ready to receive the stains and varnish. The Herford would show up beautifully if painted like the Charleston, which is shown in colors on another page.

See Terms on page 2 and General Specifications on pages 12 and 13.

The Charleston $1,472.50

Price, $1,550.00
Cash discount, 5%
Net price, $1,472.50

THERE are many good points in the Charleston, a modern square-type design. The first noticeable feature is the deep bay windows in front, both stories, also on one side. These give free sight in all directions and ample light.

The interior arrangement is one for convenience. Front entrance is gained through a large reception hall with semi-open stairway and arched entrance to large living room. This feature has proven popular, as it can be used for one room and still retain the convenience of two.

The kitchen has proved attractive to busy housewives. A rear entrance leads to the back porch, while the grade entrance at the side leads to the out-

Facing and above: The foursquare dwelling adapted to varying family budgets, 1917. Aladdin Company Archive, Clarke Historical Library, Central Michigan University.

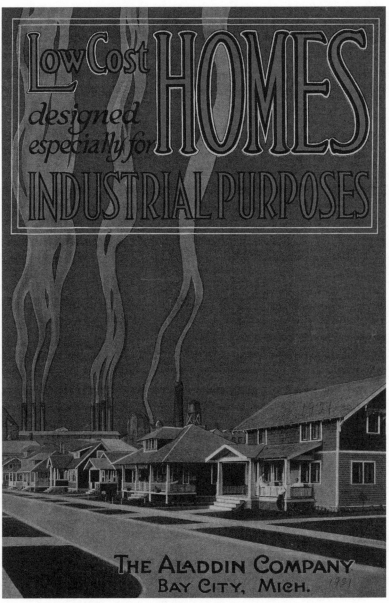

"Industrial" homes for both family and corporate consumers, 1920. Aladdin
Company Archive, Clarke Historical Library, Central Michigan University.

The Aladdin garden party, representing the community of homeowners forged by the company's consumers. 1917. Aladdin Company Archive, Clarke Historical Library, Central Michigan University.

THE SORT OF HOMES WE SHOULD HAVE IF OUR HOUSES WERE
LIKE OUR CITIES

Zoning as household
organization. Cartoon
from *The American
City*, 1923.
Library of Congress.

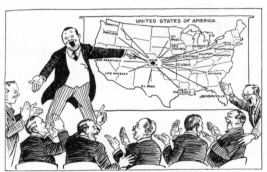

The Boosters' Ideal—"Let's Put Our City on the Map"

How to Design a City,
a cartoon from
The American City, 1928.
Library of Congress.

The Planners' Ideal—"Let's Put the Map on Our City"

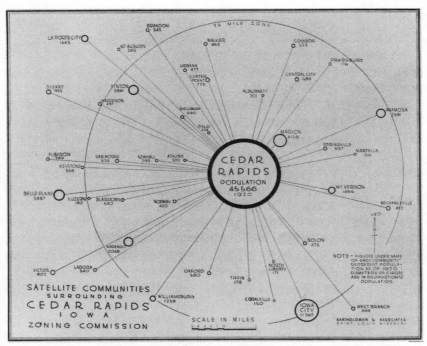

A city as a regional hub, illustration by Harland Bartholomew and Associates in *A Comprehensive Plan for Cedar Rapids, Iowa,* 1931. Harland Bartholomew and Associates Collection, University Archives, Washington University in St. Louis.

The campaign for uniform streetscapes, a byproduct of zoning. Cartoon in *The American City,* 1923, Library of Congress.

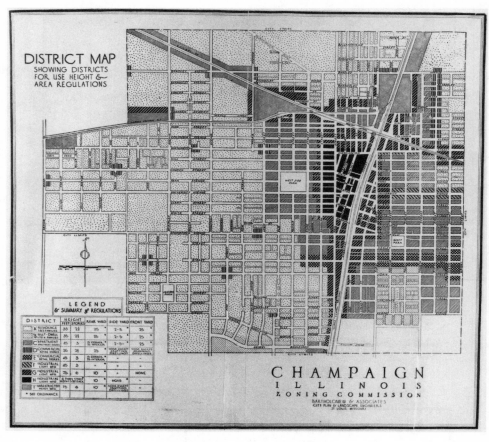

Zoning map for Champaign, Illinois, 1926. Harland Bartholomew and Associates Collection, University Archives, Washington University in St. Louis.

The components of the comprehensive plan: Streets, Transit, Transportation, Public Recreation, Civic Art, and Zoning. Harland Bartholomew and Associates, *Comprehensive Plan for Memphis, Tennessee,* 1924, Library of Congress.

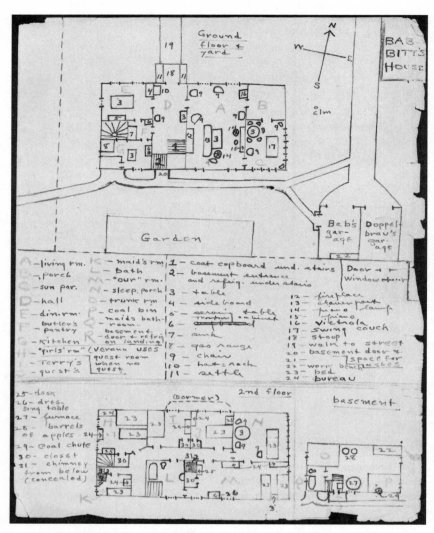

George F. Babbitt's house, drawn by Sinclair Lewis. Lewis's fictional vision of a typical American house recalls the house plans of the Aladdin Company. Dorothy Thompson Papers, Syracuse University Libraries.

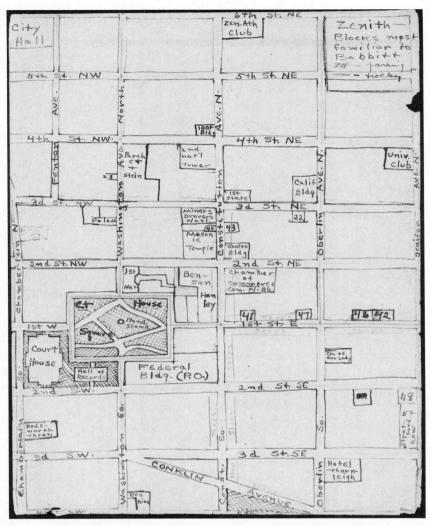

Map of places most familiar to Babbitt, drawn by Sinclair Lewis. The
urban grid sketched by Lewis is reminiscent of typical zoning plans.
Dorothy Thompson Papers, Syracuse University Libraries.

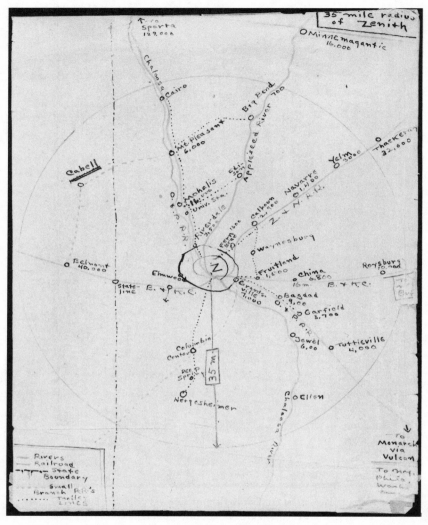

Map of satellite communities to Zenith, Sinclair Lewis. Lewis's notion of the hierarchy of communities in the fictional state of Winnemac echoes Harland Bartholomew's schematic drawing of the communities surrounding Cedar Rapids. Dorothy Thompson Papers, Syracuse University Libraries.

CHAPTER THREE

THE STANDARD OF INVESTMENT

Mail-Order Homes

In the late summer and early fall of 1915, A. J. Smith of Richmond, Virginia, built a house. It measured 22 by 30 feet; it had two stories and a hipped roof. The house was known as a box house or square-type house, even though its footprint was not an exact square. The first floor had a living room, dining room, and kitchen, arranged around a small entry hall; the second floor had three bedrooms and a bathroom. The house was fronted by a small porch and was painted cream on the first story of the exterior and brown on the second story, and had white trim. At about the same time, W. A. Moberly of Tama, Iowa, built a house. It had the exact same dimensions and room configurations, and even the same exterior paint colors. In Greenwich, Ohio, a month or so later, J. W. Kirk built an identical house. While by the 1910s, it was common to have multiple houses of the same specifications within a residential subdivision, the experience of Smith, Moberly, and Kirk was a little different. Here were three people, in radically different communities, strangers and probably destined to remain that way, all building the same home. In fact, they not only built these homes, but bought them, choosing from a catalogue, as they might have also selected household furnishings, clothing, or other consumer goods. The house model that Smith, Moberly, and Kirk picked was identified by a name and, as the historian's good fortune would have it, that name was "The Standard."[1]

While houses like "The Standard" were designed by architects and built by contractors, they were also manufactured and sold to individuals in the same way as countless other consumer goods. Large industrial firms used economies of scale to produce houses, or rather the pieces that together made up a house, and to distribute them across the country. This mail-order architecture, or kit-house, business comprised a significant part of the market in new houses in the 1910s and 1920s.[2] A variety of house models were presented in catalogues showing the floor plan, a sketch or photograph of the exterior, and sometimes other interior views. With some companies, modifications could be made to the original specifications; reversing a floor plan, enlarging a porch, including a small addition—all of these were common requests. The houses were available in a variety of paint colors, so that even in its standard form, a house displayed some personal choice. While Smith, Moberly, and Kirk had remarkably similar homes, there were dozens of other owners with houses almost, but not exactly, the same. What all of these owners shared, however, was a commitment to owning their own home, even if it meant giving up some degree of individuality.

Prospective owners viewed the decision not just in terms of creating a family nest, but also as a business prospect, making an investment in real estate. While shelter magazines of the period weighed the choice to build a new home specifically for one's family or buy one already made to someone else's specifications, the mail-order trade offered a third alternative, at a considerably lower cost. One could buy a standardized plan to be constructed of standardized parts, but make small adaptations as needed or desired. Because of the lower prices, primarily of materials but also of simplified labor, the option of homeownership was extended to those who might not otherwise be able to afford it. Families might secure bank loans, or more quickly access building and loans association funds, because of the lower costs involved. Whether spending significant savings or taking advantage of credit, new homeowners recast their attitudes toward spending and debt as necessary steps to investment, just as a business firm might do until it established itself. It was these dual associations—of family and business united through homeownership—to which mail-order house manufacturers tied their products.[3]

No one understood the importance of these associations better than two brothers, William and Otto Sovereign, of Bay City, Michigan, who effectively split the two sides of the business—factory production and marketing—under their respective leadership. As the company legend had it, William came up with the idea for mail-order houses, not from the portable house industry, but from knock-down boat companies that were thriving in Bay City. Located on the edge of timber country, but also easily accessible to transport, Bay City was a logical place for such an industry to grow. William, trained for the bar but uninspired by it, saw a future in parallel companies that would produce not boats but houses; as he pointed out to his brother, the latter was a much larger potential market. Otto, trained in advertising, took William's idea and ran with it, to ensure that this potential market was as large as possible. Together they formed the North American Construction Company, later known as the Aladdin Company. With no training in architecture or design between them, the brothers founded in 1906 the company that started the mail-order architecture business and remained a leader in the trade, bested only by the Sears, Roebuck Home Construction Division. Unlike most of its competitors, Aladdin survived the two World Wars and the Great Depression, and continued in business until the 1980s. In 1906, the brothers ran the company from their parents' kitchen and had no holdings of lumber or tools and equipment; they contracted with a lumberyard to cut pieces based on their specifications. Though this lumberyard later evolved into the competing firm of Lewis Manufactured Homes, the Sovereigns quickly amassed their own plants not just in Bay City, but also in regional timber centers across the country and in Canada.[4]

The mail-order house trade had several antecedents, but they supported different aspects of the trade. On the one hand, the catalogues seemed the latest in a line of architectural plan books that had existed for generations. Plan books had given way to mail-order plan services, which were popularized by their inclusion in popular periodicals, such as *Ladies' Home Journal*.[5] For consumers, the act of buying parts precut to fit plans was a logical next step from buying the plans themselves. There may have been a particular appeal of the mail-order product in its "do-it-yourself" quality. The earliest advertisements of mail-order firms stressed the ease in putting up the home, that it could be accomplished, with "no tool but a hammer," by oneself, with friends, or if necessary, with the help of an "ordinary man" rather than a skilled laborer. As one early catalogue for Aladdin assured prospective customers, "Put up an 'Aladdin' Yourself: Don't hesitate to send for an 'Aladdin' house because you fear it is difficult to put up. There is no back breaking, muscle racking, sawing, measuring, figuring or fitting to do. We do all that in our mill. Your 'work' is driving nails."[6]

For those owners whose livelihood involved manual labor, the act of building their own house transformed a skill associated with the working classes into a status associated with the middle classes.[7] For those purchasers who earned their living by nonproductive labor, the tangible side of the trade may have been an attraction. Those who did build the houses themselves spoke of the satisfaction involved. For example, "Geo. D. Kellogg, post office clerk, 2520 Warren Avenue, Chicago, bought a lot, arranged to have an Aladdin house shipped during his vacation and erected and completed it himself during his two weeks of vacation. The work was a change, was easy and pleasant and at the same time he had the satisfaction of constructing with his own hands his own home and saving nearly one-half the cost." Under the heading "This Man Enjoyed His Work," these words appeared in a pamphlet of testimonial stories focusing on the ease of building a mail-order home.[8] Other purchasers, at least in towns and cities, however, did hire others to build the structures, making their home-building project an extension of the work they did, this time managing the production of their own home by methods similar to those they used to manage industrial or office work. Even when the work was "managed" rather than done by the owner, there was still a much closer relationship to the final product than when buying a home in a planned subdivision. With a kit house, the owner made decisions about siting, color, plan, and orientation, even if the actual construction work was not carried out personally.

Whatever the work process, buying unseen goods (or parts) for the important investment in one's own home was certainly an adjustment to be reckoned with by marketing departments. From the production side, mail-order homes might be seen as a next step in the evolution from portable homes: small cabins or sheds used for vacation cottages or farm buildings. These portable homes, transported in pieced-together panels, were fitted together and secured with bolts, which could be as easily undone as done, a part of their convenience. Thus, while production methods might have been similar for these "knock-down" houses and the new lines of mail-order buildings, manufacturers of the latter actually wanted to distance themselves from the former. Mail-order houses were designed to be not portable but permanent. Once built, they should show no difference from "traditional construction methods"; once up, they were not to be taken down. The Aladdin Company detailed the parts of each kit in its catalogues:

> A complete house means all lumber cut to fit accurately for the foundation timbers, the joists, studding and rafters, the siding, the flooring; the porch timbers, joists, flooring, columns, railing, steps; the roofing, roof sheathing; doors, half glass for outside and paneled for all inside openings, windows, with glass in place; window sash, inside and outside window trim and inside

and outside door trim, moulded base board for all inside rooms, weather moulding for trimming all outside doors and windows, all hardware, mortised locks for all inside doors; handsome burnished art brass locks and hinges for outside doors, nails for entire house, paint for two coats inside and outside and plaster board for lining entire house inside.[9]

To make all these parts and coordinate their assembly and to convince potential buyers of their worth were two different tasks. The production and marketing of such an industry raised different sets of issues for its executives, and both sides of the business needed to be attended to in order to be successful.

INVESTED IN HOMES

The connection to family is what made homeownership so important. The Aladdin Company implied that only within a home of one's own could the true expression of family bonds occur. As one catalogue asked, "Did you ever really consider the wonderful difference in the meaning of the words house and home? A house is a structure to live in. Home—the dearest place on earth—is that structure that is a part of you—made so by its association with your family, their joys and sorrows, their hopes and aspirations, visible expression of yourself, your tastes and character."[10] A house was more than a mere shelter; as one's home, it could be furnished and decorated as best expressed each familial unit that together created the new professional managerial class. As one Aladdin publication exclaimed, "Your Own Home! no other ideal of the family is so sweet as this . . . down through all the ages of civilization, a home for the shelter and seclusion of loved ones has ever been the first and foremost object of the family."[11] Owning one's own home was presented as a part of the standard of living, perhaps the most important part. While a house might seem out of the realm of comparison with other consumer goods, the trade sought to ensure this primary position.

One of the major competing purchases in the 1920s was a family car. Aladdin started a campaign to convince prospective buyers that the purchase of an automobile should follow the purchase of a home, not precede it. As one broadside expressed simply, "Own a home first—then indulge in the luxuries." An elderly couple was pictured worrying over their bills, representing the "worry, fear and debt" associated with buying a car while the home represented savings of rent and "peace, happiness and comfort."[12]

Economists supported this idea by pointing out the financial stability of homeownership; for example, in his study of farmers, Ellis Kirkpatrick wrote, "House ownership gives access to a certain amount of land usually, and both represent fairly stable economic values which, like investments, can be drawn upon to meet different emergencies or unexpected needs."[13] A home was not a luxury; it represented the convenience and comfort that were part of the standard of living.

To be sure, homeowners had responsibilities that those living in rented dwellings did not, but these responsibilities were portrayed as having attendant privileges. Owning one's house meant making all choices oneself; as the Aladdin Company explained, "That family is, indeed, unfortunate that has never felt the joy of planning a new home; of considering this feature and discussing that one; of looking over views and studying floor plans; of deciding what size and shape and arrangement are best adapted to their particular needs. It is worth much sacrifice, if that is necessary, to feel the freedom of a home of your own."[14] Aladdin did allow for such a process of choice, whether it meant choosing one of the house plans from the catalogue or further adapting it with additions, built-in furnishings, and modifications to the original plan. The "freedom" of individual expression of a family's needs and desires stemmed from the very standardization of house parts that made the houses affordable to a broader market. Once this freedom was attained, further choices arose about decorating and furnishing— these elements were presented as making a house a home. The company elaborated on this idea in a booklet devoted to interiors:

> You have envied a friend his home because it was his own, and he had the right to fix it up exactly to suit himself and his wife . . . What keen enjoyment there is in the right to plan and make "home" likable and livable and comfortable! No landlord to beg for new paper or plumbing; nobody else to consult when you believe a window-seat here or a clothes closet there will add to looks and convenience. Simply necessary to agree on what you want, and do it. Then every penny you spend counts in improving your own investment.[15]

Thus, even the personal decisions of home decorating were one aspect of making a good business investment.

In their marketing materials, the Sovereigns echoed the larger cultural push toward homeownership as an important American ideal. Starting in the Progressive Era, but solidifying after World War I, the aspiration toward homeownership was increasingly a tenet of American middle-class culture.

At the end of the 1920s, the primary theorist of the domestic economy, Hazel Kyrk, summarized recent arguments in favor of homeownership, many of which betray a search for stability in a changing society:

> Strong arguments are made for home ownership. Mr. [Herbert] Hoover has called it the foundation of a sound economic and social system. American communities pride themselves on a high percentage of home ownership. It connotes order, good citizenship, prosperity, good housing. Home owners it is said are a stable, conservative group with a stake in the community and interest in its development. Home ownership is a widely accepted symbol of a family's thrift, industry and financial success. It is the goal that perhaps more frequently than any other, families have deliberately set up as the one they desire to attain.[16]

The mail-order architecture firms picked up on all of these arguments in their own promotions and, with their lower prices, tried to provide broader access to all of these benefits. Calvin Coolidge wrote, for an article in *The Delineator*, "It is of little avail to assert that there is an inherent right to own property unless there is an open opportunity that this right may be enjoyed in a fair degree by all." Writing as vice president in 1922, Coolidge went on to say that the moment was right for such a campaign, as materials were available, credit was ready, and the spirit of "endurance and sacrifice" had been learned in the Great War.[17] In broadening the base of those who could afford to buy houses with their lower prices, Aladdin and the other mail-order firms contributed to the message being passed along by their collaborators—federal government, popular magazines, and an odd coalition of "club-women, the clergy, financial interests, municipal officials, and the labor organizations."[18] Led in part by the magazine *The Delineator*, this coalition consolidated many of the strands of the push toward homeownership into the Better Homes in America campaign, a series of exhibition houses, magazine articles, and government pamphlets all serving to educate and encourage potential homeowners.[19] One of the strongest voices in this campaign was Herbert Hoover, at the time secretary of commerce, who called homeownership a "primal instinct in us all."[20]

The Aladdin Company underscored the positive aspects of homeownership: "We feel sorry for the poor deluded beings called Flat-Dwellers. They think they are fortunate to shed all the usual responsibilities of a home. But in freeing themselves of these responsibilities, they by the same action free themselves of all the pleasures and comforts." The company went on to describe the pleasures of family gatherings in front of the hearth and the "fun in the new garden, the opening of the first buds, spading a little patch of soil, patting tenderly the earth over the fresh planted seeds—and the first sprout!"[21] Clearly, this appeal was aimed at those whose choice about whether to buy a home was based on lifestyle rather than finances. The passage reflects the common prejudices toward apartment life, portrayed as valuing expediency above the joys of domesticity, even when the latter might require additional effort. Aladdin tried in its extensive advertising and promotions to show that it offered both modern, efficient dwellings and settings for traditional family experiences.

Aladdin took part in a larger cultural campaign against the economic futility of rent, symbolized by the stereotyped figure of the landlord. For example, one whole edition of *Aladdin's Weekly* was dubbed the "Anti-Landlord Issue." The cover depicted a cigar-smoking, slickly dressed man, who represented the financial waste of a family renting a home.[22] This same message was delivered to American families through a variety of publications, from shelter magazines to tracts issued by the federal government. A tenant wrote to the magazine *Country Life* in 1912:

> Renting is a convenience to me but it has several disadvantages. I have had my experiences with exacting landlords, and have been obliged to move several times, rather than pay an increase in rent. All this has been expensive and annoying, and as a tenant I feel always at the mercy of my landlord. All the money I have paid out for rent and moving vans would have bought me a house had I decided to make a purchase several years ago. So in a measure I am loser.[23]

As the embodiment of wasted spending in an era that eschewed the concept of waste, the landlord was posed as the antithesis of the settled breadwinner, supporting a family in their own home.

In its simplest statement, the anti-rent campaign averred, "home is never really home until you own your own."[24] Homeownership was promoted as the cure for all kinds of ills, ranging from wasted spending to the problems of child rearing to political unrest. Homeownership would prevent frequent "moving days" seen as disruptive to family life. As one reader wrote to the real estate columnists of *Country Life*, "There is one feature about renting that too many people do not consider. Constant moving has an unsettling effect upon children. If a man has his own permanent habitation, and can teach his children to love it, so much the better for them. If he anchors in one place his children are bound to absorb the atmosphere and make friend-ships that will be of advantage to them as they grown older."[25] This empha-sis on child rearing was just one more way in which the family was estab-lished as the basic unit of the market in terms of both domestic spaces and domestic goods.

The prolific and popular novelist, Kathleen Norris, addressed the issues of homeownership and family budgets in her 1917 work, *Undertow*. In de-picting Nancy and Bert Bradley, Norris also prescribed the value of owning rather than renting property. After the real estate agent Bert receives a large commission, the Bradleys evaluate their family finances:

> So the Bradleys had a bank account. And even before the precious money was actually paid them, and deposited in the bank, Nancy knew what they were going to do with it. There was only one sensible thing for young persons who were raising a family on a small salary to do. They must buy a country home.
>
> No more city, no more rent-paying for Nancy and Bert. The bank account had just five figures. Nancy and Bert said that they could buy a lovely home anywhere for nine thousand, and have a whole thousand left for furniture and incidentals.[26]

While Norris inculcated beliefs about homeownership and appropriate ex-penditures for middle-class family homes in her readers, she also warned of overreaching the family budget. Nancy and Bert wind up buying a more expensive home than the bank account supports and struggle constantly to keep up. Aladdin and other mail-order companies could benefit from such literary advice, which encouraged potential buyers to seek out less expensive routes to homeownership.

Mail-order homes were bought as an economical route to homeowner-ship—no Aladdin prices in the 1910s reached "five figures" and quite a few had only three figures. Aladdin houses were available, for the most part, on a cash-only basis; purchasers paid 25 percent down and the remainder on delivery, with a five percent discount if the whole sum was paid up front. The company explained that this cash-only policy kept the prices lower for all. In the regular lumber trade and traditional home construction industry, prices were raised to compensate for inevitable loss due to defaulted credit, but Aladdin needed to figure in no such cushion as long as it maintained its cash-only policy. As the company explained, "we have no bad accounts and are therefore not obliged to take from the man who pays to make up for the man who doesn't pay."[27] Still, the company also assured, "This is an invariable rule and is not meant to be a reflection on your financial standing."[28] Though they would not originate from the manufacturer, loans were certainly acceptable; the company actually gathered information about how its customers financed their purchases by sponsoring an essay contest on the topic.

Presumably, buyers secured bank loans or went through building and loan associations in order to have this money available up front. Starting at the turn of the century, popular periodicals printed articles outlining different means of saving, and borrowing, money for the purpose of a house purchase. By the 1920s, there were over 7,000 building and loan associations across the country, together securing mortgages worth $2 billion. These cooperative societies helped erase the stigma formerly associated with mortgages and credit arrangements in general. As one financial adviser wrote in *House and Garden* in the 1920s, "Today the mortgage is not considered a tyrant, but a servant—a financial device by which homeownership may be hastened . . . Instead of something to be ashamed of, the mortgage is now, in some one of its forms, the customary method of financing new building."[29] While an initial outlay may have been more than an average rental, Aladdin prices were low enough that within a few years, these loans could be paid off at the same rate as monthly rent charges. Most advice on financing recommended that housing costs equal one-fifth of income, regardless of whether the cost went to pay rent or the homeowner's combination of mortgage payments, maintenance, insurance, and taxes.[30]

The company actually promoted its products to financiers, particularly manufacturers who might finance, or influence local banks to finance, homes for their workers. As Elbert Hubbard, noted proponent of the Arts and Crafts movement and domestic values, wrote in promotional materials for the Aladdin Company, "Here is an absolute safe deal for the financier. A good workingman should own his home. By doing so, he becomes a better citizen and a better workman . . . Here is a combination of finance with the humanities which, in a degree, a great many cities and towns have overlooked. It spells mutuality, reciprocity, helps the individual, helps the manufacturer, helps the town."[31] By this reasoning, there was risk neither to the ultimate homeowner nor to the financier of that home.

Admittedly, Aladdin houses could be, and clearly were, bought as investment properties to be rented. Despite the "anti-landlord" rhetoric and the presentation of the joys of creating one's own family nest, the house-as-investment idea did sometimes go beyond the family home.[32] In a seemingly contradictory stance, Aladdin also promoted the idea of buying Aladdin homes as rental units. Of course, from a business standpoint, it was a pitch that made sense, encouraging multiple purchases in a market where presumably each customer really needed only one product. Whether owners occupied their first Aladdin home and then decided to invest savings into others, or whether purchasers might "experiment" with a product not actually for their own use, Aladdin assumed that investment in one's own home and investment in rental properties were two sides of the same coin. As they wrote about those who might have doubts about the Aladdin product: "Ask them if they think a hard-headed business man would buy one of our houses in 1910 and come back in 1912 and order 27 houses. That's what one big New York business man did."[33] How Aladdin squared the argument that landlords' fees were a waste of money with the persuasion that one might become a landlord with an Aladdin property was unclear, but in either case, the safety of the investment was promoted.

One difference was that the company presented the option as an investment of relatively small-scale savings from salaried employment in other fields, rather than a speculative real estate venture on a large scale. The burgeoning professional-managerial class was the target of such an appeal: "As an investment for salaried men, home owning is the most popular. Speculation in stocks and bonds is more or less a game of chance for the salaried man with a limited sum of money. A home for renting purposes is far the wisest. It enables you to be close to it and in a position where you can watch its development." Whether the house was to be immediately turned around and sold, in which case the savings of the Aladdin system would benefit the buyer, or kept as a long-term holding with yearly rental fees coming in, house buying, like homeownership, was presented as virtually risk-free.[34]

Furthermore, the behavior stemming from owning property went beyond family relations to issues of citizenship and patriotism. The emphasis on homeowning stemmed from a strong faith in environmental determinism and the belief that ownership brought control over and pride in one's domestic surroundings. As the writers of *Aladdin's Magazine* explained, "We know that environment does much to mold our thought and actions. We are a more perfect reflection of our surroundings than we suspect." The editors exploited stereotypes of tenement life to juxtapose with homeownership, never acknowledging the range of housing that might exist in any given community. Rather, a stark contrast was posed:

Carelessness in talk and general demeanor follow in the wake of improper housing. The most uncouth would not dare stick his muddy brogans on the top of a finely polished mahogany table, or expectorate on a valuable rug. But in a hovel, where there was no restraint of refinement, would the same individual have any hesitancy about propping his feet on a barrel, and expectorating on saw dust? Most assuredly not—he would do both.

But in a well arranged home there is both good taste and comfort. Such surroundings subtly impart happiness and refinement.[35]

While, many, if not most, Aladdin homeowners did not own a mahogany table or a valuable rug, they did possess the "well arranged home" that these objects represented.

Beyond the four walls of the house, homeownership would provide an investment in a local community. A newly settled owner in a New Jersey suburb wrote to *Country Life* in 1912 about his pleasure not only in his new home, but his new status as a freeholder:

It is a good thing for a man to have some civic responsibilities. He will, as a rule, if he has any civic pride at all, try to see that the right men run the town, even if he does not take more than voter's part in its affairs. He will want to have good school, proper sanitary arrangements, and see that the ordinances are enforced. By doing so he is protecting his property, besides helping to make the town a more desirable place to live in. On the whole I think it is an advantage for a growing town to have a majority of the citizens own their houses, because they naturally take more interest in its affairs, and try to improve their private property in order to enhance its value.

A family that owned their own home became a part of the community in a way that renters did not, as their own "welfare and progress" became inextricably linked to that of the community.[36]

Homeownership would also create a new form of community, of shared interests, across the country. The investment would presumably evolve into an allegiance to larger institutions, the nation and the national government, as a means of protecting one's investment. Hoover's support of the campaign stemmed from a faith in the links between the home and the cultivation of citizenship; he wrote, "It is mainly through the hope of enjoying the ownership of a home that the latent energy of any citizenry is called forth."[37] Elbert Hubbard concurred:

Patriotism is more than the resistance of a foreign invader. It is pure, whole-hearted love of your family, home and country—a zealous interest in its laws and government . . . When a man buys a lot and erects a home upon it, you may count upon him as being a useful citizen. Henceforth this is his home: here are bound up his interests. The house he lives in becomes "my little place." The town he lives in "my town." He belongs to things—he becomes an asset to the community, the state, the country—"my country."[38]

Thus, some of the justifications for homeownership were profoundly conservative measures, aimed at solidifying the status quo.

Hubbard elaborated with a parable of two anarchists "sent out of Europe for Europe's good." After the two arrived in New York, one remained there while the other moved to Iowa. After a year, the New Yorker wrote the Iowan to find out "how the revolution was coming on." The Iowan replied, "Nothing doing in the anarchist line. Have married and bought a house." As Hubbard explained it, "the moral is that revolution to a man happily married loses itself in a fadeaway. The man with a wife and a house is interested in exactly the other thing. What he wants is peace, good order and safety."[39] Though the risk of buying property was presented as minimal, homeowners were still encouraged to do anything they could to protect both their financial investment and their family home. The maintenance and improvement of domestic property became one of the bonds of middle-class communities at the turn of the twentieth century.

SOVEREIGNS OF STANDARDIZATION

While led by the specific strengths of each of the Sovereign brothers, the marketing and production of Aladdin homes were of course intertwined: Otto used the efficiency of William's factory production as a selling point while William chose what to design and put into production based on Otto's thorough recording and analysis of the market. They touted both of their innovations as part of the "Aladdin system," writing in a small pamphlet of testimonial letters distributed in 1908, "We originated and perfected an absolutely new system of constructing and marketing Homes. Our record—perfect satisfaction—proves its success."[40] Aladdin expanded quickly in terms of material holdings, products offered, and resulting sales. Beginning with a small two-room cabin that William designed using his mother's bread board as a rule, the product line grew to dozens of models in a variety of styles by a decade after the company's founding. The company did advertise factory efficiency and elimination of waste, yet they achieved these aims not through minimizing the number of products produced but through standardizing the parts that made up those products.

This efficiency and thriftiness, which would be passed along to the consumer in lower costs, supported the company's business-like approach, even as it sold domestic structures. The epitome of business sense was expressed as a form of science. Each aspect of the business was to be carried out and managed efficiently, as stated in this catalogue copy:

> The Aladdin system is simply exact science applied to house building.
>
> Scientific design to eliminate wasteful lengths of material being necessary to build the house.
>
> Scientific cutting of lumber to utilize every inch in the log.
>
> Scientific salesmanship, to eliminate unnecessary profits—to useless middlemen. Science seeks to find the shortest route between two points—cause and effect. Scientific business management seeks to find the lowest cost between raw material and the consumer. The Aladdin plan has achieved this.[41]

Issuing this copy just a few years after the publication of Frederick Winslow Taylor's *Principles of Scientific Management,* Aladdin invoked the ideas of the well-known efficiency expert, adapted for its own trade.[42] Part of the scientific approach was the rationalization of production through the use of machines. The company made a virtue of machine production over handicraft. Aladdin referred to its similarities to the skyscraper, a trusted structure whose parts were milled by machine, with more pragmatic, efficient, and economical results. The machine was the route to these results, as the company described:

> The Aladdin System of Construction is Built on this Principle—modern power-driven machines can do BETTER work at a lower cost than hand labor. Then every bit of work that CAN be done by machines SHOULD be so done. The steel worker with a little hack-saw trying to cut to fit the steel girders of the modern skyscraper would be no more out of place than the modern carpenter cutting sills, joists, and rafters. The skyscraper framework is cut to fit by machines in the steel mills, marked and numbered ready for erection. The lumber in the Aladdin house is cut to fit by machines in the Aladdin mills, marked and numbered ready for erection.[43]

The machine was just one aspect of the achievement of "science" within the company.

The need to maintain an aura of domesticity in an otherwise scientific production system separated the mail-order architecture trade from other manufacturing lines. Though in 1915, the company included in one of its publications the slogan "What Henry Ford has done for the motorist, ALADDIN has done for the home builder," in fact it maintained an important distinction.[44] Aladdin did not expect all of its customers to want to live in the domestic equivalent of a Model T. In an anecdote recorded by Otto Sovereign in his memoirs, Norvel Hawkins, general sales manager of Ford Motor Company, badgered him to adopt the Ford plan of selling only one product. In a 1916 meeting, Hawkins was shocked to learn that Aladdin offered about sixty different models in its yearly catalogue; as Sovereign quoted him, Hawkins exclaimed "My God, and you call yourselves manufacturers of a standardized product! How can you accomplish economy in production when you have such a diversity in your product?" Sovereign explained, "We have standardized on the parts which go to make up our various designs"; the houses were designed on standard modules, so that precut lumber could be used in any of the models. The cutting of wood, the main industrial process, was then the same for any of the final "products" because the "product" was in fact not a manufactured good, but the specific assortment of these standardized parts, selected to produce a certain whole, when shipped to the building site. The company explained its production process and its economic efficiency: "Aladdin houses are designed so that mill-run lengths are used almost throughout. Using mill-run lengths makes unnecessary the cutting to waste of good lumber. We reduce waste in everything down to less than two per cent. That's one reason why we can furnish No. 1 Huron Pine in every house at such low figures."[45]

Despite these arguments, Ford's Hawkins still protested that, like the Model T, Aladdin should adopt "one model, one size, one price." Again, Sovereign explained that not only was the production process different for cars and houses, but consumption patterns were different as well: "a five passenger car accommodates 90 per cent of the families in this country. A house to accommodate five people must have three bedrooms. You probably don't know that 65 per cent of the homes in this country have only two bedrooms. A lone product would lose us either 65 per cent or 35 per cent of our market." Of course, the Sovereigns' differentiation went beyond number of bedrooms; not only were two- and three-bedroom houses shown in the Aladdin catalogues, but multiple versions of them. Each year during the 1910s, there were as many as ten different models of foursquares, either three- or four-bedroom, usually ranging from about $800 to $2,000.[46] Sovereign's explanations to Hawkins could have served as the model for George Soule in his definition of "standardization" for the 1934 *Encyclopaedia of the Social Sciences.* He wrote, "A row of undistinguished, identical houses may result from a standard architectural plan, even though the materials from which these houses are made are chosen from an array of building materials in which standardization has made little progress. But a large variety of house plans and styles may be elaborated from building materials which result from highly standardized manufacturing processes."[47] Soule captured the distinction between standardization in module parts and in design on which the Aladdin Company was based.

If the Ford Motor Company could not serve as a model, the issue for the Aladdin Company and its competitors was how to make standardization in domestic architecture palatable. The company stopped competing with professional architects, and agreed with them, that the two were serving different markets. In 1919, Aladdin reprinted in its own company magazine an article that had originated in *Building Age* and then ran in *Literary Digest,* which addressed the relationship between the standardized process of the kit-house trade and the architectural profession. Considered the "first acknowledged and publicly printed endorsement of the Aladdin system of Construction on the part of architects," the article accepted the role of standardization in house design as a means of lowering housing costs. While for the most part an extended quotation of the original article, Aladdin took one important liberty in its choice of subtitles. The last section of the article, written from the perspective of the traditional architect, stated that "it is no use shutting our eyes" to the increasing prevalence of standardization, but Aladdin, in picking up this section, titled it "No Use Shutting Their Eyes," distancing itself from the traditional architectural practices that added costs to the consumer.

The original author admitted that in the traditional architectural practice, architects could charge multiple times at full cost for a set domestic design; in contrast, "the plan-foundry steps in at this point and effects economies to a great degree by the elimination of this duplication. The mail-order house goes further and effects a saving by manufacturing these houses in quantities, thus obtaining the economical advantages of quantity production." Standardization would bring about "more stable fashions in house designs," by promoting the economies of similarities between homes rather than the distinctions of differences. A new vision of the architectural profession was possible which, "If carried to its extreme, . . . will tend . . . to eliminate architects, builders, and dealers as independent workers. Instead, these men will be employed by large corporations." This corporate, or even industrial, setting for design was portrayed through Aladdin's choice of illustrations; a photo of company executives, entitled "The Brains"; a photo of a sawmill, entitled "The Machine"; and finally a picture of an Aladdin home, entitled "The Product."

Nonetheless, this vision was perhaps an extreme one. While such "corporations" might serve a large audience, a vocal minority would still strive for the individuality that a house designed by an independent architect would create. The difference between these groups was presented as an economic one; as one architect was quoted as saying: "Architecture, as I know it, is a luxury. I burn the midnight bulb to help make it so for my wealthy clients." Thus, standardization stood as the best option for reaching the broadly distributed middle class, and certainly as an excellent option to create housing for workers. And still there would always exist "the class which can never be satisfied by standardization" and the architectural profession would do well to court them. As for companies like Aladdin, they could seek a middle ground; as the article explained, "The man who can afford to buy, not rent, a house has certain definite ideas that he wants for the personal convenience of himself and his wife. If he can afford it, he will pay extra for those conveniences." Aladdin catered to a broad audience by making an initial purchase cheaper to begin with, widening the pool of the "men" described here.[48] For those who could afford to buy a house, but not the extras, Aladdin was a great option. Aladdin owners may not have been buying the nicest house money could buy, but they were convinced they were buying the nicest house they could get for their money. As one satisfied customer, Mrs. Margaret Kaufman of Missouri, wrote to the company, "We rather feel about our Aladdin house like we do about our Dodge car—at the price they are in a class by themselves."[49] And even for those who could afford the extras, Aladdin catered to them with special options for houses, such as higher-grade trim, built-in furnishings, elaborate arches or doorways, additions, porches, and even adjustments to the floor plan. The economies of the original standardized plan stood, but could be layered with details that made the home more individualized.

Another of Aladdin's selling points was good design. One part of the savings the company claimed stemmed from the designers' fees; with mass-produced housing, this fee was, in essence, shared by all those buying the same house model. Judging from a profile of one Aladdin designer, Charles Edwin Poole, the company's designers were not necessarily trained architects, a fact the company presented as a benefit. The profile of Poole focused in particular on his design for an Aladdin bungalow called the Marsden, but the logic of its argument regarding bungalow design would apply equally well to the larger box houses built along similar lines. The line of argument was that these "practically new" forms of architecture constituted an "unestablished profession" different from the study of the Colonial, Italian, Greek, or other styles. A person trained in those historic styles was not best equipped to create a modern home that was efficient and convenient on the one hand and respectful of family needs on the other. In essence, the company argued that a trained architect would focus too much on "style" and not enough on the actual living conditions that a house would foster. Even if an architect designed a simple bungalow, it would be in accordance to the aesthetic description, "a building made of squared logs and shingled"; according to Aladdin, this approach would "fail to please." Instead, a designer such as Poole was a "'home man,' a man who loves his family, one who takes his greatest pleasure in a home of comfort and convenience."[50] Aladdin still touted the strength of its designers' work as a key element in its success, but they were developing new forms of domestic space, and did not need traditional architectural education to do so. Rather than historical precedents, the Aladdin designers looked to comfort and efficiency as their guidelines; a description of the foursquare Hudson asked, "Can you imagine a better utilization of space than is obtained in the plan of the Hudson? The constant thought of Aladdin designers is toward giving a maximum of convenience and comfort for the lowest possible cost."[51] Aladdin played on the skepticism toward architects who placed their own advancement over the financial constraints of their clients.

The domestic visions of the designers and the science of the machines and business systems had to be reconciled into a cohesive whole. The company's engineers and managers, led by the expert "Board of Seven," carried out this coordination. The company explained the board's role:

Before this Board of Seven comes every Aladdin house for the acid test of perfection. No detail escapes the keen and searching analysis of these experts. The designer must prove his plans to the complete satisfaction of, First, the

Master Designer, for accuracy; Second, the Master Builders, for practicability, strength and structural harmony; Third, Factory Experts, for elimination of waste, standardization of lengths, and economy of costs. Unless the cost of these high-priced men's time could be spread over a hundred or more houses of each design it would be prohibitive. No other organization can afford to subject each house design to this searching and costly inspection.[52]

Here, the Board of Seven was lauded more for its engineering knowledge than its aesthetic sensibility. However, they too brought their home lives to their work. A few years later, the company explained, "the officers of The Aladdin Company are family men who have children of their own, so are the employees who design and make Aladdin houses. Therefore we are proud to say that there is just enough wholesale sentiment about this organization to make us strive to put into every Aladdin Home those physical qualities of beauty and comfort which mean so much to children."[53] Again, the ability to understand the sentiment of the home was the quality lauded among Aladdin employers and employees, balanced by their obviously shrewd business sense.

An unstated factor in the acceptance of standardization may well have been the attention paid to the concept during World War I, the time when the *Building Age/Literary Digest* article appeared. In addition to fostering a larger acceptance of standardized goods, World War I certainly had an impact on the company's business, in terms of large government and corporate contracts, some shifts in the company's practices, and a change in its public image. Otto Sovereign was quoted along with E. Mapes, secretary of the Cream of Wheat Company, department store king John Wanamaker, and Hugh Chalmers of the Chalmers Motor Car Company in newspapers throughout the country in 1914, promising that what was at that point the European war could bring only prosperity for the United States. As these representatives of the trade in standardized food, shelter, clothing, and means of mobility assuaged the fears of smaller businessmen, they also brought recognition to their own companies.[54] The war brought the metaphor of winning, not just to the company but its customers, as a testimonial letter from George C. Hillman of New York attests; he wrote, "This is the only house built here this year, but next year I feel there will be 6 or 7 more built and all will be Aladdin . . . You are like our Army that was on the other side. You can't be beat."[55] At the same time, Aladdin started to attract government commissions and other war-related contracts, such as a large development at Hopewell, Virginia, planned by the Dupont Company for gunpowder works.

As the war went on, though, the company was certainly affected by rapid shifts in the national economy. Until that point it had always printed prices directly in its catalogues, but in 1918, the company started including prices on tear sheets inside the front cover of the catalogue, which could be, and were, changed from month to month; in the 1917 catalogue, prices were guaranteed only until April 1 of that year.[56] Particularly for farmers, 1917 brought a brief window of opportunity when crops brought much higher prices than before but inflation of other goods had not caught up. The company produced a huge, brightly colored broadside letting farmers know that if they bought immediately and thought of their purchases in bushels of crops sold, they could not get a better bargain. A Charleston-model foursquare that had cost "4987 bushels of oats in 1914" could be bought for only "2456 bushels" at that moment. In this particular historical context, Aladdin focused its efforts on the rural market, pitting it against the urban one:

> If the prices of farm products do not go down soon, the prices of all other things will quickly be raised in proportion—and your golden opportunity will be forever lost. City folks will have to raise the prices of their things in order to buy food at the present prices . . . But while the prices of your products are up and other products are not up, *you* have a tremendous advantage. It means your products have double purchasing power. Your new house, or barn, at *half price* is another way to look at it. It's one of the rare chances of a lifetime.[57]

As soon as the United States entered the war, the company predicted coming embargoes on timber and freight transportation, and again stressed immediate purchasing as an opportunity that would soon become rare. The single year 1919 brought rapidly rising prices to Aladdin products, and the company used the threat of these rising prices to encourage immediate sales. Aladdin's marketing work appeared to pay off, as in 1918, the company sold close to 2,800 houses, which was the equivalent of over 2 percent of all housing starts in the United States.[58]

The aggressive advertising and promotions done in the years of World War I only heightened an already strong marketing strategy, but put in place several tactics that would continue to be used by the company, such as "sales" on discontinued house styles. But as soon as the war was over, the company used a "happy days are here again" approach to once again advocate new home building. In the mid-1920s the company started narrowing the number of models it produced, to create even more of a standardized product than it had previously. As Otto Sovereign wrote in a follow-up letter after catalogue distribution in 1927, "It isn't a big catalog, is it? BUT—it's crammed with big things for the home builder. If we printed a great big catalog we couldn't price our houses so far below all other dealers and manufacturers. We would either have to raise our prices or sacrifice quality, and you wouldn't like that. A few designs, big production, carefully manufactured with Henry Ford economy, and HIGH QUALITY, make a friend and a booster of EVERY customer." While Norvel Hawkins had not been able to convince the Sovereigns, World War I did. Tightened production conditions could be made economically viable with heightened marketing efforts.

In its varied promotions, the Aladdin Company offered at least two different stories of its origins. The two corporate creation myths both addressed the building process, but in different ways. As already recounted, Otto credited William with having transferred the idea of the knock-down boat industry to houses. But in some early publicity materials, a different link was established, to prior building systems that implied strength, permanence, and distinctive design, all based in construction of standardized parts. This campaign started with a reference to skyscrapers, stating that a small-town midwestern boy (presumably William Sovereign) used to venture into the city and became fascinated by the piles of precut steel that together fit into the frame for a skyscraper:

> Always on visits to the nearby cities, he spent much of his time around the large office buildings in the course of construction. He was much interested in seeing the mighty steel frame work and the massive masonry fit nicely together under the hands of the steel workers and masons; each piece having been prepared before arrival, miles away in the steel mills and stone quarries. Surely he thought, if this can be done in these great buildings of steel, concrete, and stone, the same idea can be carried out in the ordinary dwelling house of frame construction.[59]

Time and money could be saved by consolidating the cutting process—one would not see workmen cutting steel on an urban building site, so why should houses still be built this way?

In making this point clear, Otto specifically identified Aladdin homes with the Woolworth building, whose magnificence and stability could not be questioned. As one brochure encouraged, "If any one tells you Aladdin houses are an experiment just smile at them. Ask them if experiments survive eight years of critical public use. Ask them if the modern steel office buildings in big cities are experiments. Same identical system of construction."[60] This quest to identify with permanence in the built environment led the company all the way back to the Pyramids, claiming that precut stones were used in just the same way that precut wood was for Aladdin houses. In one of its early catalogues the company stressed the permanence of Aladdin homes: "When erected an Aladdin house will last for several generations."[61] The word *generations* not only specified a period of time but also implied the connection to family. An Aladdin home could be an investment and begin a family association with a particular place, creating "an estate," much as heirloom silver could be passed from generation to generation.[62]

With new designs being introduced constantly, the company could still make claims for the originality of their product, even while affirming its standardized form. Of the Willamette, a foursquare model introduced in 1919, the company wrote:

> And in the Willamette, one of the newest Aladdin designs, a very good definition of the word "individuality" can be found. Look at the illustrations on the opposite page, picturing a Willamette that stands in Aladdin Town, and then stop and think if there is another house in your city or town that is like it.
>
> We think not, for the Willamette is a new design and created with the idea of giving to those who ask for something a little "different," just that.
>
> Thoroughly American in architecture, it is a home anyone can well be proud to identify as "My Home."[63]

By presenting new models, even if slight variations on old ones, the company could make such claims. Certainly, Aladdin was not advocating a stripped down, unadorned box as the solution to affordable housing; the "home men" may not have been trained in traditional architectural styles, but they maintained an eye for aesthetics. The company was supported in these claims by popular periodicals, declaring the stock woodwork of large-scale mills to be "excellent designs . . . well made and architecturally correct."[64] Again, Aladdin countered the assumption that good design was necessarily tied to the high price of an architect. As one testimonial letter, from Mrs. Fred Towl of Arkansas, averred, "One thing that especially pleased me was that all the small details are correct, for instance, the eaves are the correct width and the brackets which hold the eaves are 'different' from the ordinary house, and unless you hire a first class architect to design your house and pay him a good fee extra, you miss these details."[65] The ability to offer variety helped make the standardization of home construction palatable to consumers.

The selection made by Kirk, Moberly, Smith, and many others over time was a square-type house or box house, now commonly called a foursquare.[66] The name referred to the geometric shape of the floor plan and volume of the house, particularly in contrast to the irregular plans and massing of Queen Anne- and revival-style houses that preceded it in popularity among American house dwellers. The foursquare did indeed often rise from a perfectly square footprint, or at least a rectangle with perpendicular sides close in measurement to one another. The house had two stories topped by a hipped roof; the side walls of the foursquare were also roughly square, with no gable ends to break the cubelike volume. The fenestration, at least in the front of the house, was usually symmetrical, though there might be one projecting bay window, and a porch often preceded the front entry. Shelter magazines proclaimed such houses the most cost-effective of the day; as an article in *Country Life* explained, "If you could build a square box, cut holes in it for the doors and windows, and put a flat roof on top you would have a house that costs the least to build . . . Let the plan be as nearly like a box as can be."[67] While the foursquare was not quite this rudimentary—for example, the "flat roof" was replaced by a hipped roof—it was the closest approximation to this description as was commonly built.

The foursquare was an older sibling to the wildly popular bungalow; it had a family resemblance in its flared columns supporting the porch and brackets under the eaves, but in general was a larger form with a more traditional interior floor plan. Many considered the box house even more cost-effective, even if slightly larger, than the bungalow; the expense of a full second story was said to be worth the added privacy and efficiency of heating.[68] While the bungalow brought the public and private spaces of a house in close proximity, and removed divisions between rooms with a more open plan, the box house maintained distinctions in room use. Three or four bedrooms and a bathroom occupied the second floor, while the living room, dining room, kitchen, and sometimes an extra bedroom or den comprised the first-floor rooms. True to the later name, the foursquare often had four roughly square rooms on each floor, though sometimes there were three rooms with one being a large rectangle running the full width or length of the house and serving as a living room or a master bedroom. Box houses often maintained some sort of entry or central hall space separating and mediating between the rooms. And still, the foursquare was a less formal plan than some other styles of its era; while often maintaining a pantry and a firm division between the work space of the kitchen and the rest of the first floor, the house was not designed with service passages. Divisions of work and leisure were not between groups of people to be spatially separated, but were temporally separated. The assumed audience for these homes was the nuclear family.

Regardless of the interior floor plan, the room arrangement was not apparent from the outside of the house. Unlike some earlier styles with jutting bays and turrets, the box house was designed "from the outside in"— the overall form determined the arrangement of space within it. While there were certainly precedents in domestic architecture for this type of design, such as Georgian or Federal architecture, the foursquare may also have shown the influence of public buildings of the day. From factory buildings to downtown business blocks to banks and hotels, rectilinear plans and massing were common in cities and towns across the country. A description of one of Aladdin's foursquare models explained:

> In design the Rochester is truly American—simple, strong, and substantial; conservative lines bespeak dignity and personality of which this design is a shining example. Its features are not composed of novelties that come and go, but are made up of the careful touches that have stood the test with home builders for many years. The Rochester has the added advantage in point of design of being square in shape, which always expresses massiveness and strength.[69]

Aladdin staked its claim for helping to create a national architecture, both by labeling these qualities "American" and by promoting nationwide distribution of its products.

If the exterior proportions connoted strength, the resulting interior projected efficiency, a watchword of the day. From the floor plan to the roof line, the interior space of such geometric buildings could be divided into regular units, seen to provide the most efficient use of space; each resulting space could be assigned its own task or user. On the domestic scale, these units also lent more privacy than was available in the more open plan bungalow. As a catalogue description of the Kingston, a large four-bedroom foursquare, explained, "This square type of house offers you one of the greatest values in modern house construction. Every available inch of space is utilized to its full capacity. A glance at the floor plan will immediately convince you that the arrangement of rooms could not be bettered."[70] The box houses were large enough to provide bedrooms for the members of the shrinking middle-class family and almost always included a separate bathroom. This second-floor design in particular was similar to the upper floors of hotels or office buildings, with similar-sized individual rooms around a central core to maximize privacy and provide natural light to the rooms.

The well-ordered foursquare illustrated the attention to efficiency as applied not only to the production of houses but to their use as well. As one plea for efficient building explained, "efficiency directs that the room most used is the most important and should be given the first consideration. That is, of course, the living room. It must have the best location in the house, must be well lighted, aired and especially it must be planned for comfort . . . Simplicity, sanitation and comfort prevail." While the division between living and dining rooms might be a decorative arch rather than a closing door, this arch "makes the work easier and distributes an even light in the home."[71] The division was there nonetheless, and both spaces were always included in the room designations presented by designers. The pragmatics of daily life were considered as important as style to middle-class consumers. These pragmatics touched on many of the same issues of health and hygiene as those faced by the enameled cast-iron and sanitary pottery industries. Not only specific parts of the home, but the overall design needed to address these issues; as Aladdin writers explained, "It is a well recognized fact that there is a close relationship definitely established between health, happiness, and the home . . . Good ventilation and light, too, are vital things in a home. Fresh air and sunshine promotes health and vigor. Every Aladdin Home is designed so as to get an abundance of both." This emphasis on light, air, sanitation, neatness, and efficiency was bolstered by similar descriptions in architectural, sociological, and economic texts; in a study of industrial workers' living conditions, Frank Streightoff concurred, "A good house . . . should invite the inflow of enough good air for ventilation; it should welcome the drying, cheering sunlight; it should facilitate the sanitary disposal of waste materials; it should encourage cleanliness by making neatness possible; and it should be well supplied with water."[72]

The foursquare fit such descriptions of modern dwellings offered by both the Aladdin Company and less interested parties. Commenting on the wastefulness of overly large houses with unused space, the company declared "the modern home is like a good business. It has resources enough for the unexpected emergency but carries no dead surplus investment."[73] While the passage was certainly meant metaphorically, it could be read as a literal description of the spatial qualities of the building, and what they shared with "a good business," such as a factory or office building. As Aladdin wrote, "The wonderful doctrine of efficiency has taken hold of the home builder's plans and changed them in many ways . . . Since efficiency has made builders realize the cost per square foot, waste space has been eliminated in the modern home."[74] As far as "work space" in these homes went, primarily the kitchen and pantry area, these too were models of efficiency; as Mabel Lorenz Ives wrote of her foursquare kitchen, "our Standard kitchen is a really charming workshop, wherein I spend fewer hours than formerly and accomplish my tasks with scarcely a waste [sic] step or motion." Ives went on to say that her kitchen had room for a "small but growing library of books on cookery, household management, dietetics and chemistry, with plenty of room for Uncle Sam's invaluable free bulletins on all problems that perplex even us elder housewives."[75] These books and bulletins all supported and augmented the lessons offered by the mail-order firms, that efficiency should be a primary consideration when choosing a home.

The simple geometry of the rooms of the foursquare afforded this efficient room arrangement. A description of the Aladdin Rochester echoed Ives's concerns: "In planning a home, the housewife, besides giving deep thought to the exterior appearance, takes a greater interest still in the interior arrangement. Housewives in general have placed their stamp of approval on the interior of the Rochester. The arrangement is ideal—convenient and comfortable, minimizing housework."[76] These two attributes—convenience and comfort—situated the foursquare home as a worthy purchase to achieve the national standard of living. Donn Barber, an architectural columnist for *The Delineator,* wrote, "A house should be skillfully planned, primarily for convenience. To arrange any house conveniently, the logical relationship between the various departments of a home should constantly be kept in mind." Good relations between the "living," "sleeping," and "service and storage" areas of the home, as well as the "circulation spaces connecting them," would result in efficient daily routines.[77] Not only minimal work but cost savings stemmed from the clean lines of the foursquare; as the description of the Liberty foursquare model explained in 1923, "To avoid the wasting of a single penny is a duty we all owe to our families and ourselves. To accomplish this object in the building of a home is the most laudable of all ambitions. Aladdin designers set about the task of creating a structure in which there would not be wasted one foot of material—one inch of space. Waste material, or waste space, means wasted dollars for the owner."[78] Because most kit-house customers were already inclined toward savings, this emphasis on the value of a foursquare was of particular importance.

Because of its simple geometry, the foursquare could also be adapted to a variety of scales; for example, an eighteen-foot square home and a thirty-two-foot square home could be designed on the same basic lines but appeal to very different sectors of the market, who would still be buying the same style. The style may have stood as an aspiration for those living in bunga-lows and other smaller houses. First-time home buyers may have been particularly engaged by the opportunity to buy a model that was visually similar to larger homes. Present in communities with smaller homes, for example, in industrial towns, where they may have served as managers' res-idences, foursquares were visually accessible to a broad sector of the public. The foursquare might be the perfect compromise home for the future ide-alized by domestic theorist Elbert Hubbard when he wrote, "In the future, the house of the capitalist will be smaller, and the house of the workingman will be larger and more comfortable."[79]

The popularity of the form also may have stemmed from its hybrid na-ture. Neither too big nor too small, neither too formal nor too casual, the box house was the perfect transition between traditional and modern in an era that could be characterized much the same way. As one foursquare dweller stated of her home, "it combines all the best that I enjoyed in my apartment with all I longed for on the farm."[80] The building could blend aesthetically into a variety of settings—it could serve as the premier house in a community of bungalows without being ostentatious but could also hold its own in a community of more massive homes. This chameleon qual-ity in itself constituted "good taste" to architects such as Barber, who in-structed the readers of *The Delineator* that in densely built neighborhoods, constructing a house in "keeping with" the "character" of "its community" was of great importance.[81]

CORNERING THE MARKET

Whatever the style or size of the buildings, the unity achieved through the production and marketing was symbolized by Otto Sovereign's focus on a brand name. Even in its first few years when the company was officially titled the North American Construction Company, the houses were known as Aladdin homes. Otto later wrote that he selected the name to conjure up the tale of the genie who speedily built a dream house for Aladdin and his new wife; the genie thus invoked the establishment of new family homes. While at first this connection was left to the consumer's imagination to make, within the company's first decade it included the Aladdin story in its catalogues, and used the image of a genie liberally in its publications. The "magic" of the genie was the necessary bridge between two potentially contradictory qualities: the rapidity with which Aladdin homes could be built and their permanence.

The company used several other icons besides the genie to express the strength of the business. The first company-produced periodical sent to Aladdin owners was known as *The Wedge,* and many of the company's catalogues carried the same inverted triangle symbol as this monthly periodical. At its most literal, the wedge was the first step of the Aladdin process, used to cut timber in the local forests. These timber centers provided cheaper materials than might otherwise be available, even if they had to be transported. As one architect explained to readers of *The Delineator* in 1922, "Now . . . with our developed industry and railways reaching every corner of the land, it often proves more expensive to use local materials than to bring others from a distance."[82] The wedge represented the areas of the country most suitable to providing raw materials for the housing trade, even the housing trade in areas far removed from these timber centers.

The company also used the wedge to symbolize its antimiddleman campaign. In addition to removing the middleman of the landlord, Aladdin drove a wedge between home buyers and the middlemen of local lumberyards and contractors, who could add considerably to the price of a house. Avoiding the middleman and consequently charging less money for a house was one of Aladdin's prime sales pitches; one of its early catalogues had on its cover the slogan: "Manufacturers Create Value—Middlemen Add Cost."[83] Aladdin frequently promoted the idea that because the goods went "Straight from the Forest to Your Home" several layers of fees and profits were removed. Under the heading "A Few Figures That Will Surprise You," the company traced the path of $100 worth of goods (their "real value" in cost of production) through the jobber's, wholesaler's, and retailer's costs of handling and profit, to show that an item was ultimately purchased by the customer for over twice its original value. The "legitimate selling price" was at the first level: the "real value" plus a 10 percent profit for the producer. The company estimated that by eliminating the intermediate steps of profits, Aladdin customers saved as much as $600,000 in one year.[84]

Aladdin pressed Elbert Hubbard into service to convince readers that rather than paying "carpenters, boss carpenters, supervisors, designers, architects" as well as for "insurance, storage, cartage, transportation" costs that get added to materials, buying an Aladdin home made financial sense. Invoking ready-to-wear clothes and Ford cars as precedents (though not necessarily models), Hubbard wrote, "The standardization of building houses is one of the great economics of modern times. Only a corporation equipped with ample capital, big resources and wide experience back of them could possibly encompass a business of this kind."[85] Testimonial letters included in promotional materials often estimated the amount of money buyers believed they saved by buying an Aladdin model, in 1912 ranging from the $150 saved by a Detroit, Michigan owner to the $600 saved by a Chicago owner.[86] Aladdin's wedge also appealed to a broad rural audience with a graphic image of a man milking a cow branded with the Aladdin wedge and the slogan "Aladdin Houses Save Money." The entire drawing was captioned "Direct from the Producer."[87]

Unlike the case of silverplate flatware, where the manufacturer had to negotiate between different forms of retail distribution that were at odds with one another, in the new mail-order house trade, the manufacturer called all forms of retail sales into question, advocating direct purchase from the manufacturer instead. The company posed directly the question of what consumers were buying for their money, depending on whom they bought it from. Situating the Aladdin purchaser in both a family and a business community, the company advised readers:

> Join the big Aladdin family of shrewd buyers. Make your every dollar bring you one hundred cents value in your home. Don't let the local dealers and middlemen and contractors grab a big portion of your dollar for the privilege of handling fifty cents worth of goods.
>
> Your dollar is as good as the dealers and will buy as much as theirs if you buy from the original producer, the manufacturer, same as they do.
>
> Aladdin houses offer you this opportunity. Surely you will accept it.[88]

This "opportunity" led to a potential democratization in the market of homeowners. As one early Aladdin publication explained, "Many a workman or man of moderate means would like to own his home who has not the money (from $1,200 to $1,500) to buy a cottage already built," but Aladdin offered the same end result for a fraction of that cost.[89]

Aladdin's emphasis on saving money was layered on top of the fact that its building process was already considered the most economical; frame houses designed to accommodate standard size lumber and stock doors, windows, and trim were declared the most cost-effective route toward home-ownership by numerous voices. One magazine article stated simply, "the house owner should understand that when he is limited in purse and must get absolutely the biggest house for the least money he would better stick to timber and build a frame house."[90] Aladdin's wedge promised that the "biggest house" could be still bigger. The money-saving wedge also came to symbolize, self-referentially, its own role as a recognizable icon, as when the company asked in 1912, "Is it to be wondered, then, that the Aladdin Wedge, our famous little triangle trade mark, is biting deeper and deeper into the consciousness of the great American public?"[91]

The Sovereigns used a number of different media to make the company's mark on this "consciousness." Unlike a manufacturing firm such as Reed & Barton, which relied on its highly paid sales staff to be the front line for the company's distribution of goods through jewelry retail outlets, Aladdin and other house companies did not employ sales staff or retail distributors. The company's yearly catalogue, along with other promotional mailings, acted as the salesman. Sent directly to the general public, rather than to potential retailers with specific knowledge of the goods shown, the annual catalogue included a wealth of information besides simply the style and price of houses. The catalogues explained the Aladdin system of construction and its influences, shared comments of satisfied customers, and offered further assistance with all aspects of homemaking, from landscaping to furnishing. While perhaps not produced with the artistic impact of the late nineteenth-century silver catalogues, the Aladdin missives were in their own way a reflection of the varied aesthetic sensibility of the company. In the 1910s and 1920s, covers ranged from a small simple graphic set against a colored ground to an ethereal scene of relaxation set on the lawn of an Aladdin home.

While the interior layout and design were similar from year to year, different backgrounds were inserted behind the images and text about specific models. Each page had the floor plan, exterior facade images, and copy about the specific qualities of that model. The exterior pictures were either drawings, or whenever possible, photographs of actual built structures, either sent in by Aladdin owners or taken of models built locally in Bay City, and its suburban communities, called "Aladdin Town" by the company. In 1917, the company began using cutaway interior drawings in its layouts, echoing the floor plans, though perhaps easier to read, and also suggesting possible fur-

nishing arrangements for the houses. The company considered these drawings a substitute for the opportunity to actually "visit" an Aladdin home:

> Walk into the homes, inspect the living rooms, notice the placing of dining
> room furniture, then peep into the bedrooms of the Aladdin Homes shown
> on the following pages. Yes, even the kitchen shows an arrangement for
> efficiency.
>
> This is the result of Aladdin's tireless efforts to bring complete information
> on Aladdin Homes to you, to make it possible for you to visit each Aladdin
> Home and mark its distinctive features, compare them and then select the
> home of your liking.[92]

Like the Kohler Company, which tried to create model bathrooms in showrooms and advertising, the Aladdin Company used its catalogues to approximate the experience of actually seeing its houses. The catalogue served as a
real estate tour, so that prospective buyers could choose the house that best
suited them.

In order to reach a broad national audience with its catalogues, the Aladdin Company had to tap into networks that already had a continental reach.
One obvious way of doing this was through the ever-increasing trade in
popular periodicals. The company estimated that in 1912 alone, its advertisements were distributed through forty publications with a combined circulation of 150 million. It is impossible to say how many people saw these
ads; while many of the readers of these publications would have read several
of the periodicals, it is also likely that more than one reader saw each copy.
Nonetheless, at a time when the national population was less than that circulation figure, this reach of the Aladdin name and image is impressive.[93] As
various types of journals, such as farm periodicals, women's magazines, and
Sunday newspaper supplements, became popular ways of sharing a national
culture, Aladdin could use these journals as bases for its advertisements.
In the first decades of the company's existence, Aladdin executives experimented with magazine and newspaper advertising, searching for the journals, or combinations of them, that would best draw potential customers.
The different journals, or types of journals, might represent different sectors
of the market for houses, ranging from a buyer in need of a farm building
to a potential investor looking to build a rental property to a family looking
for a home of their own. Otto Sovereign's staff kept meticulous track of just
these sorts of distinctions. With a slightly different advertising list from year

to year, the company kept track not only of how many inquiries, and sales resulting from those inquiries, a specific journal's ads brought in, but also the average house cost of sales from each specific journal, a rough index of the type and size of building being purchased, and thus the market being reached. With these records, the company could choose where best to place its many advertising dollars, as well as what to advertise in which journals.[94]

The marketers congratulated themselves when they placed a successful advertisement in a prime location; as the company crowed to the readers of *The Wedge,* "Seven thousand four hundred seventy-eight letters were received from a single Aladdin house advertisement in February. Pretty good evidence of the power of good advertising, and the wonderful appeal of a good article."[95] Sharing this news was a form of thanks for the advice of current owners as to what periodicals they were most fond of and whose advertising they most valued; such opinions were solicited regularly from "Aladdin people." As *The Wedge* asked its readers with promise of some reward, "What magazines do you read? which do you like the best? which have you the most confidence in? these are questions that are very important to the advertising department, and if [you] will give us their ideas on this subject, the advertising dept will show its appreciation in a way you will like. Won't you just answer those three questions?" With the company spending as much as $7,500 for a single ad in February 1914, successful placement, or "advertising value," in the eyes of prospective customers was crucial.[96] These questions guided the choices of Otto Sovereign's staff, who assumed that their own previous buyers were a good sample market.

Using trusted periodicals was important because advertising carried the associations of the journal to the image of the companies that advertised on its pages. While the periodicals carried the actual advertisements, they also featured articles and images that contributed to readers' ideas about houses and homes. Frequent reading of these magazines—their fiction, their advertisements, their advice columns—might shape what buyers were looking for in a home. Periodicals were one site where both the value of homeownership and ideas about certain styles and types of housing could be introduced on a broad scale. Reprinted in *The Wedge* was a letter to the editor of *Good Housekeeping,* attributing a customer's faith in the Aladdin product to the magazine's reputation. The buyer wrote:

> The letters from "Advertising Land" (into which we've just made the most delightful excursion) were especially interesting to me, for I was bubbling

over to tell you how we pinned our fate to the *Good Housekeeping* guarantee, and bought an "Aladdin" house.

After I had sent the draft for it, and began to realize the risk we were taking, my temperature would rise and I'd feel pretty nervous, but one reading of the guarantee would bring about a normal condition.

In due time the house came, and in just six weeks we were living in it.

The writer offered to vouch for the satisfaction of Aladdin homes to other "housed but homeless" readers, just as the magazine's guarantee had vouched for the company to this writer.[97] By reprinting this letter, the company extended the *Good Housekeeping* guarantee even to those who did not read the magazine, and shared the various channels through which news of the Aladdin Company was rapidly spreading.

In addition to evaluating the ad placement, the company tried to evaluate the content of specific ads, particularly in relation to their context in certain journals. An ad campaign such as, "Own this home for $289," used primarily in Sunday newspaper supplements, might be appropriate in places where an image of a bigger model might not be, and vice versa. However, Aladdin also saw homeownership not as a one-time experience but as a progression; the $289 wonder might be just the first step on the path toward a bigger home, such as one of their foursquare models. When the company announced to their homeowners that they had just completed a "Great Advertising Campaign," for the $289 house, they explained:

> The result is a compact, cozy little five-room cottage, at a price within the reach of a good many more people than could have purchased it at the former price . . . The house will find favor with a large class of men and women who can erect this house on their lot and live in it until they have accumulated sufficient money for the completion of a larger house. In this way they will stop their rent bills, get on their own ground and feel that they are occupying a home of their own.
>
> The five-room house is the average size house for the average size American family. It contains living room, dining room, kitchen and two bedrooms.

This particular campaign was aimed at urban buyers, whose first investment would have to be a city lot; it was carried in "twenty of the big metropolitan newspapers in the largest cities in the country" that "have a combined circulation of over five million subscribers and cover the entire section of the country east of the Mississippi river."[98] This five-room house was a "starter" home, with a similar proportion of public to private space in the company's room designations as its larger homes. It was meant to inculcate the values of property and home that might later be translated into larger purchases, such as foursquare models.

The company, and by extension its customers, evaluated a specific advertisement's success by the number of inquiries, and eventual sales, it brought in, in relation to its size, and thus, cost. For example, of the three top-drawing ads in 1913, the one in the end deemed "most successful" was the smallest of the three. The advertising copy read, "Does Your Neighbor Live in an Aladdin House?: If he does live in an Aladdin house, perhaps you would like to know it and to look it over. Aladdin houses are scattered over the entire country. Practically every community has an Aladdin customer who is proud of his home, proud of his judgment and glad to show his house."[99] This advertisement took the personal message of "your neighbor" and placed it in a national context, in "practically every community." Laura Castle of Ripley, New York, wrote the company in 1912, addressing the need for this two-prong push: "You may publish my letter with my name and any doubting thomas may write to me and I will tell them what I think of the Aladdin houses. How glad I am that I ran across your ad. You should certainly advertise in all the magazines."[100] While she was content with the association with a magazine and correctly predicted that magazines would give the company a broad reach, she also recognized that for those more risk-averse than she, a personal commendation of the company, as well as its product, would go far. This balance in scales of approach—the personal and the collective—was an effective means of accentuating the shared values of a burgeoning group of people across the country.

The balance between efficiency and domesticity achieved in the production phase of the Aladdin Company was echoed in their marketing tactics. The company had to walk a fine line between presenting itself as a sound industry, run along business principles of efficiency and economy, and as a company that fostered the elements of home—often represented as a haven from the industrial climate of the day. The Sovereigns had to present their own interests as infused with values appropriate to both home and business. One way of straddling this line was to promote the company's integrity in its line of trade: "Integrity means *moral soundness;* it means honesty; it means *freedom from corrupting influence or practice;* it means *strictness in the fulfillment of contracts, uprightness, square dealing.* The Aladdin policy of doing business endeavors to live up to the strictest meaning of *Integrity.* The customer must be well served—must be satisfied—must be pleased—*must be a friend.*"[101] "Moral soundness" and "freedom from corrupting influence" were just the sorts of values to be promoted in the home, thus it made sense that a business that sold homes should adopt them as well.

The Department of Service was one of the company's means of fostering a sense of community, or even family, among its customers. The department offered advice, free of charge, on interior design, landscaping, house siting, color choices, and other decisions associated with homeownership. In suggesting that customers use this benefit of Aladdin ownership, the company likened the department to the advice of family and friends: "You like to talk with your family, your friends, about the home you are planning on. Talk with us; write us about it . . . We have been of help to hundreds and hundreds of our friends."[102] The "family" in question was made up of Aladdin owners; the company exclaimed in 1913, "We have added over four thousand new friends to the big Aladdin family," and it expected to add 10,000 more in the coming year.[103] The Department of Service and the company's publications did the kinwork for this extensive and extended family. In explaining the amazing statistics of the company's sales in the 1910s, with doubling and tripling in sales per year, the company wrote, "*You* know that this wonderful growth would be impossible for any manufacturing institution, or any business house, unless customers became friends—unless real *service* was rendered—honest value, square business methods, and integrity prevailed." This notion of service was one of the important ways in which a sense of community was fostered. The Department of Service helped create a community out of disparate homeowners living in a wide variety of locales.[104]

Another facet of this extended "family" was the correspondence exchanged within it. The company sent its missives in the form of *The Wedge*, and later *Aladdin's Weekly* and *Aladdin's Monthly.* From its owners, the company received testimonial letters, used in its advertisements and catalogues, and even compiled booklets composed solely of hundreds of these letters. As the company stated in the first of these pamphlets, printed in 1908, "The most convincing proof of the value of an article is the opinion of the person who spent his money on it. Next to seeing or using an article itself, the experience of the man who has bought, seen and used it, is valuable."[105] The almost formulaic missives that Aladdin frequently printed suggest that the company solicited these letters and raised particular questions to be addressed: What model did you buy? How long did it take you to erect the house? How much money do you think you saved by buying an Aladdin home? Do others in your area own Aladdin homes? Would you be willing to show your home to others considering an Aladdin purchase? While the similarity of the responses may seem a bit numbing, in many ways that uniformity was the point of the publications, to show the general satisfaction with the product by people across the country, and to show the values that Aladdin homeowners shared. As one catalogue asked, "Shall we give you bankers, congressmen, postmasters, city, State, or National Government officials, or, better than all, shall we refer you to customers who have tested our integrity, customers in your own neighborhood? The proof is yours for the asking."[106] The earliest testimonials were signed and attributed to a home city, and though later published only with a home state designation, they still suggested the geographic breadth of the community that was bound by their domestic environment. For example, the 1914 Aladdin catalogue contained a two-page spread entitled "Kind Words from Aladdin Owners." The pages displayed eighteen letters from fifteen states, stretching from Maine to California. A 1919 booklet entitled "What do Aladdin Owners think of their Aladdin Homes?" contained 547 letters arranged by the owner's home state, including forty-two states.[107]

The message of the testimonial booklet as a whole was not only to tell potential customers "you'll save money with an Aladdin home" or "your home will be efficiently constructed" but also to say, "if you make this purchase, you are joining this sector of hundreds of happy Aladdin homeowners." Interestingly, Aladdin explained that one of its reasons for no longer publishing home cities of letter writers was their value as a body of consumers: "Another consideration which restrains us in quoting complete addresses is that these people being home owners represent a very desirable list for circularizing features, and personal solicitations which we have found that people frequently object to, and we therefore cannot be contributing factors in subjecting our customers to anything that might develop into an annoyance."[108] The "very desirable list" was of course the status of being homeowners, and thus, presumed purchasers of a wealth of household goods. Though the company tried to protect its consumers in this way, the consumers were in fact often willing to vouch for the company. As J. W. Hall of Saginaw, Michigan, wrote, "I certainly advertised your houses down there [at Point Lookout], people coming every day to look at the place. One day I had thirteen callers before dinner. Hope it results in some business." Aladdin homeowners described themselves as "boosters" and enjoyed their participation in the company's success.[109]

Of course, not all of Aladdin's selling points were revealed through this person-to-person communication. In some of its earliest publications, Aladdin announced the assurances of local banks, the mayor of Bay City, and the secretary of the local Board of Trade, to attest to the security of the company and the honesty of its business dealings. It also sought commissions with some sort of institutional backing that might inspire trust with potential customers. In an early company pamphlet devoted to testimonial letters, one of the letters included was from a doctor at the Easton, Pennsylvania sanitarium, expressing his satisfaction with the Aladdin cottage he had purchased and assuring he would buy others. Though some companies might have avoided a connection to failing health, the "eminent specialist . . . at the head of his profession" would certainly be trusted to promote comfortable living conditions. In the same booklet was a letter from Raymond D. Fisk, building his Aladdin home in Boonton, New Jersey. After his own words of praise was appended a description of Fisk's position as being "associated with W.C. Russell, Jr., which firm is a large importer of coffees and makes a specialty of selling direct to the people all over the United States." Fisk was someone who knew and understood the mail-order business, had earned his own livelihood from it, and was thus in a position to evaluate Aladdin's business and product. A letter from him might mean all the more to prospective buyers because of his business associations. These ties to business and the professions balanced the more neighborly approach of the Aladdin "family."[110]

Like Reed & Barton and Kohler with their hotel commissions, Aladdin recognized that its large, institutional buyers were important not only as a means of adding to the company's sales but as a way of establishing faith in the company. As early as 1908, Aladdin inserted into its small catalogue the following offer: "We invite mining companies, manufacturers, etc., to get our quotation, in quantities, for houses for their workmen. They can be erected in a few days."[111] In 1915, Aladdin secured a large contract with the Dupont Company, which was building a new plant at Hopewell, Virginia, trying to meet the increasing demand for explosives during World War I. Unlike some of the stereotyped industrial towns of both earlier and later generations with large numbers of limited house models, Dupont made full use of Aladdin's range of styles, ordering a variety of models, including sev-

eral square-type houses. In addition to announcing these large-scale commissions, Aladdin also advertised its awards and selections from various fairs
and competitions, most notably a contract to build the Michigan State building at the Panama-Pacific Exposition. Aladdin also offered a model home at
the Panama-Pacific, an award-winning example of its system of building.[112]
Much like the separate hotel trade catalogues of the silverware companies,
Aladdin began producing "special interest" catalogues, such as the 1920 publication, *Low Cost Homes Designed Especially for Industrial Purposes*.[113] Additional pamphlets followed, ranging from circulars for industrial housing to
a selection of homes for narrow lots, designed for urban streets or residential subdivisions, or homes adapted to the southern climate.

Even when addressing these specific market sectors, the company's main
goal was to appeal to buyers across the country. Architects noted the increasing similarity of houses across the country, whether made by mail-order
firms or not. They credited eased travel by rail, widely disseminated photographic images in books and magazines, and, increasingly, film as means by
which this national taste was growing, to the point where it was "no unusual
thing to find in Illinois the brother of a house in Massachusetts and first
cousin to a . . . house in Virginia."[114] By the first issue of *The Wedge*, in 1913,
just seven years after the company's founding, Aladdin boasted that there
was not a "hole or corner in the United States where Aladdin houses are
entirely unknown." Two prime examples were used to show the breadth of
the company's reach. The editor recounted a conversation he had had in the
Palace Hotel, in which a fellow traveler surmised that with all the building
going on in the city, San Francisco "ought to be a good field for Aladdin
homes." The traveler's experience with the company had been at home in
New Jersey, where his neighbor built an Aladdin home. The recounted conversation attested to the coast-to-coast reach with similarly positive results.
Furthermore, the editor saw an Aladdin home in the middle of the desert,
at San Simon, Arizona, with only two other buildings and a water tank in
close proximity. Here the contrast was between the densely built urban areas
and the middle of nowhere, as well as the climatic differences, and how
Aladdin homes still stood up well for their purpose.[115] Being a national distributor meant not just reaching geographically across the country but also
appealing to different types of communities—rural, urban, and the small
towns in between. While some models might be more suited to certain types
of locations, foursquares seemed to transcend these differences; they were at
home on a farm or in an industrial town.

Aladdin worked on its appeals to these different markets in its promotional literature. For example, *Aladdin's Weekly* sponsored the "Small Town Preferred" issue, which presented, in the guise of a humorous story, all the problems of urban life and why village life was preferable. The humor softened any possible offense to urban dwellers (in fact, the dialect of the village booster might have offended more rural dwellers, despite the content). Though the piece never contained a specific reference to Aladdin homes, one of the problems attributed to life in the city was the ever-rising rent and the "contention that many a man's makin' a bare livin' on land that sells by the square foot when he oughta be livin' on the fat'uv land that sells by the acre."[116] Presumably "the land that sells by the acre," particularly in a "prosperous little village" where there would be less competition for business as described by the narrator, would afford greater opportunities for homeownership. Not dependent on urban markets to buy his goods, one customer, James E. Dyer of Ohio, wrote in and explained that his new Aladdin home was "all equipped with hot and cold water, lighted by the Delco light system, hot air furnace and just as though we were living in the city instead of 22 miles from Toledo. City folks stop to see our new home."[117] Other issues featured the "Back to the Farm" movement and industrial circumstances. Aladdin needed both geographic breadth and market depth to achieve its goal of being a nationwide distributor.

FAMILY BUSINESS

As much as the Aladdin Company strove to introduce itself as attuned to the values of the home, it also imagined its purchasers as smart business players. The company needed to present homeownership as a smart investment, a good decision in a family's "business." It was supported in this aim by the rhetoric of popular periodicals, declaring the family, in one instance, "a joint stock company." One author, Ruby Ross Goodnow, wrote in her six-part series on "Building the Honest House" in *The Delineator,* that "you must look upon your house as a lifetime business." Another, Emma Gary Wallace, told *House and Garden* readers of the "dividends in security and satisfaction" to be earned by investing in a house.[118] Thus, the company was able to echo strains already heard in the cultural conversation surrounding homeownership, that family values and business sense were not mutually exclusive.

A good business sense, then, was not opposed to family life, but integral to it. J. B. Hughes of Kansas well summed up the different approaches to buying an Aladdin house, as an investment and as a family home: "My dealing with the Aladdin company has been a hard headed, practical proposition of producing a home for my family and not a matter of sentiment, but now that it is through, I find that I cannot keep from being an Aladdin enthusiast and I find it hard to hold myself to plain, unsentimental language in telling of my experience."[119] The company quickly developed a way to capitalize on this enthusiasm. Though the firm often stated in its literature that the catalogue was its "only salesman," in fact it encouraged, if not technically employed, a vast secondary network of boosters.

An enticing but obscure message in the Aladdin catalogue referred to opportunities to gain immediate returns on the investment in an Aladdin home. A white-collared man was pictured at the end of the walkway to his (presumably Aladdin-made) house with an arm outstretched. Across the fold of the page, the Aladdin genie stood before a great factory building, with a bag of money in his hand. Though receiving money from a genie might seem a fantasy, the text spoke in hard financial facts. The rhetoric juxtaposed the business sense of investing wisely with the comfort and security of the home, taking repeated opportunities to assure readers of the safety of the home as an investment: "Can you imagine any place that is safer to put your money than in your own home? Can you imagine any finer investment to make with hard-earned money than to *invest it in your own home?* Of course not!" With this ground established, the company went on to suggest that the money invested in one's home could bring "an annual cash dividend check of 10%!" The lesson continued in an imagined conversation with the reader of this offer:

> "Splendid thought," you say, "but surely it's an impossible condition—too good to be true. Why I've always been taught to believe, and I do believe, that for money to earn dividends, there must be some risk, and the greater the dividend, the greater the risk. Now there is no risk whatever in putting money in your home, and yet you say it can earn a 10% dividend, more or less."
>
> True—every word.
>
> We are not seeking to violate any natural laws of finance or business, but we *are* seeking to steer them gently in the right direction.[120]

Though the plan would be explained only to those who actually purchased Aladdin homes, or "joined the Aladdin family," additional enticement was offered by examples of those who had received these dividends, such as Mrs.

E. D. Glaspie of Royal Oak, Michigan, the owner of an Aladdin Standard square-type house, who had earned $121.65 from the company. (The Glaspies were in fact prominent members of the Aladdin family; a testimonial letter from E. D. Glaspie appeared in the 1914 catalogue, and a photo of their Standard home appeared in *The Wedge* in July 1913.) A random sample of Aladdin customers revealed an average dividend payback of 7 percent on their initial investment. The unnamed plan could bring these special dividends, but the underlying message was that homeownership, even without any additional schemes, was a sound investment.

The opportunity to earn these dividends began with enrollment in a program of "co-operation" with the company. Co-operators were Aladdin homeowners who agreed to supply the company with names of potential customers. If the co-operator supplied a name before any other advertising source reached that person, and that person purchased a house, the co-operator received $20. As the company punned in the language of investments: "The principle—*simply to interest your neighbors who expect to build in Aladdin Houses.*" As the company explained its program, it had calculated the cost of selling a house at $20. (While presenting this fact, Otto Sovereign's marketing team did not waste the opportunity to explain that this figure averaged 4 percent of the house cost, a significantly lower amount than the 10 percent minimum he claimed any middle man would add as overhead to raw costs of materials, even before adding a percentage for profit.) If a co-operator sent in a name that resulted in a sale before any other form of advertising did, the advertising budget could not be credited with that sale, so that $20 could be offered to the co-operator. As the company stated, "Our intention in formulating the plan was chiefly to open a way to the many members of the big Aladdin family to receive something tangible in the way of payment for all the good work they are constantly doing for us."[121] Of all the many collaborators who supported the company's marketing messages, its consumer base was the most valuable.

While the "chief" aim may have been to encourage still more of this "good work," the fact remained that the company recognized the important role of personal referrals to its trade and wanted to codify the process of securing these referrals. The co-operators only received the money if they sent in a prospective name *first;* thus, co-operators were encouraged to send in a name the very day they learned that someone they knew was in the market for a home, encouraging word-of-mouth to travel as quickly as national periodicals. The speed of passing along possible customers' names became the one important "rule" of the plan: "The whole success of the Co-Operative Department rests upon our enforcing this rule, for if it is not strictly enforced, we will lose money every time, and would soon have to entirely abandon the Co-Operative Department."[122] In every location beyond Bay City, co-operators had the single most persuasive advertising tool, which even the company did not: their own home to show as a sample product. The company recognized this: "We have always thought that an Aladdin house itself is our best advertising medium and salesman."[123] While the houses might speak for themselves, they needed someone to show them off to their best advantage, and that was the role of the co-operator. Unable to see the mills and inspect the materials for themselves, prospective buyers could rest assured when they saw the house and heard of the honest dealings of the company.[124]

While some co-operators might simply send in the name of a friend or relative known to be in the market for a new house, glad to share in the good fortune of their new home, others were more ambitious in their solicitations, recognizing a true money-making scheme. The company encouraged this more aggressive approach, establishing a Club of Merit for co-operators who brought in $10,000 in sales to the company with their suggested buyers. Merit club members received a $100 bonus and a gold medal; the first to reach the lofty $10,000 mark would win, in addition, a trip to the Panama-Pacific Exposition, at which Aladdin was responsible for building the Michigan State Pavilion.[125] Some owners in effect established themselves as local agents of the company. The house organ sent to all purchasers was in large part devoted to the workings of the co-operators, and served as a clearinghouse for innovative ways of gaining commissions, while drumming up sales for the company. The page entitled "With the Co-operators" was devoted to suggestions from and to the ranks. For example, one homeowner wrote in, explaining that he had put a small advertisement in the newspaper; the message "Are you looking to build? Low cost readi-cut houses from forest to farm. Write O. White, Broken Arrow, Okla." ran weekly in the real estate section.[126] Aladdin immediately responded by designing advertisements in two sizes, made to fit newspaper columns, which co-operators could send for free of charge and place in their own hometown newspapers. The company would also furnish free engravings of the various house models to be inserted into newspaper advertisements.

Like the Kohler Company, Aladdin produced a variety of promotional materials, in this case for co-operators rather than wholesalers. A slide to be projected on a movie theater screen between shows was available from the company, with a place to insert the name of the local co-operator. *The Wedge* carried sample designs for cards to be handed out, containing the pertinent information to be sent in for a catalogue, and of course a space for the name of the co-operator; the cards could be ordered free of charge from the company. They were particularly useful for garnering commissions even without face-to-face contact; as *The Wedge* explained, "While the person you hand a card to may not every time be interested in building, still he will likely have an acquaintance who is and pass it on. Who ever may use the card is sure to be on your list and credited to you by us." These means made it possible for co-operators, and thus the company, to reach beyond their actual circle of acquaintances, or to let those in the circle know their "connection with the Aladdin Readi-Cut system."[127]

Through these promotions, Aladdin worked to codify, and enumerate, the extent to which "word of mouth" supported its business, just as it evaluated its other forms of advertising and publicity. While most of the networks that co-operators could tap into were local and geographically bound (especially if they relied on showing their own home), others were of kin or professional relationships, and might form a web from town to town across the country. Co-operators simply had to look out for possible circles and groups of people for whom their "service" would make sense. Again calling on the theme of investment, *The Wedge* suggested to co-operators that they approach the local building and loan association, a group already committed to saving for a home, and show how achievement of that goal could happen more quickly through the Aladdin system. Either by getting names from the loan association or by running a small advertisement addressed to these members, this group of people could be contacted and would surely bring "a great deal of profit" to the co-operator who tapped into the network. This form of target marketing is one that Otto Sovereign excelled at and built his business on; he encouraged the co-operators to think in similar ways by sponsoring a contest for "the best suggestions for helping 'to learn of prospective builders.'"[128]

The co-operator plan was presented in terms of the levels of service exchanged; co-operators were to be of service not just to the company's bottom line, but also to one another, and presumably to the prospective clients with whom they were sharing their home investment strategies. As the company used connections between its customers to build its market, so too did those customers form a sense of community based on their bond of home-ownership. A letter from a co-operator from New York demonstrates this sense of unity that transcended geographic boundaries. As reported in *The Wedge:*

> "I would like to feel better acquainted with this fine lot of men and women," he wrote, "for there is in their combined forces, the seed of great accomplishments. I may not profit in a direct and personal way by this association, but who can tell the limitations for mutual advancement that might come of such a league. Now, you people at the home of the Company, of course, have the key to this possibility, and it must be with your aid and assistance that we, scattered over the country, can get together."

The writer and the company together assumed that "all the people of the Aladdin family are progressive, wide awake, and lead their respective neighborhood in recognizing advanced and modern ideas."[129] Together these consumers formed a community based on their shared status as homeowners and their shared sense of the standard of living based in those homes.

If co-operation was one form of community cohesion, friendly competition was another. A variety of contests drew the "Aladdin people" together, even if they were competing with one another. In the rhetoric of *The Wedge,* "Aladdin" was not only a brand name, but also an adjective, meaning not just those people who owned or lived in Aladdin homes, but those who had adopted a shared lifestyle that was centered on that home. The contests were particularly aimed at "ALADDIN housewives" who could "profit by pleasant work." A yearly garden contest began with offers of free seeds from the company, as well as advice on plantings from the Department of Service, and continued with hundreds of photographs being sent in to the firm, and finally closed at year's end with four happy winners receiving cash prizes—$50 for first place, $25 for second, $15 for third, and $10 for fourth. Similarly, contests for interior decor of Aladdin homes were held. Through additional writing contests, as opposed to those with images, Aladdin solicited different types of stories of experience with the company's houses—essentially longer versions of the testimonial letters. In June 1913, *The Wedge* announced four additional contests, one for best advertisement, and three for best essays in three categories: the story of erecting an Aladdin house; the advantages of the Aladdin building system; and the process of purchasing an Aladdin home when money was borrowed to make the purchase.[130]

While spreading good will for the company, and creating camaraderie among owners who would not meet in any other way, the contests were also crucial for the photographs and essays sent in, which were used for advertising purposes. As one contest announcement stated in 1913:

> We want pretty pictures of ALADDIN houses and bungalows . . . Photographs can be easily taken of the interior of your house either by flashlight or time exposure. Give as many views as is necessary to show the house complete with the different rooms. Every housewife should take pleasure in the contest and select the corners in each room, which will make the most attractive view. This contest gives every owner a chance to win a prize and show how attractive an ALADDIN house can be made.
>
> A view looking from the living room into the dining room showing a part of each room, a cozy grouping of furniture about the fire place or a view of the bed rooms, all these will help to win a prize in the ALADDIN contest.[131]

Photographs of Aladdin houses in use as homes were the next best things to having people open their actual homes for public viewing. Rules for the garden contest explicitly stated that the house must be visible in the photographs of the gardens, and if the images included happy families so much the better. These design contests were a way to gather publicity and advertising images of the houses at their best, with minimal cost to the company. Even if co-operators did not wish to enter the contests, there was "an opportunity for Aladdin house owners to make a little spare change." The company solicited 4×5 inch negatives of both the interior and exterior of Aladdin homes, and would pay $2 per "good negative" for up to six images, three each of inside and outside a house.[132]

If Aladdin owners chose not to participate in the Co-operator Program or the contests, they were still part of "the Aladdin family." They were encouraged to include themselves in this extended family's reunions with the company's magazines serving as the actual site where these "meetings" took place. The company solicited photographs of babies born to Aladdin owners, "who are really and truly born in Aladdin houses—really truly Aladdin babies"; they were to be called "wedgelings" in keeping with the original journal's name. The wedgelings received a gold coin or a small ring from the sovereigns to mark their entry into the Aladdin family. The company simply wanted "to be proud of them, crow over them, show them off to each other in *The Wedge*."[133] A month later appeared the first "wedgeling": Loretta Nellie Gates, born in an Aladdin house in Monroe, Michigan. Baby Loretta was announced to the Aladdin family with great fanfare:

Observe the gentle dignity with which she contemplates the world. She is perfectly satisfied with her choice of parents, her comforts and her home. The future is as bright as the eyes that peer so seriously into the camera. She is reposing comfortable in the snowy folds of her faultless baby dress.

Miss Loretta is the possessor of a bright and shining gold piece, for has she not distinguished herself by being the first Aladdin baby reported, the first Aladdin baby in Monroe, the first Aladdin Wedgeling, and the first to have her picture in the Wedge? A distinction to be proud of![134]

Little "Sally Aladdin," the daughter of one of the Sovereign brothers, was the leader of this little pack, frequently appearing in *The Wedge* to welcome her new friends into the homes that shared their origins with her own. If the home was for the nuclear family, then Aladdin homeowners could be an extended family, to occasionally "visit" with, even if only through these publications. In one instance the photographs of three otherwise unrelated wedgelings were shown together as if through three openings in one large frame, as indeed a "family" might show three siblings.[135] Another shared view of home life in Aladdin houses was captured in a small promotional book of "Aladdin's Favorite Recipes," a collection of "recipes of extraordinary merit from Aladdin's housewives," covering all parts of a meal from Marsden Turtle Soup, submitted by Mrs. Orr Swinehart of Ohio; to a meat-and-potatoes main course called Aladdin "Three-In-One" from Mrs. David Reed of New York; to Pomona Pineapple Delight, sent in by Mrs. Grace Davis of North Carolina.[136]

If the measures taken through *The Wedge* and its subsequent incarnations were self-serving to the company, they also solidified common interests among the journal's readers. From testimonial letters and photographs, Aladdin owners could easily imagine their counterparts across the country, living under a different climate and perhaps by means of a different livelihood, but at least in the spatial arrangement of their homes, leading parallel lives. While soliciting photographs of its houses to use in advertisements, the company also requested photos of owners to share in *The Wedge,* as a means of "getting acquainted." The company explained:

> The Aladdin family of Co-Operators each one interested in the other's interests and friendship, but located in many parts of the United States and other countries, should be drawn closer together. We cannot all live in the same city or state, but we could be more intimately acquainted and know each other should we meet.

... In this way when we read of a Co-operator in California we have seen him—it brings him closer to us; it is a real visit he has paid each one of the large Aladdin family.

Let us start next month with a number of personal visits and enjoy the talks, friendship and faces of each other.[137]

While the company tested the parameters of its market, it also helped that market to imagine itself as a community with shared interests and values, and shared ways of expressing those values in its built environment, particularly the intimate environment of domestic space. While earnings might vary from place to place, and different occupations might carry different social rank from one locale to another, a national standard of living could be expressed through the increasing standardization of domestic architecture. The mail-order market was one way in which this nationalization occurred.

Kit-house companies used standard modular parts to produce a variety of houses, allocating domestic space in different ways to appeal to a broad market, while still keeping costs low. Distribution of these parts by railroad allowed for specific house types, such as the foursquare, to become a shared feature of the national landscape, transcending regional traditions of construction. Still, the small variations available even in mass-produced housing were emblematic of the personal choices that were available to those who owned their own houses, while the solidity of the structures emphasized a sound investment. Variety and standardization actually went hand in hand, as the latter made the former financially viable. Marketing campaigns frequently combined the ideals of business and family—interlacing two seemingly opposed concerns of American culture.

Those who advocated homeownership, ranging from government officials to editors of shelter magazines, believed that the investment aspect was important to inculcate not only fiscal responsibility, but also civic responsibility. House manufacturers also stressed this point by trying to form a community of their purchasers. The Aladdin Company fostered the closest and most direct collaborative effort of the companies examined thus far, enlisting current owners to promote their positive experiences to prospective owners. Who better to uphold not just the homes themselves but the idea of homeownership? Word of mouth was envisioned to spread not just locally but nationally; as networks of kin, occupation, or other affinity increasingly spread across the country, so might Aladdin's houses. It was deemed a "comfort" to own one's home, not a luxury, and thus this common aspiration stood at the center of the standard of living.

While flatware provided a frame to organize space at an intimate level and bathroom fixtures determined the design of a room, the ultimate goal in the organization of personal space was the single-family home. The idea of privacy presented in a closed circle at a table, or the walls of a bathroom, was magnified in the idea of owning one's own home. Working on an assumption that the family was the basic unit of society, the single-family house provided a spatial reflection of this social organization. In the early twentieth century, zoning plans would codify boundaries around whole districts of these houses, representing the standard of living in urban form.

CHAPTER FOUR

THE STANDARD OF MANAGEMENT

Zoning Plans

"Does your city keep its gas range in the parlor and its piano in the kitchen?" When Herbert S. Swan, secretary of the New York City Zoning Committee, asked this question in April 1920 to the readers of *The American City,* a journal of civic affairs, he presumed that their answer, upon thinking through the metaphor, would have to be "yes." He further presumed that this answer was unacceptable. Swan continued his comparison: "In what city can we not find gas tanks next to parks, garages next to schools, boiler shops next to hospitals, stables next to churches, or funeral establishments next to dwelling houses? What would be considered insanity if practiced in the ordinary house is excused as an exercise of individual liberty when practiced in the city at large. And yet misplaced buildings are to be condemned much more than out-of-place pieces of furniture."[1] Figuring the hometown as a home was a popular way to convince city and town residents to consider design on a civic scale. A few years after Swan asked his leading questions, the Pittsburgh Citizens Committee on City Planning translated the comparison into a cartoon, issued through the local press. The cartoon depicted a house in which the presumed owner smoked a cigar and read the newspaper in the living room of his home, but rather than reclining in the upholstered chair depicted under a fringed lamp, he sat in a bathtub. The piano was, as Swan had earlier quipped, in the kitchen, the kitchen sink in the bedroom, and, perhaps most improbable of all, the family car was somehow stowed in a garage located in the attic of the house. The caption read "The sort of homes we should have if our houses were like our cities."[2] The cartoon implied that just as the private home was ordered with some guiding hand to design it, so too did the city need management of its constituent parts.

Both Herbert Swan and the Pittsburgh Citizens Committee had the same idea for how this management should be achieved: zoning. Zoning was an urban planning measure with a regulatory effect. It established a series of boundaries within the city, creating and separating districts in which different uses of land were permitted.[3] The earliest building regulations that can be considered forms of zoning were restrictions placed on height and occasionally on use—for example, Washington, D.C.'s 1899 ordinance limiting buildings to the height of the U.S. Capitol, a similar restriction passed in Boston in 1904, and a 1909 Los Angeles ordinance regulating property use. New residential subdivisions often placed restrictions on building size and usage in the form of covenants applicable to owners.[4] But the method of combining use, height, and area regulations to classify urban land use was new to the 1910s. After much planning and negotiation, New York City passed a zoning code in 1916, stemming from public health concerns regarding accessibility to light and clean air, safety concerns over necessary open space for fire breaks, and a desire to stabilize land values and protect real estate investments. In the comprehensive form that it took on in the New York City ordinance, zoning regulated the use, height, and area of construction on any vacant lot in the municipality, as well as major reconstruction of existing structures.[5] Zoning was based in a vision of urban planning that was "scientific" and "well-managed," with emphasis on efficiency and integrated systems. Earlier planning practices, particularly for parks, civic centers, and street systems, had also exhibited this emphasis.

A survey of American planning and zoning completed under the auspices of the Harvard University Urban Planning Program in 1929 documents the widespread adoption of zoning in the 1920s. By the year of publication, a short 13 years after the first zoning ordinance was passed in New York City, over 750 municipalities in the United States had adopted zoning codes, and the numbers continued to increase rapidly through the early 1930s. The Department of Commerce under Secretary Herbert Hoover drafted model enabling legislation for zoning, first issued in 1924, easing the process by which municipalities could gain the power to enact such ordinances; by the end of the 1920s, 47 states and the District of Columbia had adopted enabling legislation of some sort, whether based on this model or not.[6] That zoning codes could be adopted in such a large number of communities suggests the range of cities and towns that must have engaged in this planning process.

Although the 1920 Census is recognized as the first to declare the United States as an urban nation, the official definition of "urban" was any incorporated municipality with a population over 2,500. In the 1920 Census, only 60 American cities had populations over 100,000, and by 1930 this number had risen to only 81 cities. Clearly, most of the 750 communities to implement zoning codes were small cities. Looking back on the first 20 years of zoning, one planner claimed that zoning ordinances had been most effective when passed in cities with a population under 75,000, allowing a plan for direction of growth before it occurred haphazardly. As *The American City* explained to its readers, "It may be assumed that the protection of residential districts from value-destroying encroachments is just as desirable in the place of 2,000 population as the place of 200,000." More important, zoning was most effective if undertaken as part of a comprehensive plan, in order to coordinate districts with the street plan, transportation and local transit routes, and other local concerns.[7]

The firm of Harland Bartholomew and Associates (HBA), whose clients provide a cross-section of municipalities engaged in comprehensive planning and zoning, serves as a window into the nationally shared enthusiasm for zoning. Harland Bartholomew was one of the most prolific American planners, and the firm he established in 1917 continues to this day to provide planning and engineering services.[8] Even in the first decades of its existence, HBA worked in a variety of cities and towns across the United States and Canada, completing about fifty comprehensive plans by the early 1930s. The range of these communities, from small residential suburbs to regional hubs for agricultural districts to larger cities based in an industrial economy, shows how widespread the appeal of comprehensive planning and zoning was. In a plan for Binghamton, New York, Bartholomew explained the purpose of his work, writing in language typical of the Progressive Era, that when "properly administered," a city plan "will make possible the gradual and economical development of an efficient city which will provide good living conditions for all of its citizens, be everywhere attractive, and free from the physical defects that hamper commerce and industry." He pointed specifically to the zoning ordinance to promote "the health, safety, morals, and general welfare of the community," in other words, the given community's standard of living.[9] From Utica, New York, to Glendale, California, with stops such as Knoxville, Grand Rapids, Michigan, and San Antonio along the way, the firm used similar methods and to a certain extent recommended similar programs. The zoning ordinances all exhibited the beliefs that a community should be structured with a separation of functions; that growth was a positive thing if well-managed; and that a city's physical manifestation, economic well-being, and quality of life were interrelated.

At the time of Bartholomew's entry into the field of urban planning, there was barely a field to enter. He was one of a growing group of individuals with training in architecture, civil engineering, landscape architecture, or other related fields who together forged the new profession at the beginning of the twentieth century. Bartholomew did have a few well-known predecessors in laying out new towns, and even creating comprehensive plans, such as the Olmsteds, John Nolen, and Cass Gilbert. These men created the nascent academic programs in urban planning, for example, at Harvard University and the University of Illinois, that they themselves had not had the opportunity to attend. Bartholomew's training was in civil engineering. He had attended Rutgers for a few years and worked for the U.S. Army Engineering Corps as a leadsman on a river survey and harbor maintenance crew in New York. The first job that he considered to be in his own field was working for E. P. Goodrich, a consulting engineer. Bartholomew worked for Goodrich on harbor projects in Portland, Oregon, and Los Angeles. After Goodrich and architect George B. Ford secured a contract with the city of Newark, New Jersey, Bartholomew undertook his first comprehensive planning work there. He stayed in Newark for a few years, continuing to work for the city after Goodrich's contract was completed. Bartholomew credited Goodrich as an important influence, and even while forging his own path, retained a vision of urban planning that was informed by engineering.

In 1917, Bartholomew was hired by the Citizens' City Planning Committee of St. Louis to serve as engineer, and later became secretary to the official city plan commission; he opened his own consulting firm based in St. Louis the same year.[10] While continuing his relationship with the City of St. Louis until mid-century, Bartholomew accepted dozens of contracts for comprehensive plans across the country, the firm itself becoming one conduit through which information about planning and zoning was distributed. Although HBA occasionally worked for private developers, and later would do a bulk of its work for the federal government designing military bases, in the early years of the firm, the majority of the clients were municipalities, either a city planning commission or a citizens' group trying to garner support for planning efforts.

Although the consumers of zoning plans were municipalities, zoning applied to privately owned space. Earlier planning efforts had centered on municipally owned land and buildings, but these holdings made up only 25 to 40 percent of urban space in most American cities. As more comprehensive visions of the city took hold, planning advocates introduced the benefits of regulation over privately owned land as well. It was one thing for a municipality to improve and rationalize the property it owned in the form of streets, street railway lines (when municipally owned), parks, schools, and the like, even when such measures required public support for the fund-raising to carry out such projects. It was another matter for citizens to develop and build their own properties in accordance with a legal scheme that dictated possible areas for possible uses and vice versa. In one of his earliest plans for the adoption of zoning, then known as "districting," Bartholomew wrote:

> Unquestionably the interests of the whole community require a form of control over the development of the entire city, which shall enable all to enjoy the benefits of urban life without prohibitive expense and without unwarranted, detrimental health conditions. Such control, to be effective, must be public . . . American cities, and the majority of property holders in them, have but recently come to realize the absolute necessity of intelligent centralized control of city growth. Districting is the name given to the first attempt at such control.[11]

The basic tenet of zoning was to separate the different functions of a city into different geographic areas, with corresponding height limitations and lot area guidelines.

In most cities and towns, the use classifications were separated into three general categories: industrial, commercial, and residential.[12] These three categories corresponded to the three sectors of daily life in any community—production, distribution, and consumption. While we often think of a town's commercial district—location of stores and professional blocks—as a site of consumption, I would argue that these spaces are in fact sites of distribution of goods and services; these goods are produced in the industrial areas and consumed in the home. In terms of the physical structure of most municipalities, the heart of the city was the commercial district, or aptly named "central business district," ranging from a block-long Main Street in small towns to a densely constructed urban core in large cities. Circulation patterns, whether streets or transit, focused on these areas and radiated from them. Residential areas surrounded these cores, with decreasing density (of both architecture and population) the farther one traveled. Industrial areas lurked on the outskirts, or along major transportation routes.[13] Zoning did not create this landscape, which long predated the planning measure.[14] Rather, zoning was designed to codify and refine the basic spatial relationships in times of growth.

Zoning was presented as an insurance that growth would occur in a beneficial way. The economic gain from business and industry would occur without the attendant social problems that seemed to be following fast in many American cities, which one planner called the "inevitable blight of ugliness and squalor that usually follows industrial growth."[15] The cities both affected by the encroachment of industry and trying to stay its impact were not only experienced in daily life, but also represented in the literature of the day. In his 1920 novel *Moon-Calf,* author Floyd Dell juxtaposed the "unrestricted" city of Garth with the well-planned Port Royal. Dell created the fictional Garth:

> Garth was a nightmare—the inconceivably hideous product of unrestricted commercial enterprise; its centre was occupied by the vast, bare, smoke-begrimed structures of the greatest plough-factory on earth; a little fringe of desultory shops, insulted and apparently pushed aside by incessantly switching trains of freight cars, gave way to a drab, monotonous area of cheap and hastily-constructed workingmen's dwellings, each house exactly like the next, street after street and mile after mile—while afar, set almost inaccessibly upon the hills like the castles of robber barons, could be discerned the houses where the plough-magnates lived.

By contrast, Port Royal "had a kindlier aspect," stemming from its ordered arrangement of streets, "its great parks, its public buildings, even its shops and homes." Dell was just one of many authors outside the realm of planning who brought the field's concerns to public attention.[16]

Planners and citizens alike named a variety of benefits that zoning could achieve in a given community. Economic arguments about the preservation of property values provided one approach.[17] Another stemmed from public health concerns about overcrowding, in both living and working conditions. Poor working conditions and traffic snarls in densely constructed downtowns resulted from the increasing height of commercial buildings, while workers needing to live near industrial centers crowded into tenements.[18] Increasingly, however, the reasons for zoning were not so much to prevent these ills as to preserve what was positive about a city's existing organization, usually its neighborhoods of single-family homes. The impulse to protect the "civic and social values of the American home" was upheld by the California State Supreme Court as a legitimate reason for zoning.[19] And finally, zoning was a way for residents to show their commitment to the continued growth and prosperity of their hometowns; to implement a zoning ordinance was a shorthand version of demonstrating this commitment to others.[20] Zoning would protect and enhance the standard of living of urban dwellers whose cities adopted the planning measure.

Ideas about zoning and the image of the city it codified were distributed through a variety of channels. Within a city or town, speeches at community meetings, exhibits of visual aids, and the local press all promoted these ideas. On a national level, the planners physically traveled from town to town by train; local civic leaders read *The American City* and other journals to share ideas across the country; and conventions of professionals brought town boosters together. As a by-product of this national distribution, standardization in American urban planning emerged as cities and towns across the country designed their ordering systems in remarkably similar ways. A unified vision of what it meant to be a city, and perhaps an American city, arose in this era. Though some similarities, particularly from the Midwest to the west, were rooted in original gridded town plans, the 1910s and 1920s brought a uniform plan for organization to cities. This is not to say that all cities began to look alike, though this is a common criticism leveled at American cities, but the similarity of the plans does suggest a common vision shared by municipal planners and civic groups. This vision, of a city that preserved family homes while allowing for economic growth, was widely accepted but did have bounds: it was primarily a middle-class vision. Implicit in Herbert Swan's description of a community as a house was the assumption that readers would be able to envision family life in a single-family home, and recognize its icons. A gas range, a piano, the space of a parlor all conjured up a standard of living shared by a new class of managers and professionals. It was this standard that these planners, managers, and salesmen hoped to ensure in the community as a whole through zoning.

MANAGING THE CITY

Zoning invested the notion of the public good with a personal consequence and responsibility. As Bartholomew wrote in a plan for Jackson, Michigan, "The old belief that a city was merely a place in which large numbers of men congregated with a common understanding that it was 'each man for himself' has passed, and the more democratic doctrine that, as the city grows, the welfare of the individual becomes more dependent upon the welfare of all, has taken its place."[21] As the idea quickly spread from the largest American metropolis to small towns across the country, zoning became not so much a way to reform urban problems as a way to manage the growth of smaller cities and towns. From concerns over public health and safety, zoning grew to be a policy that regulated growth, protected economic investment, and presented the single-family residential district as a neighborhood ideal in all but the largest cities. Models of industry and business, particularly the concept of scientific management, became useful for forming new visions of the city, as were the emphases on growth and reform that marked the Progressive Era. The practice of zoning seemed to contradict established laissez-faire business practices and yet was often largely supported by the business community. It is not surprising that in trying to improve their home communities as they had improved their businesses, a new class of managers and credentialed professionals would apply their own styles of doing work to the city, all the while protecting their own investments of property and business.

Even the common form of local governance was increasingly modeled on corporate structures. The adoption of the city manager form of government was a municipal trend that contributed to the rise of city planning, zoning, and Bartholomew's booming business in the 1920s. Under the city manager plan, citizens elected a small city council on a nonpartisan ticket. The council then appointed and supervised a city manager, who in turn oversaw the workings of the various city departments and named their department heads. Because the manager position was essentially administrative and not elected, it was considered "professional" rather than "political"; good managers kept their positions for long periods of time, assuring continuity in municipal government. The city manager plan became increasingly popular in the 1920s.[22] As Bartholomew and his peers moved around the country, they collected references from the city managers of different cities to whom they could refer prospective clients. Bartholomew himself on occasion spoke to conventions of city managers. A longtime partner in the HBA firm, Eldridge Lovelace, suggested that over time as managers moved from position to position across the country, with strong ties to HBA, they would give the firm repeat business in different locales. This network of new middle-class professionals appears to have been one avenue down which the ideas of planning and zoning generally, and the HBA firm specifically, traveled.

If the city was imagined as a business, particularly an industrial firm, zoning could be likened to scientific management. Scientific management was a newly codified form of industrial organization that advocated the separation of work into discrete tasks, arranged for maximum efficiency of the whole process. Standardization of all parts of work would replace "rule of thumb" methods in order to achieve "maximum prosperity." Frederick Winslow Taylor, the popularizer of these practices in numerous lectures and his book *The Principles of Scientific Management,* suggested that his theory of management could be applied to all aspects of daily life, not just industrial work. He wrote that his aim was to "prove that the best management was a true science, resting upon clearly defined laws, rules, and principles, as a foundation."[23] Planning was one form of management, with the city as its object rather than industrial work. As Bartholomew said to residents of Des Moines, Iowa, "The problem . . . is not one of spreading out the city but making more efficient use of what you now have."[24] The other sections of city planning were like the different stages of industrial work; zoning was the system to manage them.

In creating these working plans, Bartholomew's first employer, E. P. Goodrich, was an influence not only in the type of work he did but also in how it was organized, on a consultant basis. Bartholomew appears to have looked on the work of consultants in a special light, as a subfield of their chosen profession. Consultants could enter a municipality with a fresh perspective, diagnose its ills and weaknesses, prescribe solutions, and predict its promise. Of equal importance were the planners who remained working in a place over a long period of time, making sure that changes were made and plans were implemented, but these two positions were distinct. Bartholomew's professional practice combined the positions of "outside expert" and "community insider," but he more frequently played the former role. While Bartholomew and his partners made extensive visits to the various towns for which they produced plans, they also assigned a junior member of the firm to take up residence for the two- to two-and-one-half-year process that complete comprehensive planning and zoning took. For example, HBA's contract with the "municipal corporation" of Dallas, Texas, in 1928 called for work on the plan to be completed within two years of the contract date, "during which time the Parties of the First Part [HBA] will place a technically qualified local representative in the city of Dallas to direct the preparation of information and planning studies and who will also give such other services as will be helpful to the work of the City Planning Commission in securing the adoption, acceptance and execution of the city plan."[25] These "resident engineers," as they were called, often remained in the towns, becoming employees of the municipal government, secretaries to city planning and zoning commissions, and, in some cases, long-term consultants to private planning groups.

In this way, planners all over the country were trained in Bartholomew's firm and his planning methods. Bartholomew admitted that this was an expensive way to run a business, having to continually train new employees and then pass them along to cities, but it appears to have been successful for the firm as well as for the communities involved. Working for HBA was often a route into one of the increasing number of municipal planning jobs across the country. The Dallas contract also stipulated that, whenever possible, local draftsmen be engaged by HBA. In these ways, HBA managed to have both the loyalty and trust of a person familiar with the specific location and the clout and experience of the outside expert who had worked in a variety of cities. While HBA did provide this evaluation of the conditions of specific cities, in the process the firm promoted certain definitions of community types. Foremost among these community designations was the "industrial city," a label that Bartholomew applied to municipalities such as Utica, New York, and South Bend, Indiana; the industrial city was not only a community based in an industrial economy but also a spatial arrangement of clearly organized constituent parts.[26]

The process of creating a zoning ordinance began with an extensive study phase reminiscent of Taylor's explanation: "The managers assume the burden of gathering together all of the traditional knowledge which in the past has been possessed by the workmen and then of classifying, tabulating, and reducing this knowledge to rules, laws, and formulae."[27] Before zoning plans were begun, questionnaires were sent out, polling opinions of building and usage regulations, while resident engineers and city officials compiled local data. While some of these studies, and particularly mapping projects, dealt strictly with features of the built environment, such as building heights or street widths, others dealt with uses of the city's components, such as traffic counts, types of housing, population density, trolley time zones, or the light projection in all parts of the city. The planners began the process by charting the use of every property in the city with the following classifications:

single-family, two-family, and multifamily dwellings; light and heavy industry; business and commerce; railroad property; parks and cemeteries; public and semi-public buildings; city-owned property; and vacant and undeveloped lots.[28] The contract between HBA and the City of Dallas called for over fifty separate computations of the status of land use, ranging from the percentage of the population housed in single-family residences to retail street frontage per hundred persons in the central business district to a special study of apartments, in order to arrive at a zoning ordinance that would pass the required test of "reasonableness."[29] Once a tentative zoning code was determined, all sites that did not conform to it were mapped, fine tuning the original designations so as not to cause hardship in particular districts. Such studies backed the planners' claims that zoning upheld the general development trends of the cities in which they worked instead of creating wholly new schemes on paper. The remainder of the comprehensive plan also entailed a wide variety of studies, ranging from traffic counts and transit ridership to usage of parkland and community demographics. This study phase in fact made up much of the two- to two-and-one-half-year process of creating a comprehensive plan.

Once this background study was completed, for either Taylor or Bartholomew, the next step was to find the best way to order the institution under examination. The simplest statements of scientific management as outlined by Taylor dictate that component functions of any process should be broken down into discrete steps and each one made to work most effectively in its own right, together contributing to the health and productivity of the whole. Starting with the idea of separating out the functions of daily life into use districts, we can also see in Bartholomew's work the attempt to further analyze each sector of the city. For example, what institutions would contribute to the smooth functioning of a residence district without detracting from its domestic character? How much commercial street frontage would meet the needs of the growing population without overreaching and leading to failing businesses and blight? Just as Taylor's followers determined the numbers of employees working particular times on particular tasks to reach a certain output, Bartholomew's followers projected specific spatial allocations and relationships between districts.

If business and industry provided the models for how to manage the growing city, they also became the criteria on which to evaluate the success of that management. One argument used to garner support for planning efforts was that just as businesses care about planning and design, so too should municipal entities. Addressing the importance of calculating urban growth over time and planning well for it, Bartholomew wrote in a 1925 report for Des Moines, Iowa, "The sort of anticipatory planning which is being done by the engineer of the telephone company, the water company and the electric company should be duplicated and carried even further by the municipality itself."[30] The growth of that city and the success of its business and industry supported one another.

The commissioners applied the models of competition learned in the arena of business and management to the cities in which they lived. Familiar with selling goods and services to one another and to their communities, the city planning and zoning boards commissioned Bartholomew to "package" their hometowns to sell as well. In a plan for Lansing, Michigan, from 1921, Bartholomew explained the importance of good design:

> A city is "sold" by its so-called beauty spots. Men have learned to make art and beauty and attractiveness pay. The seller of real estate adds to the price of a lot because it is so situated that he can point to the dignity and character of nearby homes. The automobile manufacturer aims to produce a car of pleasing proportions. Power and speed alone will not sell his cars. Similarly a city must give more thought to "design." Mere multiplication of factories and warehouses will not create a perfect city.[31]

The language of competition between cities suffused not only the comprehensive plans themselves, but also other sites of booster rhetoric such as accounts of the planning process in local newspapers and directories.

Boosters concerned themselves with broadly publicizing the positive aspects of their hometowns, and worked toward creating more of these attributes. Usually local businessmen, boosters sought continued growth and prosperity for their communities; local chambers of commerce and other civic groups often coordinated the efforts. Ironically, their publicity campaigns often stressed both what was unique about a specific place and what made it just like other cities, often ones perceived to be bigger and better. Geographical location, topographical features, climate, new homes, conditions for trade, natural resources, characteristics of the citizens, and, perhaps most important, promise for the future—any and all of these aspects of a city were used to convince visitors to consider that city as a new place to live and work, while convincing current residents to maintain their investment there. Popular novelist Booth Tarkington invoked the familiarity of boosters' rhetoric in his 1924 work, *The Midlander*, a quasi-sequel to *The*

Magnificent Ambersons. The female protagonist, Martha Shelby, parodies the oratorical tendencies of chamber of commerce members: "Oh you know the speeches they make: 'A city of prosperity, a city of homes, a city that produces more wooden butter-dishes than all the rest of the country combined! Yes, ladies and gentlemen, the finest city with the biggest future in the whole extent of these United States!'"[32]

Boosters often made specific comparisons to other cities, particularly in the same region, to set off their own. L. B. Jeffries, industrial secretary of the Des Moines Chamber of Commerce, favorably compared the trade territory of his town to the well-recognized distribution center of Chicago; explaining Des Moines's location as halfway between the center of the national population in Indiana and the center of area in Kansas, he wrote that Des Moines "is the immediate logical market and trade center for this extensive territory, its competitors, including Chicago (385 miles distant), being on the outer rim."[33] These specific claims were set into a general rhetoric of the beauty, opportunity, and progressive nature of cities and towns.

Zoning provided one way for boosters to claim these qualities for their cities. The act of zoning showed the town to be progressive, while its effects would preserve local beauty, order, and economic well-being. If reformers saw the act as a corrective measure against the ills of urban life, and a class of managers saw it as a preventive means of avoiding these ills, boosters presented a third way of viewing zoning. They were proactive: zoning was a way to not only avoid problems but also bring prosperity. Chicago businessman Charles Ball stated the trend clearly for the Chicago City Club: "Zoning sells a town. An unzoned city is like a dead stock of goods on the shelves."[34] A cartoon in *The American City* in 1928 showed the relationship between boosters and the planners they hired to create comprehensive plans for their towns. While the planners, dressed in conservative dark suits, work with eyes cast downward upon a tabletop size map of the city, the boosters jocularly applaud one flashily dressed spokesman as he points to the central location of their hometown on a map of the United States. The planners' ideal was to "put the map on our city" while the boosters' was to "put our city on the map."[35]

The boosters' competitive language does beg the question of what cities were competing for, or to whom they were selling. Having properly zoned industrial districts close to necessary resources, such as waterways or the railroad, along with sites for employees to live, would be a draw to industrialists looking to establish new factories. Bartholomew's clients wanted to use zoning both to attract more industry to their towns and to keep it within bounds. Bartholomew explained the importance of city planning to industry in a plan for East St. Louis, Illinois:

> It is now a generally accepted fact that the industrial city wishing to attract new industries as well as to retain its present ones must offer to the manufacturer not merely good industrial sites, low freight rates and switching charges, and public utility services at economical prices, but the city must also offer to the employees of industries good living conditions, good housing conditions, ample recreation facilities, and those other things which will tend to make life in that city pleasant.[36]

City planning, and particularly zoning, would create a system for organizing urban space in such a way that industry could provide an economic base without overtaking residential and recreational spaces.

Certainly related to the competition for industry was the more general competition for population. In an era when local success was equated with population growth, cities sought to attract new residents and homeowners, particularly at a time when rural residents were moving to cities in large numbers. With a zoning ordinance in place, town boosters could ensure the sanctity of their single-family residential districts as safe and appealing places to live and as places that would retain investment value on property, no matter how large the population grew. Growth was applauded as representing the health of a city and a way to gauge the success of that city in relation to others. The plans that were done in the first fifteen years or so of Harland Bartholomew's consulting career exhibit an incredible faith in the continued growth of American cities. The planner himself believed that some sort of prediction of population growth was a necessary first step to planning, and especially zoning, in order to evaluate the quantity and percentage of space in any given community that was required for residential space as well as commercial needs.

Despite the needed base number for such calculations there was no exact science of obtaining it and local constituents were often in disagreement. The HBA plans projected population increase based on growth in comparable cities, but also mentioned the numbers planned for by the local utilities and Bell Telephone, frequently even higher.[37] The Des Moines Zoning Commission publicized these projections, stating, "Expressed in a different way, [the projected growth] means a new city practically the size of Cedar Rapids or Davenport, built on the outskirts of Des Moines today."[38] The booster mentality toward population size, regardless of the scale of the town, was captured in contemporary fiction, as characters tended to exaggerate a population figure that might then be "corrected" by the omniscient narrator. In Tarkington's 1899 novel, *The Gentleman from Indiana,* he wrote, "Natives of this place have sometimes remarked, easily, that their city had a population of from five to six thousand souls. It is easy to forgive them for such statements; civic pride is a virtue." In a slightly later novel, similarly centering on a midwestern newspaper editor, author Samuel Hopkins Adams wrote of "a city of two hundred thousand inhabitants, claimed (one hundred and seventy-five thousand allowed by a niggling and suspicious census)."[39] Bartholomew recalled this cultural trend toward civic boosterism when he wrote in correspondence later in his career, "It is especially difficult to recapture . . . the climate in earlier times with respect to population. In the 1920's it was next to impossible to get any city plan commission to agree on a ceiling of future growth." This assumption of population growth lasted until the Depression, when, as Bartholomew wrote, "the concept of any probable future growth was pretty well shattered in the minds of most people."[40] Nonetheless, the optimistic projections of the 1920s brought an interest in zoning to manage this growth, an interest that ironically outlasted the optimism on which it was based.

Finally, communities could sell themselves not just to individuals or families looking for a new home but to other whole communities, as a model for a quality of life. For example, in the plan for Hutchinson, Kansas, Bartholomew explained the town's responsibility to provide for outlying rural areas without the amenities of an "industrial city," whether commercial opportunities, parkland, or additional employment. He wrote:

> Even more than the 25,000 people residing within the corporate limits are concerned in this matter. As many people as live in the city itself make up the population of Reno County alone outside Hutchinson. Its trade territory is enormous, containing many times as many people as the city. For the most part they are wheat farmers and trades people of smaller communities. They come to Hutchinson to enjoy the facilities which only a city of considerable size can support. Hutchinson owes something to this larger population.[41]

At the same time, a town like Hutchinson was served in similar ways by larger regional cities such as Wichita, Kansas City, or Chicago.[42] Zoning, though primarily focusing on the needs of the community supporting the measure, also took into account potential regional growth in area, population, and industrial products. While the problems of industrial environments were recognized, the primacy of urban settings in this era was obviously growing. What remains striking then is not the willingness but the desire for communities to accept the designation of "industrial city." For perhaps industrial city meant not just a community with industry as its economic base, but a city that was actually organized like an industry, one in which each function had its own designated space on the landscape and could be managed in relation to one another. Zoning was one way for communities to achieve this cultural meaning of the term.

THE SINGLE-FAMILY STANDARD

The image of a city with "everything in its place" was a common one in the culture of the early twentieth century. Urban planners were aided in their task of promoting zoning by the popular representations of the era, which often described "zoned" cities, even if not referred to as such. In Sinclair Lewis's *Babbitt*, the title character's morning drive to work showed Zenith to be zoned into residential, commercial, and industrial districts, with further specification of each of these classes. Lewis wrote:

> [Babbitt] admired each district along his familiar route to the office: The bungalows and shrubs and winding irregular driveways of Floral Heights. The one-story shops on Smith Street, a glare of plate-glass and new yellow brick . . . The market gardens in Dutch Hollow, their shanties patched with corrugated iron and stolen doors. Billboards with crimson goddesses nine feet tall advertising cinema films, pipe tobacco, and talcum powder . . . Across the belt of railroad-tracks, factories with high-perched water tanks and tall stacks . . . Then the business center, the thickening darting traffic, the crammed trolleys unloading, and high doorways of marble and polished granite.[43]

That Babbitt "admired" these districts, even those that seemed less than admirable, was also a sign that he admired the very concept of *having* districts, as might many of Lewis's readers.

The zoning code that became Bartholomew's standard developed over the course of the 1920s. Starting with separate use, height, and area regulations, the firm began to coordinate the three aspects of zoning into a series of classes that regulated all three at once; nonetheless, the plans remained fairly simple, usually with a maximum of eleven classes. The geographic distribution of these zones, while certainly varying with the local townscape, did follow general trends. Since most local industry was already coordinated with transportation access, areas along railroads and waterways and on the outskirts of cities were zoned industrial. In addition to the central business district, commercial districts were zoned along major streets radiating from downtown. The sectors in between these major streets were left for residential development. While based on existing conditions, zoning codes regulated unplatted land as well, attempting to regulate future growth and to prevent the juxtaposition of buildings considered uncomplementary in use or size by the planners or their employing civic groups.

Within the broad use classifications, zoning ordinances usually made additional distinctions, particularly within the residential category. One of the hallmarks of zoning ordinances was the creation of residence districts classified by the numbers of families the specific buildings housed, with corresponding regulations for the height of buildings, the area of a lot a building could occupy, and thus the land area per family.[44] Much as the family was seen as a primary unit of consumption of goods, family spaces were a primary unit of the city. At the most basic, this practice might mean splitting single-family homes from multiple-dwelling buildings, but at its most complex it could mean a four-tier residence classification, for single-family homes, two- to four-family dwellings, and different scale apartment complexes. These different types of housing were accompanied by different requirements for building height and population density, with the acceptable measure of area per family dwindling as one went down the residence scale. As a general rule, multifamily dwellings were closer to the downtown, while the outlying areas in the directions opposite industrial development were zoned single-family, with low height restrictions and large requirements for lot size per family. These classifications not only split residence districts off from places of work, but further divided residences, often in terms of social and economic status that was in turn in loose accordance with the types of work done by the people who lived in them. As industrial production increasingly divided types of work from one another, the divisions of the workplace were reflected in the organization of other facets of life, including residential neighborhoods.

The category deemed the highest and best use by planners was a class of single-family homes; as Bartholomew wrote in a plan for Grand Haven, Michigan, "The 'A' Residence district, restricted to single-family dwellings and correlated uses of property, is the highest classification and represents the ultimate ideal in city development which the zoning ordinance is designed to encourage."[45] The single-family district was said to encourage homeownership by the occupants, and exemplified in built form the family unit as the basis of community structure. In the words of the California State Supreme Court in a 1925 decision upholding zoning, "The establishment of single-family residence districts offers inducements not only to the wealthy but to those of moderate means to own their own homes. With ownership comes stability, the welding together of family ties, and better attention to rearing of children."[46] One of the few, but interesting, distinctions between different cities' zoning codes was whether their "A" residence class allowed for only single-family or one- and two-family homes, a difference that revealed the common housing stock already existing in a town. For example, the "A" residence district in San Antonio, Texas, included both one- and two-family dwellings; the explanation was that, especially in areas closest to the central business district, single-family homes were not a big enough return on the investment in land and construction costs.[47] However, a provision for single-family districts was the standard. In either case, larger dwellings, housing over two families, and apartment buildings were always separated into distinct regions of the city by zoning regulations, as were commercial and industrial structures, considered an "undesirable presence" in residential neighborhoods.[48]

The use classifications in zoning codes illustrated one set of definitions of what constituted a community for early twentieth-century citizens. Much of the rhetoric that embroidered the zone plans makes clear that a district of single-family homes was seen as a sanctified space to be protected; such districts were not to be encroached upon by apartment dwellings, by commerce, and certainly not by industry. In a plan for Grand Haven, Michigan, Bartholomew wrote, "The zone plan, by showing appropriate locations for neighborhood commercial groups, will very effectively encourage the proper development of residential neighborhoods. It will prevent the scattering of stores, garages, filling stations and the like, and concentrate these community-serving interests in spots where they can thrive without having a detrimental effect on residential property values."[49] Thus, service to the community was acknowledged but still not deemed worthy of inclusion within a boundary of residential space. The role of these services in residence districts could be contentious, as when the Northwestern Bell Telephone Company fought against zoning in Des Moines, Iowa, because the proposed ordinance would zone out their substations and branch offices from residence districts, while they believed such stations in areas of high usage were necessary to good service.[50]

While separating out commercial and industrial sites that were seen to detract from the residential character of a community, there were a few institutions that obviously were thought to add to that character. Predominant among these institutions were schools and churches, and sometimes libraries, which were allowed with intermingle with single- and two-family structures, while providing places for those families themselves to intermingle. A wider variety of "educational, philanthropic, or eleemosynary" institutions were permitted in multiple-dwelling unit districts, but not single-family districts, perhaps indicating the primacy of the family as a unit over institutions that catered to particular sectors of the population. For example, clubhouses, hotels, and charity organizations were permitted in areas where homes were perceived as smaller and not as able to provide social spaces but were not allowed in single-family residential districts.[51]

While single-family districts were described in terms of their cultural, and even moral, influence, multifamily districts were portrayed as a consequence of economic realities. Apartment districts were increasingly seen as a necessity, as long as they were separated from single-family residence districts. Bartholomew explained in a plan for Des Moines, Iowa, that as central business districts grew, so too would the numbers of people who worked there, and "the cost of providing public utilities, streets, transit facilities and the like" to house these workers at a distance was too high. Land close to the central business district was most sensibly zoned for apartments to house these workers. However, Des Moines also lauded itself for ranking first in the nation in home ownership at the time the report was made, and this trend was certainly encouraged.[52] Apartments were accepted only where they did not "intrude" on single-family residences. As Bartholomew wrote in a plan for Glendale, California, "apartments have appeared here and there, and wherever this has happened in districts of single-family homes, the residential surroundings have been injured. As a result there are now many blocks of attractive and modern homes marred by the intrusion of one or more apartments."[53] Robert Whitten, a Cleveland-based planning and zoning consultant, stated in no uncertain terms: "The apartment house and the one- or two-family house cannot exist side by side."[54] For zone planners and their clients, the best way for apartments to be nonintrusive was to be clustered together, apart from other forms of housing.

The financial situations of urban dwellers both reflected and created other differences between residence classes. Further discussion of the reasons for the spread of apartment buildings was given in a report for Louisville, Kentucky, in which the planners cited the following:

> the changing economical conditions such as the increase in the number of employees of large corporations who are not permanently located, the larger number of families in which both the husband and wife are employed, smaller families, high cost of domestic help, the tendency of elderly people to seek smaller, more convenient quarters after their children are grown, the practice of several single men or women renting an apartment instead of residing in lodging houses, together with the added conveniences and facilities available in modern apartment buildings.[55]

This description shows the cultural impact of the "economical conditions": most notably that living situations were not tied to a nuclear family unit to the extent they were in single-family houses. Whitten summed up a popular view of apartment living, echoing the advocates of homeownership: "The apartment house is very well suited to the housing of adults. It is not well suited to the rearing of children. From the nature of the case, children are a nuisance in an apartment house, and the apartment house is an injury to the children."[56] Different age brackets or wage structures characterized these spaces, resulting in more heterogeneous neighborhoods. This image of apartment living was put forward not only by writers on civic or planning policy, but also in popular literature. Toward the end of Sinclair Lewis's *Babbitt*, the title character carries on a flirtation with not just the young widow Tanis Judique, but her whole circle of friends and their "bohemian" lifestyle. This subset of Zenith society was marked in part by their inhabitance of apartments, strictly separated from Babbitt's family life in the subdivision of Floral Heights.[57]

In addition to these residence classifications, the distinctions between commercial and industrial classes also indicate what the boundaries of community were seen to be. While in later years, the social prescriptions of residence districts would be questioned on the basis of economic and racial segregation, in the early years of zoning, controversy, if it existed at all, arose within the business sector. Commercial zoning had to strike a balance between the projected business needs of a growing population and the hazards of "overzoning" of these spaces. Bartholomew explained:

In the zoning plan it has been the endeavor to supply an amount of commercial frontage that would correspond to the present ratio. Experiences of other cities have shown that if an area is zoned for commercial purposes over and above the amount that approximates the accepted ratios, the stores supplying the necessary frontage will be scattered and portions of the area will remain vacant. No one will wish to use the remaining area for residential purposes, and consequently, property values will depreciate and the land will not yield any financial return. For these reasons great care must be exercised against providing too much area for commercial use.[58]

An attempt was made to establish a standard for how much commercial street frontage per hundred persons a community "should" have. In a report from the early 1930s, Bartholomew claimed that the average ratio of commercial frontage was fifty-five to sixty feet per one hundred persons. This street frontage was to be further divided between about twenty-five feet in the downtown central business district and the remainder in secondary commercial centers located within walking distance of residential districts. One guideline was the placement of small commercial districts so that all residents would be within walking distance of a food market.[59]

In the zoning plans completed by HBA through the 1920s, as in many American townscapes, the "downtown" or central business district was zoned commercial, and industrial districts were more likely to be found along waterways, along railroad lines, and generally on the outskirts of the geographical boundaries of the town or city. But some of the distinctions in the uses allowed in these two districts were subtle. For example, a bakery with fewer than five bakers was deemed commercial, whereas one with more than five bakers was considered light industry. Thus, the small-scale business whose market could ostensibly be the local community and could viably sell all their products there was accepted in the commercial heart of the city. The firm that produced a supply of goods exceeding local demand, that was producing for some sort of "export" outside the community, was deemed industrial and relegated to physical points outside of the community center. The industrial site as a place of work was in a less central and accessible location than the commercial site as a place of distribution of goods and services. While most of the rhetoric surrounding the placement of industrial sites centered on either the convenience of transport or the protection of residence districts from pollution, the effect was also this removal of industrial work. One way to correct for this separation was by linking areas with appropriately placed transit systems, running inexpensively enough for daily use by workers. Though the achievement of this ideal might be questioned, zoning proponents lauded the place of zoning in a larger comprehensive plan to coordinate such needs.[60]

While the purpose of zoning was usually stated in terms of separating seemingly incompatible features of urban life, it also meant a concentration of similar types within the zones. District boundaries not only zoned out difference, but also zoned in homogeneity. In social terms this situation could mean groupings of dwellings along the lines of economics, occupational groups, or family structure. In aesthetic terms, it could mean an enclave unified at the least by building height and setback line, and at the most by architectural style. Bartholomew clearly considered uniformity in architecture to be a positive trait to a streetscape, particularly in residence districts. One way to achieve this uniformity was by separating residential and commercial spaces, with their differing architectural types. Thus, it was not just that commerce was unseemly in a residential neighborhood, but that the presence of buildings with storefronts extended out to the street line ruined the effect of a residential streetscape. In Bartholomew's opinion, this "scattering of stores promiscuously . . . hurt the appearance of a good many residence streets," as well as the city as a whole. Bartholomew recommended the concentration of local neighborhood stores into groupings at the intersections of larger streets that serve the neighborhood; he wrote, "Their design is being studied and many real estate promoters are building structures of uniform type at such points. When thus constructed they have architectural merit and become a credit to the neighborhood which they serve."[61]

Concentration of similar architectural types was an aesthetic goal of zoning. The Pittsburgh Citizens Committee on City Planning issued a cartoon to illustrate the need for separation among architectural types. Personifying the buildings as standing on a street, the artist depicted a happy skyscraper trying to get in line with unhappy houses, a stone-faced grocery store, and a garage so lost in its own smoke that it could not emote; "General Efficiency" rode by them on horseback, studying his battle plan of zoning.[62] Even within residence districts Bartholomew felt compelled to argue for neighborhood cohesion, perhaps recognizing that architecture could both reflect and influence a homogeneous grouping of citizens. As he wrote in one plan, "the mixture of architectural styles and the haphazard placing of buildings of all sizes along the same street is responsible for the disturbing effect found on

some streets . . . this is a matter that is subject to no control other than public taste."[63] Many of his plans included examples of how homeowners could
comply with the zoning regulations in their district and how the "typical"
house lot should be laid out. Thus, zoning would not only regulate the use
of land within a given community, but also guide or suggest specifically how
building on that lot should occur, ensuring the aesthetic unity that planners
of the day favored. A unified street façade would represent the shared standard of living of those who lived in a given community.

   While aspiring to the financial success and recreational and cultural opportunities of urban areas, Americans were also wary of the problems they
perceived in large cities. Zoning, particularly as one phase of a comprehensive plan, promised a way to reap that success without causing the blight
often associated with industry, and because of that promise was adopted at
an overwhelming rate in all areas of the country. Debates on whether that
promise was ever realized are, of course, ongoing, with proponents and
detractors of the concept going head to head not only with one another, but
also with those who say that zoning has not made a bit of difference in
American urban development.[64] Beyond its impact in specific places, however, zoning has significance as a national movement. Zoning codes were
attempts by planners and the municipal and civic groups that hired them to
define communities and the relations within and between them. These
groups envisioned a balance of economic and cultural progress and social
stability that they wanted to embed in the very landscape of their hometowns.

PACKAGING THE PLAN

The rapid acceptance of zoning across the country suggests that advocates
were particularly successful in their explanations of the necessity of the
measure. It is difficult from an early twenty-first-century perspective that
takes zoning as a starting point for much urban development to remember
that the regulation of private property was a radical idea in the early twentieth century. Planning advocates were careful to explain the benefits of
their work and situate their efforts in larger national trends, particularly the
ideology of progressivism. Through urban planning, the Progressive Era
ideal of reform took on its most literal meaning; planners would "re-form"
the physical space of the city to create what they perceived to be better living and working environments. Zoning regulations were most effective

when placed in the context of comprehensive city plans. These comprehensive plans provided the "packaging" for zone plans, and, in turn, were "sold" to the public through a variety of public education campaigns.

In order to carry out reforms in a spatial sense, Bartholomew insisted that city planning had to be an interdisciplinary endeavor. Calling himself a "city plan engineer," he hired a landscape architect and architect to round out his own expertise. Bartholomew contributed to one of the early urban planning programs, teaching at the University of Illinois as a professor of civic design. He began teaching in 1918, filling a spot recently vacated by the death of Charles Mulford Robinson, the prolific writer and theorist of civic art. Robinson seems best remembered for his attention to "art" and Bartholomew certainly held onto that aspect of the profession, considering city planning to be both a science and an art. However, Bartholomew bristled at the idea that what he was doing was only about beautification or surface details and sought to distance himself from the form of planning that had been dubbed the City Beautiful movement.[65] He strove to affect the very structure of the city or town through designs for districts or zones, well-apportioned and related to one another. In other words, planning was not a luxury, but a necessity for the continued success of urban life.

Still, early in his career, Bartholomew recognized that zoning would work best as part of a larger, comprehensive plan. Trying to consult solely on zoning plans in Omaha, Detroit, and Washington, D.C., he found the planning measure ineffective without the support that a larger plan could garner.[66] Bartholomew recognized the importance of weaving a zone plan into a larger comprehensive plan for growth, and that this comprehensive plan must include those details that were the hallmarks of city beautiful planning: civic centers, attractive boulevards and carefully constructed vistas, and parks. Perhaps the difference between the two approaches was not in fact in the elements of the plans but in the degree of cohesion in which they were put together. Bartholomew quickly arrived at a template for his comprehensive plans: a six-part program including a major street plan, a transit plan, a transportation plan, public recreation, civic design or appearance, and zoning. This program was shared broadly by those concerned with city planning; *The American City* used this same enumeration to explain "What City Planning Is" in 1920.[67]

Bartholomew explained zoning in the context of broader plans: "It is the whole plan that counts, and to consider streets, transit, transportation, recreation or the creation of districts for industry, commerce or residence without considering its relation to the others, is to ignore the basis upon which the entire plan is based and to fail to grasp the full purport of the city plan."[68] Each part of the comprehensive plan was interwoven with the zone plan, both supporting and being supported by it. Zoning was a tool for managing the other five constituent parts of the comprehensive plan. Just as the idea of zoning spread from city to city across the country, so too did the arrangement of streets, transportation, transit, recreation facilities, and civic beautification projects. The parts that made up the whole of the city plan became standardized and contributed to a shared image of the American city.

Zoning provided a form of oversight for the other areas of planning. It supplied a legally binding section of the plan, but the other parts sometimes served to make the regulations more palatable. Popular projects such as park and playground improvements were used to "sell" the importance of urban planning and its more prosaic component of zoning. However, the importance of placing zoning in a larger context was not just a public relations ploy. The broader comprehensive plan, adopted by much of the urban planning field, was a necessary measure to uphold the legality of zoning, particularly after the 1926 U.S. Supreme Court decision in *Euclid v. Ambler*.[69] As the concept of a city's regulation of the uses of private property was challenged, police power was upheld only if "reasonable," and part of the proof of reasonability was having a definite plan for the growth of the city that directed the drawing of district boundaries. The comprehensive plan was thought to safeguard against zoning ordinances that favored specific economic interests within the community. State enabling legislation for zoning often made the larger envelope of a comprehensive plan a necessity. The subsections of the comprehensive plan were usually drafted one at a time, and released for comments from the local commission, relevant departments of the municipal government, and other interested parties. Then, after revisions were made, the six sections—major streets, transit, transportation, parks and recreation, civic beauty, and zoning—were compiled to produce a final plan.

Bartholomew, like many of his colleagues, started his reports with the major street plan. This vision for the means of distribution of people and goods throughout the community would become the basis for all other planning. Bartholomew and his associates studied the existing street patterns and traffic counts and tried to ascertain methods by which traffic could circulate more efficiently. The street plan became the basis not only for the transit and transportation plans but also the recreation plans, as boulevards and parkways had to be coordinated with the street design. And finally the street plan became the basis for creating zoning districts. Bartholomew wrote in his plan for Grand Haven, Michigan, in 1923:

> The plan of streets and the zone plan cannot be considered separate and distinct items. They are closely related. The successful application of one depends very greatly upon the execution of the other. Neither involves expensive improvements or changes in things as they are. They are forward-looking measures. They are preventative. Their purpose is to make Grand Haven a more attractive city to industries, to business, to the home owner, and to the summer residents.[70]

While some early zoning codes assigned restrictions to sides of streets, or particular blocks thereof, HBA-designed codes had designations for each lot in a city's street system, with broad districts bounded by the streets themselves.

Much as the zoning ordinances considered commercial property an "intrusion" in residential districts, the street plan saw certain types of traffic as suited to different types of areas. Describing the small town of Anchorage, Kentucky, as "distinctly residential in character," Bartholomew recommended following his scheme for a major street plan that fit into the surrounding Louisville regional highway plan in order to preserve that character; he wrote, "Unless certain properly located streets are designed to accommodate fast moving and heavy traffic, quiet residential streets will likely be usurped by vehicles having no occasion in the neighborhood."[71] In other areas, Bartholomew supported business growth through zoning. In Hutchinson, Kansas, he noted that most of the wide streets were directed east-west, pushing virtually all north-south traffic onto one street, Main Street, which in turn determined the commercial area of the town. The business district was confined to one long strip, a situation Bartholomew deemed "by no means a healthy sign in a thriving city like Hutchinson."[72] A reworking of the street system and the encouragement of a broader business district through commercial zoning thus went hand in hand. Both residential and commercial areas were positive developments, but best if separated with appropriate traffic patterns for each. Zoning codified the spatial separation of work and leisure spaces that contributed to other aspects of the standard of living.

Bartholomew presented a scheme of three types of streets: radials, major through streets, and purely local streets, which should be narrow for residential and local commercial uses. His description of this hierarchy showed the way it was intended to correlate with the zone plan:

> The principal radial streets are those affording direct short-line connections between the business district and the several residential and industrial districts . . . The secondary major streets are those affording direct crosstown connection between different parts of the city. The minor streets are those used for residential or industrial purposes where little or no through traffic is expected, such traffic as is accommodated originating chiefly upon the minor street itself.[73]

Bartholomew's work in the late 1910s and 1920s had special resonance, as he and so many of his contemporaries struggled to determine the role of the private automobile in cities. Bartholomew seemed to accept that the car was there to stay, and worked to accommodate increased vehicular traffic. Nonetheless, in his correlation of street capacity with use districts, he clearly anticipated the journey to work (at least industrial work) taking place by streetcar, rather than private automobile.

Transit plans dealt with local circulation issues. For the most part, the central focus of these plans was the streetcar system, though as the 1920s progressed, the firm devoted more energy to the role of buses in the overall transit system. While acknowledging the growing role of the private automobile, planners also had to admit that the streetcar still carried the vast majority of riders each day while causing only a small percentage of traffic. Circulation patterns had to fit the existing travel patterns, provide access to places of work and leisure, be evenly distributed for access from all parts of a community, and allow for the expansion of the inhabited parts of a community. Buses were thought of as most useful for extensions of routes otherwise served by streetcars, in order to accommodate expansion at a lower rate of investment. Bus routes that competed with streetcars were discouraged, as were multiple competing streetcar routes. Again the transit plan and the zone plan were linked; transit services made the expansion of residential districts possible, while the establishment of the zone plan would make clear where new lines would best serve the growing population.[74]

Transportation plans dealt with the interaction between municipal travel patterns and intercity transport, primarily the railroads, though in some places waterways. One of the big issues for towns served by multiple railroads was trying to get those carriers to coordinate, at the very least on a

Union Station, and preferably on lines and yards. Bartholomew also focused on the elimination of grade crossings; though expensive, increasingly it was deemed necessary for the safety and beauty of cities and towns. The zone plan served as a guide in these investments. For example, the elimination of grade crossings was most important in or near residential and commercial districts, and new train stations ideally would be incorporated into the downtown civic center.

The timing of this phase of urban planning was such that for virtually all the towns that HBA worked in, the railroad was already a given that the planners had to incorporate into their designs. As a general rule, areas traversed and served by the railroad became logical sites for industrial or unrestricted districts in the zone plan. In the plan for Grand Rapids, Michigan, Bartholomew explained the natural link between railroads and industrial districts as follows: "Along the railroads and on the large areas adjacent have been provided districts for industry—heavy or unrestricted industry. Within these districts can be located those factories which may be considered objectionable because of various reasons and such large plants as need yards for material storage which might prove dangerous in built-up neighborhoods, and those industries which need switching facilities and special loading devices."[75] Similar concerns were applied to waterfront areas in cities that had industrial growth along waterways. These transportation systems effectively became barriers between industrial districts and areas reserved for less intensive, more picturesque uses.

In trying to distance his own form of city planning from the maligned City Beautiful movement, Bartholomew had to be particularly careful in his descriptions of parks and aesthetic improvements to the city, the two main purviews for which the earlier movement was known. He broadened the notion of park planning to encompass recreation systems, and declared these to be a necessary part of any community. In a plan for Utica, New York, Bartholomew stated:

> It was not long ago that parks here were generally opposed by the people on the ground that they were luxuries, decorative features too expensive for the city to have . . . It is obvious, however, that old prejudices against parks and playgrounds have practically disappeared. There is a widespread realization of the fact that open spaces and grounds for recreation are required in the modern city. They render a health-building, nerve-restoring, ameliorating service that is no less valuable to city-dwellers than the service performed by pavements, street lights, water supplies and similar necessities.[76]

Bartholomew based his recreation plans on classifications of a community's population, categorized by age. He believed that there should be a variety of recreation facilities corresponding to the needs of these different groups of the population. Just as material objects and certain types of buildings made the transition from luxury items to necessities, Bartholomew classified these recreation areas as "necessities."

The park plans were important to the overall comprehensive plan, including the zoning plan, because they demarcated potential future growth for municipally owned park land, which was coordinated with other community needs through the zone plan. For example, if plans for a large-scale park were in place, that reserve of land could be placed so that it would not abut an industrial district. Bartholomew's recreation schemes built from Frederick Law Olmsted's notions of park systems.[77] They included community centers, supervised playgrounds, ball fields for organized sports, large pleasure gardens and parkways, and pleasure drives linking the other sites. Bartholomew looked to links with other municipal institutions, particularly the school system; playgrounds, ball fields, and sometimes community centers were seen as logical extensions of the use of school grounds. These classifications were tied to the zone plan, as Bartholomew saw a particular need for play space in areas with higher population density. He wrote, in rhetoric typical of the Progressive Era, "Public recreation facilities are necessities in the modern city; the thickly-built-up neighborhood is full of play impulses demanding outlet . . . This restraint of natural play desires cannot but effect the efficiency of the city as a living, producing, marketing organism."[78] Thus, availability of public recreation sites was particularly important in multi-family residence districts. Recreation spaces could also serve as a public influence on groundskeeping, plantings, and general upkeep in otherwise privately tended districts.

In addition to a general scheme for parks and other recreation facilities, HBA usually included in comprehensive plans more detailed suggestions for beautification of the city or town's physical plant. Bartholomew explained the relation between the overall design of the city structure through zoning and the smaller points of civic beautification. He wrote of the results of the comprehensive plan, including zoning:

> there will result greater uniformity of development and a more balanced type of growth which, in itself, will exemplify one of the primary essentials of good design—the adaptation of form to function. In addition, however, there are certain phases that should receive special attention, such as the grouping of

public buildings (civic center) at a strategic location; the regulation of poles and wires, signs and billboards; and a system of street tree planting. When these are properly done, the city's appearance is greatly improved. An attractive city not only stimulates civic pride but it also has a direct value in drawing growth and in brightening the municipality's good name among cities.[79]

In sections entitled "Civic Art" or "The City's Appearance," Bartholomew and his associates made suggestions for everything ranging from the burying of wires to the regulation of signage to plantings to war memorials. This last consideration arose increasingly in the wake of World War I; Bartholomew advised how best the progressive city might commemorate the Great War. However, in these arenas of recreation and civic art, the firm did not contract for the actual carrying out of such plans but rather advised on suitable designs and sites. Bartholomew believed that his plans could be successfully adopted only with the support of local architectural, landscape, and engineering firms, and did not want to compete with them for the implementation of his plans. Bartholomew's "product" was an image for the city, a plan for its development. It would be up to others to sell the actual services needed to carry through this image.

In all parts of the comprehensive plan, there was an acknowledgment that private property contributed to the overall impression of the city, as much as the physical well-being of the city had an impact on individual owners and dwellers. In sections of plans dedicated to the civic art or appearance of a town, planners began broadening their prescriptions from those that included only public spaces such as civic centers and memorials and started advocating for proper care of lots surrounding homes, stores, and even factories. The influence of larger institutions on smaller property owners was noted, for example, in the case of Champaign, Illinois, where the University of Illinois was credited with providing a model for homeowners on how to plan "a good lawn and a bit of planting." Whether in the outward appearance of the city or its overall structure as determined by zone plans, "improving the city's appearance is a matter of collective responsibility. City and county officials can only do certain things. In the main they can go no farther, however, than the people wish them to go."[80] In his plan for Binghamton, New York, Bartholomew stated that approximately 75 percent of any city's geographic area was privately owned, and that in order to make a city attractive in the broadest sense of the term, the owners of that bulk of the property must be committed to the city's overall well-being.[81]

Public education campaigns were used to garner support for planning and zoning; the responsibilities of the planners in these campaigns were often laid out in their contracts with the community. For example, HBA's contract with Cedar Rapids called for "a series of final maps and drawings in exhibition form to be used for educational purposes" in addition to the plan itself.[82] The contracts also often stipulated the final printing of the report as an attractive, well-bound book that could be broadly distributed to community members. Both the design and the language of these plans were intended to persuade the audience of residents of the importance of the proposed changes and suggestions. For example, *The Lansing Plan* showed close attention to eye-catching design; who could resist the charming children seemingly asking for recreation areas protected from industrial pollution? The plan for Hutchinson, Kansas, was illustrative of the dramatic writing that could be included to rally public interest; the report opened with the description of Hutchinson's origins: "Less than fifty years ago bleached buffalo bones and horns driven in the sand marked the streets of Hutchinson . . . A long line of stakes disappeared eastward and westward from the flat, sandy site, however, and for those who knew held the chief promise of the future city. These stakes marked the line of the new Santa Fe Railroad." The implication was that through city planning and zoning measures, residents, at least "those who knew," could have the same influence on the future of the town as its founder, C. C. Hutchinson.[83] These educational materials were distributed to all age groups, including school children, as in Evansville, Indiana, where a Planning Primer was distributed to eighth grade and high school civics classes, along with the preliminary reports that Bartholomew's team produced.[84]

Beyond preparing these printed materials, Bartholomew and his staff gave dozens of public talks and attended community meetings devoted to civic improvement. Those appearances were well-covered by the local press, lending Harland Bartholomew authority as an "expert." For example, when Bartholomew visited the Madison, Wisconsin Kiwanis Club, the *Wisconsin State Journal* announced the talk of the "Planning Expert"; similarly, a front-page headline in the *Des Moines Register* referred to him as "Zoning Expert."[85] Part of Bartholomew's task was to act as a salesman for his firm; though HBA did not advertise in the sense of placing ads in print media, the firm certainly did broadcast in other ways. As Bartholomew traveled from town to town on business, he also gave speeches to national meetings and published articles in periodicals ranging from *The American City* to *Forbes* to *Independent Woman;* these and other publications also covered his projects.[86] Though perhaps not buying advertising space, Bartholomew was actively engaged in publicity, for not only his firm but also the concepts of comprehensive planning and zoning.

Many of the facets of comprehensive planning would eventually require funding; this money could be raised most easily by bond issues, and thus needed citizen approval. The campaigns to educate the residents of the town were also seen as important in keeping community leaders, particularly elected officials, engaged in the process. Community support would create electoral pressure, ensuring that the plans would move on to the implementation stage.[87] The zoning ordinance needed a different type of compliance; the ordinance needed to be available to public comment as part of the process of declaring it a reasonable exercise of the police power. As part of the zoning process in Chattanooga, Tennessee, the *Chattanooga Daily Times* announced, "Members of the city commission yesterday expressed the hope all citizens interested would attend the next meeting and if displeased with any provision discuss the question with the commission so that dissatisfaction in the future may be reduced to a minimum."[88] The public comment period made legal contestation of zoning less likely.

Glendale, California's lengthy process of public comment exemplifies the establishment of zoning ordinances across the country. After HBA drew up the zoning ordinance, it was published in the local newspaper with a request for petitions and comments about it. A week later, four public hearings were held in the four different quadrants of the city to provide an opportunity for petitioners to present their views. For the town of Glendale, HBA had suggested limiting space allocated to business districts and recommended rezoning some of these areas as apartment districts. The current owners would be able to keep their stores there but in the future the properties would be reclassified as residential, albeit a residential use that still afforded an investment opportunity. Nonetheless, the reclassifying of areas that were traditionally business areas incited the most public outcry. The City Planning Commission (CPC) gathered letters and petitions signed by 798 Glendale residents (out of a population numbering 13,576 in 1920); 251 of these made "general criticisms but no specific requests," 409 made "definite requests for changes and were sustained," and 138 made requests which were denied. The CPC was quick to point out that these figures meant that 75 percent of those who asked for specific changes were granted those requests.

Thus, in presenting the revised ordinance to the Glendale City Council for approval, the CPC acknowledged the influence of public sentiment:

> In view of this attitude of property owners we have revised our district plan and are recommending that practically all the property now zoned for business be retained, not for the reason that we believe it to be to the best interest of the property owners and the city, but because of the insistent demand of the property owners.
>
> We think it fair however to state that the original plan as submitted by Harland Bartholomew and Associates was undoubtedly a scientifically and economically sound method for the zoning of our city . . . in making such changes we do not wish such action to be construed as any disagreement with their judgment which is based upon experience in preparing zoning plans for over forty cities in all parts of the country.[89]

The Glendale process showed that compromises were often necessary for zoning ordinances to be passed; scientific planning could only go so far in the face of the citizenry. Clearly the Glendale CPC preferred that these changes be made rather than face an in-court battle. Even with precedent in favor of municipal zoning, the expensive process that could shake public support for other parts of the city plan was to be avoided. The Glendale example also exemplified the extent to which disagreement over a proposed zoning ordinance occurred within the business community, not between the managerial class of the planning and zoning commissions and other socioeconomic sectors. The impetus for and oversight of urban planning usually originated within this managerial and professional community.

COMMUNITIES AS CONSUMERS

To say that HBA's plans for a wide variety of American cities and towns were remarkably similar is not an indictment of the firm. Bartholomew not only used city managers, planning commissioners, and local bankers as references for his work, but also sent copies of past plans to prospective clients, making clear what "product" was being sold. The similarities were more a comment on the desires of these clients—the civic groups and municipal commissions for whom they worked—to structure their cities in similar ways. The process of comprehensive planning and zoning in American cities and towns often originated with a small group of local citizens, usually drawn from business and professional sectors of the city. Some form of citizens' committee regarding city planning, whether its own entity or under the auspices of a local civic organization or chamber of commerce, began to drum up support for civic improvement. This support provided the impetus for government officials to become engaged in the process. Bartholomew virtually insisted on having some sort of civic body in place to ensure the support of local citizens. If the push for city planning had not started with such a group, but rather directly with the municipal government, he recommended the formation of one.

The function of such a group was initially to promote the ideas of comprehensive planning and zoning within the community and sometimes went so far as to hire an outside consultant. Bartholomew defined the role of the citizens' committee: "to stimulate public interest in the importance of city planning, the numerous advantages that would accrue from its practice, and to show what other cities have done. This is a preliminary process of public education. It is usually necessary in order to stimulate and justify recognition of the subject by the city government." For example, the Citizens' City Planning Committee originally hired Bartholomew for his permanent job in St. Louis, and only after municipal funds were appropriated did he become a city employee. While an official municipal commission on city planning usually replaced the citizens' committee, the two groups occasionally coexisted, with the citizens' committee acting in an advocacy and public relations role.[90]

One of the seeming ironies of the move to include private property within the purview of urban planning through zoning is that it occurred simultaneously with the shift to planning being undertaken by municipal entities rather than, or in addition to, private civic or commercial groups. Prior to zoning, private citizens could regulate one another only through mutual agreements, such as restrictive covenants. The novelist Kathleen Norris summed up the mixed feelings about restrictions on private property in her 1917 work, *Undertow*. As her protagonists, Nancy and Bert Bradley look for a home, they receive a lesson in contemporary real estate practice:

> It was no use, the agents told Nancy, to think about a pretty, shabby, old farmhouse, for those had been snapped up. If she found one, it would be a foolish investment, because it probably would be surrounded by unrestricted property. Restrictions were great things, and all developments had them in large or small degree. There were developments that obliged the purchaser of land to submit his building plans to a committee, before he could build.

Nancy laughed that she shouldn't care for *that*. And when restrictions interfered with her plans she very vigorously opposed them. She told Bert that she would not consider places that did not allow fences, and chickens, and dogs.[91]

While Nancy chafes at the thought of rules governing her own property, the real estate agents have already seen the wave of the future and advocate restrictions, even if only within a specific development, in order to protect property investments.

These local restrictions, however, were not proving to be strong enough deterrents for larger-scale situations, such as the encroachment of industry on housing. Charles M. Fassett, who had served as both mayor and head of the chamber of commerce of Spokane, Washington, wrote:

> The right of a citizen to do what he will with his own property is gradually yielding to the larger right of the community. Private property in city land is not so sacred as it used to be . . . Now we are ready to go another step, in saying that the use made of land shall be so regulated that it shall not infringe a neighbor's right of usage, or the common interests of the community . . . Zoning is the latest expression of the desire to make a city more livable for all its inhabitants by the reasonable application of a wholesome law.[92]

As the city moved toward the acceptance of zoning as a legitimate planning measure, the welfare of the community was to be placed above the rights of the individual.[93] The city government could speak to the importance of community compliance and issues of communal good in a way that one subset of that community could not. Only a governing body had the power to have all citizens comply with the ideas of planning codified by the zoning ordinances. Plans were not effective if they existed solely on paper; only the city had the ability to coordinate all the necessary parties and the regulatory and financial power to implement the plans.

Local officials and citizens alike recognized that the most expensive areas to "plan" were those that in fact need to be "replanned," particularly where both municipal and private developments needed adjustments in order to accommodate larger schemes. For example, in order to widen a street, the city would impinge on private ownership but its doing so would ultimately benefit the public at large.[94] The sooner a comprehensive plan and a zoning ordinance were adopted, the more efficiently and economically urban order could be established, another reason why smaller cities were at an advantage in the city planning process. An editorial in the *Chattanooga Daily Times* in

1927 compared the city's own progress in urban planning to that of Chicago, stating, "Chattanooga is more fortunate than Chicago in that it has begun to give attention to its development . . . it will cost a great deal more to correct undesirable growth in the future than it would cost to prevent it by proper regulation and direction now while the future city is 'forming.'" Planning in a small town or city was seen as a "big opportunity," but only if both municipal officers and a corps of concerned citizens were behind the effort.[95]

While many of the first comprehensive plans drawn up in the United States were supported by private groups, perhaps best known in the Commercial Club of Chicago's support of Daniel Burnham's work there, the types of plans that Bartholomew created would eventually depend on municipal support for their implementation. Bartholomew believed in the need for municipal control, writing, "The ineffectiveness of private restrictions to insure stability of growth is well known. Only through public control of a city's growth by adherence to an intelligent and reasonable city plan can the future of the community's welfare be insured."[96] Though Bartholomew conceived of zoning as a design tool, at the same time he recognized the need for its legal status; if private property was to be regulated on a large scale, those regulations needed to be effective. Thus even when he contracted with private planning groups, Bartholomew advocated for and advised on the ways to engage in planning at a municipal level. Lawyer Edward Bassett wrote of a city plan: "It is not only made *for* the city and *of* the city, but it is made *by* the city. Private individuals as such cannot make it or change it or end it."[97] While these municipal plans needed cooperation to be drafted, they could also carry much stronger power once implemented.

In order for a municipality to enact a zoning ordinance, however, it needed to secure legislative authority to do that from its state government. In some places, zoning ordinances preceded these state measures, but then were at much greater risk of being contested. As explained by Bartholomew in a plan for South Bend, Indiana, produced just after Indiana passed its enabling legislation in 1921,

> Our legislatures have generally been reluctant to equip cities with regulatory measures in city building unless the need for such was clearly evident and in the interests of the community as a whole. The continued and unprecedented growth of American cities is constantly bringing about new social and economic problems, the solution of which requires broader community powers.

This our legislatures and courts have come to recognize and within the last decade the majority of states have enacted various city planning laws.[98]

Zoning enabling legislation affirmed that zoning was a legitimate use of the police power, just as other nuisance and public health and safety regulations were. The zoning legislation was in itself an impetus to comprehensive planning, as having a plan in place was one way to prove the "reasonableness" by which zoning cases were tested. Many of Bartholomew's comprehensive plans mention the achievement of state enabling legislation as one prod to their work.[99]

While several states passed enabling legislation of their own design before this point, in 1924 the federal government took a role in the process, by issuing model legislation for those enabling acts. The Standard State Zoning Enabling Legislation was followed by the Standard Town Planning Enabling Legislation in 1927. Thus, the impetus toward zoning had a national endorsement from the secretary of commerce and later president Herbert Hoover. The nation's foremost engineer and manager set the Commerce Department to the task of issuing and endorsing the model enabling legislation that would allow cities to engage in zoning and comprehensive planning. The Commerce Department continued to pave the way for zoning codes by issuing informational pamphlets and other public education materials. The department also kept track of its success. It was constantly charting the growth of the planning and zoning movements, and its statistics then found their way back into planners' reports, adding further justification and assurance to communities engaging in the practice. Several of Bartholomew's early reports quote Hoover or mention information taken from the Commerce Department handbooks.[100] In these ways a national model was established from which zoning ordinances could be easily adapted.

At first, government involvement in planning and zoning might mean the local city council or board of aldermen, until legislation was passed to authorize a city planning commission. For example, in Lansing, Michigan, the City Council hired Bartholomew but then also appointed a commission to be "constantly in consultation" with him.[101] The CPC was not necessarily to be an administrative part of the government but rather an advisory one, and one that could coordinate the needs of other parts of the city government affected by city planning. The commission needed to coordinate not only with the planning consultant, but also with the various arms of the municipal government involved in planning, such as the public works department and the parks department. In the words of Bartholomew, "One of the greatest obstacles to extensive result-getting in city planning is that it involves cooperation of numerous city departments. City planning is of such magnitude and ramification that it cannot be the sole function of a single governmental agency . . . The city plan commission should indeed be the place in the city government where all policies with respect to directing physical growth should be determined upon."[102] In some states, zoning enabling legislation preceded legislation to authorize planning commissions, meaning a series of commissions working with the planner. In Des Moines, in accordance with the Iowa State Zoning Enabling Legislation of 1923, a zoning commission was appointed. Although Iowa did not pass legislation authorizing a planning commission until 1926, the original zoning commission had already contracted with HBA for a full-scale comprehensive plan, recognizing that without it a zoning code could not be prepared effectively. The work of the Zoning Commission was passed on to the City Planning and Zoning Commission when the latter group was formed in 1926.[103]

Once enabling legislation was passed for its creation, the CPC usually was the arm of the municipal government that hired consultants to produce a city plan, and worked with them throughout the process to secure needed information and build public support. Plans for Evansville, Illinois, stated clearly what the local commission could and could not do in accordance with state legislation passed in 1921:

> the primary duty of the City Plan Commission is to anticipate the future expansion of Evansville, to plan a larger, better city. It cannot directly involve the city in additional expense, cannot issue bonds, cannot raise taxes. It can only act as an impartial investigator of the effect of the physical structure of the city upon the health, comfort and well-being of its citizens. It can only advise and recommend and urge the officials elected by the people themselves to make timely improvements.[104]

The planning commission was also the body that would oversee the actual implementation of the plan. Advocating for the creation of a permanent city planning commission in Grand Rapids, Michigan, the sitting board argued that if they were not made a permanent municipal entity, the planning and zoning project "might as well be dropped right now."[105] Although these commissions were structured somewhat differently from place to place, they often had a few slots designated by role, such as representatives from the park, public works, or school board, and other slots appointed by the mayor from the local citizenry for their interest and dedication to the issue.[106] Recognizing that both the municipality itself and the enthusiasm of its citizens played vital roles in achieving the adoption of comprehensive plans, Bartholomew quoted in a plan for South Bend, "As has well been said 'A city is as progressive as its leading citizens.'"[107]

The city planning commissions were not only municipal entities, but also collections of individuals, whose own ideas about planning and zoning could be influential. Bartholomew acknowledged the uniform work that his clients were seeking in a letter to his biographer late in his career; he wrote:

> I cannot emphasize too much the fact that I was not at complete liberty to introduce unusual new ideas and concepts in city planning, nor were the city plans produced exclusively my own work. We made a practice of having members of the city plan commissions participate extensively in the preparation of the comprehensive plan. I am not trying to offer excuses but I am merely endeavoring to say that the technical level of most plans was limited to what we could get the members of planning commissions to accept. Since this was such a new field, we seldom found a commission which was willing to venture far from traditional habits and trends. Occasionally we would find an individual member of a commission who was venturesome but this was the exception rather than the rule.[108]

These commission members, communicating with one another to disseminate the "traditional habits and trends," were, as a general rule, members of the burgeoning middle classes. Eldridge Lovelace, a longtime principal with HBA who joined the firm in 1935 but has researched its earlier work extensively, recalled that the citizens most interested in planning were usually business managers and members of the professions.[109] Although there were certainly exceptions, it does appear that the majority of city planning commission members were of the professional-managerial class.

The commissions were made up of representatives of professional groups whose expertise or local influence would aid the work of the group: newspaper editors, attorneys, architects, engineers, and managers of local commercial and industrial ventures. Two professional groups were overwhelmingly represented: real estate and insurance agents, and local bankers, whose own businesses would be directly affected by their hometown's physical development and population growth.[110] The commissioners were most often men, though occasionally the wife or daughter of a local professional served as well. The board members were clearly well-respected figures in the community, the kinds of persons listed in boldface type in their local directories, but they were not necessarily the most wealthy or largest employers; as a general rule, there were many more vice presidents of local firms than presidents. Two typical boards were that of Des Moines, Iowa's Zoning Commission, whose members included two realtors, a construction company president, the general manager of a local dairy, and the manager of a local newspaper, and South Bend, Indiana's City Planning Commission, whose forces included the head of the local Studebaker plant, an architect, an attorney, a realtor, and an insurance agent, several of whom were also officers of local banks and savings and loans associations.[111]

These early commissions, often the first appointments made after a state passed legislation allowing for such municipal groups to exist, were the boards that hired planners such as Bartholomew, and then worked with them, particularly in areas of public relations. In the words of Miriam Ross, secretary for the Division of Housing and Town Planning for the Massachusetts Department of Public Welfare, wrote, "The work of the city planning commission is three-fold—planning, advising, and selling the plan."[112] The groups worked with the local press to encourage coverage of the planners' work, reprinting of maps and plans, and editorials in support of planning and zoning. As St. Louis planning advocate Walter Stevens stated to the National Conference on City Planning in 1912, there was an understanding in the press that action was needed: "We have all the papers in the city with us and following up the matter so closely that they are insisting that we shall have something beside plazas on paper."[113] The planning commissions publicized the important of planning and zoning in other ways as well. For example, in Grand Rapids, Michigan, the CPC sponsored a booth at the "City Show," a municipal fair highlighting the work of the local government. Or a commission might schedule screenings of films such as *Growing Pains,* produced by the Civic Film Service of New York City, which explained and advocated for zoning.[114]

Zoning provided both a process, arranging daily life in a city, and a product, an image of urban life. The process was to be managed; the product was to be sold. These relations of managing and selling defined communications between professional planners, planning commissions, municipal governments, citizens, and cities as a whole. City planners sold their services to civic groups and commissions in order to create plans; their work encompassed both a process of analysis and the actual planning report, with its maps and written descriptions of suggestions for the future. These groups in turn sold the plans to their constituents, in order to form an image of the city as a community that safeguarded its residential areas while encouraging industrial, and economic, growth. At the same time, the commissions had to sell the entire concept of planning and zoning to municipal governments and state legislatures in order to ensure that the plans could be legally codified. While garnering these two levels of support, the commissions managed the planning and zoning process, and thus the growth of their home communities, by coordinating the hired planners and the different sectors of the local government that were affected. Finally, the city as a whole, through its municipal government, local civic groups, and individual citizens, sold the urban image to industry and potential residents in order to build a bigger and more prosperous city.

The popular novelist Booth Tarkington laid bare this push for progress in his 1918 Pulitzer Prize-winning work, *The Magnificent Ambersons,* a novel that captured the effects of the automobile on a mid-sized midwestern city. Tarkington wrote, "The idealists planned and strove and shouted that their city should become a better, better, and better city—and what they meant, when they used the word 'better,' was 'more prosperous,' and the core of their idealism was this: 'The more prosperous my beloved city, the more prosperous beloved I!'"[115] There is no doubt that advocates for zoning were motivated by their own interests in the protection and growth of property values, but these interests were not necessarily at odds with the potential benefits in public health and safety that zoning also was said to bring. To such "idealists," city governments offered zoning as the management of its physical plant to industry and the growing population, essentially acting as a large-scale landlord—promising to keep the gas range out of the parlor, if only the newcomers would move into their new home. In many ways, the act of zoning was as important as its results; to engage in the planning was itself a sign of the progressive nature of a city.

An irony of this sort of boosterism and competition between American cities is that in adopting similar systems of organization through comprehensive planning, and specifically through zoning codes, the growth of small American cities was not only to be managed but also to be increasingly similar. Of course, some of the similarities in townscapes stemmed from an earlier point, such as the gridded platting of railroad towns. Most early zoning ordinances were based closely on already existing conditions, but their adoption suggested that growth would continue along uniform lines. At the cul-

mination of a speech to the Zenith Real Estate Board, Sinclair Lewis's character Babbitt sings the praises of the "Zip City," saying, "'I tell you, Zenith
and her sister-cities are producing a new type of civilization. There are many
resemblances between Zenith and these other burgs, and I'm darn glad of
it!'"[116] Lewis's parodic depiction of his character and that character's community resonated because its portrayal of an American town in the early
twentieth century was recognizable. Ultimately the similar zoning codes
promoted a standard of living agreed upon at least by municipal planners
and civic groups, one in which industry could not encroach upon residential space, commercial districts coordinated with transit lines, and single-
family residential neighborhoods stood as a common aspiration. Zoning
almost certainly did not achieve this end for all residents of any given community. But the attempt to do so created a landscape of familiarity across
the country, a landscape on which was inscribed a national standard of
living.

City planning, especially zoning, affected the very structure of a city and
how it would function economically, socially, and culturally. Although zoning often codified existing land-use patterns, it did so by legally regulating
the use of privately owned space. Just as so many of the material goods and
spaces of the turn of the twentieth century encouraged some sort of separation of function or task, zoning effected these divisions on a grand scale.
The separation of urban functions into producing, distributing, and consuming zones was believed to be the best form of management in the era in
which zoning codes were first developed. If consumer goods, and the houses
that contained them, offered a visible means of organizing space and social
activities on a relatively small scale, within a room or building, zoning
offered a way to plat all those individual buildings—domestic, commercial,
and industrial—in a cohesive way.

To broaden the market for their services, city planners traveled across the
country and advertised to clients at a variety of scales. The burgeoning profession of city planning needed to convince municipalities and community
groups that its services were not a luxury but of great importance to any
given city. Planners worked closely with local municipal officials and also
citizens' groups; HBA advocated the involvement of the latter, recognizing
that collaboration would make adoption and implementation more feasi-
ble. Local business interests dominated the citizens' groups, bringing their
ideals of management and corporate reform to literal fruition in cityscapes

and townscapes across the United States. If good management of daily life was a very abstract ideal, it was materialized in urban form.

Boosterism encouraged friendly competition, but also aspiration to greater population and greater wealth. While the purveyors of consumer goods promised that individual benefits would reap larger social and cultural good, planners and boosters did the opposite. A zoned city would grow in a managed, and manageable, way that would benefit its citizens. A zoned city would embody the American standard of living.

THE STANDARD OF LIVING, REVISITED

Facts and Fictions

On 29 November 1929, the American novelist Sherwood Anderson wrote to his future wife, Eleanor Copenhaver, about a new book by Robert and Helen Merrell Lynd: "We are in a strange, transient time, Eleanor dear. I have just been reading *Middletown* . . . I wonder how true it is. I have to believe that it does not get it all . . . Which is most true, a picture like that or the picture made by *Winesburg?*"[1] Anderson posed a question that was crucial to the consolidation of middle-class culture at the turn of the twentieth century: having grown and expressed themselves through the material environment, how best should middle-class communities represent, and reflect upon, themselves? One obvious way to capture the patterns of daily life and the environments in which they took place was in writing. But even in prose these descriptions could take a variety of forms, ranging, as Anderson contrasted, from the report of a social scientist to the imaginative creation of a novelist. In trying to solidify their own place in American culture, a variety of writers took up the project of describing the middle class, the group set apart from both the wealthy industrialists who financed the country's productivity and many of the workers who actually produced goods.

Anderson saw a place for the literary artist in this juncture, writing to Copenhaver, "Surely in this situation, capital on one side and labor on the other, there should be a place for the artist who wants merely to be openeyed, to receive impressions and make his pictures, wanting to serve only the central inner story and not one side or the other."[2] His stated aim, of being descriptive without being judgmental, was shared by social scientists such as the Lynds. The Lynds wrote, in the first chapter of *Middletown,* "Neither field work nor report has attempted to prove any thesis; the aim has been, rather, to record observed phenomena, thereby raising questions and suggesting possible fresh points of departure in the study of group behavior."[3] While the objectivity of both realist novels and social science surveys can be called into question, these stated goals do illustrate that in their desire to chart the cultural influences on and of middle-class communities, the two projects had much in common. The "art" and "science" of recording the middle-class standard of living were not as far away from one another as Anderson may have expressed. Just as manufacturers, marketers, and consumers of silverplate flatware, bathroom fixtures, foursquare homes, and zoning plans looked to both aesthetic design and scientific efficiency as essential elements of the products, so too did they look to both literary creativity and purportedly objective observation as a means of chronicling their culture.

The two types of projects also shared their material manifestation in books, which they helped to promote as a requisite part of the middle-class home. In trying to distinguish the homes of persons they classified as business class, even if these persons may have shared a basic income level with members of the working class, the Lynds wrote, "There is less likely to be a radio than in the more prosperous working class home, but one may come upon . . . a set of Dickens or Irving in a worn binding; the rugs are often more threadbare than those in the living room of a foreman, but text-books of a missionary society or of a study section of the Woman's Club are lying on the mission library table." The upper reaches of this group had "open book-shelves with sets of Mark Twain and Eugene Field and standard modern novels."[4] According to the Lynds, books were one marker of the cultural, not financial, differences between classes. To talk about shared ideals is to raise questions about how and through what mechanisms these ideals were shared. The methods of marketing explored in the preceding chapters, such as advertisements and public placement, constituted these mechanisms, but only in part. The standard of living was also carried through a variety of written texts, which were easily distributed nationwide and thus helped create a national community of their readers.

The contents, both fact and fiction, contained in these artifacts were the means of representing the quality of life to which many Americans aspired. They were thus both the smallest scale of material culture, to be possessed, read, handled, and displayed, and the largest, as a study of all the rest of the material environment. If the home, workplace, or leisure site was a structure in which to arrange one's possessions and the activities of daily life; and the neighborhood, town, or city was a place in which to organize these sites; then studies of the middle class provided spaces in which to consider whether these communities functioned as planned, how different communities might be alike or different, and, most simply, how people lived and related to one another. The influence of these books could be evaluated on the one hand on their scientific or literary merit and on the other hand in the same terms of marketing and sales by which the national distribution of other forms of material culture were measured. As Anderson wrote, "It would be, I think, generally admitted that, in my *Winesburg, Ohio,* I did do something to give people an insight into the lives of people of the small towns. My *Poor White* was the story of the coming of the modern industrial world to such another town . . . Although, at the time of their publication, they brought me little or no money, they have since, through cheap editions, been distributed, as you know, by hundreds of thousands."[5] In selling their books and gaining recognition in their respective fields, publishers and authors also sold, whether intentionally or not, a way of looking at and evaluating American life; they both captured and created communities.

A TIGHT FOCUS

Communities can be, and certainly were at the turn of the century, defined in myriad ways. While some communities are geographic, coinciding with physical or political boundaries, others transcend geographic lines to favor other shared qualities or affinities, such as ethnicity, occupation, political views, or leisure-time activities. Depending on these definitions, communities may be either fixed or temporal. And, perhaps most important, individuals can be present in or feel a part of several communities at once. The new transportation and communications mechanisms of the late nineteenth century enabled the formation of a sense of community between individuals or groups not physically close at hand; these mechanisms allowed for a broad distribution of the goods and services that became emblems of community participation. These innovations often brought a perceived "loss of community" to geographic areas, at the same time that they might broaden other possibilities for groupings, such as those based on occupation or on shared socioeconomic status.

As the nineteenth century melded into the twentieth, professionals in the social sciences became increasingly likely to study groups similar to their own. While retaining the methods of observation that they had employed while studying cultures different from their own, social scientists began to undertake studies of Americans, including middle-class Americans like themselves. Budgets, the cost of living, housing, and the relationship of work and family life were all topics that middle-class reformers and statisticians had surveyed at the end of the nineteenth century with an eye to the working classes. But they slowly began turning the lens on themselves as well. At the same time, the explosion of the publishing industry produced numerous stories devoted to middle-class life, some from authors who had trained as journalists to observe and report, much as their scientific counterparts had, and now applied their trained eye to characters and plot lines of their own imagination. The lives of male and female clerks, factory foremen, managers, professionals, and particularly those just attaining the status that went along with these occupations, became the subjects of numerous representations. The growth of the "middle" sector of American society was mirrored in the growth of its representation.[6]

A culmination of this shift of study subjects can be seen in a report that sharpened the focus at very close range on the exact milieu in which the author lived and worked. Jessica B. Peixotto, a professor of social economics at the University of California, authored *Getting and Spending at the Professional Standard of Living: The Cost of Living an Academic Life* in 1927. Peixotto admitted that studying a group of which she was a member challenged her training in scientific objectivity, but she believed the project was valuable to economists and to society in general. She defined her work as contributing to "the field of consumption wherein lie some of the most relevant questions of economic theory and business practice."[7] While most budget studies had focused on necessary levels for subsistence, Peixotto's work examined a level of spending at which consumer choice came into play. Indeed as a community study of a professional group, the case of academics allowed Peixotto to study the standard of living as separate from a budget study. Although she did undertake the latter, she found that the growing expectations for academics to take part in the quality of life of a more general professional culture greatly outpaced their actual salaries. Peixotto's original aim was to address this issue of academic salaries in the context of the increasingly uncloistered life that most academics led. She hoped to show that academics increasingly supported families on salaries originally designed for one person, taking her cue from a group of faculty wives who had earlier voiced similar concerns in the *University Chronicle*. While charting the actual cost of daily life, she also implicitly asked, as had these wives, if the intangible cost was too high, both on a level of personal career choice and on a cultural level, if the country would eventually lose their best and brightest to higher-paying jobs.[8]

Peixotto's work was based on two important assumptions. First, she established that the basic unit for any evaluation of the standard of living was the family, not the individual, regardless of the breadwinner's profession. While the popular image of the cloistered, ascetic academic might still hold, Peixotto argued that the reality of academic life was different:

> The fact is that the average faculty man is caught by the same influences which, to a greater or less degree, draw all effective members of modern democratic life into "standardized" ways of living . . . Family life in universities takes on continuously more of the pattern of the common life . . . With the world at large, the professor and his family have capitulated in greater or less degree to the standardizing influences that play unremittingly upon the purchasing public to extend their wants.[9]

Second, she explained that the standard of living was aspired to, not necessarily met; when it was met, the yearly salary was often augmented by independent income or credit. When Peixotto asked rhetorically what the American standard of living cost a family a four, she gave a firm answer: "It costs about $7000 a year." But Peixotto went on to disassociate this figure from that of annual income. She wrote:

> True, current statistics tell us that in our prosperous United States only one percent of the nation can command an income of $10,000 or more; that scarcely three percent of our people have $5,000 or over to spend. But the question is not of income. $7,000 is the sum needed to satisfy a set of desires for goods and services, desires that at the present time influence widely and profoundly the way men earn their money and the way they spend it.

In trying to explain this new standard and from where it evolved, Peixotto pointed to the cultural value placed on a rising standard of living. She particularly noted that the "comfort standard" stemmed from the availability of mass-produced goods, as well as to "new, pervasive, persuasive" business practices inducing greater purchasing than in past generations. As the mechanism that made this new system run, she pointed to credit. Perhaps most important, Peixotto considered this a "new single standard" to which all aspired. She wrote of her predecessors in the field of budget studies, "The several 'lower' standards most often considered are actually planes of living but not standards of living. In this study, the standard in question is designated a professional standard." Academics were expected to have the cultural capital to interact with other professionals. As among the lowest paid of the salaried professionals, they proved to be the perfect test case for explaining class distinctions based on organization of life, rather than income.[10]

Academics were expected, in short, to lead middle-class lives, but if this life were defined in terms of earnings, the occupational group would not measure up. As Peixotto wrote of her work, "As a cost of living study, its immediate serviceability seems to be to show decisively that the salaries offered the faculty of the university under investigation, and in all probability the faculties of most universities, are below the amount required if an accepted standard of living for professional men is to be paid for out of those salaries." And yet, Peixotto also asserted, academics were a valued group in American society: "Not only does the public want the class; it wants the members of the profession to look like other people; to behave like other people; to take their place on even terms with other professionals."[11] But again, purchasing power, including purchasing on credit, outweighed actual salaries in the social evaluation system. Peixotto chose not to address the issue of whether this situation was good or bad; she did not want to address the question of whether the "comfort standard" was too high. Rather, she asserted its existence and addressed how the occupationally defined community of academics functioned within that set of standards.

Peixotto used the terms *professional, comfort,* and *middle-class* alternately to define her concept of the standard of living. She distinguished the comfort level from both subsistence and luxury levels, and attributed this quality to the middle class about which she chose to study and write. Peixotto explained the distinctions on either end of the spectrum: "The way faculty families want to live, that is, the 'standard' of living they ascribe to themselves has, I think, never raised any challenge of luxury living. On the contrary, it has been usual to recognize it as a scale of living where emphasis falls on wants for that class of needs most commonly indicated by the dubious term, 'higher goods.'" The "higher goods" encompassed the conveniences and comforts widely thought to constitute the standard of living. The wants of the faculty wives who were Peixotto's original inspiration seem simple enough:

food of the simplest with very occasional meals away from home; clothing of a quality sufficiently good to keep from being "ashamed"; a house large enough to make it unnecessary "to move again before the birth of the second baby,"— a house with at least two bedrooms,—desirably with a study, and some quarters for help. The house operation allotment, it was decided, ought to be enough to include payments of water, light, fuel, laundry, repairs (including the garden and its upkeep), and some surplus for service. Income ought to furnish at least a minimum of savings, set at 10%. Maintenance of health was set at a minimum cost of $120 . . . The right to satisfy a modest desire for books, music, the theatre, travel and entertainment of friends was taken for granted.[12]

This definition was certainly not extravagant, but it also went beyond simple subsistence, to encompass comfort. The list of "wants" took into account not just the life lived on a particular income, but the perception of how that life was lived; the outward appearances of clothing, a garden, or public outings were important parts of the "standard." The issue of "higher goods," those above subsistence levels, was what Peixotto considered uniquely American about her subjects. The American value system of the day, stemming from the tenets of the Gilded Age and Progressive Era, encouraged an aspiration to professional life and an ever-rising standard of living, accessible to as many as possible.[13] As Peixotto explained, there were no scientific means for measuring actual "needs," beyond the barest requirements of food, bodily warmth through clothing, and shelter. Thus, "safety in deciding on a reasonable scale of living lies in an appeal to current ideas of the proprieties in the use of goods. There seems good ground for contending that the only fair gauge of any standard of living . . . is the way of living most widely accepted as 'right and proper' for a given class."[14] And indeed those who lived by the "standard" contributed, at least in part, to its definition.

While Peixotto's book may not have been widely read outside of academic communities, the American author Robert Herrick brought similar issues to a more general readership in his 1926 novel, *Chimes,* about faculty life at a newly formed midwestern college. Like Peixotto, Herrick knew of what he wrote; in addition to being a prolific novelist, he was an English professor at the University of Chicago. Herrick portrayed in fiction the same distinction between the social standing and the actual financial circumstances of university professors that Peixotto presented in her budget study. Herrick's work bordered on the sociological or even psychological, sketching in great detail the characters who comprise the university faculty and administration, while the plot lines were rather thin. In fact, some readers of the book, particularly in the Chicago area, were consumed with this party game aspect of guessing the real-life counterparts to Herrick's not-always-flattering fictional characters. (In an uncanny coincidence, Herrick's work features a young female social scientist named Jessica.) Nonetheless, in presenting this academic enclave, Herrick also addressed where that enclave fit into the larger professional community. As the main character, Beamon Clavercin, strove to improve his standing among academics, his wife was concerned with improving the standing of academics in the town at large. Herrick wrote of this familial tension:

> They had been going into the city pretty often; whenever he demurred Louise proved to him triumphantly that it was advantageous for him to become known and seen in the company of influential people ... There were comparatively few of the faculty who were invited into the city ... It was a kind of aristocracy worth striving for. She already dreamed of buying a lot on Beechwood Terrace, quite a nicely settled street near the campus, and some day having their own house,—oh, quite small but *chic*,—where they could ask people Sundays and for occasional dinners. While he shared to some extent this ambition to be known, to meet interesting and influential people,—and knew that such social opportunities helped unduly in the university,—he had an uneasy feeling that this was not the road to high scholarship and to consideration by real scholars.[15]

Ultimately, Louise's dream of "occasional dinners" triumphs, despite Clavercin's meager salary in comparison with that of many of his neighbors. The family's financial standing and social standing were not one and the same.

One of *Chimes*'s crucial scenes occurs at a dinner party given in honor of a former professor who has left the university to work in finance. As he describes his life in glowing terms and advises his former colleagues to follow his lead away from the ivory tower, the others chafe, struggling over how important money should be in their career choices. Through this character of Aleck Harding, Herrick provided the example of the temptation to get away from the university that Peixotto warned of in her own work. The professors were uncomfortable with the "cigar, the monogrammed cigar case, the finely cut sleeve of the banker's coat ... palpable symbols to all of what Harding had sought in life, material achievements rather than the intangibilities." Still, as one of them explained, "we must live in the world as we find it, reasonably free from anxieties."[16] This freedom from "anxiety" would come from providing not just the means of family subsistence, but rather familial comfort.

A WIDE-ANGLE LENS

While Peixotto and Herrick focused on communities defined by occupation, they also addressed the geographic areas in which their respective "studies" take place. Other authors focused more tightly on a geographically bounded community, taking in a broader range of individuals and families within it. Arguably the best known of these community studies was the Lynds' groundbreaking 1929 work, *Middletown: A Study in Modern American Culture. Middletown* paved the way for later studies such as Lloyd Warner's *Yankee City* series in the 1940s, and Herbert Gans's *The Levittowners* in 1967. While other sweeping studies had appeared previously, such as Margaret Byington's *Homestead* or the multifaceted Pittsburgh Survey, these works differed from *Middletown* in several respects. The earlier projects had grown out of the reform efforts of the Progressive Era, undertaken and funded by groups such as the Russell Sage Foundation. They focused specifically on the conditions of industrial work and the plight of laborers, charting conditions in order to make improvements in the future. As much as these works were descriptive, they were also prescriptive; they were closely connected to projects such as training in household economics and budgeting.

The *Middletown* project was hardly without cultural biases; it had in fact started as a more focused investigation of the relationship between cultural change and religious observance, funded by the Institute of Social and Religious Research.[17] However, it grew into an exercise designed to study a whole community's functioning for its own sake. While the earlier studies had focused on problems of work, *Middletown* in many ways focused on what might be called the problems of leisure—particularly how developments in transportation and communications affected family life and community life. To be sure, these developments, such as family ownership of a car or movie-going with peer groups replacing family-centered meals, did stem from the conditions, both economic and social, of the industrial era. But coming as it did at a slightly later date, the study charted "second-wave" changes of social and cultural factors, rather than the specific changes of daily life patterns stemming from industrial labor. The Lynds considered how a family income was earned, but simply as one of six major categories of study: Getting a Living, Making a Home, Training the Young, Using Leisure, Engaging in Religious Practices, and Engaging in Community Activities. The Lynds stressed the ability to consume, and the choices made about consumption, rather than the work that earned the income to do so. *Middletown* both reflected and helped entrench this shift in the meaning of the standard of living, from a measure of adequate earnings to a measure of desired consumption.

In masking the actual site of the study, and drawing out the generalities of social and cultural life, rather than a specific site with specific historical circumstances (such as the aftermath of the Homestead strike), the Lynds lent their project a national importance it might not otherwise have had. Middletown was in fact Muncie, Indiana, but it could have been any number of places, in a day and age when not only food, household furnishings, and clothing were distributed nationwide, but also the methods of ordering both buildings and communities were shared from coast to coast. The Lynds recognized the multiplicity of communities to which any individual weighed allegiances on a day-to-day basis.[18] Nonetheless, they defined the object of their study as the community of Middletown, where that community corresponded to the political designation of the city.

Within that broad community, and despite the myriad potential subsets of it, the Lynds drew one primary distinction: between the working class and the business class. As the authors defined these groups, "Members of the first group, by and large, address their activities in getting their living primarily to things, utilizing material tools in the making of things and the performance of services, while the members of the second group address their activities predominantly to people in the selling or promoting of things, services, and ideas." This second group assisted the citizens of Middletown in transforming their daily work into the other five components of their lives, supplying "the multitude of non-material institutional activities such as 'credit,' 'legal contract,' 'education,' 'sale for a price,' 'management,' and 'city government.'" The Lynds also included in this group "users of highly skilled techniques," such as architects and surgeons, and "other professional workers," such as lawyers and engineers, because "the business interests of the city . . . dominate and give their tone" to these types of work. In early drafts of the study, the Lynds actually referred to these groups as "tool users" and "non-tool users," terminology that received unanimous criticism from the institute's editorial advisers. What the Lynds eventually termed the business class corresponds to what was later called the professional-managerial class.[19]

The Lynds avoided the tripartite designations of lower, middle, and upper classes as not truly representing the experience of daily life in Muncie. Their rejection of the tripartite class division, despite encouragement from their advisers to use them, stemmed primarily from their belief that in a town the size and stature of Muncie, there was no true upper class, as might have existed in a metropolitan area.[20] The Lynds' business class, when considered in a national context rather than a local one, corresponded with a middle-class standard of living. While the categories of working class and business class were characterized by their modes of work, the Lynds explored how those differences in work were a shorthand reference to two different systems of prioritizing and ordering the components of daily life; the distinctions between them transcended income level.

The Lynds saw the decades around the turn of the century as the time when the industrial revolution reached American "villages and towns, metamorphosing them into a thing of Rotary clubs, central trade councils, and Chamber of Commerce contests for 'bigger and better' cities." In order to have a sense of belonging in this "middle" realm, citizens of Muncie had to see themselves in a broader context and think about what they shared with their counterparts across the country. Certainly, their material environment was one large aspect of this shared experience. The Lynds painted these national parallels of daily life experience writ large:

> Every aspect of Middletown's life has felt something of this same tendency: standardized processes in industry; nationally advertised products used, eaten, worn in Middletown homes; standardized curriculum, text-books, teachers in the schools; the very play-time of the people running into certain molds with national movie films, nationally edited magazines, and standardized music contests.[21]

Like Peixotto, the Lynds looked to mass media, and particularly advertising, as a spur to the acceptance of standardized goods, and new credit plans such as installment purchasing, "which turns wishes into horses overnight," as the means by which these goods were so quickly consumed.[22]

The new lifestyle was the reflection of "industry, this new trait in the city's culture that is shaping the pattern of the whole of living."[23] While this standardization affected all groups, the Lynds further suggested that the business class was more able to partake in this standardized lifestyle—whether the acquisition of goods, the organizing of them in their environments, or the valuing of them in daily life—and more likely to derive a sense of community from it. The Lynds explained:

> the sense of "belonging," of fitting their world—none the less real psychologically though possibly based on nothing more substantial than symbols—appears to be growing more rapidly among the business class than among the workers. The one group gives more easily with the stresses to which the group is subject, because its members have built their lives about these dominant stresses at more points; it does the "civic" thing easily, because civic values are its values at so many points.[24]

Although in Muncie, members of what the Lynds considered the working class far outnumbered the business class, it was the latter group that established social and cultural norms. The values placed on etiquette, privacy, investment, and management, among others, were the values of both business and the Lynds' business class. And they were represented by the "symbols" of material goods and physical environments used and occupied by that class.

Sherwood Anderson may have had a special reason for scrutinizing the Lynds' work, as they quoted from his writings several times in their book. His fictional descriptions were offered to best express the nature of the community being "scientifically" rendered as Middletown, specifically the "simplicity" of its "early pioneer life" and its later booster spirit. The exact question of "real" American life that he called into question in the sociologists' work, they themselves called into question by using his literary voice to describe their subject of study. While stressing that they could only describe the one place of their study, they allowed that the novelist could generalize in a way that might capture a multitude of communities. The Lynds could not fabricate a "typical city," which, as they wrote, "strictly speaking, does not exist," but looked for a model "having many features common to a wide group of communities." Anderson, Herrick, or any of their counterparts, however, could perhaps create a community more "typical" than any "real" town could be, by creating such common features as the setting for their works. While the Lynds wrote only of the singular Middletown, they described Anderson as depicting the "tenor of life in these Middletowns."[25]

Still, even before the book's publication, Clark Wissler, of the Museum of Natural History in New York and one of the Lynds' primary advisers, commented, "The real kick of the manuscript comes from its impressionism, in that respect it falls almost in the class of a novel." When the book was pub-lished, to wide critical acclaim, reviewers often compared *Middletown* to novels, whether explicitly or implicitly discussing the literary qualities of the book. For example, the columnist of "Some Rattling Good Stories" in *Good Housekeeping* wrote, "it reads as smoothly and goes by as quickly as a first-person story in a magazine . . . For me, at least, it was a good story." Another commentator enthused that the "zestful, humorous language, rich in meta-phor, combines with an unusual degree of imagination," an interesting de-scription of a study purported to be based on "scientific" principles. A fan from the Muncie area wrote, "I yearned over it almost as I would a fat Russ-ian novel." No reviewer made the comparison as colorfully as H. L. Mencken, who wrote in the *Baltimore Evening Sun* in the first weeks after the book's release, "A book full of entertainment and instruction is 'Middletown' . . . it is as exhilarating as even the dirtiest of the new novels." Still, many of these same reviewers also commented on the "scientific" or "anthropological" methodology and aims.[26]

Perhaps no one so effectively combined the stances of the novelist and the social scientist in describing the American middle class as did Sinclair Lewis. In 1920, Lewis wrote the critically acclaimed and wildly popular novel *Main Street,* which pictured an Everytown, USA, named Gopher Prairie. In *Main Street,* the setting of Gopher Prairie is as much a character in the novel as its main player Carol Kenicott. If *Middletown* was described as a novel, the language used by other authors, critics, and adoring fans to describe the work echoed the rhetoric of the social sciences. F. Scott Fitzgerald wrote to Lewis after the publication of *Main Street,* "The amount of sheer data in it is amazing!"[27] The British novelist John Galsworthy, who undertook a sim-ilar project of portraying the middle class in his own home nation, wrote to Lewis, "You have used the exhaustive method, I think, with absolute fitting-ness to your theme—no other could have served you half so well . . . Every country, of course, has its main streets, all richly deserving of diagnosis, but America is lucky to have found so poignant and just and stimulating a diag-nostician. (There is such a word isn't there?)."[28] Walter Lippman, at the time associate editor of the *New Republic,* called *Main Street* "as good a novel as it is good sociology."[29] Even Lewis himself referred to the book as "an un-usually factual picture of American life."[30]

Lewis himself repeatedly expressed the admiration of social scientists' recording of American life, noting *Middletown* and its successor, *Middle-town in Transition,* among his list of the books that "might equip us to scan the complexities of civilization."[31] Years after the publication of his own masterworks, Lewis would continue to look favorably upon the methods of social science. In a scathing review of Louis Bromfield's *Pleasant Valley,* written in the mid-1940s, he wrote in particular that Bromfield might learn from the newly published study *Plainville USA* and its author,

> James West, an anthropologist. He spent a year and a half studying, as impartially as though it were a Pacific isle, the people and customs of a village of 275 in the Southern Middlewest. He reports with a quick and easy style that makes these details as fascinating as village gossip upon their occupations, finances, sex manners, family squabbles, religious ways, and what the young people do and want to do.[32]

These categories of study not only loosely corresponded to the Lynds' course of study in *Middletown,* but also provided the basic outlines of Lewis's own descriptions of the fictional communities of Gopher Prairie and Zenith.

Lewis's work process for his novels was as much a "study" as that supporting the publication of *Middletown.* The plethora of materials that went into the writing of Lewis's next work, *Babbitt,* gives an example of the considerations that went into the author's "fiction." Having thoroughly documented small town or village life in *Main Street,* Lewis accepted the challenge of many of his friends and reviewers, and went on to try to capture a bigger city through his acutely descriptive prose. *Babbitt* was set in a city named Zenith, in a mythical midwestern state named Winnemac in later novels; again Lewis focused as much on the setting as the character, even briefly considering "Population, 300,000" as the title of the book.[33] Before writing the novel, Lewis sketched out all the characters and their interrelations, and imagined the city, as any novelist might before beginning an actual narrative draft. But Lewis's preparation went well beyond those simple tasks. He collected clippings from the real estate section of a variety of newspapers, noting the names of suburban developments, advertising practices, and typical price ranges, to lend accuracy to the portrayal of his title character's profession of real estate. He noted the weather at different seasons of the year in different cities, in order to best create his composite picture of Zenith's climate. He clipped notices of social highlights, ranging from college sporting events to private parties, to better represent the leisure time of his characters. He noted dress, speech, and favorite foods to incorporate into his novel. In short, Lewis carefully covered the six main categories of community life outlined by the Lynds in *Middletown.* Creating composite settings and situations from his studies was a complementary form of representation to the Lynds' sample quotations and tabulated statistics. In fact, an excerpt from *Babbitt* was included in a textbook entitled *American Standards and Planes of Living,* edited by Thomas Eliot and published in 1931.[34]

Lewis not only imagined the city of Zenith but also drew it, in a series of maps; similarly, he made floor plans of houses and offices that figured prominently in the novel. These maps depicted Lewis's vision of a typical middle-class professional, in a typical American city like Middletown. The drawings of Babbitt's house, in the Floral Heights subdivision, are similar to the Aladdin Company's floor plans and cutaway drawings. Lewis drew both the outlines of the house, including a formal dining room, living room, sun porch, bedrooms for each family member (though one room is designated the "girls' room," another note says that "Verona [the older daughter] uses guest room when no guest"), and two bathrooms, and the furnishings of these rooms. Maps of the surrounding neighborhood highlight the concentration of "Babbitts" as a character type rather than a family name. Maps of the downtown of Zenith demarcate the monuments of Babbitt's daily life, including his office and the club and hotels where he dines. Finally, maps drawn at larger scales show Zenith to be a city zoned as Harland Bartholomew might have planned it, and show Zenith's role as a center for satellite communities. Lewis used these graphics as a guide for his own written depiction of the American standard of living.[35]

Many reviewers commented that Lewis represented a quality of life already in existence. As the theorist of domestic economies, Hazel Kyrk, wrote, "Given the setting any one who is at all sensitive to the concrete manifestations of contemporary culture can, without reading the book, describe the Babbitts' home, its location, its layout and architecture, the furnishings found in living-room, bedroom, dining-room, and bathroom down to the placing of the furniture and the colors of the rugs and walls." Kyrk actually had similar thoughts about the Lynds' subject of study: "Anyone who knows Middletown can describe the food, clothing, housing and recreation of the families living there."[36] Beyond the general descriptions of *Middletown* as novelistic and *Babbitt* and *Main Street* as sociological, the books were specifically compared to one another by numerous commentators. As Maxwell Lerner asked in *The Literary Review,* "Is it accident or the authors' intention that when I am reading about Middletown I seem to be revisiting Zenith, where I first met Babbitt?" Another reviewer, Elsie McCormick, warned of

Middletown: "If the book had been published as a novel, the author would have been severely criticized for following so closely in the spoor of Sinclair Lewis." While Lewis was considered an inescapable influence on the Lynds, their work became the "true" yardstick against which Lewis's realism was measured.[37]

Many reviewers noted Lewis's biting critique of contemporary American culture and in using *Middletown* as a measure of veracity for that critique betrayed their own ambivalence toward their society: could the level of standardization that Americans had achieved really be considered an achievement?[38] Both the positive and negative answers to that question yielded fruitful avenues for the consideration of American communities, their consumption of material goods, and the values that those goods symbolized. Images of a materialistic, conformist American society received extensive attention and concern in the post–World War II period in a variety of works ranging from the journalistic rant of John Keats's *The Crack in the Picture Window* to Hebert Gans's sociological study, *The Levittowners,* to Sloan Wilson's novel (and the Nunnally Johnson film adaptation), *The Man in the Gray Flannel Suit.* Such critiques of contemporary culture and the economy that underpins it continue today in wildly popular books such as Naomi Klein's *No Logo* or John De Graaf, David Wann, and Thomas Naylor's *Affluenza.*[39]

Still, while some authors questioned the proliferation of standardized goods, many Americans asserted that standardized goods democratized material well-being, an idea encompassed by the phrase "the American dream." While the standard of living is still an important concept, its role as a shared icon fueling American consumers was rivaled if not eclipsed by the American dream. That this shift began during the Great Depression is surely not a coincidence; at a time when the standard of living was seen to retrench, a dream was perhaps a better name for common aspirations. From James Truslow Adams's *The American Epic,* which popularized the term, to Nixon and Khrushchev's "Kitchen Debate," to the Disney Corporation's planned community of Celebration, Florida, the American dream has held an important place in the political and popular culture of the United States.[40]

While broadening access to material culture, standardized production of goods could also encourage individualism rather than conformity. As Thomas Eliot explained in his *American Standards and Planes of Living,* any consumer could form a "unique *combination* of standardized elements."[41] Eliot's stance explained the selection for his textbook of a particular passage from *Babbitt* in which the link between standardized possessions and standardized lives was hotly debated. The questions surrounding standardization and consumption in American culture were not easy ones. Perhaps the best summation on standardization was offered by the economist Stuart Chase, a contemporary of Lewis and the Lynds: "Look this word in the face hereafter. When you hear it named, find out the specific project involved, analyze its implications, and praise it or damn it intelligently instead of blindly."[42]

SELLING THE STANDARD OF LIVING

Whatever their legacy, the authors who offered their reflections on the American standard of living, whether from an academic or artistic perspective, were not immune to the sales techniques that made other products so desirable. At the same time that his novels satirized the booster mentality that advertised and marketed goods, services, and whole communities, Lewis took an active role in the advertising and marketing of his novels. He was willing to waive early royalty fees if the funds were put toward the advertising budget for his books. In almost constant contact with his editor, Alfred Harcourt, Lewis did everything from suggesting ad copy (often well before the books were even finished), to drafting letters to prospective reviewers that could be sent out under the press's name, to proposing elaborate schemes whereby certain authors known to like his books would contact other authors to request testimonial quotations for publicity materials. Always thinking on his feet, Lewis strove to turn potential competition into support. For example, when a few months after the publication of *Main Street,* he noticed reviewers starting to compare other books favorably to his own, he suggested the following ad copy as "very fresh, but . . . effective": "THANKS FOR THE COMPLIMENT! Three big books of the spring season are all being advertised as 'Better than *Main Street.*' This admission that during the four months since it was published, *Main Street* has become the standard for comparison is received with gratitude." He also recognized that book design could serve as a form of branding, for both author and publisher. After the success of *Main Street,* he recommended "exactly the same" cloth cover for *Babbitt;* he wrote, "we'll try to begin to make lines of books, all in that blue and orange, across library shelves. I know I like to have all my Conrads in the same binding."[43] While the author had a particularly close relationship to Alfred Harcourt and his fledgling publishing company, Lewis's interest in marketing his own books was, of course, not unique.

So too did the Lynds, particularly Robert, become involved in the promotion of their book; as the former managing editor of *Publishers Weekly,* Robert Lynd certainly knew the book trade. When Trevor Bowen of the Institute of Social and Religious Research wrote Lynd in 1928 that he would negotiate for royalties if and when the study had sold 5,000 copies, he perhaps thought that event unlikely. However, whether due to favorable reviews or aggressive marketing, the book sold remarkably well: over 1,000 copies were sold at bookstores in the first two months after publication and well over another 1,000 were sold as textbooks across the country in the 1929–30 academic year. When Robert Lynd requested sales figures at the end of the 1950s, well over 50,000 copies of the book had been sold.[44] The reviews and marketing came together in print advertisements with quotations pulled from reviews from well-known authors or journals, as well as in a premium run by *The New Republic,* offering a savings on a subscription with a purchase of the book.[45] While Robert Lynd generally appreciated his publisher's attempts to sell copies of *Middletown,* he did draw the line at their use of Mencken's "dirty novel" description; he wrote, "Such publicity does not help me professionally and I do not believe this sort of emphasis helps the book. The cumulating emphasis of the reviews is that 'nobody interested in American life can afford to miss this book.' Wouldn't some such appeal as this chop as much wood as the 'dirty novel' appeal?" He and Helen went through all the reviews and pulled out what they considered to be more appropriate quotations, typed them up, and sent them off; their exact list appeared in later advertisements. Other advertising materials drew on the course adoptions, quoting university professors.[46]

Other targeted marketing was perhaps more surprising. Not only was *Middletown* sold using contemporary advertising techniques, the book actually became a marketing tool. Advertisements placed in *The Tide* and *Printer's Ink* appealed to the advertising industry to use the book as a market survey. One ad approached the audience: "ADVERTISERS,—it would cost you $50,000 to get this information!" Testimonial quotes came not from general interest magazines or academics but from trade periodicals such as *Advertising and Selling, Chain Store Review,* and *Retailing.* The copy explained that *Middletown* was "the book every advertising man has always said he'd go out and do for himself if he ever had time." Other firms jumped on the Lynds' bandwagon for their own public relations. *McCall's* magazine capitalized on the attention paid to Muncie in the wake of *Middletown's* publication and issued a brochure entitled "Living on McCall Street in 'Middletown.'" The brochure depicted photographs of every household in

Muncie—"the 'Middletown' of Dr. and Mrs. Lynd"—that subscribed to *McCall's*. The town exemplified "by far the most important group of people sociologically and market-wise in America." Others would refer to similar groups as "Babbitts."[47]

In fact, Lewis and the Lynds shared not only subject matter but also their publisher, Harcourt, Brace. If their book titles were compared to one another in book reviews, they were also seen together in advertisements. The Harcourt, Brace marketing department placed advertisements in such major journals as *The Nation, The New Republic,* and *The New York Times,* that featured the press's new releases, including *Middletown,* alongside Lewis's latest novel, *Dodsworth.* On 7 September 1929, Harcourt, Brace took out a full-page ad in *The Saturday Review of Literature* introducing a sort of party game based on "ten important books" that they published. Ten authors were depicted reading one another's books. Anyone who could correctly match all ten authors to their pictures would win the book of their choice from the list of ten. The copy read, "The critics have acclaimed them. They are continual best-sellers. They have been recommended by the American public for your permanent library. Your bookseller will show them to you."[48] Thus, while the books reflected contemporary American culture, they were also part of the standard of living, a prospective purchase suggested by the public at large for a permanent place in their homes.

Though it is hard to gauge the social influence of any given book, we do know that *Main Street, Babbitt,* and *Middletown* were immensely popular books in their day.[49] From the 1920s through the middle of the century, Lewis, and to a somewhat lesser degree the Lynds, achieved the status of public figures in American culture. Lewis and Robert Lynd both took part in a forum in the November 1929 *McCall's* entitled "What's Right with America," in which Henry James Forman interviewed "the most famous authorities, the most alert observers." As Harcourt, Brace strove to sell as many books as possible, it was also selling the picture of life in American small towns that Lewis and the Lynds presented, through what critic Maxwell Lerner called "the literature of national introspection."[50] These authors recognized that the commercial processes of distribution paralleled the cultural processes of establishing a standard of living. Both processes linked the production and consumption of American material life, and both supported the flourishing of the American middle class.

:: NOTES ::

INTRODUCTION

Sinclair Lewis, *Babbitt* (1922; rpt. New York: Penguin Books, 1996), 12.

1. Joseph Corn offered helpful comments on this idea of consumer collaboration at the Business History Conference, Palo Alto, Calif., March 2000. Hazel Kyrk, *Economic Problems of the Family* (New York: Harper & Bros., 1929), 377; Thomas Eliot, ed., *American Standards and Planes of Living: Readings in the Social Economics of Consumption* (Boston: Ginn & Co., 1931), 10.

2. Edward T. Devine, *The Normal Life* (New York: Survey Associates, 1924), 1. On the difficulty of defining the standard of living, see also Ellis Lore Kirkpatrick, *The Farmer's Standard of Living* (New York: Century Co., 1929), 11–15; and Philip Ayres, "The Standard of Living," *Charities* 9, no. 10 (6 September 1902): 216. On the standard of living as it applies to both individuals and communities, see also Frank Hatch Streightoff, *The Standard of Living Among the Industrial People of America* (Boston: Houghton Mifflin Co., 1911), 3; and Eliot, 3. Excellent work in the field of economics describes the standard of living, its influence, and its use in comparing different historical periods, regions, or communities in economic terms; still, these authors tend to take the concept itself as a given, while I attempt to situate its emergence and use historically. See, for example, Amartya Sen, *The Standard of Living*, ed. Geoffrey Hawthorne (Cambridge: Cambridge University Press, 1987); and Clair Brown, *American Standards of Living* (Cambridge: Blackwell, 1994). While economists such as Brown do explore means of quantifying the standard of living, they tend to do so in retrospect or as a comparative tool. This study focuses more on the use of the term within a given historical moment, when its translation into enumerable data is less stable.

3. The *Oxford English Dictionary* dates the term *standard of living* to 1903. The term was apparently used slightly earlier in the American context; see, for example, Ayres. The term *standard of life* was used still earlier; see, for example, F. Spencer Baldwin, "Some Aspects of Luxury," *The North American Review* 168, no. 507 (February 1899): 155.

4. Carl Brinkman, "Standards of Living," in *The Encyclopaedia of the Social Sciences*, ed. Edwin R. A. Seligman (New York: Macmillan, 1934), 14:322.

5. Ibid., 14:323.

6. Lawrence Glickman, "Inventing the 'American standard of living': Gender, Race, and Working-Class Identity, 1880–1925," *Labor History* 34, nos. 2–3 (Spring–Summer 1993): 221.

7. Ira S. Wile, "Standards of Living," *Journal of Home Economics* 5 (December 1913): 417; Kyrk, 424–25.

8. For a more thorough discussion of consumer credit, see Lendol Calder, *Financing the American Dream* (Princeton: Princeton University Press, 1999); and Martha Olney, *Buy Now, Pay Later: Advertising, Credit, and Consumer Durables in the 1920s* (Chapel Hill: University of North Carolina Press, 1991).

9. Baldwin, 155. For strikingly similar categorizations of the planes of living, see Kyrk, 372, 387; Streightoff, 2; Thomas Francis Moran, "Ethics of Wealth," *American Journal of Sociology* 6, no. 6 (May 1901): 824; S. Agnes Donham, "Conscious Standards," in Eliot, ed., *American Standards and Planes of Living*, 477–78.

10. Streightoff, 2.

11. Wile, 410–11; see also Baldwin, 155; Kyrk, 376; Streightoff, 2; Mary Hinman Abel, "Community and Personal Standards," in Eliot, ed., *American Standards and Planes of Living*, 183.

12. Mark Twain and Charles Dudley Warner, *The Gilded Age: A Tale of To-day* (Hartford: American Publishing Company, 1874).

13. This process of incorporating goods into the standard of living was quite a different one from the notion of "conspicuous consumption" coined by Thorstein Veblen. While Veblen's leisure class sought to own goods or use services that would make them stand out from their peers, the middle class described by those who theorized the standard of living sought to meet the same bar as everyone else. Veblen, *The Theory of the Leisure Class: An Economic Study of Institutions* (1899; rpt. New York: Modern Library, 1934).

14. I take these terms from two classic works on the Progressive Era: Richard Hofstadter, *The Age of Reform* (New York: Vintage, 1955); and Robert Wiebe, *The Search for Order, 1877–1920* (New York: Hill and Wang, 1967). For additional background on the Gilded Age and the Progressive Era, see Steven J. Diner, *A Very Different Age: Americans of the Progressive Era* (New York: Hill and Wang, 1998); Nell Irvin Painter, *Standing at Armageddon: The United States, 1877–1919* (New York: W. W. Norton, 1987); Alan Trachtenberg, *The Incorporation of America: Culture and Society in the Gilded Age* (New York: Hill and Wang, 1982).

15. Helen Campbell, *Prisoners of Poverty: Women Wage Workers, Their Trades and Their Lives* (1887; rpt. Westport, Conn.: Greenwood Press, 1970); Walter Wyckoff, *The Workers: An Experiment in Reality* (New York: Charles Scribner's Sons, 1897); Robert Chapin, *The Standard of Living of Workingmen's Families in New York* (New York: Charities Publication Committee, 1909); Robert S. Lynd and Helen Merrell Lynd, *Middletown: A Study in Modern American Culture* (New York: Harcourt, Brace and Co., 1929). Daniel Horowitz traces this expansion of scope in the study of household

budgets from the working class to the middle class in *The Morality of Spending: Attitudes Toward the Consumer Society in America, 1875–1940* (Baltimore: Johns Hopkins University Press, 1985). For historiography of the burgeoning social sciences, see Dorothy Ross, *The Origins of American Social Science* (Cambridge: Cambridge University Press, 1991); Maurine Greenwald and Margo Anderson, eds., *Pittsburgh Surveyed: Social Science and Social Reform in the Early Twentieth Century* (Pittsburgh: University of Pittsburgh Press, 1996); Martin Bulmer, Kevin Bales, and Kathryn Kish Sklar, eds., *The Social Survey in Historical Perspective, 1880–1940* (Cambridge: Cambridge University Press, 1991); Sarah Igo, "America Surveyed: The Making of a Social Scientific Public, 1920–1960" (Ph.D. diss., Princeton University, 2001).

16. Christine Frederick, "New Wealth, New Standards of Living and Changed Family Budgets," *Annals of the American Academy of Political and Social Science* 115 (September 1924): 79; see also Kirkpatrick, 6–8 and passim.

17. Edna Ferber, *Fanny Herself* (New York: Frederick A. Stokes Co., 1917), 52–53.

18. See, for example, *Des Moines Register,* 3 June 1925, 7; 18 June 1925, 6.

19. Jean-Christophe Agnew explicates the historical meanings and theoretical underpinnings of the market in "The Threshold of Exchange: Speculations on the Market," *Radical History Review* 21 (Fall 1979): 99–118. Regina Lee Blaszczyk has deftly examined the communications between manufacturer and consumer in *Imagining Consumers: Design and Innovation from Wedgwood to Corning* (Baltimore: Johns Hopkins University Press, 2000). Sally Clarke is also exploring this theme in her forthcoming work, *Consumer Negotiations.*

20. The culture of these salespersons has begun to be examined by historians, and they are familiar as characters such as Theodore Dreiser's Charles Drouet in *Sister Carrie* (1911). For the purposes of this project, however, I am more interested in the actual means and patterns of their travel, and the scope of the territory covered. See, for example, Timothy Spears, *100 Years on the Road: The Traveling Salesman in American Culture* (New Haven: Yale University Press, 1995); and Earl Sharris, *A Nation of Salesmen: The Tyranny of the Market and the Subversion of Culture* (New York: W. W. Norton, 1994).

21. Wayne Fuller, *RFD: The Changing Face of Rural America* (Bloomington: Indiana University Press, 1964) and *The American Mail: Enlarger of Common Life* (Chicago: University of Chicago Press, 1972).

22. Eliot, 7–8; Kirkpatrick, 38; Stuart Chase, "One Dead Level," in Eliot, ed., *American Standards and Planes of Living,* 800.

23. The studies that have been done to date on the history of marketing provide an excellent starting point, but these works have tended to look at early brand names and consumable goods, such as food products and soap. Work on advertising has tended to focus on the design of advertising itself rather than the relation between advertising and the physical distribution of products. On the history of marketing, see Susan Strasser, *Satisfaction Guaranteed: The Making of the Mass Market* (New

York: Pantheon Books, 1989); Richard Tedlow, *New and Improved: The Story of Mass Marketing in America* (New York: Basic Books, 1990); Pamela Laird, *Advertising Progress: American Business and the Rise of Consumer Marketing* (Baltimore: Johns Hopkins University Press, 1998); Nancy F. Koehn, *Brand New: How Entrepreneurs Earned Consumers' Trust from Wedgwood to Dell* (Boston: Harvard Business School Press, 2001); Blaszczyk. For works more specifically on advertising, see Stuart Ewen, *Captains of Consciousness: Advertising and the Social Roots of American Culture* (New York: McGraw-Hill, 1977); Roland Marchand, *Advertising the American Dream: Making Way for Modernity, 1920–1940* (Berkeley: University of California Press, 1985); T. J. Jackson Lears, *Fables of Abundance: A Cultural History of Advertising in America* (New York: Basic Books, 1994). For durable goods, see Martha Olney, *Buy Now, Pay Later: Advertising, Credit, and Consumer Durables in the 1920s* (Chapel Hill: University of North Carolina Press, 1991). For background on department stores, see William Leach, *Land of Desire: From the Department Store to the Department of Commerce: The Rise of America's Commercial Culture* (New York: Pantheon Books, 1993); Susan Porter Benson, *Counter Cultures: Saleswomen, Managers, and Customers in American Department Stores, 1890–1940* (Urbana: University of Illinois Press, 1986); Hrant Pasdermadjian, *The Department Store: Its Origins, Evolution, and Economics* (New York: Arno Press, 1976).

24. Newel Howland Comish, *The Standard of Living: Elements of Consumption* (New York: Macmillan Co., 1923), 110.

25. On magazines, consumer culture, and gender, see Richard Ohmann, *Selling Culture: Magazines, Markets, and Class at the Turn of the Century* (London: Verso, 1996); Ellen Gruber Garvey, *The Adman in the Parlor: Magazines and the Gendering of Consumer Culture, 1880s to 1910s* (New York: Oxford University Press, 1996); Jennifer Scanlon, *Inarticulate Longings: The Ladies' Home Journal, Gender, and the Promises of Consumer Culture* (New York: Routledge, 1995); Leland M. Roth, "Getting the Houses to the People: Edward Bok, *The Ladies' Home Journal,* and the Ideal House," in *Perspectives in Vernacular Architecture, IV,* ed. Thomas Carter and Bernard L. Herman (Columbia: University of Missouri Press, 1991). For specific material on images and printing technology, see David Clayton Phillips, "Art for Industry's Sake: Halftone Technology, Mass Photography and the Social Transformation of American Print Culture" (Ph.D. diss., Yale University, 1996). For background on the increasing trade in American fiction, see David Minter, *A Cultural History of the American Novel* (New York: Cambridge University Press, 1994); Joan Shelley Rubin, *The Making of Middlebrow Culture* (Chapel Hill: University of North Carolina Press, 1992); James L. W. West III, *American Authors and the Literary Marketplace* (Philadelphia: University of Pennsylvania Press, 1988); Archibald Hanna, *Mirror for the Nation: An Annotated Bibliography of American Social Fiction, 1901–1950* (New York: Garland, 1985). See also Kirkpatrick, 37; Comish, 114; Kyrk, 377.

26. Kirkpatrick, 15.

27. Wile, 410; Eliot, 194; Simon Patten, "The Standardization of Family Life," in Eliot, ed., *American Standards and Planes of Living,* 194–95; Kyrk, 381.

28. Joseph Jacobs, "The Middle American," *American Magazine* 63 (March 1907): 526; Kyrk, 380.

29. J. Anthony Lukas cites a 1991 survey in which 93 percent of Americans polled perceive of themselves as members of the middle class; see *Big Trouble: A Murder in a Small Western Town Sets Off a Struggle for the Soul of America* (New York: Simon and Schuster, 1997), 13. A frequently cited survey that acknowledged the middle class as the American norm was "The Fortune Survey," *Fortune* 21 (February 1940) 14; in this survey 79 percent of those polled identified themselves as members of the middle class.

30. See, for example, Joan Wallach Scott, *Gender and the Politics of History* (New York: Columbia University Press, 1988); Denise Riley, *"Am I That Name?": Feminism and the Category of "Women" in History* (Minneapolis: University of Minnesota Press, 1988); Gail Bederman, *Manliness & Civilization: A Cultural History of Gender and Race in the United States, 1880–1917* (Chicago: University of Chicago Press, 1995); Mark C. Carnes and Clyde Griffen, *Meanings for Manhood: Constructions of Masculinity in Victorian America* (Chicago: University of Chicago Press, 1990); Michael Omi and Howard Winant, *Racial Formation in the United States: From the 1960s to the 1990s* (New York: Routledge, 1994); Matthew Frye Jacobson, *Whiteness of a Different Color: European Immigration and the Alchemy of Race* (Cambridge, Mass.: Harvard University Press, 1998).

31. For background and historiography of the American middle class, see Burton Bledstein and Robert Johnston, eds., *The Middling Sorts: Explorations in the History of the American Middle Class* (New York: Routledge, 2001); Joan Shelley Rubin, *The Making of Middlebrow Culture* (Chapel Hill: University of North Carolina Press, 1992); Stuart Blumin, *The Emergence of the Middle Class: Social Experience in the American City, 1760–1900* (New York: Cambridge University Press, 1989); John S. Gilkeson Jr., *Middle-Class Providence, 1820–1940* (Princeton: Princeton University Press, 1986); Karen Halttunen, *Confidence Men and Painted Women: A Study of Middle-Class Culture in America, 1830–1870* (New Haven: Yale University Press, 1982).

32. Lynd and Lynd, 478–79.

33. See, for example, David Hounshell, *From the American System to Mass Production, 1800–1932* (Baltimore: Johns Hopkins University Press, 1984); Merritt Roe Smith, *Harpers Ferry Armory and the New Technology: The Challenge of Change* (Ithaca: Cornell University Press, 1977); Alfred Chandler, *The Visible Hand: The Managerial Revolution in American Business* (Cambridge, Mass.: Belknap Press, 1977); Daniel T. Rodgers, *The Work Ethic in Industrial America, 1850–1920* (Chicago: University of Chicago Press, 1978).

34. David Noble, *America by Design: Science, Technology and the Rise of Corporate Capitalism* (New York: Knopf, 1977), 80–81.

35. Kyrk, 373, 376–77; Lucy Maynard Salmon, *History and the Texture of Modern Life: Selected Essays,* ed. Nicholas Adams and Bonnie G. Smith (Philadelphia: University of Pennsylvania Press, 2001); Jules Prown, "Mind in Matter: An Introduction to Material Culture Theory and Method," in *Material Life in America, 1600–1860,* ed. Robert Blair St. George (Boston: Northeastern University Press, 1988), 17–37.

36. In *Economic Problems of the Family,* Kyrk brilliantly theorized the role of the family in the American economy; in pointing out that the family was "the primary social unit . . . the primary economic group . . . the major consuming unit," Kyrk explained that in the 1930 Census, only 2.4 percent of the U.S. population lived "otherwise than in private households" and only 1.9 percent lived alone (2). See also Eliot, 469; Kirkpatrick, 21–22.

CHAPTER ONE. THE STANDARD OF ETIQUETTE

1. Foster Coates, "How Delmonico Sets a Table," *Ladies' Home Journal* 8, no. 12 (November 1891): 10; Amy Lyman Phillips, "Famous American Restaurants," *Good Housekeeping* 48, no. 1 (January 1909): 22–31; Jennifer Scanlon, *Inarticulate Longings: The Ladies' Home Journal, Gender, and the Promises of Consumer Culture* (New York: Routledge, 1995); Charles L. Venable, *Silver in America, 1840–1940: A Century of Splendor* (Dallas: Dallas Museum of Art, 1994), 127–28; Arthur M. Schlesinger, *Learning How to Behave: An Historical Study of American Etiquette Books* (New York: Macmillan, 1946), 30–33.

2. Fiske letter book, letter to E. M. Wheeler, 18 January 1877, Vol. 148, 24, Reed & Barton Collection, Manuscript Collection no. 597, Baker Library, Harvard University Graduate School of Business Administration, Cambridge, Mass. (Subsequent references to this collection will be designated R&B, with appropriate locating information.) The Fiske letter books are fifteen volumes of copies of letters sent from a manager at the Reed & Barton Company in Taunton, usually to branch offices and salesmen; the books are paginated, and the copies dated, but the precise recipients of the letters are occasionally unclear.

3. John F. Kasson, "Rituals of Dining: Table Manners in Victorian America," in *Dining in America, 1850–1900,* ed. Kathryn Grover (Amherst: University of Massachusetts Press, 1987), 115.

4. Earlier notions of sets of eating implements did exist. For example, in the 1400s, "apostle spoons" were produced in sets of thirteen, each one representing one of the apostles and Jesus. However, the idea of a set in which all forms matched one another in some way, and all groups of forms matched as well, was a later innovation. See James Cross Giblin, *From Hand to Mouth: Or, How We Invented Knives, Forks, Spoons, and Chopsticks, and the Table Manners that Go With Them* (New York: Thomas Crowell, 1987), passim; see especially chapters 3 and 5.

5. *Coin silver* was the term used for wares made out of silver melted down from

coins; the Tariff of 1842 stipulated that duty on luxury goods had to be paid in gold or silver specie, increasing the flow of coins into the United States. Venable, 19–20, 140.

6. Dorothy and Ivan Rainwater, *American Silverplate* (Nashville: Thomas Nelson, 1968), 18; Edmund P. Hogan, *An American Heritage: A Book about the International Silver Company* (Dallas: Taylor Publishing Company, 1977), 16.

7. The Tariff of 1842 assessing a 30 percent tax on imported luxury goods also bolstered the market for domestic products. Venable, 299.

8. Ibid., 19–20; Rainwater and Rainwater, 19, 29; Giblin, 61; *Jewelers' Circular and Horological Review* 19, no. 1 (February 1888): 21.

9. Philip Scranton, *Endless Novelty: Specialty Production and American Industrialization, 1865–1925* (Princeton: Princeton University Press, 1997), 108–21.

10. George Sweet Gibb, *The Whitesmiths of Taunton: A History of Reed & Barton, 1824–1943* (Cambridge, Mass.: Harvard University Press, 1943), 272; also see listing for Reed & Barton Company in Massachusetts, Vol. 10, 759, 855, 1010, R. G. Dun & Co. Collection, Baker Library, Harvard University Graduate School of Business Administration, Cambridge, Mass. (Subsequent references to this collection will be designated R. G. Dun, with appropriate volume and page citations.)

11. "The Record of Last Year," *Jewelers' Circular and Horological Review* 19, no. 1 (February 1888): 38; 15, no. 1 (February 1884): 3.

12. Hogan, 65; Gibb, 187–88, 254–55.

13. Clifford E. Clark Jr., "The Vision of the Dining Room: Plan Book Dreams and Middle-Class Realities," in Grover, ed., *Dining in America*, 142–71; Susan Williams, *Savory Suppers & Fashionable Feasts: Dining in Victorian America* (New York: Pantheon Books in association with the Strong Museum, 1985), 51–90; Venable, 124–25.

14. Robert Herrick, *The Real World* (New York: Macmillan Co., 1901), 12, 158.

15. Venable, 128–30; Williams, *Savory Suppers,* 93–128.

16. *Manual of Etiquette for the Use of Schools and Academies* (New York: D&J Sadlier & Co., 1888), 20; F. Oswald, ed., *Manual of Good Manners* (Baltimore: Kreuzer Bros., 1874), 47–48; Mrs. Julia M. Bradley, *Modern Manners and Social Forms* (Chicago: James B. Smiley, 1889), 179; Christine Terhune Herrick, "Home Dinners without a Servant," *Harper's Bazar* 40, no. 12 (December 1906): 1168; Anna Wentworth Sears, "Good Form—The Points That Tell," *Harper's Bazar* 33, no. 44 (3 November 1900): 1728–29; Robert De Valcourt, *The Illustrated Book of Manners: A Manual of Good Behavior and Public Accomplishments* (Cincinnati: R. W. Cornell & Co., 1865), 128.

17. De Valcourt, 137.

18. Kasson, 119–39; Williams, *Savory Suppers,* ix, 21–22, 75–78; Venable, 137–39; Schlesinger, passim.

19. De Valcourt, iii.

20. Sears, 1728.

21. Mrs. Burton Kingsland, "Dinners, Luncheons and Teas: Covering Every Point in Connection with Each," *Ladies' Home Journal* 17, no. 5 (April 1900): 22.

22. G. H. Sandison, *How to Behave and How to Amuse: A Handy Manual of Etiquette and Parlor Games* (New York: Christian Herald, 1895), 35; "On Setting the Table," *Harper's Bazar* 37, no. 4 (April 1903): 390–91; Florence Howe Hall, "How to Set the Table," *Harper's Bazar* 41, no. 5 (May 1907): 492–93; C. T. Herrick, "Entertaining Without Service," *Harper's Bazar* 41, no. 11 (November 1907): 1120–24; Christine Terhune Herrick, "How to Serve a Dinner," *Harper's Bazar* 40, no. 7 (July 1906): 660–64; Herrick, "Home Dinners without a Servant," 1165–68; Kingsland, 22; De Valcourt, 137.

23. Herrick, "How to Serve a Dinner," 660.

24. Mrs. Burton Kingsland, "Courtesy and Good Manners in the Home," *Ladies' Home Journal* 18, no. 1 (December 1900): 32.

25. Herrick, "Home Dinners without a Servant," 1167; Mrs. S. T. Rorer, "The Training of a Waitress," *Ladies' Home Journal* 17, no. 10 (September 1900): 22; Kingsland, "Courtesy and Good Manners," 32; Bradley, 203.

26. De Valcourt, 249.

27. Oswald, 53–54.

28. Sandison, 11; see also, Kingsland, "Dinners, Luncheons and Teas," 22; Sears, 1728; De Valcourt, 129; Bradley, 189; *The Guide to Politeness* (New York: George Blackie and Co., 1875), 30.

29. De Valcourt, 129.

30. Theodore Dreiser, *Jennie Gerhardt* (1911; rpt. Cleveland: World Publishing Co., 1954), 199.

31. Eleanor Hallowell Abbott, *The White Linen Nurse* (New York: Century Co., 1913), 165.

32. Williams, *Savory Suppers*, 10–12.

33. "Fashions in Jewelry," *Jewelers' Circular and Horological Review* 16, no. 12 (January 1886): 396; 15, no. 11 (December 1884): 341; 17, no. 4 (May 1886): 117–18, 124; 17, no. 5 (June 1886): 149, 159.

34. Venable, 139–40.

35. Hogan, 39.

36. "Growth of Art Appreciation," *Jewelers' Circular and Horological Review* 17, no. 3 (April 1886): 71. For the influence of auctions on public taste, see Katherine C. Grier, *Culture & Comfort: Parlor Making and Middle-Class Identity, 1850–1930* (Washington, D.C.: Smithsonian Institution Press, 1997), 28.

37. Clipping in scrapbook, Vol. 206, R&B.

38. "Official Awards, Sydney International Exposition," Box A-11, R&B.

39. Brochure, 1881, Box D-30, File: F.2: Christmas Booklets, 1878–1881, Display and Other Advertising 1870–1900, R&B; Venable, 136–39.

40. Venable, 13, 20, 26, 74–79; Rainwater and Rainwater, 20; Giblin, 60–61;

Dorothy Rainwater, "Victorian Dining Silver," in Grover, ed., *Dining in America*, 177; Williams, *Savory Suppers*, 76–78.

41. Venable, 74, 82; Scranton, *Endless Novelty*, 10–11; Philip Scranton, "Diversity in Diversity: Flexible Production and American Industrialization, 1870–1930," *Business History Review* 65 (1991): 27–90. Regina Lee Blaszczyk also deals with the issue of batch or flexible production in *Imagining Consumers: Design and Innovation from Wedgwood to Corning* (Baltimore: Johns Hopkins University Press, 2000).

42. Gibb, 184–85, 189, 254–55.

43. Ibid., 180; Venable, 93.

44. Account book, Vol. 66, 122–23, 152–53, R&B; quotation from, Massachusetts, Vol. 10, 759, R. G. Dun; see also Gibb, 184.

45. *Reed & Barton, Artistic Workers in Gold and Silver Electro Plate, Illustrated Catalogue*, 1885, Vol. D-29, 293, R&B.

46. Gibb refers to the "increasingly prominent place the flatware came to occupy in the American home" at this time. Gibb, 189, 254–55; Rainwater and Rainwater, 30; Venable, 93.

47. Gibb, 254–55.

48. M. T. Rogers letter book, letter to E. M. Wheeler, 14 August 1878, Vol. 167, 14, R&B. The M. T. Rogers letter books are ten volumes of copies of letters sent from a manager at the Reed & Barton Company in Taunton, usually to branch offices and salesmen; the books are paginated, and the copies dated, but the precise recipients of the letters are occasionally unclear.

49. Fiske letter book, letter to Calvin Harris, 6 March 1878, Vol. 160, 3, R&B.

50. M. T. Rogers letter book, letter to Calvin Harris, 16 November 1878, Vol. 170, 37–38, R&B.

51. M. T. Rogers letter book, letter to Calvin Harris, 14 November 1878, Vol. 170, 27–28, R&B.

52. *Reed & Barton, Artistic Workers in Gold and Silver Electro Plate, Illustrated Catalogue*, n.p.; for background on the rise of brand names, see Nancy F. Koehn, *Brand New: How Entrepreneurs Earned Consumers' Trust from Wedgwood to Dell* (Boston: Harvard Business School Press, 2001); Susan Strasser, *Satisfaction Guaranteed: The Making of the American Mass Market* (New York: Pantheon Books, 1989); John Phillip Jones, *What's in a Name? Advertising and the Concept of Brands* (Lexington, Mass.: D. C. Heath, 1986).

53. Fiske letter book, letter to Calvin Harris, 26 April 1878, Vol. 160, 40; 14 May 1878, Vol. 160, 49, R&B.

54. Venable, 14.

55. "A Word for Makers of Fine Goods," *Jewelers' Circular and Horological Review* 16, no. 10 (November 1885): 300–301; Gibb, 251–54; Rainwater and Rainwater, 30–31, 432; Venable, 151.

56. "The American at Work, IV: Among the Silver-Platers," *Appleton's Journal* 5 (December 1878): 484.

57. "Art Work in Silver," scrapbook, Vol. 206, R&B.

58. Gibb, 251.

59. "Fashions in Jewelry," *Jewelers' Circular and Horological Review* 16, no. 10 (November 1885): 323–34.

60. Although this series referred to patterns in sterling silver, the design principle held for silverplate as well. The series began in *Jewelers' Circular and Horological Review* 30, no. 10 (10 April 1895): 19–23, and continued weekly.

61. George Howard letter book, letter to Reed & Barton home office, 26 July 1902, Vol. 181, 5; letter to Reed & Barton home office, 15 August 1902, Vol. 181, 22, R&B. The George Howard letter book contains copies of letters sent from Reed & Barton's Philadelphia office; the book is paginated and the copies are dated.

62. Price list, Box B. A-10, File: R&B Papers re: Products 1860–1875, R&B; Gibb, 255–56; Venable, 136.

63. William Dean Howells et al., *The Whole Family: A Novel By Twelve Authors* (New York: Harper and Brothers, 1908), 300.

64. Susan Williams, "Introduction," in Grover, ed., *Dining in America*, 22; Williams, *Savory Suppers*, 78.

65. "Oddity in Design," *Jewelers' Circular and Horological Review* 16, no. 2 (March 1885): 59.

66. *Electro Gold and Silver Plate Catalogue*, 1882, Vol. D-1, 68, R&B.

67. See, for example, *Jewelers' Circular and Horological Review* 16, no. 4 (May 1885): iii; Fiske letter book, letter to Calvin Harris, 14 June 1878, Vol. 161, 3, R&B; Gibb, 255–56.

68. M. T. Rogers letter book, letter to Calvin Harris, 6 December 1878, Vol. 171, 19, R&B; Gibb, 216–19.

69. Venable, 140; Hogan, 72.

70. "Fashions in Jewelry," *Jewelers' Circular and Horological Review* 17, no. 5 (June 1886): 153.

71. *Jewelers' Circular and Horological Review* 16, no. 9 (October 1885): xxiv.

72. The excessive variety created by the many companies in competition with one another led to some call for reform in the early twentieth century. As part of the Department of Commerce's evaluation of waste in industry under Secretary Herbert Hoover, flatware manufacturers agreed in 1926 to limit the number of pieces made in any one pattern; but this limit was to fifty-seven pieces—from today's perspective it is hard to imagine such a variety considered a hindrance. Although this voluntary restriction applied to sterling silver, it had implications for silverplate as well. See Venable, 271.

73. Gibb, 213–14.

74. Quoted in a Reed & Barton brochure, in scrapbook, Vol. 204, 202, R&B.

75. "A Word for Makers of Fine Goods," *Jewelers' Circular and Horological Review* 16, no. 10 (November 1885): 300–301.

76. Gibb, 191–92; Hogan, 110.

77. The task of designing exhibits at World's Fairs and other competitions was similar to that of designing show windows. See William Leach, *Land of Desire: From the Department Store to the Department of Commerce: The Rise of America's Commercial Culture* (New York: Pantheon Books, 1993), 39–70.

78. Correspondence and notes, Box B. A-10, File: Reed & Barton Documents—International Exhibition, Philadelphia 1875–76, R&B; Massachusetts, Vol. 10, 759, R. G. Dun; Gibb, 200; Venable, 107–19.

79. "1876 Centennial," Vol. 205, R&B.

80. *Jewelers' Circular and Horological Review* 16, no. 1 (February 1885): 9; 16, no. 2 (March 1885): 43–44, 62; Reed & Barton's decision not to participate in the Exposition at New Orleans was no doubt also related to the huge expenditure for their 1885 catalogue.

81. *Jewelers' Circular and Horological Review* 19, no. 1 (February 1888): 25.

82. Clipping from *Harper's Weekly,* 23 December 1876, in Box B. A-10, File: Reed & Barton Documents—International Exhibition, Philadelphia 1875–76, R&B.

83. Fiske letter book, letter to Calvin Harris, 6 February 1877, Vol. 149, 1; letter to Calvin Harris, 30 July 1877, Vol. 153, 13, R&B.

84. "New Illustrated Spoon and Fork Price List," 1880, Box D-30, File: F.2: Christmas Booklets, 1878–1881, Display and Other Advertising 1870–1900, R&B.

85. Fiske letter book, letter to Calvin Harris, 26 September 1877, Vol. 154, 54, R&B.

86. Venable, 45; *Jewelers' Circular and Horological Review* 16, no. 1 (February 1884): 3.

87. Brochures, trade cards, and other ephemera, Box D-30, File: F.2: Christmas Booklets, 1878–1881, Display and Other Advertising 1870–1900, R&B.

88. Venable, 101; Gibb, 203–4.

89. Hogan, 24–25.

90. Fiske letter book, letter to Calvin Harris, 9 June 1877, Vol. 151, 49; letter to Calvin Harris, 14 June 1877, Vol. 151, 61, R&B; *Goulding's New York City Directory* (New York: Goulding, 1876).

91. Fiske letter book, letter to Calvin Harris, 20 June 1877, Vol. 152, 7; letter to Calvin Harris, 31 August 1877, Vol. 153, 59, R&B.

92. Fiske letter book, letter to Calvin Harris, 3 January 1877, Vol. 148, 19; letter to Calvin Harris, 24 February 1877, Vol. 148, 39; letter to Calvin Harris, 14 April 1877, Vol. 150, 41; letter to Calvin Harris, 12 May 1877, Vol. 151, 11; letter to Calvin Harris, 28 August 1877, Vol. 153, 52, R&B.

93. "A Splendid Specimen of American Book Making," undated clipping from *The Evangelist,* in scrapbook, Vol. 206, R&B.

94. Fiske letter book, letter to Calvin Harris, 30 April 1877, Vol. 150, 61; letter to Calvin Harris, 21 July 1877, Vol. 153, 4, R&B.

95. Fiske letter book, letter to Calvin Harris, 26 July 1877, Vol. 153, 10; letter to Calvin Harris, 5 September 1877, Vol. 154, 8, R&B.

96. *Reed & Barton, Artistic Workers in Gold and Silver Electro Plate, Illustrated Catalogue,* n.p.

97. Leaflet, Box D-30, File: F.2: Christmas Booklets, 1878–1881, Display and Other Advertising 1870–1900, R&B.

98. Howells et al., 13.

99. Clippings in scrapbook, Vol. 206, n.p., R&B.

100. "To the Editor," typescript, Vol. 204, 174, R&B.

101. Clipping in scrapbook, Vol. 206, n.p., R&B.

102. Massachusetts, Vol. 10, 855, R. G. Dun.

103. George Howard letter book, letter to Reed & Barton home office, 12 August 1902, Vol. 181, 18, R&B; Venable, 26.

104. George Howard letter book, letter to Charles Flood, 10 September 1902, Vol. 181, 45, R&B.

105. Fiske letter book, letter to Calvin Harris, 6 February 1877, Vol. 149, 5; letter to Calvin Harris, 3 April 1877, Vol. 150, 30, R&B.

106. George Howard letter book, letter to Reed & Barton home office, 12 August 1902, Vol. 181, 18, R&B.

107. *Jewelers' Circular and Horological Review* 16, no. 11 (December 1885): 344; 19, no. 2 (March 1888): 25–26.

108. Gibb, 190; Venable, 102–3, 235.

109. Advertising list, scrapbook, Vol. 204, R&B; Gibb, 199, 224.

110. *Reed & Barton, Artistic Workers in Gold and Silver Electro Plate, Illustrated Catalogue,* 329.

111. Advertisement, scrapbook, Vol. 216, R&B.

112. Ibid.

113. Ibid.

114. "Fashions in Jewelry," *Jewelers' Circular and Horological Review* 17, no. 3 (April 1886): 97.

115. Fiske letter book, letter to Calvin Harris, 17 April 1878, Vol. 160, 35, R&B.

116. *Jewelers' Circular and Horological Review* 16, no. 2 (March 1885): 43.

117. "Electros" [Record Book], Vol. 188, R&B; Fiske letter book, 7 June 1877, Vol. 151, 42, R&B.

118. Advertisement, Box D-30, File: F.2: Christmas Booklets, 1878–1881, Display and Other Advertising 1870–1900, R&B.

119. Venable, 237.

120. Gibb, 220–23; Venable 226–27; Hogan, 43.

121. See, for example, *Jewelers' Circular and Horological Review* 30, no. 3 (20 February 1895): 17; 30, no. 10 (10 April 1895): 14–15; 30, no. 15 (15 May 1895): 15.

122. George Howard letter book, letters to Reed & Barton home office, 27 August 1902, 4 September 1902, 6 September 1902, 12 September 1902, Vol. 181, 34, 40, 42, 46, R&B.

123. "The Channels of Trade," *Jewelers' Circular and Horological Review* 16, no. 3 (April 1885): 66.

124. George Howard letter book, letter to Reed & Barton home office, 5 August 1902, Vol. 181, 12, R&B.

125. George Howard letter book, letter to Reed & Barton home office, 19 August 1902, Vol. 181, 26, R&B.

126. In 1881, salesmen's licensing fees, which had been assessed by states and counties, were challenged and deemed unconstitutional by the U.S. Supreme Court, further encouraging companies to send their own salesmen out. Venable, 43–47, 93. For more information about the earlier reliance on wholesalers, see Gibb, 153–56, 163–65; George Howard letter book, letter to New York Ship Building Co., 3 September 1902, Vol. 181, 39, R&B.

127. Oscar Lewis and Carroll D. Hall, *Bonanza Inn: America's First Luxury Hotel* (New York: Alfred A. Knopf, 1939), passim, especially chapter 1, "Show Place."

128. For whole section, see letters of Joseph H. Rines, Box: B. A-10, Folder: Reed & Barton Letters—Correspondence with agents, domestic and foreign, 1866–1875, R&B. See also Gibb, 189.

129. Gibb, 217–18; Hogan, 65; Williams, *Savory Suppers,* 8. Katherine C. Grier discusses the influence of public spaces on the popularization of upholstered furniture in *Culture & Comfort;* see particularly, chapter 1, "Imagining the Parlor," 22–63.

130. *Jewelers' Circular and Horological Review* 16, no. 10 (November 1885): 314; 16, no. 12 (January 1886): 389–90.

131. *Electro Gold and Silver Plate Catalogue,* 68.

132. Gibb, 256.

133. Scrapbook, Vol. 206, R&B; Payroll Expense 5/1/1905–5/1/1906, Box A-4, File 2: Payrolls, 1829, 1903–15 & Estimates 1874–76, R&B; Gibb, 217–18.

134. Scrapbook, Vol. 206, R&B.

135. George Howard letter book, letter to W. H. Woodward, 31 July 1902, Vol. 181, 10; letter to W. H. Woodward, 23 July 1902, Vol. 181, 2–3; letter to Reed & Barton home office, 26 August 1902, Vol. 181, 33, R&B.

136. George Howard letter book, letter to W. G. Price, 24 July 1902, Vol. 181, 4; letter to Daniel Test, 29 July 1902, Vol. 181, 7; letter to Carey Thomas, 15 August 1902, Vol. 181, 23; letter to Old Dominion Steamship Co., 18 August 1902, Vol. 181, 24, R&B.

137. *Reed & Barton, Artistic Workers in Gold and Silver Electro Plate, Illustrated Catalogue,* n.p.; Gibb, 187. Though beyond the scope of this chapter, Reed & Barton

did a significant trade abroad, particularly in South America; portions of the 1885 catalogue were printed in Spanish; see also Gibb, 235–47.

138. Fiske letter book, letter to Calvin Harris, 3 April 1878, Vol. 160, 31, R&B; Gibb, 229–33.

139. Fiske letter book, letter to Calvin Harris, 27 June 1878, Vol. 161, 10; letter to Calvin Harris, 22 July 1878, Vol. 161, 29, R&B.

140. Gibb, 234; "Trade Centers," *Jewelers' Circular and Horological Review* 16, no. 5 (June 1885): 129–30; "Trade Gossip," 30, no. 10 (10 April 1895): 24.

141. It is possible that in 1878, the year after an unusually large expenditure for the 1877 catalogue, Reed & Barton managers thought it best not to produce and hold a large stock; nonetheless, it is apparent that this practice, of producing for orders, was acceptable. M. T. Rogers letter book, letter to E. M. Wheeler, 1 May 1878, Vol. 165, 12, R&B.

142. Fiske letter book, letter to E. M. Wheeler, 21 March 1877, Vol. 150, 3, R&B; letter to Calvin Harris, 13 March 1878, Vol. 160, 14, R&B.

143. Contract with New England Telephone Company, Box B. A-10, File: Reed & Barton, Miscellaneous Papers, 1843–1874, R&B; *Jewelers' Circular and Horological Review* 15, no. 7 (August 1884): 228.

144. "The Record of Last Year," *Jewelers' Circular and Horological Review* 19, no. 1 (February 1888): 38.

145. H. W. Graves, letter to Reed & Barton Company, 11 May 1881, Box B. A-10, File: Reed & Barton letters—correspondence with agents, domestic and foreign, 1866–1875, R&B.

146. George Howard letter book, letter to Reed & Barton home office, 5 August 1902, Vol. 181, 11, R&B.

147. Postcard, Box D-30, File: F.2: Christmas Booklets, 1878–1881, Display and Other Advertising 1870–1900, R&B.

148. Fiske letter book, letter to [??] Oxton, 21 March 1877, Vol. 150, 4, R&B.

149. M. T. Rogers letter book, letters to Calvin Harris, 14 February 1878, 27 February 1878, Vol. 163, 34, 47, R&B.

150. H. W. Graves, letter to Reed & Barton Company, 11 May 1881, Box B. A-10, File: Reed & Barton letters—correspondence with agents, domestic and foreign, 1866–1875, R&B; Gibb, 210.

151. George Howard letter book, letter to Reed & Barton home office, 11 August 1902, Vol. 181, 17, R&B.

152. George Howard letter book, letter to Reed & Barton home office, 12 August 1902, Vol. 181, 18, R&B.

153. De Valcourt, 128.

154. R. C. Chapin, "The Influence of Income on Standards of Life," *American Journal of Sociology* 14, no. 5 (March 1909): 638–39.

155. Newel Howland Comish, *The Standard of Living: Elements of Consumption*

(New York: Macmillan Co., 1923), 99, 101; Royal Meeker, "Minimum Quantity Budget Necessary to Maintain a Worker's Family of Five in Health and Decency," in *American Standards and Planes of Living: Readings in the Social Economics of Consumption,* ed. Thomas Eliot (Boston: Ginn & Co., 1931), 518–19.

CHAPTER TWO. THE STANDARD OF HEALTH AND DECENCY

1. F. Oswald, ed., *Manual of Good Manners* (Baltimore: Kreuzer Bros., 1874), 33.

2. Newel Howland Comish, *The Standard of Living: Elements of Consumption* (New York: Macmillan Co., 1923), 97; Harry Laidler, "How America Lives: A Living Standard," in *American Standards and Planes of Living: Readings in the Social Economics of Consumption,* ed. Thomas Eliot (Boston: Ginn & Co., 1931), 486. Nancy Tomes explores these relations between cleanliness, hygiene, and good health in *The Gospel of Germs: Men, Women, and the Microbe in American Life* (Cambridge, Mass.: Harvard University Press, 1998).

3. Seneca Egbert, *A Manual of Hygiene and Sanitation* (Philadelphia: Lea Brothers & Co., 1898), 24.

4. The Kohler Company of Kohler, Wisconsin, is the descendent of several companies, with histories stretching back to the 1870s. For the purposes of this chapter, the earliest company under consideration is Kohler, Hayssen & Stehn, formed in 1879, the first to produce enamelware bathroom fixtures. The company was reorganized and incorporated in 1901 as J. M. Kohler Sons Company, and in 1913, changed its name to the Kohler Company. Although the bulk of this chapter concerns the period of the J. M. Kohler Sons Company, I do use the designation "Kohler" or "Kohler Company" at times, as there is a direct lineage and the Kohler Company in fact claims its originating date as 1873.

5. Copy of *The Sheboygan Times,* n.d.; copy of *The Sheboygan Herald,* 13 May 1897, Folder 1–052: 658.3: Kohler, Hayssen & Stehn: Labor Relations & Personnel Mgmt., Kohler Company Archives, Kohler, Wis. (All subsequent references to this archive will be designated KCA, with appropriate locating information.)

6. For background on the Better Homes in American campaign, see Blanche Halbert, *The Better Homes Manual* (Chicago: University of Chicago Press, in cooperation with Better Homes in America, 1931); Janet Anne Hutchison, "American Housing, Gender, and the Better Homes Movement, 1922–1935" (Ph.D. diss., University of Delaware, 1989); Karen Altman, "Consuming Ideology: The Better Homes in American Campaign," *Critical Studies in Mass Communication* 7, no. 3 (September 1990): 286–308.

7. John I. Jegi, *Practical Lessons in Human Physiology, Personal Hygiene, and Public Health for Schools* (New York: Macmillan, 1903), 307.

8. Egbert, 2. For other contemporary definitions of hygiene, see, for example, Jegi, 3; George Wilson, *Health and Healthy Homes: A Guide to Domestic Hygiene*

(Philadelphia: Presley Blakiston, 1880), 169; Kenelm Winslow, *The Home Medical Library* (New York: Review of Reviews Co., 1907), 5:219; W.M.L. Coplin and D. Bevan, *A Manual of Practical Hygiene Designed for Sanitary and Health Officers, Practitioners, and Students of Medicine* (Philadelphia: P. Blakiston, Son, & Co., 1893), 91–92; Frederick W. Smith, *Essentials of Practical Hygiene* (Syracuse: n.p., 1908), 11, 93; Maurice Le Bosquet, ed., *Personal Hygiene* (Chicago: American School of Home Economics, 1907), 1; Louis J. Cooke, *Manual of Personal Hygiene* (Minneapolis: H. W. Wilson Co., 1910), n.p.

9. Smith, 93; see also Le Bosquet, 2; Jegi, 311–12; Charles Harrington, *A Manual of Practical Hygiene for Students, Physicians, and Medical Officers* (Philadelphia: Lea Brothers & Co., 1901), 692.

10. Smith, 13; see also Lillian Brandt, "Sanitary Progress," *Charities* 12, no. 13 (2 April 1904): 361.

11. Florence Nesbitt, "The Chicago Standard Budget for Dependent Families," in Eliot, ed., *American Standards and Planes of Living,* 524; George M. Kober, *Industrial and Personal Hygiene* (Washington: President's Homes Commission, 1908), 97.

12. Maureen Ogle offers valuable insight into the incorporation of plumbing fixtures into domestic spaces, focusing on the convenience of linking individual households to larger sanitation systems, in *All the Modern Conveniences: American Household Plumbing, 1840–1890* (Baltimore: Johns Hopkins University Press, 1996).

13. Oscar Kroos, letter to Walter Kohler, 19 January 1914, Folder: 1–053: 651.5: 48: J. M. Kohler Sons Co.: Office Files—Kohler Co., KCA.

14. Simon Nelson Patten, "The Crisis in American Home Life," in Eliot, ed., *American Standards and Planes of Living,* 367.

15. William Allen, "Sanitation and Social Progress," *American Journal of Sociology* 8, no. 5 (March 1903): 632; see also Brandt, 361; Winslow, 5:216–17.

16. Martha Cutler, "Modern Bathrooms," *Harper's Bazar* 41, no. 2 (1907): 167–68.

17. *Kohler Sales Helps,* promotional booklet, 1915, 1–3, Folder: 2–100: 658.84: Kohler Co.: Plumbing—Sales Action Manual, KCA.

18. Copy of Kohler, Hayssen & Stehn Manufacturing Company Catalogue, n.d., inside front cover, Folder: 1–051: 609: Kohler and Silberzahn: General History, KCA; Trudi Jennes Eblen, "A History of the Kohler Company of Kohler Wisconsin 1871–1914" (M.S. thesis, University of Wisconsin, 1965), 5.

19. Broadside, n.d., Folder 1–052: 659.13: Kohler, Hayssen & Stehn: Advertising, KCA.

20. Eblen, 5.

21. In 1884, hollowware and enameled goods accounted for $16,676 out of total sales of $39,962; in 1887, they amounted to $50,214 out of $69,538. Eblen, 15 (Table III), 22, 36–38, 41, 58.

22. Billheads dated 10 September 1895, 1 June 1896, Folder: 1–052: 659.13: Kohler, Hayssen & Stehn: Advertising; copy of 1902 catalogue, Folder: 1–052: 609: Kohler, Hayssen & Stehn: General History, KCA.

23. Philip Scranton, *Endless Novelty: Specialty Production and American Industrialization, 1865–1925* (Princeton: Princeton University Press, 1997), 10–11; "Diversity in Diversity: Flexible Production and American Industrialization, 1870–1930," *Business History Review* 65 (1991): 27–90. Regina Lee Blaszczyk also deals with the issue of batch or flexible production in *Imagining Consumers: Design and Innovation from Wedgwood to Corning* (Baltimore: Johns Hopkins University Press, 2000).

24. Blaszczyk explores Kohler's introduction of color into the production of bathroom fixtures; see 194–206.

25. Walter Kohler, letter to Oscar Kroos, 5 February 1914, Folder: 1–053: 651.5: 48: J. M. Kohler Sons Co.: Office Files—Kohler Co., KCA.

26. Walter Kohler, letter to Kohler Co. New York office, 21 May 1910, Folder: 1–053: 651.5: 49: J. M. Kohler Sons Co.: Office Files—J. M. Kohler Sons Co.—New York Office; Walter Kohler, letter to Kohler Co. home office, 21 April 1911, Folder: 1–053: 651.5: 50: J. M. Kohler Sons Co.: Office Files—W. J. Kohler, KCA.

27. Copy of advertisement in *Plumbers' Trade Journal,* Folder 1–052: 659.13: Kohler, Hayssen & Stehn: Advertising, KCA.

28. Oscar Kroos, letter to Walter Kohler, 24 January 1914, Folder: 1–053: 651.5: 48: J. M. Kohler Sons Co.: Office Files—Kohler Co.; Oscar Kroos and Roy J. Miller, letter to Walter Kohler, 20 April 1911, Folder: 1–053: 651.5: 50: J. M. Kohler Sons Co.: Office Files—W. J. Kohler, KCA.

29. Copy of advertisement in *Plumbers' Trade Journal.*

30. Eblen, 59–60.

31. *Kohler Sales Helps,* 1–2.

32. Copy of advertisement in *Plumbers' Trade Journal.*

33. Advertisement in *The Metal Worker,* 22 April 1905, in scrapbook, Folder: 1–053: 659.03: J. M. Kohler Sons Co.: Advertising, KCA.

34. *Kohler of Kohler News* 1, no. 2 (December 1916): 5, KCA.

35. W. B. Clark, letter to Walter Kohler, 23 January 1914, Folder: 1–053: 651.5: 20: J. M. Kohler Sons Co.: Office Files—W.B. Clark, KCA.

36. George Leland Hunter, "Inside the House that Jack Built," *Country Life* 25 (November 1913): 66.

37. C. W. Armes Jr., letters to Walter Kohler, 12 March 1907, 24 March 1909; Walter J. Kohler, letter to C. W. Armes, 25 March 1907, Folder: 1–053: 651.5: 4: J. M. Kohler Sons Co.: Office Files—C. W. Armes Jr., KCA.

38. Walter Kohler, letter to William Barth, 31 October 1908, Folder: 1–053: 651.5: 9: J. M. Kohler Sons Co.: Office Files—W. H. Barth, KCA.

39. Eblen, 66–68.

40. Walter Kohler, letter to Kohler Co. home office, 20 December 1907, Folder: 1–053: 651.5: 50: J. M. Kohler Sons Co.: Office Files—W. J. Kohler, KCA.

41. *Kohler of Kohler News* 1, no. 1 (November 1916): 7; 1, no. 2 (December 1916): 5, KCA.

42. Walter Kohler, letter to William Barth, 9 November 1908, Folder: 1–053: 651.5: 9: J. M. Kohler Sons Co.: Office Files—W. H. Barth, KCA.

43. William Barth, letter to Walter Kohler, 11 November 1908, Folder: 1–053: 651.5: 9: J. M. Kohler Sons Co.: Office Files—W. H. Barth, KCA.

44. *Kohler of Kohler News* 1, no. 1 (November 1916): 7; 1, no. 2 (December 1916): 5, KCA.

45. B. Francis Dashiell, "The Septic System for Sewage," *House and Garden* 40 (August 1921): 52.

46. Walter Kohler, undated telegram (c. February 1909), Folder: 1–053: 651.5: 49: J. M. Kohler Sons Co.: Office Files—J. M. Kohler Sons Co.—New York Office, KCA. For a broader discussion of the importance of show windows, see William Leach, *Land of Desire: From the Department Store to the Department of Commerce: The Rise of America's Commercial Culture* (New York: Pantheon Books, 1993), 39–70.

47. Walter Kohler, letter to William Barth, 5 May 1909, Folder: 1–053: 651.5: 49: J. M. Kohler Sons Co.: Office Files—J. M. Kohler Sons Co.—New York Office, KCA.

48. Walter Kohler, letter to Kohler Co. home office, 20 December 1907, Folder: 1–053: 651.5: 50: J. M. Kohler Sons Co.: Office Files—W. J. Kohler, KCA.

49. Walter Kohler, letter to Kohler Co. home office, 15 May 1911, Folder: 1–053: 651.5: 50: J. M. Kohler Sons Co.: Office Files—W. J. Kohler, KCA.

50. Walter Kohler, company memorandum, 14 December 1911, Folder: 1–053: 651.5: 22: J. M. Kohler Sons Co.: Office Files—Colwell Lead Co., KCA.

51. *Kohler Sales Helps*, 1.

52. Walter J. Kohler, letter to Hughes and Co., 6 June 1911, Folder: 1–053: 651.5: 42: J. M. Kohler Sons Co.: Office Files—Hughes and Co., KCA.

53. Walter Kohler, letter to Oscar Kroos, 5 February 1914, Folder: 1–053: 651.5: 48: J. M. Kohler Sons Co.: Office Files—Kohler Co., KCA.

54. Walter Kohler, letter to Oscar Kroos, 31 January 1914, Folder: 1–053: 651.5: 48: J. M. Kohler Sons Co.: Office Files—Kohler Co., KCA.

55. Walter Kohler, letter to Oscar Kroos, 29 January 1914, Folder: 1–053: 651.5: 48: J. M. Kohler Sons Co.: Office Files—Kohler Co., KCA.

56. Walter Kohler, letter to Oscar Kroos, 30 January 1914 (re: West Co., Salt Lake City); letter to Oscar Kroos, 30 January 1914 (re: Western National Supply Co., San Diego), Folder: 1–053: 651.5: 48: J. M. Kohler Sons Co.: Office Files—Kohler Co., KCA.

57. Walter Kohler, letter to Oscar Kroos, 29 January 1914, Folder: 1–053: 651.5: 48: J. M. Kohler Sons Co.: Office Files—Kohler Co., KCA.

58. Walter Kohler, letter to Oscar Kroos, 30 January 1914 (re: Western National

Supply Co., San Diego), Folder: 1–053: 651.5: 48: J. M. Kohler Sons Co.: Office Files—Kohler Co., KCA.

59. Walter Kohler, letter to Oscar Kroos, 5 February 1914, Folder: 1–053: 651.5: 48: J. M. Kohler Sons Co.: Office Files—Kohler Co., KCA.

60. Walter Kohler, office memorandum, 3 January 1911, Folder 1–053: 658: J. M. Kohler Sons Co.: Corporate Structure, KCA; Eblen, 69–70.

61. Walter Kohler, letter to Kohler Co. home office, 12 May 1911; Oscar Kroos, letters to Walter Kohler, 11 May 1912, 18 May 1912, Folder: 1–053: 651.5: 50: J. M. Kohler Sons Co.: Office Files—W. J. Kohler; Oscar Kroos, letter to Walter Kohler, 24 January 1914, Folder: 1–053: 651.5: 48: J. M. Kohler Sons Co.: Office Files—Kohler Co., KCA.

62. Walter Kohler, letter to Oscar Kroos, 28 January 1914, Folder: 1–053: 651.5: 48: J. M. Kohler Sons Co.: Office Files—Kohler Co., KCA.

63. Walter Kohler, letter to Kohler Co. home office, 14 April 1911, Folder: 1–053: 651.5: 50: J. M. Kohler Sons Co.: Office Files—W. J. Kohler, KCA.

64. Kohler Company, *Porcelain Enameled Iron Sanitary Ware: Catalog K* (Kohler, Wis.: n.p., 1914), 8–19. On the importance of separate bathroom, see Coplin, 357; Comish, 97; Laidler, 486; Nesbitt, 524.

65. For some sense of the plethora of advice on bathing, see John H. Girdner, "Care of the Human Body," *Munsey's Magazine* 24, no. 5 (February 1901): 677–80; Woods Hutchinson, "Baths and Bathers," *Cosmopolitan* 45, no. 3 (August 1908): 305–10; C. Gilman Currier, *The Art of Preserving Health: Outlines of Practical Hygiene Adapted to American Conditions* (New York: E. B. Treat, 1893), 355; Alvin Davison, *The Human Body and Health: An Elementary Text-Book of Essential Anatomy, Applied Physiology, and Practical Hygiene for Schools* (New York: American Book Co., 1908), 187–88; Anna Galbraith, *Personal Hygiene and Physical Training for Women* (Philadelphia: W. B. Saunders Co., 1911), 21–33; George D. Bussey, *A Manual of Personal Hygiene* (Boston: Ginn & Co., 1917), 49–52; George Newton, *Practical Hygiene for Home and School* (Cedar Falls, Iowa: n.p., 1914), 8–11; Walter L. Pyle, ed., *A Manual of Personal Hygiene* (Philadelphia: W. B. Sanders & Co., 1900), 60–69; John Harvey Kellogg, *The Household Manual* (Battle Creek, Mich.: Office of the Health Reformer, 1875), 23; Wilson, 172–74; Coplin, 92–93; Smith, 93; Harrington, 692; Kober, 107–8; Winslow, 4:15–21; Le Bosquet, 137–41; Jegi, 156–59.

66. Robert De Valcourt, *The Illustrated Book of Manners: A Manual of Good Behavior and Public Accomplishments* (Cincinnati: R. W. Cornell & Co., 1865), 27.

67. Booth Tarkington, *The Magnificent Ambersons* (1918; rpt. New York: Bantam Books, 1994), 4.

68. Walter Kohler, letters to Oscar Kroos, 30 January 1914, 31 January 1914, Folder: 1–053: 651.5: 48: J. M. Kohler Sons Co.: Office Files—Kohler Co., KCA.

69. Oscar Kroos, letter to Walter Kohler, 6 February 1914, Folder: 1–053: 651.5: 48: J. M. Kohler Sons Co.: Office Files—Kohler Co., KCA.

70. [signature illegible], letter to Walter Kohler, 23 February 1914, Folder 1–053: 651.5: 82: J. M. Kohler Sons Co.: Office Files—J. J. Vollrath Mfg. Co., KCA.

71. Eblen, 49–50.

72. Oscar Kroos, letter to Walter Kohler, 16 February 1912, Folder: 1–053: 651.5: 50: J. M. Kohler Sons Co.: Office Files—W. J. Kohler, KCA.

73. *Kohler of Kohler News* 2, no. 8 (June 1918): 10, KCA.

74. W. B. Clark, letter to Walter Kohler, 23 January 1914, Folder: 1–053: 651.5: 20: J. M. Kohler Sons Co.: Office Files—W. B. Clark; Walter Kohler, letter to Kohler Co. home office, 20 December 1907, Folder: 1–053: 651.5: 50: J. M. Kohler Sons Co.: Office Files—W. J. Kohler, KCA.

75. Walter Kohler, letters to Kohler Co. home office, 12 May 1911, 21 May 1911, Folder: 1–053: 651.5: 50: J. M. Kohler Sons Co.: Office Files—W. J. Kohler, KCA.

76. Walter Kohler, letter to Kohler Co. home office, 12 May 1911, Folder: 1–053: 651.5: 50: J. M. Kohler Sons Co.: Office Files—W. J. Kohler, KCA.

77. Walter Kohler, letter to Kohler Co. home office, 10 April 1911, Folder: 1–053: 651.5: 50: J. M. Kohler Sons Co.: Office Files—W. J. Kohler, KCA.

78. "The Tonsor," brochure, n.d., Folder: 1–053: 659.03: J. M. Kohler Sons Co.: Advertising, KCA.

79. See, for example, *Kohler of Kohler News* 1, no. 1 (November 1916): 4; 1, no. 5 (March 1917): 17; 2, no. 6 (April 1918): 10, KCA.

80. *Kohler of Kohler News* 3, no. 3 (January 1919): 9, KCA.

81. Sinclair Lewis, *Babbitt* (1922; rpt. New York: Penguin Books, 1996), 131.

82. Walter Kohler, letter to Oscar Kroos, 29 January 1914, Folder: 1–053: 651.5: 48: J. M. Kohler Sons Co.: Office Files—Kohler Co., KCA.

83. *Kohler of Kohler News* 1, no. 2 (December 1916): 5, KCA.

84. Walter Kohler, letters to Oscar Kroos, 28 January 1914, 5 February 1914, Folder: 1–053: 651.5: 48: J. M. Kohler Sons Co.: Office Files—Kohler Co., KCA.

85. *Kohler of Kohler News* 1, no. 1 (November 1916): 5, KCA.

86. Walter Kohler, letters to Kohler Co. home office, 24 April 1911, 12 May 1911, Folder: 1–053: 651.5: 50: J. M. Kohler Sons Co.: Office Files—W. J. Kohler, KCA.

87. On the history of mass marketing and advertising, see, for example, Nancy F. Koehn, *Brand New: How Entrepreneurs Earned Consumers' Trust from Wedgwood to Dell* (Boston: Harvard Business School Press, 2001); Susan Strasser, *Satisfaction Guaranteed: The Making of the Mass Market* (New York: Pantheon Books, 1989); Richard Tedlow, *New and Improved: The Story of Mass Marketing in America* (New York: Basic Books, 1990); Pamela Laird, *Advertising Progress: American Business and the Rise of Consumer Marketing* (Baltimore: Johns Hopkins University Press, 1998); Blaszczyk; Thomas Hine, *The Total Package: The Evolution and Secret Meanings of Boxes, Bottles, and Cans, and Tubes* (Boston: Little, Brown and Co., 1995); Stuart Ewen, *Captains of Consciousness: Advertising and the Social Roots of American Culture* (New York: McGraw-Hill, 1977); Roland Marchand, *Advertising the American*

Dream: Making Way for Modernity, 1920–1940 (Berkeley: University of California Press, 1985); T. J. Jackson Lears, *Fables of Abundance: A Cultural History of Advertising in America* (New York: Basic Books, 1994); Martha Olney, *Buy Now, Pay Later: Advertising, Credit, and Consumer Durables in the 1920s* (Chapel Hill: University of North Carolina Press, 1991).

88. "Memorandum of Advertising Schedule for 1920: Plumbing Ware Only," Folder 1–211: 659: Kohler Co.: Advertising Management and Budget, KCA.

89. Walter Kohler, letter to Oscar Kroos, 29 January 1914, Folder: 1–053: 651.5: 48: J. M. Kohler Sons Co.: Office Files—Kohler Co., KCA; Eblen, 71–72.

90. "Memorandum of Advertising Schedule for 1920: Plumbing Ware Only."

91. "The Well-Equipped Bath," *House and Garden* 40 (August 1921): 58–59.

92. Hunter, 66.

93. J. M. Kohler Sons, Catalogue "A," 1908, KCA.

94. "Bring Your Bathroom Up To Date," *The Delineator* 83 (July 1913): 42.

95. Cutler, 165.

96. Charles G. Norris, *Bread* (New York: E. P. Dutton and Company, 1923), 244.

97. The one exception to the "rule of children" in Kohler's 1915 advertising campaign was an ad featuring a drawing of the Kohler plant that was placed only in architectural periodicals. See *Kohler Sales Helps,* 17.

98. Ibid., 9.

99. See, for example, *Manual of Etiquette for the Use of Schools and Academies* (New York: D&J Sadlier & Co., 1888); Frank Overton, *Personal Hygiene* (New York: American Book Co., 1913); Charles Stowell, *A Primer of Health: Practical Hygiene for Pupils in Primary and Lower Grades* (New York: Silver, Burdett & Co., 1906); L. N. Millard, *The Wonderful House that Jack Has* (New York: Macmillan Co., 1908).

100. *Kohler Sales Helps,* 9, 10.

101. Ibid., 7.

102. Ibid., 11.

103. Ibid., 12, 13; Ruby Ross Goodnow, "New House Designs from Out West," *The Delineator* 83 (November 1913): 21.

104. *Kohler Sales Helps,* 1, 19.

105. Ibid., passim, quotation from p. 27.

106. "Memorandum of Advertising Schedule for 1920: Plumbing Ware Only."

107. *Kohler of Kohler News* 2, no. 11 (September 1918): 13, KCA.

108. John R. Commons, "Standardizing the Home," *Journal of Home Economics* 2 (February 1910): 23–29.

109. Kohler Company Advertisement, *Saturday Evening Post* 194 (8 April 1922): 60.

CHAPTER THREE. THE STANDARD OF INVESTMENT

1. Aladdin Company Sales Records, 1915, Part 1, no. 3879–no. 4575, Aladdin Company Archives, Clarke Historical Library, Central Michigan University, Mount Pleasant, Mich. (Subsequent references to this collection will be designated ACA, with appropriate locating information.)

2. For a more in-depth discussion of the mail-order house trade, see Robert Schweitzer and Michael W. R. Davis, *America's Favorite Homes: Mail-Order Catalogues as a Guide to Popular Early 20th-Century Houses* (Detroit: Wayne State University Press, 1990); and Cheryl DeCosta Evans, "American Ready-Made Housing in the Early Twentieth Century" (M.S. thesis, University of Nebraska, 1982).

3. Hazel Kyrk, *Economic Problems of the Family* (New York: Harper & Bros., 1929), 418. For a more thorough discussion of consumer credit, see Lendol Calder, *Financing the American Dream* (Princeton: Princeton University Press, 1999); and Martha Olney, *Buy Now, Pay Later: Advertising, Credit, and Consumer Durables in the 1920s* (Chapel Hill: University of North Carolina Press, 1991).

4. Schweitzer and Davis, 70.

5. On the early history of architectural plan books, see Dell Upton, "Pattern Books and Professionalism," *Winterthur Portfolio* 19 (Summer–Autumn 1984): 107–50.

6. "Aladdin Knocked Down Houses . . . ," pamphlet, inside cover, Box 1, Folder: 1908: Catalogs and Brochures, ACA.

7. Humphrey Tonkin offered helpful questions and comments on this point in response to a presentation at the Whitney Humanities Center, New Haven, Conn., October 1998.

8. "How Three Chicago School Teachers Built Their Aladdin Home," pamphlet, 1911, 10, Box 1, Folder: 1911 Booklet, ACA.

9. Catalog no. 18, Fall 1909, 2, Box 1, Folder: 1909 Catalogs, ACA.

10. Catalog no. 24, Spring 1913, 91, Box 1, Folder: 1913: Catalogs and Brochures, ACA.

11. "Aladdin Interiors," pamphlet, 1914, Box 1, Folder: 1914a, ACA.

12. Broadside, Box 2, Folder: 1925 Follow-up, ACA.

13. Ellis Lore Kirkpatrick, *The Farmer's Standard of Living* (New York: Century Co., 1929), 126.

14. "Aladdin Interiors," Box 1, Folder: 1914a, ACA.

15. "Aladdin Interiors," Box 1, Folder: 1912: Aladdin Interiors, ACA; Kyrk, 418.

16. Kyrk, 417.

17. Calvin Coolidge, "A Nation of Home-Owners," *The Delineator* 101 (October 1922): 17.

18. "A Nation-Wide Building Boom," *Literary Digest*, 19 April 1919, 13.

19. Blanche Halbert, *The Better Homes Manual* (Chicago: University of Chicago

Press, in cooperation with Better Homes in America, 1931). For a broad discussion of the Better Homes campaign, see Janet Anne Hutchison, "American Housing, Gender, and the Better Homes Movement, 1922–1935" (Ph.D. diss., University of Delaware, 1989); and Karen Altman, "Consuming Ideology: The Better Homes in American Campaign," *Critical Studies in Mass Communication* 7, no. 3 (September 1990): 286–308. Faith Williams, a faculty member at Cornell University and a consultant to Robert and Helen Merrell Lynd in their research for *Middletown*, wrote, "The Homemaking section of the *Delineator* is edited and largely written here at Cornell, and some really original scientific material is here put up in simplified form." Faith Williams, undated memorandum to Robert Lynd, Container 7, File: Comments on Manuscript, Robert and Helen Merrell Lynd Papers, Manuscript Division, Library of Congress, Washington, D.C.

20. Herbert Hoover, "The Home as an Investment," *The Delineator* 101 (October 1922): 17; Regina Lee Blaszczyk has discussed Hoover's involvement in American housing in "From House to Home: Herbert Hoover and the American Standard of Living, 1921–1928," in *Herbert Hoover: Re-evaluating the Evidence*, ed. Timothy Walch (West Branch, Iowa: Herbert Hoover Presidential Library, forthcoming).

21. *The Wedge* 1, no. 2 (April 1913): 9, Box 7, ACA. All issues of *The Wedge*, a house organ of the Aladdin Company, are housed in Box 7, ACA; subsequent references to articles in *The Wedge* will be identified solely by volume, issue, date, and page number.

22. *Aladdin's Weekly* 8, no. 1 (7 February 1920): cover, Box 7, ACA.

23. Charles Molesphini and Walter B. Hayward, "Real Estate: Renting Versus Buying," *Country Life in America* 22 (1 September 1912): 74.

24. "Aladdin Interiors," Box 1, Folder: 1914a, ACA.

25. Molesphini and Hayward, 74.

26. Kathleen Norris, *Undertow* (Garden City, N.Y.: Doubleday, Page and Company, 1917), 100.

27. Catalog, no. 18, Fall 1909, 2.

28. Catalog, no. 18, Fall 1909, inside back cover.

29. Emma Gary Wallace, "Shall You Build Buy or Rent?" *House and Garden* 40 (September 1921): 36. See also Harland H. Allen, "Laying the First Foundation," *House and Garden* 48 (September 1925): 80, 118; Newel Howland Comish, *The Standard of Living: Elements of Consumption* (New York: Macmillan Co., 1923), 279–83; Frank Hatch Streightoff, *The Standard of Living Among the Industrial People of America* (Boston: Houghton Mifflin Co., 1911), 113–15; Kyrk, 420–22; Calder, passim.

30. "The Home that Fits the Income," *Literary Digest* 69 (23 April 1921): 64; Harland H. Allen, "How Much House Can We Afford?" *House and Garden* 48 (November 1925): 84.

31. Elbert Hubbard, "Houses While You Wait," *The Wedge* 1, no. 2 (April 1913): 5.

32. "Building Homes as Real Estate Investments," *House and Garden* 43 (January 1923): 116–18.

33. Brochure, Box 1, Folder: 1913: Catalogs and Brochures, ACA.

34. Rene Fredericks, "Home Building as an Investment," *The Wedge* 7, no. 3 (May 1916): 9, 18.

35. "Let Us Have Homes: For the Children's Sake—Childhood Impressions are Deep and Lasting," *Aladdin's Magazine* 9, no. 27 (30 April 1921): 5, Box 7, ACA.

36. Molesphini and Hayward, 74, 76; Wallace, 36.

37. Hoover, 17.

38. Hubbard, 5.

39. Ibid.

40. "What Buyers of Aladdin Houses Think of Them," 1908, Box 1, Folder: 1908: Catalogs and Brochures, ACA.

41. Catalog no. 24, 96.

42. Frederick Winslow Taylor, *The Principles of Scientific Management* (1911; rpt. New York: W. W. Norton and Co., 1967).

43. Catalog no. 25, "The New Home," 1914, 3, Box 1, Folder: 1914 Catalogs, ACA.

44. *The Wedge* 5, no. 3 (1915): 4.

45. Catalog no. 18, 1.

46. Otto E. Sovereign, *Fifty Million Dollars on a Shoestring: A Tale of Fifty Years in Business (and Fifty Years of Fun)* (n.p., 1951), 25. This entire tale was told in Sovereign's book under the chapter heading, "Exploding the One-Design Production Method."

47. George Soule, "Standardization," in *The Encyclopaedia of the Social Sciences,* ed. Edwin R. A. Seligman (New York: Macmillan, 1934), 14:319.

48. For all quotations in preceding three paragraphs, see "A Better Day for the Home Builder," *Aladdin's Weekly* 7, no. 5 (1 March 1919): 5, Box 7, ACA.

49. "What Do Aladdin Owners Think of Their Aladdin Homes?" Box 2, Folder: 1919a: Brochures, ACA.

50. *The Wedge* 6, no. 5 (February 1916): 3–4.

51. Catalog no. 28, 1916, 33, Box 1, Folder: 1916 Catalog, ACA.

52. Catalog no. 25, 9.

53. "Let Us Have Homes," 5.

54. "Here's Proof of Prosperity," *The Wedge* 4, no. 2 (October 1914): 4.

55. "What Do Aladdin Owners Think of Their Aladdin Homes?"

56. Leaflet in Catalog no. 29, 1917, Box 1, Folder: 1917 Catalog; Catalog no. 30, 1918, Box 1, Folder: 1918 Catalog, ACA.

57. Broadside, Box 1, Folder: 1917a, ACA.

58. Price lists, Box 2, Folder: 1919a Brochures, ACA; see also Schweitzer and Davis, 81.

59. Untitled pamphlet, 3, Box 1, Folder: 1912: Aladdin Interiors, ACA.

60. Brochure, Box 1, Folder: 1913: Catalogs and Brochures, ACA.

61. Catalog no. 18, 2.

62. Donn Barber, "Good Taste in American Homes," *The Delineator* 101 (September 1922): 18.

63. Catalog no. 32, 1919, 98–99, Box 2, Folder: 1919 Catalogs, ACA.

64. "To Offset the High Cost of Building," *Country Life* 36 (June 1919): 116, 118.

65. "What Do Aladdin Owners Think of Their Aladdin Homes?"

66. For analysis of other house types manufactured by the Aladdin Company, see Scott Erbes, "The Readi-Cut Dream: The Mail Order House Catalogs of the Aladdin Company, 1906–1920" (M.A. thesis, University of Delaware, 1990).

67. "To Offset the High Cost of Building," 114.

68. Wallace, 36.

69. Catalog no. 30, 86.

70. Catalog no. 24, 36.

71. *The Wedge* 7, no. 3 (May 1916): 12.

72. "Let Us Have Homes," 5; Streightoff, 69.

73. *The Wedge* 1, no. 2 (April 1913): 9.

74. *The Wedge* 7, no. 3 (May 1916): 12.

75. Mabel Lorenz Ives, "My Standard Kitchen," *Aladdin's Weekly* 8, nos. 2–4 (28 February 1920): 6, Box 7, ACA.

76. Catalog no. 30, 87.

77. Barber, 90; Kirkpatrick, 138.

78. "Aladdin Homes," pamphlet, 1923, 5, Box 2, Folder: 1923 Catalogs, ACA.

79. Hubbard, 5.

80. Ives, 6.

81. Barber, 90.

82. Ibid., 18.

83. Catalog no. 18, cover.

84. *The Wedge* 1, no. 2 (April 1913): 9.

85. Hubbard, 4.

86. "Aladdin Interiors," pamphlet, 1912, Box 1, Folder: 1912—Aladdin Interiors, ACA.

87. *The Wedge* 1, no. 3 (May 1913): 9.

88. "How Three Chicago School Teachers Built Their Aladdin Home," 10.

89. "Aladdin Knocked Down Houses . . . ," 9.

90. "To Offset the High Cost of Building," 114–18.

91. *The Wedge* 1, no. 1 (March 1913): 7.

92. Catalog no. 29, 14.

93. *The Wedge* 1, no. 1 (March 1913):7. The national population, according to the 1910 Census, was 92,228,496; see Donald B. Dodd, *Historical Statistics of the States of*

the United States: Two Centuries of the Census, 1790–1990 (Westport, Conn.: Greenwood Press, 1993).

94. Advertising source records, ACA.

95. *The Wedge* 1, no. 1 (March 1913): 8.

96. *The Wedge* 1, no. 5 (July 1913): 11; see also *The Wedge* 3, no. 1 (March 1914): 10.

97. *The Wedge* 1, no. 2 (April 1913): 11.

98. *The Wedge* 1, no. 4 (June 1913): 3.

99. *The Wedge* 2, no. 1 (August 1913): 2.

100. Untitled pamphlet, 15, Box 1, Folder: 1912: Aladdin Interiors, ACA.

101. Catalog no. 25, 3 (emphasis original).

102. "Aladdin Interiors," 1912.

103. Brochure, Box 1, Folder: 1913: Catalogs and Brochures, ACA.

104. Catalog no. 25, 3. The historian Sam Bass Warner has written that this idea of service is one that binds communities together. See Warner, *Streetcar Suburbs: The Progress of Growth in Boston, 1870–1900* (Cambridge, Mass.: Harvard University Press, 1978), xi.

105. "What Buyers of Aladdin Houses Think of Them."

106. Catalog no. 25, 3.

107. "What Do Aladdin Owners Think of Their Aladdin Homes?"

108. "Aladdin Homes: Some Interesting Facts about Aladdin Service," pamphlet, 1922, 12, Box 2, Folder: 1920a, ACA.

109. Catalog no. 25, 92–93.

110. "What Buyers of Aladdin Houses Think of Them."

111. "Aladdin Knocked Down Houses . . . ," 9.

112. *The Wedge* 5, no. 1 (April 1915): cover.

113. *Low Cost Homes Designed Especially for Industrial Purposes,* Box 2, Folder: 1920, ACA.

114. Barber, 18, 90.

115. *The Wedge* 1, no. 1 (March 1913): 7.

116. D. G. Baird, "City or Village, "*Aladdin's Weekly* 8, no. 7 (20 March 1920): 3–4, Box 7, ACA.

117. "What Do Aladdin Owners Think of Their Aladdin Homes?"

118. Lida A. Churchill, "The Home a Joint Stock Company," *The Delineator* 88 (January 1916): 24; Ruby Ross Goodnow, "Why Consult an Architect—and How?" *The Delineator* 83 (November 1913): 7; Wallace, 78.

119. "What Do Aladdin Owners Think of Their Aladdin Homes?" Jan Cohn explores these two views of the house, as property and as home, in *The Palace and the Poorhouse: The American House as Cultural Symbol* (East Lansing: Michigan State University Press, 1979), 213–44.

120. Catalog no. 26, 1915, 30–31, Box 1, Folder: 1915 Catalog, ACA.

121. *The Wedge* 1, no. 1 (March 1913): 5.

122. Catalog no. 26, 30–31; *The Wedge* 1, no. 2 (April 1913): 7; 2, no. 1 (September 1913): 9.

123. Untitled pamphlet, 7, Box 1, Folder: 1912: Aladdin Interiors, ACA.

124. *The Wedge* 1, no. 3 (May 1913): 9.

125. *The Wedge* 3, no. 1 (March 1914): 3.

126. *The Wedge* 1, no. 2 (April 1913): 7.

127. *The Wedge* 1, no. 5 (July 1913): 2; 3, no. 1 (March 1914): 2; 2, no. 4 (December 1913): 10.

128. *The Wedge* 2, no. 4 (December 1913): 10.

129. *The Wedge* 1, no. 1 (March 1913): 5.

130. *The Wedge* 1, no. 1 (March 1913): 3; 1, no. 4 (June 1913): 5.

131. *The Wedge* 1, no. 1 (March 1913): 3.

132. *The Wedge* 1, no. 5 (July 1913): 12.

133. *The Wedge* 1, no. 1 (March 1913): 7.

134. *The Wedge* 1, no. 2 (April 1913): 2.

135. *The Wedge* 6, no. 5 (February 1916): 4.

136. "Aladdin's Favorite Recipes," Box 1, Folder: 1916a, ACA.

137. *The Wedge* 3, no. 1 (March 1914): 7.

CHAPTER FOUR. THE STANDARD OF MANAGEMENT

1. Herbert S. Swan, "Does Your City Keep Its Gas Range in the Parlor and Its Piano in the Kitchen?" *The American City* 22, no. 4 (April 1920): 339.

2. Cartoon reprinted in *The American City* 28, no. 2 (February 1923): 142.

3. Lawyer Edward M. Bassett, involved with comprehensive zoning since its inception in New York City, wrote that city planning is in fact the legislative power that allows for the designation of different land for different uses. Edward M. Bassett, "What Really Is City Planning?" *The American City* 34, no. 5 (May 1926): 470.

4. Seymour I. Toll, *Zoned American* (New York: Grossman Publishers, 1969), see esp. chapters 6 and 7. See also *Louisville, Kentucky Zoning Report*, 1930, 2–3, Series 1, Box 6, Harland Bartholomew & Associates Collection, Research Collection no. 8, Washington University Archives, St. Louis, Mo. (Subsequent references to this archival collection will be designated HBA, with appropriate series and box or volume number.)

5. Toll, 172–87. See also Carol Willis, *Form Follows Finance: Skyscrapers and Skylines in New York and Chicago* (New York: Princeton Architectural Press, 1995); and David Ward and Olivier Zunz, *The Landscape of Modernity: Essays on New York City, 1900–1940* (New York: Russell Sage Foundation, 1992).

6. Toll, 201–2; *Louisville, Kentucky Zoning Report*, 1930, 2–3.

7. Theodora Kimball Hubbard and Henry Vincent Hubbard, *Our Cities, Today and To-morrow: A Survey of Planning and Zoning Progress in the United States*

(Cambridge, Mass.: Harvard University Press, 1929), 162; Donald B. Dodd, *Historical Statistics of the States of the United States: Two Centuries of the Census, 1790–1990* (Westport, Conn.: Greenwood Press, 1993), 443–62; Harland Bartholomew, "Twenty Years of Zoning: A Brief Appraisal of Benefits and Shortcomings," typescript of article for the *Engineering News Record*, 1937, in *Articles by Harland Bartholomew: Volume 2: 1930–1958*, Series 4, Box 1, HBA; "Fifteen Million People Live in Zoned Cities," *The American City* 28, no. 2 (February 1923): 201; W. D. Freeman, "The Big Opportunity of the Small Town," *The American City* 36, no. 1 (January 1927): 88; "The Big Opportunity of the Small Town," *The American City* 37, no. 5 (November 1927): 630; quotation from "No Town Too Small for City Planning," *The American City* 29, no. 1 (July 1923): 1–2.

8. A 1921 article in *The American City* shows Bartholomew's early involvement in the zoning movement; of the prominent firms listed as zoning consultants to American cities and towns, Bartholomew had the most clients except for the Technical Advisory Corporation, a significantly larger firm headed by Bartholomew's original employers, E. P. Goodrich and George Ford. "The Remarkable Spread of Zoning," *The American City* 25, no. 6 (December 1921): 456–58.

9. *Comprehensive City Plan for Binghamton, New York*, 1, 13, Series 1, Box 2, HBA.

10. Harland Bartholomew, letters to Norman Johnston, 6 December 1960, 9 April 1962, Series 3, Box 1, File: Correspondence: Norman Johnston/Harland Bartholomew & Associates: 1960–72, HBA; Eldridge Lovelace, *Harland Bartholomew: His Contributions to American Urban Planning* (Urbana: University of Illinois Department of Urban and Regional Planning, 1993), 1–12; Norman John Johnston, "Harland Bartholomew: His Comprehensive Plans and Science of Planning" (Ph.D. diss., University of Pennsylvania, 1964), 87–133.

11. Harland Bartholomew, *Problems of St. Louis, Being a description, from the city planning standpoint, of past and present tendencies of growth with general suggestions for impending issues and necessary future improvements* (St. Louis: City Plan Commission, 1917), 66.

12. A fourth designation of "unrestricted" space did exist, but was in fact conceived as industrial space. The most intensive and most intrusive uses of land could take place there; examples of uses allowed only in unrestricted areas were blast furnaces, fat rendering plants, rolling mills, rock crushers, or the manufacture of ammonia, celluloid, explosives, sauerkraut, soap, or vinegar. Other sections that were exceptions to the zoning ordinance were reserves of space used for municipal purposes, such as schools and parkland.

13. The exceptions to this general characterization were zoning codes in agricultural regions that had "productive" space for agriculture separate from, or in place of, industrial districts; agricultural districts were more closely integrated with residential areas. Still, in the sample comprised of Harland Bartholomew's clients into

the early 1930s, this type of zoning rarely occurs. The only other types of productive activity specifically enumerated as allowable in residential districts were gardening, small-scale truck farming, and nurseries, but this gesture was more a nod to the vestiges of home production than an acceptance that residential areas would house major agriculture.

14. Sam Bass Warner has explained that the growing late nineteenth-century city is an expansion of the "walking city," not a radical replacement of it; see Warner, *Streetcar Suburbs: The Process of Growth in Boston, 1870–1900* (Cambridge, Mass.: Harvard University Press, 1978), 3. The pattern can be seen going back even to the structure of the New England town, driven by efficient economic usage of the land, as described by Joseph Wood, *The New England Village* (Baltimore: Johns Hopkins University Press, 1997), passim.

15. "Comprehensive City Plan Des Moines, Iowa," 1928, 1, Series 2, Labeled Black Binders, Vol. 14, HBA. (Subsequent references to the Labeled Black Binders in Series 2 will be designated LBB.)

16. Floyd Dell, *Moon-Calf* (New York: Alfred A. Knopf, 1920), 156–57.

17. "New Zoning Law Up For Passage," *Chattanooga Daily Times,* 20 January 1927, 7.

18. "Skyscrapers to be Opposed By Zoning Board," *Des Moines Register,* 2 June 1925, 18; Charles F. Fisher, "Zoning as a Traffic Safety Measure," *The American City* 30, no. 2 (February 1924): 144–45.

19. "A Supreme Court on the Civic and Social Values of Single-Family Residence Districts," *The American City* 32, no. 6 (June 1925): 683.

20. For a variety of explanations for zoning, see (protection of investment) "Comprehensive City Plan for Glendale, California," 1928, 4, Series 1, Box 4; (avoidance of overcrowding) "Major Streets Mishawaka, Indiana," 1925, 15, Series 1, Box 7; (advertisement for the city) Chamber of Commerce, "Report of the Committee on a City Plan, Hutchinson, Kansas, " n.d., Series 2, LBB, Vol. 26; (combined reasons) "Comprehensive Plan for Stockton, California," c. 1932, 200, Series 2, LBB, Vol. 58, Part 1, HBA.

21. "Preliminary Report on the Public Recreational Facilities of Jackson, Michigan," 1920, 1, Series 2, LBB, Vol. 27, Part 2, HBA.

22. H. W. Dodds, "Thumb-Nail Sketches of the Four Principal Types of City Government," *The American City* 28, no. 4 (April 1923): 353–54; "How the City Manager Plan is Working—I," *The American City* 33, no. 3 (September 1925): 293–96; "How the City Manager Plan is Working—II," *The American City* 33, no. 4 (October 1925): 406–8. For a historical overview of this development in municipal government, see Bradley Robert Rice, *Progressive Cities: The Commission Government Movement in America, 1901–1920* (Austin: University of Texas Press, 1977).

23. Frederick Winslow Taylor, *The Principles of Scientific Management* (1911; rpt. New York: W. W. Norton and Co., 1967), 7 and passim.

24. "Build City for 500,000, Says Bartholomew," *Des Moines Register*, 16 May 1925, 2.

25. Contract between Harland Bartholomew and Associates and Municipal Corporation of Dallas, Texas, 3, Series 5, HBA.

26. *A Report on the Transportation Facilities of Utica, New York*, 1927, 7, Series 2, LBB, Vol. 62; *Major Streets: Present and Proposed, South Bend, Indiana*, 1924, 13, Series 1, Box 10, HBA.

27. Taylor, 36.

28. "The Grand Rapids City Plan," 1923, Series 2, LBB, Vol. 23, HBA; see also "Remaking and Zoning Omaha in Progress," *Morning World Herald*, 1 January 1920, 16; "Survey of Social and Living Conditions Essential to Wise City Planning," *The American City* 31, no. 3 (September 1924): 227.

29. Contract between Harland Bartholomew and Associates and Municipal Corporation of Dallas, Tex.

30. "A Preliminary Major Street Plan for Des Moines, Iowa," 1925, 17, Series 1, Box 3, HBA.

31. *The Lansing Plan: A Comprehensive City Plan for Lansing, Michigan*, c. 1923, 48, Series 2, LBB, Vol. 34, HBA.

32. Booth Tarkington, *The Midlander* (Garden City, N.Y.: Doubleday, Page and Co., 1924), 50.

33. *Polk's Des Moines and Valley Junction Directory* (Des Moines: R. L. Polk & Co., 1925).

34. Of course, there were not clear-cut divisions between reformers, managers, and boosters, and many individuals incorporated all three stances into their civic work. *The American City* 26, no. 3 (March 1922): 279; "Did You Ever Stop to Think—," *The American City* 27, no. 5 (November 1922): 403.

35. Cartoon in *The American City* 38, no. 1 (January 1928): 99.

36. *A Comprehensive City Plan for East St. Louis*, 1920, 55, Series 2, LBB, Vol. 16, HBA.

37. The Bell Telephone system actually served as a source of information for planners and urban commissioners; known for elaborate predictions of community demographics, the company was said "to cooperate with city officials, chambers of commerce, and other organizations for community betterment." See "Forecasting the Future of a City," *The American City* 27, no. 2 (August 1922): 152.

38. "Figures Are Announced by Zoning Expert," *Des Moines Register*, 6 April 1925, 1.

39. Booth Tarkington, *The Gentleman from Indiana* (New York: Doubleday & McClure Co., 1899), 2; Samuel Hopkins Adams, *The Clarion* (Boston: Houghton Mifflin, 1914), 19–20.

40. Harland Bartholomew, letter to Norman Johnston, 30 November 1961, Series

3, Box 1, File: Correspondence: Norman Johnston/Harland Bartholomew & Associates: 1960–72, HBA.

41. *Parks and Recreational Facilities, Hutchinson, Kansas,* 1920, 1–2, Series 2, LBB, Vol. 26, HBA.

42. For a broader discussion of core-periphery relationships in North American cities, see Michael Conzen, *Frontier Farming in an Urban Shadow: The Influence of Madison's Proximity on the Agricultural Development of Blooming Grove, Wisconsin* (Madison: State Historical Society of Wisconsin, for the Department of History, University of Wisconsin, 1971); and William Cronon, *Nature's Metropolis: Chicago and the Great West* (New York: W. W. Norton, 1991).

43. Constance Perin, *Everything in its Place: Social Order and Land Use in America* (Princeton: Princeton University Press, 1977); Sinclair Lewis, *Babbitt* (1922; rpt. New York: Penguin Books, 1996), 27.

44. I am using the words *class, district,* and *zone* interchangeably to designate the units of the zoning codes.

45. "A Major Street and Zoning Plan for Grand Haven, Michigan," 1923, 25, Series 1, Box 5, HBA.

46. "A Supreme Court on the Civic and Social Values of Single-Family Residence Districts," 683.

47. *A Comprehensive City Plan for San Antonio, Texas,* 1933, 185, Series 1, Box 9, HBA.

48. *The Grand Rapids City Plan,* 1927, 25, Series 2, LBB, Vol. 23, HBA.

49. "A Major Street and Zoning Plan for Grand Haven, Michigan," 24–25.

50. "Phone Company Fights Zoning," *Des Moines Register,* 10 June 1925, 1.

51. "City Plan for Hutchinson, Kansas," c. 1920, 9, Series 2, LBB, Vol. 26, HBA.

52. "Comprehensive City Plan Des Moines, Iowa," 1, 198–99.

53. "Comprehensive City Plan for Glendale, California," 170.

54. Robert Whitten, "The Zoning of Apartment and Tenement Houses," *The American City* 23, no. 2 (August 1920): 140; see also "A Supreme Court on the Civic and Social Values of Single-Family Residence Districts," 683.

55. *Louisville, Kentucky Zoning Report,* 32.

56. Whitten, 141.

57. Lewis, 250–53, 284–308.

58. *Zoning for Troy, Ohio,* 1931, 23–24, Series 1, Box 10, HBA.

59. Ibid., 23–24; "Skyscrapers to be Opposed By Zoning Board," 18; Robert Kingery, "Determining the Size of Retail Districts in Zoning Cities and Villages," *The American City* 36, no. 3 (February 1927): 246–48.

60. Thomas Adams, "Efficient Industry and Wholesome Housing True Aims of Zoning," *The American City* 24, no. 3 (March 1921): 289.

61. "Comprehensive Plan for Champaign, Illinois," 1926, 63–64, Series 2, LBB, Vol. 8, HBA.

62. Cartoon reprinted in *The American City* 28, no. 3 (March 1923): 266.

63. "Comprehensive Plan for Champaign, Illinois," 64.

64. Patricia Burgess has argued effectively for the need to examine not just the passage of zoning ordinances, but their implementation and effects. See Burgess, *Planning for the Private Interest: Land Use Controls and Residential Patterns in Columbus, Ohio, 1900–1970* (Columbus: Ohio State University Press, 1994).

65. Lovelace, 12; Johnston, 28–29; Harland Bartholomew, letter to Norman Johnston, 27 September 1962, Series 3, Box 1, File: Correspondence: Norman Johnston/Harland Bartholomew & Associates: 1960–72, HBA. For Charles Mulford Robinson and his aesthetic approach to urban planning, see his best known works, *The Improvement of Towns and Cities* (New York: G. P. Putnam's Sons, 1902) and *Modern Civic Art; or, The City Made Beautiful* (New York: G. P. Putnam's Sons, 1903). For background on the City Beautiful movement, see William H. Wilson, *The City Beautiful Movement* (Baltimore: Johns Hopkins University Press, 1989).

66. Johnston, 140.

67. "What City Planning Is," *The American City* 22, no. 3 (March 1920): 223.

68. Harland Bartholomew, *Zone Plan for St. Louis* (St. Louis: City Plan Commission, 1919), 14; Russell Van Nest Black, "Can Intelligent Zoning Be Done Without a Comprehensive City Plan?" *The American City* 38, no. 4 (April 1928): 108–9.

69. Toll, 213–53.

70. "A Major Street and Zoning Plan for Grand Haven, Michigan," 11.

71. "Report on Major Streets and Railroad Grade Separations, Anchorage, Kentucky," 1930, 3, 10, Series 2, LBB, Vol. 1, HBA.

72. "An Introduction to the City Plan and a Preliminary Report on a Major Street System for Hutchinson, Kansas," 1920, 10, Series 2, LBB, Vol. 26, HBA.

73. *A Comprehensive Plan for East St. Louis,* 1920, 5, Series 2, LBB, Vol. 16, HBA.

74. *The Lansing Plan,* 38.

75. "The Grand Rapids City Plan."

76. "A Plan for the Systematic and Economical Development of Recreational Facilities for Utica, New York," c. 1924, 7, Series 2, LBB, Vol. 62, HBA.

77. For background on Olmsted and park systems, see Cynthia Zaitzevsky, *Frederick Law Olmsted and the Boston Park System* (Cambridge, Mass.: Belknap Press, 1982).

78. "Preliminary Report on the Public Recreational Facilities of Jackson, Michigan," 2.

79. *Comprehensive City Plan for Binghamton, New York,* 14.

80. "Comprehensive Plan for Champaign, Illinois," 65–66.

81. *Comprehensive City Plan for Binghamton, New York,* 278.

82. Contract between Harland Bartholomew and Associates and City of Cedar Rapids, Iowa, Series 5, HBA.

83. "An Introduction to the City Plan and a Preliminary Report on a Major Street System for Hutchinson, Kansas," 1.

84. "Indiana Puts Planning Primer in Public Schools," *The American City* 35, no. 2 (August 1928): 232–33.

85. "Planning Expert Talks to Kiwanians," *Wisconsin State Journal*, 7 November 1921, 8; "Figures Are Announced by Zoning Expert," 1; "Taubert Explains Zoning System," *Des Moines Register*, 20 May 1925, 1.

86. Interview with Eldridge Lovelace, 12 June 1997, University City, Mo. See also *Articles by Harland Bartholomew*, Series 4, Box 1, HBA.

87. Miriam I. Ross, "A Primer of City Planning Progress and Legislation," *The American City* 28, no. 2 (February 1923): 132.

88. "Delay Passage Zoning Ordinance," *Chattanooga Daily Times*, 21 January 1927, 8; "Commission Will Vote on Zoning Ordinance," *Chattanooga Daily Times*, 18 January 1927, 5.

89. "Comprehensive City Plan for Glendale, California," 18, 24, 321–22.

90. Harland Bartholomew, "Getting Results in City Planning and Zoning," speech for National Municipal League and American Civic Association, Pittsburgh, Pa., 19 November 1925, typescript, 2–5, in *Speeches by Harland Bartholomew: 1918–1959*, Series 4, Box 1, HBA.

91. Kathleen Norris, *Undertow* (Garden City, N.Y.: Doubleday, Page and Company, 1917), 101–2.

92. Charles M. Fassett, "Assets of the Ideal City," *The American City* 24, no. 4 (April 1921): 345.

93. *Problems of St. Louis*, xi–xv.

94. Ibid., 26.

95. "A Plan in Time," *Chattanooga Daily Times*, 5 January 1927, 4; Freeman, 88; "The Big Opportunity of the Small Town," 630.

96. *Zone Plan for St. Louis*, 16.

97. Bassett, 470.

98. *Major Streets: Present and Proposed, South Bend, Indiana*, 17.

99. *Zoning for Troy, Ohio*, 4.

100. *Public Recreation Facilities in Evansville*, 1927, 5, Series 1, Box 4, HBA; "A City Planning Primer," *The American City* 36, no. 1 (January 1927): 89–95; "Fifteen Million People Live in Zoned Cities," 201; "No Town Too Small for City Planning," 1–2; Edward M. Bassett, "Fields of Progressive Legislation for Better City Planning," *The American City* 31, no. 6 (December 1924): 525–27; Frank B. Williams, "The Progress of City Planning Law During 1923," *The American City* 30, no. 2 (February 1924): 188–91. Both Bassett and Williams suggested that part of the problem in litigation over zoning ordinances stemmed from weak enabling legislation; Williams further implied that enabling acts that followed the federal model were more successful protection against legal challenges to ordinances.

101. *The Lansing Plan.*

102. Bartholomew, "Getting Results in City Planning and Zoning," 5–6.

103. "Comprehensive City Plan Des Moines, Iowa."

104. *A System of Major Streets for Evansville, Indiana,* 1925, 5, Series 1, Box 4, HBA.

105. "St. Louis Expert is Recommended by City Planners," *Grand Rapids Herald,* 16 January 1921, 3.

106. *A System of Major Streets for Evansville,* 5, 56.

107. *Major Streets: Present and Proposed, South Bend, Indiana,* 13.

108. Harland Bartholomew, letter to Norman Johnston, 30 November 1961.

109. Interview with Eldridge Lovelace, 12 June 1997, University City, Mo.

110. Much attention was given to the special role of real estate agents in advocating for zoning. See "New Zoning Law Up For Passage," *Chattanooga Daily Times,* 20 January 1927, 7; Henry R. Brigham, "The Realtor and the Community," *The American City* 28, no. 2 (February 1923): 147–48.

111. *A System of Major Streets for Evansville,* 5, 56; *Polk's Des Moines and Valley Junction Directory, Polk's South Bend City Directory* (Indianapolis: R. L. Polk and Co., 1923); for other examples, see *Binghamton City Directory* (Binghamton, N.Y.: Calvin-Kelly Directory Co., 1932); *Bennett's Evansville City Directory* (Evansville, Ind.: Bennett Directory Co., 1928); *Lansing City Directory* (Lansing: Chilson McKinley & Co., 1921); *Schenectady & Scotia Directory* (Schenectady: H. A. Manning Co., 1924); *Polk's Stockton, California City Directory* (San Francisco: R. L. Polk of California, 1932).

112. Ross, 132.

113. *Proceedings of National Conference on City Planning* (Boston: National Conference on City Planning, 1912), 114; Robert Whitten, "Atlanta Adopts Zoning," *The American City* 26, no. 6 (June 1922): 542.

114. "The 'City Show' in Grand Rapids," *The American City* 22, no. 3 (March 1920): 248–50; "Film on Zoning Wins Widespread Approval," *The American City* 28, no. 1 (January 1923): 60.

115. Booth Tarkington, *The Magnificent Ambersons* (1918; rpt. New York: Bantam Books, 1994), 245–46.

116. Lewis, 165.

CONCLUSION

1. Charles E. Modlin, ed., *Sherwood Anderson's Love Letters to Eleanor Copenhaver* (Athens: University of Georgia Press, 1989), 28. Anderson refers to his own novel, *Winesburg, Ohio,* originally published in 1919.

2. Modlin, 37.

3. Robert S. Lynd and Helen Merrell Lynd, *Middletown: A Study in Modern American Culture* (New York: Harcourt, Brace and Co., 1929), 3.

4. Lynd and Lynd, 101–2.

5. Modlin, 36.

6. For background on the middle class and the culture of books and reading, see David Minter, *A Cultural History of the American Novel* (New York: Cambridge University Press, 1994); Joan Shelley Rubin, *The Making of Middlebrow Culture* (Chapel Hill: University of North Carolina Press, 1992); James L. W. West III, *American Authors and the Literary Marketplace* (Philadelphia: University of Pennsylvania Press, 1988); Archibald Hanna, *Mirror for the Nation: An Annotated Bibliography of American Social Fiction, 1901–1950* (New York: Garland, 1985).

7. Jessica B. Peixotto, *Getting and Spending at the Professional Standard of Living: A Study of the Costs of Living an Academic Life* (New York: Macmillan, 1927), vii. Similar studies of other universities include Yandell Henderson and Maurice Davie, eds., *Incomes and Living Costs of a University Faculty* (New Haven: Yale University Press, 1928); and John H. McNeely, *Salaries in Land-grant Universities and Colleges* (Washington, D.C.: U.S. Government Printing Office, 1932). See also Daniel Horowitz, *The Morality of Spending: Attitudes Toward the Consumer Society in America, 1875–1945* (Baltimore: Johns Hopkins University Press, 1985), 138–48.

8. Peixotto, chapter 1: "The Pay Check and the Professor," 1–27, passim; see also 39–40.

9. Ibid., 11.

10. Ibid., viii–ix; Mary Hinman Abel discusses teachers, clerks, and ministers in this same category; Abel, "Community and Personal Standards," in *American Standards and Planes of Living: Readings in the Social Economics of Consumption,* ed. Thomas Eliot (Boston: Ginn & Co., 1931), 185; see also Ellis Lore Kirkpatrick, *The Farmer's Standard of Living* (New York: Century Co., 1929), 202–3.

11. Peixotto, xi, 21.

12. Ibid., 39–40.

13. Ibid., 33–37.

14. Ibid., 44.

15. Robert Herrick, *Chimes* (New York: Macmillan, 1926), 51–52.

16. Ibid., 180–86.

17. Robert S. Lynd, letter to Galen Fisher, 7 April 1924, Lynd papers, RSL to Galen Fisher, 7 April 1924, Container 7, File: General Correspondence 1923–60, Robert and Helen Merrell Lynd Papers, Manuscript Division, Library of Congress, Washington, D.C. (Subsequent references to this archival collection will be designated LP, with appropriate container and file location.) See also Horowitz, 148–52; and Richard Wightman Fox, "Epitaph for Middletown: Robert S. Lynd and the Analysis of Consumer Culture," in *The Culture of Consumption: Critical Essays in American History, 1880–1980,* ed. Richard Wightman Fox and T. J. Jackson Lears (New York: Pantheon Books, 1983).

18. Lynd and Lynd, 478–79.

19. For example, Faith Williams, a faculty member at Cornell University, recommended the terms *industrial* and *professional or commercial*: Williams, letter to Robert Lynd, 13 May 1926, Container 7, File: General Correspondence 1923–60, LP. See also Trevor Bowen, "Notes," 6 May 1927, Container 7, File: Comments on Manuscript, LP; S. Went, "Small City Study Notes," 26 May 1927, Container 7, File: General Correspondence 1923–60, LP. Barbara and John Ehrenreich, "The Professional-Managerial Class," *Radical America* 11 (March–April 1977): 7–31; 11 (May–June 1977): 7–22.

20. Galen Fisher, "Notes on Small City Manuscript," 6 May 1927; and S. Went, "General Comments," 5 May 1927, both in Container 7, File: Comments on Manuscript, LP.

21. Lynd and Lynd, 6, 22–23 (see especially n. 3), 491.

22. Ibid., 81–82 (see especially n. 18).

23. Ibid., 87.

24. Ibid., 495.

25. Ibid., 3, 12, 487.

26. "Minutes of Conference on Mr. Lynd's Manuscript," typescript, Container 7, File: General Correspondence 1923–60; Clarendon Ross, letter to Robert and Helen Merrell Lynd, 26 June 1929, Container 7, File: General Correspondence 1923–60; Clipping from June 1929 edition of *Good Housekeeping,* Container 12, File: Middletown Reviews; unsigned typescript, Container 11, File: Reviews; Clipping of H. L. Mencken, "A Treatise on the Americano," *Evening Sun,* 14 January 1929, Container 12 , File: Middletown Reviews, LP.

27. F. Scott Fitzgerald, letter to Sinclair Lewis, 26 January [1921], Sinclair Lewis Papers, Beinecke Rare Book and Manuscript Library, Yale University, New Haven, Conn. Subsequent references to this collection will be designated SLP.

28. John Galsworthy, undated letter to Sinclair Lewis, SLP.

29. Walter Lippman, undated letter to Sinclair Lewis, SLP.

30. Harrison Smith, ed., *From Main Street to Stockholm: Letters of Sinclair Lewis, 1919–1930* (New York: Harcourt, Brace and Co., 1952), 27.

31. Sinclair Lewis, "Too Much Fate for America," typescript for 11 October 1937 issue of *Newsweek,* SLP.

32. Sinclair Lewis, "The Boxers of M. Voltaire," typescript no. 358–59, 6, SLP.

33. Smith, 77.

34. Sinclair Lewis, "Americanism as Standardization" [excerpt from *Babbitt*], in Eliot, ed., *American Standards and Planes of Living,* 814–18.

35. The planning notebook for *Babbitt* is part of the Sinclair Lewis Papers at the Beinecke Rare Book and Manuscript Library, Yale University, New Haven, Conn., but the maps are part of the Dorothy Thompson Papers at the Syracuse University Library, Syracuse, N.Y. The maps are reproduced in Helen Batchelor, "A Sinclair

Lewis Portfolio of Maps: Zenith to Winnemac," *Modern Language Quarterly* 32 (December 1971): 401–8.

36. Hazel Kyrk, *Economic Problems of the Family* (New York: Harper & Bros., 1929), 379.

37. Clippings of reviews of *Middletown* by Maxwell Lerner, Elsie McCormick, Hamilton Fyfe, Myron Garrett, Willoughby Walling, Container 12, File: Middletown Reviews, LP.

38. For example, see clippings of reviews by R. L. Duffus and H. L. Mencken, Container 11, File: Middletown Reviews, LP.

39. John Keats, *The Crack in the Picture Window* (Boston: Houghton Mifflin, 1957); Herbert Gans, *The Levittowners: Ways of Life and Politics in a New Suburban Community* (New York: Pantheon Books, 1967); Sloan Wilson, *The Man in the Gray Flannel Suit* (New York: Simon and Schuster, 1955); Nunnally Johnson, dir., *The Man in the Gray Flannel Suit* (Twentieth Century Fox, 1956); Naomi Klein, *No Logo: Taking Aim at the Brand Bullies* (New York: Picador, 2000); John De Graaf, David Wann, and Thomas Naylor, *Affluenza: The All-Consuming Epidemic* (New York: Berrett-Koehler, 2001).

40. James Truslow Adams, *The Epic of America* (Garden City, N.Y.: Blue Ribbon Books, 1931), vii; Andrew Ross, *The Celebration Chronicles: Life, Liberty, and the Pursuit of Property Value in Disney's New Town* (New York: Ballantine Books, 1999); Douglas Frantz and Catherine Collins, *Celebration, U.S.A.: Living in Disney's Brave New Town* (New York: Henry Holt and Co., 1999).

41. Eliot, 798–99.

42. Stuart Chase and F. J. Schlink, "Consumers in Wonderland," in Eliot, ed., *American Standards and Planes of Living*, 804.

43. Smith, 64, 88, and passim. One can only guess how Lewis would have spun the publication of a parody of Main Street, Carolyn Wells's *Ptomaine Street: A Tale of Warble Petticoat* (Philadelphia: J. B. Lippincott, 1921).

44. Trevor Bowen, letter to Robert Lynd, 8 May 1928; Alfred Harcourt, letter to Robert Lynd, 2 March 1929; G.M.S., sales memorandum to [??] Reid, 3 May 1960, Container 7, File: General Correspondence 1923–60; Harcourt Brace and Co., undated list of academic course adoptions of *Middletown*, Container 12 , File: Middletown Reviews, LP.

45. Bruce Bliven, letter to Robert Lynd, 7 March 1929, Container 7, File: General Correspondence 1923–60; Clipping of full-page advertisement in *The New Republic*, 6 March 1929, Container 12, File: Middletown Reviews, LP.

46. Robert Lynd, letter to Alfred Harcourt, 22 February 1929, Container 7, File: General Correspondence 1923–60; typescript of advertising copy, Container 12, File: Middletown Reviews, LP.

47. Clippings of advertisements in *The Tide* (May 1929) and *Printers' Ink* (16

May 1929); brochure for *McCall's* magazine, Container 12, File: Middletown Reviews, LP.

48. Clippings of advertisements in *The Nation, The New Republic, The New York Times,* and *The Saturday Review of Literature,* Container 12, File: Middletown Reviews, LP.

49. Frank Luther Mott lists Sinclair Lewis's *Main Street* and *Babbitt* among his lists of "Better Sellers" (books whose overall sales did not quite reach the best-seller benchmark of one percent of the population for the decade in which they were published, but did come close) although he does note *Main Street* as the annual fiction best-seller in book stores for 1921; see Mott, *Golden Multitudes: The Story of Best Sellers in the United States* (New York: Macmillan, 1947).

50. Clippings of Henry James Forman, "What's Right with America," *McCall's* (November 1929) and Maxwell Lerner, review of *Middletown,* Container 12, File: Middletown Reviews, LP.

A study of the standard of living is a study of the relationship between cultural and economic behavior. In the discipline of history, in the American context, one starting point for this line of inquiry is David Potter's classic text, *People of Plenty: Economic Abundance and the American Character* (Chicago: University of Chicago Press, 1954), which examines the course and impact of Americans' ideas of attaining, and perhaps exceeding, material comfort. Daniel Horowitz's *The Morality of Spending: Attitudes Toward the Consumer Society in America, 1875–1940* (Baltimore: Johns Hopkins University Press, 1985) is a model for looking at the cultural meaning of consumer behavior; his text focuses more on actual expenditure and the rising standard of living, which sparked my own interest in what it means to even have a standard of living. Lawrence Glickman, in "Inventing the 'American standard of living': Gender, Race, and Working-Class Identity, 1880–1925" (*Labor History* 34, nos. 2–3 [Spring–Summer 1993]) and *A Living Wage: American Workers and the Making of Consumer Society* (Ithaca, N.Y.: Cornell University Press, 1997), helpfully differentiates between wages, purchases, and aspirations for material goods in the formulation of the standard of living.

Historians interested in the standard of living would also do well to look to the field of economics, where John Kenneth Galbraith's *The Affluent Society* (Boston: Houghton Mifflin, 1958) stands as a counterpart to Potter's text. The Nobel Prize laureate Amartya Sen has written conceptually on the standard of living, but more on its role as a measure of welfare and economic development than in what the idea of having a standard way of life represents about a culture or historical era that adopts such an image; see, for example, *The Standard of Living*, ed. Geoffrey Hawthorne (Cambridge: Cambridge University Press, 1987) or the volume he edited with Martha Nussbaum, *The Quality of Life* (Oxford: Oxford University Press, 1987). More recently, Clair Brown, in *American Standards of Living* (Cambridge: Blackwell, 1994), has analyzed spending norms over time, investigating the difference between measured standards and the perceived quality of life. Peter Shergold shed light on the American standard of living at the beginning of the twentieth century by comparing it to living conditions, and opportunities for consumption, in Britain, in *Working-Class Life: The "American Standard" in Comparative Perspective, 1899–1913* (Pittsburgh: University of Pittsburgh Press, 1982). Such studies show that whether through skepticism toward luxury or distress over poverty, there is a level of material comfort that is considered "just right." While that level is difficult, if not impossible, to pin down, its existence is no longer questioned; for any given place, time, and community, there is a standard of living. My own question is from where and how did this concept take hold.

The phrase, and the perception of, the standard of living spread through the popular American lexicon at the beginning of the twentieth century. Many of its early uses, however, were found in the social sciences, particularly economics, sociology, and social and cultural anthropology. The earliest use of the term that I have found is in Philip Ayres's essay "The Standard of Living," written in 1902 for the philanthropic journal, *Charities* (9, no. 10 [6 September 1902]: 216). While many studies of living standards took the very concept of such a study as a given, some authors considered the meaning of the projects they carried out; for their thoughtful discussions of the meaning of the term, I have found the following studies helpful: Newel Howland Comish, *The Standard of Living: Elements of Consumption* (New York: Macmillan Co., 1923); Edward T. Devine, *The Normal Life* (New York: Survey Associates, 1924); Thomas Eliot, ed., *American Standards and Planes of Living: Readings in the Social Economics of Consumption* (Boston: Ginn & Co., 1931); Ellis Lore Kirkpatrick, *The Farmer's Standard of Living* (New York: Century Co., 1929); and Frank Hatch Streightoff, *The Standard of Living Among the Industrial People of America* (Boston: Houghton Mifflin Co., 1911). As will be apparent from the preceding pages, I have been particularly influenced by Hazel Kyrk's *Economic Problems of the Family* (New York: Harper & Bros., 1929) and Jessica Peixotto's *Getting and Spending at the Professional Standard of Living: A Study of the Costs of Living an Academic Life* (New York: Macmillan Co., 1927).

The developing social sciences, one vehicle for the popularization of the standard of living, achieved national recognition with Robert and Helen Merrell Lynd's landmark study, *Middletown: A Study in Modern American Culture* (New York: Harcourt, Brace and Co., 1929). *Middletown* was significant not only because it attempted to portray the quality of life in all sectors of an American town, but also because it captured the tensions between local and national standards. In doing so, the book found a broad audience. The Robert and Helen Merrell Lynd Papers in the Manuscript Division of the Library of Congress (Washington, D.C.) illuminate both the back story to the book's publication, in terms of its funding, advisers, and original aims, and its reception, through scores of reviews and clippings demonstrating the Lynds' rise to the position of recognized public intellectuals. Several recent projects explore the rise of the social sciences in the United States, contextualizing the Lynds and their contemporaries: Martin Bulmer, Kevin Bales, and Kathryn Kish Sklar, eds., *The Social Survey in Historical Perspective, 1880–1940* (Cambridge: Cambridge University Press, 1991); Maurine Greenwald and Margo Anderson, eds., *Pittsburgh Surveyed: Social Science and Social Reform in the Early Twentieth Century* (Pittsburgh: University of Pittsburgh Press, 1996); Daniel Horowitz, *The Morality of Spending: Attitudes*

Toward the Consumer Society in America, 1875–1940 (Baltimore: Johns Hopkins University Press, 1985); Sarah Igo, "America Surveyed: The Making of a Social Scientific Public, 1920–1960" (Ph.D. diss., Princeton University, 2001); and Dorothy Ross, *The Origins of American Social Science* (Cambridge: Cambridge University Press, 1991).

Though it was theorized in the social sciences, I argue that the standard of living was popularized and disseminated by the structures of American commerce. In situating the standard of living in the marketplace, I have looked to authors who discuss the myriad exchanges, of both goods and ideas, that take place in this physical and social space. My greatest intellectual debt is to Jean-Christophe Agnew, whose essay "The Threshold of Exchange: Speculations on the Market" (*Radical History Review* 21 [Fall 1979]: 99–118) offers fresh insight with each reading. More recently, scholars working on the boundary between business history and cultural history have explored the ideas of mediation, translation, or negotiation between buyers and sellers; important projects include Regina Lee Blaszczyk's *Imagining Consumers: Design and Innovation from Wedgwood to Corning* (Baltimore: Johns Hopkins University Press, 2000); Shelley Nickles's "Object Lessons: Household Appliance Design and the American Middle Class, 1920–1960" (Ph.D. diss., University of Virginia, 1999); and Sally Clarke's forthcoming book *Consumer Negotiations,* which was previewed in an essay by the same title in *Business and Economic History* (26, no. 1 [Fall 1997]: 101–22). These authors remind readers that consumption is driven by neither supply nor demand acting in isolation, but by the communications between the two; the economic phases of production, distribution, and consumption are cyclical rather than linear. In my own work, I am interested in what Joseph Corn has helped me term *collaboration,* through which producers and consumers together promote cultural norms encapsulated in the standard of living.

The idea of a broadly shared standard of living influences the production, distribution, and consumption of material culture on a variety of scales. Even choices surrounding the purchase or use of small objects, and the daily behavioral norms that go with them, contribute to larger cultural similarities. For the student of the quotidian activities surrounding the dining table, there is a wealth of source material to consult. I chose to start with purveyors of silverplate flatware; even in this one trade, the historical record is rich. One of the largest collections documenting the rise of silverware production is the Gorham Company Papers at Brown University. However, I did not feel I could in any way improve upon Charles Venable's insightful discussion of Gorham, and the Tiffany Company as well, in *Silver in America, 1840–1940: A Century of Splendor* (Dallas: Dallas Museum of Art, 1995). Venable's book is quite simply the best discussion to date of the production and marketing of silver and will be of use to anyone interested in not only silver, but the decorative arts more generally, as well as historians of American business. To complement Venable's work, I chose to focus on a collection of materials from the Reed & Barton Company, housed in the Historical Collections of the Baker Library at Harvard

Business School. Although these papers are not a comprehensive archive of the company, they do contain extensive materials regarding marketing and sales of silverware, as well as some papers regarding production and employment practices. These papers had formed the basis of a business history case study by George Sweet Gibb, published in 1943 as *The Whitesmiths of Taunton: A History of Reed & Barton, 1824–1943* (Cambridge, Mass.: Harvard University Press, 1943); Gibb's work still stands as an excellent model of corporate history. Since I completed my research at the Baker Library, Reed & Barton has published a newer company history, by Renee Garrelick, entitled *Sterling Seasons: The Reed & Barton Story* (Taunton, Mass.: Reed & Barton, 1998) extending the company's narrative through World War II to the present.

In addition to Venable's overview and the histories of Reed & Barton, Charles Carpenter's *Gorham Silver, 1831–1981* (New York: Dodd, Mead, 1982), Charles and Mary Grace Carpenter's *Tiffany Silver* (New York: Dodd, Mead, 1978), and Edmund P. Hogan's *An American Heritage: A Book about the International Silver Company* (Dallas: Taylor Publishing Co., 1977) contribute to the history of silver production and distribution by focusing on the other major American producers of the nineteenth and twentieth centuries. Still, understanding the role of flatware as the embodiment of shared social codes requires reading of not just the objects themselves, but the rituals of the tables at which they are set. I found Kathryn Grover's edited collection, *Dining in America, 1850–1900* (Amherst: University of Massachusetts Press, 1987) and Susan Williams's *Savory Suppers & Fashionable Feasts: Dining in Victorian America* (New York: Pantheon Books, in association with the Strong Museum, 1985) particularly helpful in contextualizing the use of flatware at mealtimes. Harvey Levenstein's *Revolution at the Table: The Transformation of the American Diet* (New York: Oxford University Press, 1988) is a great resource for thinking about the actual foods consumed. I consulted a variety of contemporary sources on etiquette and table manners, but the best way to approach these materials is through the introductions offered by Arthur Schlesinger, in his classic text, *Learning How to Behave: A Historical Study of American Etiquette Books* (New York: Macmillan, 1946) and Sarah E. Newton, in *Learning to Behave: A Guide to American Conduct Books Before 1900* (Westport, Conn.: Greenwood Press, 1994). Finally, John Kasson, in *Rudeness and Civility: Manners in Nineteenth-Century Urban America* (New York: Hill and Wang, 1990), and Karen Halttunen, in *Confidence Men and Painted Women: A Study of Middle-Class Culture in America, 1830–1870* (New Haven: Yale University Press, 1982), place table manners in their larger cultural contexts, in order to understand the ways in which these small gestures of the table are related to larger cultural standards.

Health and welfare, on the level of both the individual and the general public, are important indicators of the standard of living. By the late nineteenth century, bodily cleanliness and personal hygiene were seen as inextricably linked to this larger goal of good health. One avenue into the study of personal hygiene is to look in depth at those companies that strove to make the task easier by producing sanitary bathroom fixtures. The Kohler Company in Kohler, Wisconsin, aids historians with their accessible and well-organized corporate archive. Materials at the Kohler Archive range from the personal correspondence of company leaders, to catalogues and advertising files, to accounts of the creation of the company town surrounding the factory and span the company's history from its founding in the late nineteenth century to the present day. In examining these Kohler records, I follow in the footsteps of a number of historians of American business and culture, such as Regina Lee Blaszczyk and Janet Hutchison, as well as Trudi Jennes Eblen, whose master's thesis on the Kohler Company is particularly helpful in understanding the firm's origins ("A History of the Kohler Company of Kohler, Wisconsin, 1871–1914" [M.S. thesis, University of Wisconsin, 1965]).

Important starting points for the history of domestic plumbing include Marc Stern on the broader industry that included sanitary pottery (*The Pottery Industry of Trenton: A Skilled Trade in Transition, 1850–1929* [New Brunswick: Rutgers University Press, 1994]); Maureen Ogle on the incorporation of these fixtures into household plumbing systems (*All the Modern Conveniences: American Household Plumbing, 1840–1890* [Baltimore: Johns Hopkins University Press, 1996]); and Ellen Lupton and J. Abbott Miller on the aesthetics of plumbed spaces (*The Bathroom, The Kitchen, and the Aesthetics of Waste: A Process of Elimination* (Cambridge, Mass.: MIT List Visual Arts Center, 1992). Richard and Claudia Bushman, in their article "The Early History of Cleanliness in America" (*Journal of American History* 74 [March 1988]: 1213–38), and May Stone in "The Plumbing Paradox: American Attitudes toward Late Nineteenth-Century Domestic Sanitary Arrangements" (*Winterthur Portfolio* 14 [Fall 1979]: 283–309) link the development and use of fixtures to larger concerns about cleanliness and sanitation. The following provide a greater understanding of the place of health and welfare in American culture of the Gilded Age and Progressive Era: Andrew McClary, "Germs are Everywhere: The Germ Threat as Seen in Magazine Articles, 1890–1920" (*Journal of American Culture* 3 [Spring 1980]: 33–52); and Nancy Tomes, *The Gospel of Germs: Men, Women, and the Microbe in American Life* (Cambridge, Mass.: Harvard University Press, 1998).

Housing is perhaps the central consideration for the study of the standard of living. In studying the ways in which Americans estimated both housing generally, as well as specific house types, I was very lucky to have access to a goldmine of business records and ephemera of the North American Construction Company, later called simply the Aladdin Company. Indeed many historians of twentieth-century American housing, architecture, advertising, business, and economics would find the trip to the Clark Historical Library of Central Michigan University, which through both foresight and serendipity houses this Aladdin Company Archive, well worth their while. My own research dealt with only the first few decades of the company's existence, but the papers actually span Aladdin's history from its founding in 1906 through the 1980s, with particular strength in the postwar period. The collection houses yearly catalogues, price lists, and magazines; extensive sales records; advertising records; and architectural drawings. Smaller and more esoteric items, such as a still-vibrant paint selector card and an Aladdin homeowner recipe book, give the collection the rich texture so often missing from business archives.

The specific architectural plans of the Aladdin Company are examined at greater length in Scott Erbes's "The Readi-Cut Dream: The Mail Order House Catalogs of the Aladdin Company, 1906–1920" (M.A. thesis, University of Delaware, 1990). Cheryl DeCosta Evans surveys a variety of companies and house types in "American Ready-Made Housing in the Early Twentieth Century" (M.S. thesis, University of Nebraska, 1982). The definitive book on kit architecture is Robert Schweitzer and Michael W. R. Davis's *America's Favorite Homes: Mail-Order Catalogues as a Guide to Popular Early 20th-Century Houses* (Detroit: Wayne State University Press, 1990). Leland Roth's article, "Getting the Houses to the People: Edward Bok, *The Ladies' Home Journal,* and the Ideal House" (*Perspectives in Vernacular Architecture, IV,* ed. Thomas Carter and Bernard L. Herman [Columbia: University of Missouri Press, 1991]) is an important reading of popular and prescriptive influences shaping Americans' ideals about their homes. Useful discussions of the aesthetics and meanings of American domestic architecture include Clifford E Clark Jr.'s *The American Family Home, 1800–1960* (Chapel Hill: University of North Carolina Press, 1986); Jan Cohn's *The Palace or the Poorhouse: The American House as Cultural Symbol* (East Lansing: Michigan State University Press, 1979); Alan Gowans's *The Comfortable House: North American Suburban Architecture, 1890–1930* (Cambridge, Mass.: MIT Press, 1986); David Handlin's *The American Home: Architecture and Society, 1815–1915* (Boston: Little, Brown and Co., 1979); Clay Lancaster's *The American Bungalow: 1880–1930* (New York: Abbeville Press, 1985); Sally McMurry's *Families and Farmhouses in Nineteenth-Century America: Vernacular Design and Social Change* (New York: Oxford University Press, 1988); and Fred W. Peterson's *Homes in the Heartland: Balloon Frame Farmhouses in the Upper Midwest, 1850–1920* (Lawrence: University Press of Kansas, 1992).

These texts on domestic architecture are complemented by works that look at housing in more social and cultural terms. I find Gwendolyn Wright's *Building the Dream: A Social History of Housing in America* (New York: Pantheon, 1981) to be the most comprehensive introduction to the topic. Two collections of essays provide excellent overviews of the creation and arrangement of spaces within the home: *American Home Life, 1880–1930: A Social History of Space and Services,* ed. Jessica Foy and Thomas Schlereth (Knoxville: University of Tennessee Press, 1992), and *Making the American Home: Middle-Class Women and Domestic Material Culture, 1840–1940,* ed. Marilyn Ferris Motz and Pat Browne (Bowling Green: Bowling Green State University Popular Press, 1988). Janet Hutchison makes an important contribution to the understanding of housing in the interwar period by looking at the Better Homes in America campaign, in "American Housing, Gender, and the Better Homes Movement, 1922–1935" (Ph.D. diss., University of Delaware, 1989). Regina Lee Blaszczyk makes an explicit link between housing and the standard of living in "From House to Home: Herbert Hoover and the American Standard of Living, 1921–1928," in *Herbert Hoover: Re-evaluating the Evidence,* ed. Timothy Walch (West Branch, Iowa: Herbert Hoover Presidential Library, forthcoming).

The standard of living achieved by any given household is influenced not only by the life patterns that are carried on within the domestic space, but by the broader environment in which that housing is placed. It became clear to me early on that the ideas and ideals encapsulated by the standard of living went beyond consumer products and households, to the organization of space on the American landscape. For a sweeping look at the history of comprehensive planning and zoning in the United States, the papers of Harland Bartholomew and Associates, one of the leading firms promoting these types of planning in the twentieth century, is a logical starting point. The University Archives of Washington University in St. Louis maintains a broad collection of the firm's papers, including draft and final reports of hundreds of city plans. This excellent concentration of planning reports is augmented by a large set of Bartholomew's more theoretical writings on planning and zoning. Interest in Bartholomew and his firm has been on the rise in the academic subfield of urban planning history, because his practice spanned such a broad array of municipal clients throughout the twentieth century; historians with more general interest in urban and cultural history would find much of value in these papers as well. For an introduction to Bartholomew's planning and philosophies, two good starting points are Norman Johnston's "Harland Bartholomew: His Comprehensive Plans and Science of Planning" (Ph.D. diss., University of Pennsylvania, 1964) and Eldridge Lovelace, *Harland Bartholomew: His Contributions to American Urban Planning* (Urbana: University of Illinois Department of Urban and Regional Planning, 1993); Johnston conducted extensive interviews with Bartholomew, and Lovelace worked at Bartholomew's side for years as a principal in his firm.

To understand the context in which Bartholomew began his practice, two early surveys of planning projects in the United States provide a glimpse of the field and its parameters in the early twentieth century: *City Planning Progress in the United States,* ed. George Ford (Washington, D.C.: American Institute of Architects, 1917) and *Our Cities To-Day and To-morrow: A Survey of Planning and Zoning Progress in the United States,* comp. Theodora Kimball Hubbard and Henry Vincent Hubbard (Cambridge, Mass.: Harvard University Press, 1929). Similarly, an early text by one of the main proponents of zoning in the legal sphere still stands as an important explanation of the origins of the practice; Edward Bassett was supported by the Russell Sage Foundation in his publication of *Zoning: The Laws, Administration, and Court Decisions During the First Twenty Years* (New York: Russell Sage Foundation,

1936). Seymour Toll's book, *Zoned American* (New York: Grossman Publishers, 1969), is still a standard historical work on this aspect of city planning, joined by Constance Perin's *Everything in its Place: Social Order and Land Use in America* (Princeton: Princeton University Press, 1977). More recent discussions of zoning in local contexts are Patricia Burgess, in *Planning for the Private Interest: Land Use Controls and Residential Patterns in Columbus Ohio, 1900–1970* (Columbus: Ohio State University Press, 1994); and Carol Willis, in *Form Follows Finance: Skyscrapers and Skylines in New York and Chicago* (New York: Princeton Architectural Press, 1995). More general discussions of urban planning and its role in the Gilded Age and Progressive Era are offered by Donald Krueckenberg, in his edited volume, *Introduction to Planning History in the United States* (New Brunswick, N.J.: Center for Urban Policy Research, 1983); Neil Larry Shumsky, the editor of *The Physical City: Public Space and the Infrastructure* (New York: Garland Publishers, 1996); and William Wilson, in *The City Beautiful Movement* (Baltimore: Johns Hopkins University Press, 1989). In order to understand how planning was often carried out in accord with ideas of corporate management, it is well worth reading Frederick Winslow Taylor's *The Principles of Scientific Management* (1911; rpt. New York: W. W. Norton, 1967).

Through these four case studies, whether goods, buildings, or services are being bought and sold, certain structures of the marketplace are consistent. The past generation of business and cultural historians has produced a wealth of material on these structures. For the changing shape of the American business firm and the rise of the corporation, Alfred Chandler's *The Visible Hand: The Managerial Revolution in American Business* (Cambridge, Mass.: Belknap Press, 1977) remains the classic text with good reason. I have found Mansel Blackford's *The Small Business in America* (New York: Twayne, 1991) and Naomi Lamoreaux's *The Great Merger Movement in American Business, 1895–1904* (Cambridge: Cambridge University Press, 1985) helpful on particular aspects of the American business narrative that are important considerations when studying the turn of the twentieth century. Olivier Zunz's *Making America Corporate, 1870–1920* (Chicago: University of Chicago Press, 1990) provides a link between these new business organizations and the American economy and society at large. Research at the intersection of business and culture has been encouraged by Kenneth Lipartito in his essay, "Culture and the Practice of Business History" (*Business and Economic History* 24, no. 2 [Winter 1995]: 1–41).

Part of the story of the incorporation of consumer goods into the standard of living stems from the standardization of those goods, and the ability to produce them in large enough quantities that they could be broadly adopted. David Hounshell offers the clearest narrative of the phases of industrial production methods in his invaluable book, *From the American System to Mass Production, 1800–1920* (Baltimore: Johns Hopkins University Press, 1984). Philip Scranton gives important reminders that American firms' reliance on mass production was limited to certain types of goods; he explores the alternative of batch, or flexible, production in "Diver-

sity in Diversity: Flexible Production and American Industrialization, 1870–1930"
(*Business History Review* 65 [Spring 1991]: 27–90) and *Endless Novelty: Specialty Production and American Industrialization, 1865–1925* (Princeton: Princeton University Press, 1997).

My own work, however, focuses on the role of distribution in the creation of the standard of living. For background on the logistics and infrastructure that support American commerce, the following are still invaluable: George Rogers Taylor, *The Transportation Revolution, 1815–1860* (New York: Rinehart, 1951); and Wayne Fuller, *RFD: The Changing Face of Rural America* (Bloomington: Indiana University Press, 1964) and *The American Mail: Enlarger of Common Life* (Chicago: University of Chicago Press, 1972). Timothy Spears, in *100 Years on the Road: The Traveling Salesman in American Culture* (New Haven: Yale University Press, 1995), and Earl Sharris, in *A Nation of Salesmen: The Tyranny of the Market and the Subversion of Culture* (New York: W. W. Norton, 1994), introduce readers to those individuals who made use of these new structures to circulate goods on behalf of manufacturers. The varied distribution points between producer and consumer, and the culture of these spaces, are discussed in Susan Porter Benson, *Counter Cultures: Saleswomen, Managers, and Customers in American Department Stores, 1890–1940* (Urbana: University of Illinois Press, 1986); Boris Emmet and John E. Jeuck, *Catalogues and Counters: A History of Sears, Roebuck and Company* (Chicago: University of Chicago Press, 1950); William Leach, *Land of Desire: From the Department Store to the Department of Commerce: The Rise of America's Commercial Culture* (New York: Pantheon Books, 1993); Bill Reid Moeckel, *The Development of the Wholesaler in the United States, 1860–1900* (New York: Garland, 1986); and Hrant Pasdermadjian, *The Department Store: Its Origins, Evolution, and Economics* (New York: Arno Press, 1976).

Of course, the marketing process extends beyond the boundaries of an actual store. The following studies provide excellent overviews of the varied approaches to marketing that arose in the nineteenth and early twentieth centuries: Pamela Laird, *Advertising Progress: American Business and the Rise of Consumer Marketing* (Baltimore: Johns Hopkins University Press, 1998); Deborah Anne Federhen et al., *Accumulation and Display: Mass Marketing Household Goods in America, 1880–1920* (Winterthur, Del.: Henry Francis du Pont Winterthur Museum, 1986); Glenn Porter and Harold C. Livesay, *Merchants and Manufacturers: Studies in the Changing Structure of Nineteenth-Century Marketing* (Baltimore: Johns Hopkins University Press, 1971); Susan Strasser, *Satisfaction Guaranteed: The Making of the Mass Market* (New York: Pantheon Books, 1989); and Richard Tedlow, *New and Improved: The Story of Mass Marketing in America* (New York: Basic Books, 1990). Regina Lee Blaszczyk's study of the pottery and glass industries, *Imagining Consumers: Design and Innovation from Wedgwood to Corning* (Baltimore: Johns Hopkins University Press, 2000), has broad implications for the narrative of American marketing and the communications between producers and consumers. Nancy F. Koehn's *Brand New: How*

Entrepreneurs Earned Consumers' Trust from Wedgwood to Dell (Boston: Harvard Business School Press, 2001) and John Phillip Jones's *What's in a Name? Advertising and the Concept of Brands* (Lexington, Mass.: D. C. Heath, 1986) specifically treat the development of branding and its importance to American firms.

Advertising became the most familiar and pervasive form of marketing over the course of the late nineteenth and early twentieth centuries. Important texts for understanding this development include Stuart Ewen, *Captains of Consciousness: Advertising and the Social Roots of American Culture* (New York: McGraw-Hill, 1977); Robert Jay's *The Trade Card in Nineteenth Century America* (Columbia: University of Missouri Press, 1987); T. J. Jackson Lears, *Fables of Abundance: A Cultural History of Advertising in America* (New York: Basic Books, 1994); and the classic work by Roland Marchand, *Advertising the American Dream: Making Way for Modernity, 1920–1940* (Berkeley: University of California Press, 1985). In an era in which advertising was associated with print, it is important to examine the link between marketing and broader print culture, particularly magazines. I have found the following texts particularly helpful in considering this relationship: Ellen Gruber Garvey, *The Adman in the Parlor: Magazines and the Gendering of Consumer Culture, 1880s to 1910s* (New York: Oxford University Press, 1996); Richard Ohmann, *Selling Culture: Magazines, Markets, and Class at the Turn of the Century* (London: Verso, 1996); Jennifer Scanlon, *Inarticulate Longings:* The Ladies' Home Journal, *Gender, and the Promises of Consumer Culture* (New York: Routledge, 1995); Salme Harju Steinberg, *Reformer in the Marketplace: Edward W. Bok and* The Ladies' Home Journal (Baton Rouge: Louisiana State University Press, 1979); the classic work by Frank Luther Mott, *A History of American Magazines* (Cambridge, Mass.: Harvard University Press, 1938–68), offers a good sense of the range of periodicals in which advertising space was available.

Students of consumption are lucky in that over the past two decades, a number of excellent editors have culled the flourishing scholarship on consumption—past and present, theoretical and historical—into several extremely useful collections. Thus, for an introduction to consumer culture in the American context, I would recommend the following: Simon J. Bronner, ed., *Consuming Visions: Accumulation and Display of Goods in America, 1880–1920* (New York: W. W. Norton & Co., for the Henry Francis du Pont Winterthur Museum, 1989); Richard Wightman Fox and T. J. Jackson Lears, eds., *The Culture of Consumption: Critical Essays in American History, 1880–1980* (New York: Pantheon Books, 1982); Lawrence Glickman, *Consumer Society in American History: A Reader* (Ithaca: Cornell University Press, 1999); and Juliet Schor and Douglas Holt, *The Consumer Society Reader* (New York: New Press, 2000). Glickman's volume is distinguished by its thorough bibliography, as well as its selection of essays. It is important to remember that the standard of living charts aspiration more than actual consumption, and is perhaps even farther removed from earnings. In order to understand the gaps between wages, consumer spending, and the incentives of greater material comfort, it is important to consider the role of credit. Authors from the Lynds on recognized how important credit systems were to American consumer cycles. Lendol Calder has brilliantly synthesized both the logistics and the cultural meaning of credit in *Financing the American Dream: A Cultural History of Consumer Credit* (Princeton: Princeton University Press, 1999); this book and Martha Olney's *Buy Now, Pay Later: Advertising, Credit, and Consumer Durables in the 1920s* (Chapel Hill: University of North Carolina Press, 1991) are required reading when considering the topic of American consumption.

Much of the theoretical writing on consumer behavior in fact overlaps with work on material culture, exploring the meaning that the act of consumption—who the consumer is and what the circumstances of purchase are—lends the commodity. The classic text on this relationship is, of course, Thorstein Veblen's *The Theory of the Leisure Class: An Economic Study of Institutions* (1899; rpt. New York: Modern Library, 1934), and seemingly well on its way to becoming equally relied upon is Pierre Bourdieu's *Distinction: A Social Critique of the Judgment of Taste,* trans. Richard Nice (Cambridge: Cambridge University Press, 1984). As important as these two volumes are, ultimately they are more about the use of material culture to establish divisions than its use in community cohesion—a subtle difference but a significant one. Therefore, I would add to any reading list the following texts, for a broader variety of approaches: Arjun Appadurai, *The Social Life of Things: Commodities in Cultural Perspective* (Cambridge: Cambridge University Press, 1986); Mihaly Csikszentmihalyi and Eugene Rochberg-Halton, *The Meaning of Things: Domestic Symbols and the Self* (Cambridge: Cambridge University Press, 1981); Mary Douglas and Baron Isherwood, *The World of Goods: Toward an Anthropology of Consumption* (New York: W. W. Norton, 1979); and Grant McCracken, *Culture and Consumption: New Approaches to the Symbolic Character of Consumer Goods and Activities* (Bloomington: Indiana University Press, 1988).

Ultimately, all of these works rest on the assumption that objects, buildings, and landscapes are important reflections of the people, societies, and cultures that produced, distributed, and consumed them. The issue is often how to mine these alternative sources for the rich cultural ore they contain. For methods and examples, I have used the following models: Jules Prown, "Mind in Matter: An Introduction to Material Culture Theory and Method" (in *Material Life in America, 1600–1860,* ed. Robert Blair St. George [Boston: Northeastern University Press, 1988], 17–37); Ian M. G. Quimby, ed., *Material Culture and the Study of American Life* (New York: W. W. Norton and Co., 1978), and the remarkable writings of Lucy Maynard Salmon, most recently collected in *History and the Texture of Modern Life: Selected Essays* (ed. Nicholas Adams and Bonnie G. Smith [Philadelphia: University of Pennsylvania Press, 2001]).

When the actual objects and environments of the past are not available for study, one must turn to representations of them. The early twentieth-century studies of the standard of living mentioned above are one source for determining levels of material comfort. As a counterpoint to the statistical depictions of the standard of living found in social science studies, the more qualitative descriptions of daily life found in popular fiction are valuable. While virtually any novel from the Gilded Age and Progressive Era would betray the standards of daily life at the turn of the twentieth century, I have found works by the following authors particularly helpful: Samuel Hopkins Adams, Floyd Dell, Theodore Dreiser, Edna Ferber, Robert Herrick, William Dean Howells, Sinclair Lewis, Kathleen Norris, and Booth Tarkington. Along with other contemporaries, these authors place the daily challenges of identifying and approaching material and cultural standards at the center of their narratives. The editor and bibliographer Archibald Hanna has termed such works "social fiction" for their dominant themes of exploring cultural customs and social change. He has made life easier for historians, literary scholars, and fiction lovers alike, by cataloguing and indexing American novels from the first half of the twentieth century in *Mirror for the Nation: An Annotated Bibliography of American Social Fiction* (New York: Garland, 1985). For background reading on the place of fiction in American culture and why it serves well as a "mirror for the nation," I suggest the following books: David Minter, *A Cultural History of the American Novel* (New York: Cambridge University Press, 1994); Joan Shelley Rubin, *The Making of Middlebrow Culture* (Chapel Hill: University of North Carolina Press, 1992); and James L.W. West III, *American Authors and the Literary Marketplace* (Philadelphia: University of Pennsylvania Press, 1988). Several authors situate the development of "social fiction" in the realm of the middle class.

One of the many debates fostered by cultural and economic historians is the question of when, as well as if, the middle class emerged into the stream of American society; one extremely helpful summary of these discussions is Stuart Blumin's essay, "The Hypothesis of Middle-Class Formation in 19th Century America: A Critique and Some Proposals" (*American Historical Review* 90 [April 1985]: 299–338). I consider the following books to be essential reading on this debate: Burton Bledstein, *The Culture of Professionalism: The Middle Class and the Development of Higher Education in America* (New York: W. W. Norton and Co., 1976); Stuart Blumin, *The Emergence of the Middle Class: Social Experience in the American City, 1760–1900* (New York: Cambridge University Press, 1989); John S. Gilkeson, Jr., *Middle-Class Providence, 1820–1940* (Princeton: Princeton University Press, 1986); Katharine Grier, *Culture and Comfort: Parlor Making and Middle-Class Identity, 1850–1930* (Washington, D.C.: Smithsonian Institution Press, 1997); Karen Halttunen, *Confidence Men and Painted Women: A Study of Middle-Class Culture in America, 1830–1870* (New Haven: Yale University Press, 1982); Joan Shelley Rubin, *The Making of Middlebrow Culture* (Chapel Hill: University of North Carolina Press, 1992); Mary Ryan, *Cradle of the Middle Class: The Family in Oneida County, New York, 1790–1865* (New York: Cambridge University Press, 1981); and Pat Walker's edited collection, *Between Labor and*

Capital: The Professional Managerial Class (Boston: South End Press, 1979), which includes Barbara and John Ehrenreich's seminal essay, "The Professional-Managerial Class." The essays in Burton Bledstein and Robert Johnston's edited volume, *The Middling Sorts: Explorations in the History of the American Middle Class* (New York: Routledge, 2001), update these lines of research.

In my own study I am less concerned with the emergence of the middle class than I am with their consolidation as a national group and their influence on the material environment. In doing so, I have looked for models that relate urban and rural, or metropolitan and small town, cultures and economies. Michael Conzen's *Frontier Farming in an Urban Shadow: The Influence of Madison's Proximity on the Agricultural Development of Blooming Grove, Wisconsin* (Madison: State Historical Society of Wisconsin, 1971) is an important precursor to the classic work on this topic, William Cronon's *Nature's Metropolis: Chicago and the Great West* (New York: W. W. Norton, 1991). In envisioning the middle class as a national community, one whose members might also affiliate with a host of other communities, I have relied on the ideas presented by Thomas Bender in *Community and Social Change in America* (New Brunswick: Rutgers University Press, 1978).

The emergence of the standard of living as one of the organizing principles in the American economy coincided with the historical eras often designated the Gilded Age and the Progressive Era; the political, economic, social, and cultural narratives of these periods inform any understanding of this emergence. Two classic texts about these periods, Richard Hofstadter's *The Age of Reform* (New York: Vintage, 1955) and Robert Wiebe's *The Search for Order, 1877–1920* (New York: Hill and Wang, 1967), remain necessary as starting points in the field. Still, they have been joined over the succeeding generation by several very important studies, including Edward Ayers, *The Promise of the New South: Life after Reconstruction* (New York: Oxford University Press, 1992); Paul Boyer, *Urban Mass and Moral Order in America, 1820–1920* (Cambridge, Mass.: Harvard University Press, 1978); Steven J. Diner, *A Very Different Age: Americans of the Progressive Era* (New York: Hill and Wang, 1998); Harvey Green, *The Uncertainty of Everyday Life, 1915–1945* (New York: Harper Perennial, 1993); T. J. Jackson Lears, *No Place of Grace: Antimodernism and the Transformation of American Culture, 1880–1920* (New York: Pantheon Books, 1981); Nell Irvin Painter, *Standing at Armageddon: The United States, 1877–1919* (New York: W. W. Norton, 1987); Thomas Schlereth, *Victorian America: Transformations in Everyday Life, 1876–1915* (New York: HarperCollins, 1996); and Alan Trachtenberg, *The Incorporation of America: Culture and Society in the Gilded Age* (New York: Hill and Wang, 1982).

:: INDEX ::

Page numbers in italics refer to illustrations.